W9-BUT-413

A DIGEST
OF REPORTS
OF THE
CARNEGIE
COMMISSION
ON
HIGHER
EDUCATION

A DIGEST OF REPORTS OF THE CARNEGIE COMMISSION ON HIGHER EDUCATION

WITH AN INDEX TO RECOMMENDATIONS
AND SUGGESTED ASSIGNMENTS
OF RESPONSIBILITY FOR ACTION

McGRAW-HILL BOOK COMPANY
New York   St. Louis   San Francisco   Düsseldorf
London   Sydney   Toronto   Mexico   Panama
Johannesburg   Kuala Lumpur   Montreal
New Delhi   São Paulo   Singapore

This publication is issued by the Carnegie Commission on Higher Education with headquarters at 2150 Shattuck Avenue, Berkeley, California 94704. The views and conclusions expressed in this document are solely those of the members of the Carnegie Commission on Higher Education and do not necessarily reflect the views or opinions of the Carnegie Corporation of New York, The Carnegie Foundation for the Advancement of Teaching, or their trustees, officers, directors, or employees.

Library of Congress Cataloging in Publication Data

Carnegie Commission on Higher Education.
A digest of reports of the Carnegie Commission on Higher Education.

1. Education, Higher—United States. I. Title.
LA227.3.C38 1974   378.73   73-22231
ISBN 0-07-010103-5

This book was set in Claro by University Graphics, Inc.
It was printed and bound by Von Hoffman.
The designer was Edward A. Butler.
The editors were Michael Hennelly,
Janine Parson, and Nancy Tressel.
Milton Heiberg supervised the production.

CONTENTS

FOREWORD

In early 1967, The Carnegie Foundation for the Advancement of Teaching created the Carnegie Commission on Higher Education to examine the vital issues facing higher education in the United States as we approach the year 2000. In making its recommendations, the Commission was not asked to speak *for* higher education but rather *about* higher education and its needs and contributions in relation to the nation's social concerns and purposes.

In our deliberations we have sought out information and expert advice from scores of authorities in both this country and abroad. Some of these authorities have prepared detailed reports for us that have been published for wide distribution and are abstracted in a summary volume, *Research Reports of the Carnegie Commission on Higher Education,* which will be issued early in 1974.

We have also published the findings and conclusions of our own deliberations, not only in our final report, *Priorities for Action,* but also in 21 additional reports issued as they became available on subjects of urgent concern to higher education. Typically, these Commission reports have presented information and analysis in some detail and included specific recommendations or objectives.

This publication makes available the digests of the 21 reports the Commission itself has issued over the past six years. It also includes indexes of our recommendations both by topic headings and by the persons and agencies that have immediate interests and responsibilities for policy implementation.

While the full reports should be consulted by those who wish to have access to a comprehensive discussion of the Commission's recommendations, we believe that this digest and index will provide a useful reference for those who are interested mainly in the general trend and conclusions of the Commission's work.

CLARK KERR
Chairman,
Carnegie Commission
on Higher Education

October 1973

DIGEST
OF REPORTS

QUALITY
AND
EQUALITY

NEW LEVELS OF
RESPONSIBILITY
FOR HIGHER
EDUCATION
(DECEMBER 1968)
AND REVISED
RECOMMENDATIONS
(JUNE 1970)

Going to college, once a privilege for only a few, has become feasible, even necessary, for increasing numbers of young Americans. Enrollment in 1968 totaled almost 6 million students on a full-time-equivalent (FTE) basis. The nation's colleges and universities must provide new facilities for 3 million additional students by 1976–77, and enrollments will continue to rise until the year 2000. The heaviest costs for further expansion must be met in the period ending about 1980.

The crucial question is: Can our colleges and universities meet at the same time the nation's expectations of academic quality and its demands for equality of educational opportunity?

Financing is a critical element of the answer. Total institutional expenditures for higher education climbed from $5.2 billion in 1957–58 to about $17.2 billion in 1967–68 and are estimated at $41 billion in 1976–77. (Costs of higher education not resulting in college and university expenditures are not included in this figure. Such costs are certain subsistence payments, administrative expenditures in governmental agencies, and forgone earnings.)

Private resources have provided about half of the institutional funds required for higher education in recent years. State, local, and private sources combined now pay about four-fifths of the total higher education expenditures. The federal government pays one-fifth. The Carnegie Commission believes that increased federal support is justified by higher education's contributions to the national welfare and is essential to the effectiveness and vitality of the institutions themselves. The federal government's share of financial support for colleges and universities should rise from the present one-fifth to about one-third by 1976–77.

By 1967–68, federal aid given directly to institutions of higher education and for various student-aid programs (not including veterans' and social security education benefits) had reached almost $4 billion. The increase proposed by the Carnegie Commission for 1976–77 is approximately $10 billion greater. During the same period, the net increase in federal revenue will be about $70 billion; so we are convinced that the federal government can meet the suggested new level of responsibility for higher education without penalty to other urgent national priorities.

The best immediate means of federal aid to higher education are:

1   Grants and loans to individual students as we move toward the nation's goal of equal educational opportunity

2   Support to institutions to meet increased costs of expanding enrollment and to strengthen areas of particular national concern

3   Extension of support for research, construction, and special programs

STUDENT AID AND RELATED INSTITUTIONAL GRANTS

EDUCATIONAL OPPORTUNITY GRANTS

One of the most urgent national priorities for higher education is the removal of financial barriers for all youth who enroll in our diverse colleges and universities, whether in academic or occupational programs.

The Commission recommends strengthening and expanding the present program of educational opportunity grants based on need by providing:

▪ That the level of funding be increased so that all college students with demonstrated need will be assured of some financial aid to meet expenses at institutions which they select.

▪ That grants based on need be available for a period not to exceed four years of undergraduate study and two years of study toward a graduate degree (December 1968, p. 19).[1]

The Commission recommends the following maximum grants:[2]

$1,000 per year to students working for a recognized undergraduate degree or certificate, generally for not more than four years, but for a longer period up to a maximum of six years.

$2,000 per year to students working toward a graduate degree or postgraduate certificate or credential, generally for no more than two years, but for a longer period up to a maximum of three years for students in professional programs requiring three years beyond the bachelor's degree (June 1970, pp. 5, 6).

SUPPLEMENTARY MATCHING GRANTS

To encourage commitment of funds from private, state, and local government sources for undergraduate educational opportunity grants, the Commission recommends

. . . that an undergraduate student holding an educational opportunity grant and receiving added grants from nonfederal sources be given a supplementary federal grant in an amount matching the nonfederal grants but not exceeding one-quarter[3] of the student's original educational opportunity grant (June 1970, p. 5).

FEDERAL SCHOLARSHIP GRANTS TO INSTITUTIONS

To provide greater flexibility, and permit adequate coverage of individual hardship cases, the Commission recommends

. . . that each college and university be given a scholarship fund for needy students equal to 10 percent of the total sum of educational opportunity grants (not including supplementary matching grants) held by students at that institution (December 1968, p. 22; June 1970, p. 6).

[1] Page references are to pages in full report.

[2] In the 1968 report, the Commission had recommended a lower grant ($750 per year) for students in the first two years, and also a lower grant for graduate students ($1,000 per year).

[3] In December 1968, the proportion recommended was one-half.

WORK-STUDY PROGRAM
The Commission strongly endorses the work-study program and recommends that this form of federal assistance should be continued.

In its December 1968 report, the Commission recommended that federally supported programs for part-time employment for students be sufficient to enable students who meet the need criteria determined by the federal government to earn up to $500 a year.

Specifically, the Commission recommends

. . . continuation and expansion of the work-study program with federal funding sufficient to enable those undergraduate students who meet, in general terms, the federal need criteria to earn up to $1,000 during the academic year, working not more than the equivalent of two days per week (June 1970, p. 6). Off-campus assignments of educational importance, such as tutorial work, should be encouraged (December 1968, p. 23).

THE FINANCIAL AID PACKAGE
Together with a loan program (reviewed beginning on page 6) the Commission views the various financial aid programs discussed in this report as integral elements of a financial aid package. The components of the package can be combined in a variety of ways to meet the needs of different students. To permit greater flexibility in the use of the funds provided, the Commission recommends

.˙. . that each college and university be given a scholarship fund for needy students equal to 10 percent of the total sum of educational opportunity grants (not including supplementary matching grants) held by students at that institution, such funds to be allocated by the institution to students as determined by the institution's own definition of student need (December 1968, p. 22; June 1970, p. 6).

AID TO VOCATIONAL AND TECHNICAL STUDENTS
Many vocational and technical students are now ineligible for federal financial aid. In the June 1970 revision of *Quality and Equality* the Commission recommends

. . . that existing legislation be revised to enable all postsecondary vocational and technical students to apply for grants on the basis of need regardless of whether such students are enrolled in community colleges, area vocational schools, or public adult schools. Work-study programs should also be available to vocational and technical students in all these institutions, and, in addition, to students in proprietary schools. To participate in either of these programs each institution should be officially recognized as providing a particular program in which the student is enrolled at an acceptable standard of instruction (June 1970, pp. 6–7).

VETERANS' AND OTHER NATIONAL SERVICE BENEFITS
The Commission recommends

. . . that the Veterans' Educational Benefit Programs be continued and that benefits under such programs be revised automatically to keep pace with rising living and educational costs (June 1970, p. 19).

To encourage students to seek noncollege alternatives early in their years following secondary school attendance, the Commission recommends

. . . that a national service educational benefit program be established making educational grants available for service in various programs such as the Peace Corps or Vista, with the amount of the benefits set at some percentage of veterans' educational benefits (June 1970, p. 19).

COUNSELING AND INFORMATION PROGRAM

The National Defense Education Act of 1958 authorized a program for guidance, counseling, and testing of students. One of its purposes was to encourage students with outstanding aptitudes and ability to complete secondary school, to qualify for admission, and to enter institutions of higher education.

The Commission recommends that the present federal aid program of guidance, counseling, and testing for identification and encouragement of able students be expanded and that funding for the program be increased to $30 million in 1970–71, rising to $40 million in 1976–77 (December 1968, p. 24).

GRADUATE TALENT SEARCH AND DEVELOPMENT PROGRAM

Some students who have completed undergraduate training are not adequately guided or prepared for the graduate education that they need or desire. As a partial remedy to this situation, the Commission recommends

. . . that certain universities be selected on the basis of program proposals submitted to national panels to undertake specific graduate talent search and development programs, and that federal funding be made available for such programs in the amount of $25 million in 1970–71, rising to $100 million in 1976–77 (December 1968, p. 25).

DOCTORAL FELLOWSHIP PROGRAM

Because of the great importance of encouraging the most able students to continue graduate studies at the highest level, the Commission recommends

. . . a doctoral fellowship program with selection based upon demonstrated academic ability without reference to need, with fellowships in the amount of $3,000 annually for a maximum of two years to graduate students advanced to candidacy for a Ph.D. or equivalent research doctorate . . . (December 1968, p. 26; June 1970, p. 15).

The total number of such first-year fellowships awarded should equal one-half of the average of the national total of doctorates earned in the fourth, third, and second year preceding the year in which the fellowships are awarded. In each year an additional number of fellowships equal to 10 percent of the total just described would be allocated for expansion into neglected or developing fields[4] (June 1970, p. 15).

[4] In the 1968 report it was recommended that the number of first-year fellowships equal three-fourths of the national total of earned doctorates in the previous year (December 1968, p. 26).

The growth and acceptance of the doctor of arts degree for students primarily interested in a teaching career is encouraged by the Commission through its suggestion that a specified number of fellowships be made available each year to students in that program (June 1970, p. 16).

NATIONAL STUDENT LOAN BANK
The desirability of federal participation in loan programs has already been recognized in the National Student Defense Loan program established in 1958 and the Guaranteed Loan Program established in 1965. Together, these had outstanding loans over a billion dollars by 1966–67. These programs are hampered, however, by inadequate funding, limitations of eligibility in terms of need, and 10-year repayment periods.

As a supplementary source of student aid, in *Quality and Equality: Revised Recommendations* issued in June 1970, the Commission recommends that the federal government charter a National Student Loan Bank, a nonprofit private corporation to be financed by sale of governmentally guaranteed securities. The proposed bank would be self-sustaining, except for administrative costs and the cost of cancellations of interest that might occur because of low income of borrowers, and of principal for any reason other than death. We propose that about $3 billion in new loans be authorized for the first two years of the bank's existence. After the first two years, new annual obligation levels would be set each year by agreement between the directors of the bank and the Secretary of the Treasury.

The bank would make loans available to postsecondary students in amounts not to exceed $2,500 per year up to a total of $6,000 for undergraduate studies and $10,000 for graduate studies.[5] No student would be eligible to obtain more in loans, all types of grants, and work-study payments in any year than his cost of education, including subsistence costs, as officially recognized by the institution in which the student was enrolled.

Under the proposed program, borrowers would repay loans by paying at least three-fourths of 1 percent of income each year for each $1,000 borrowed until the total loan and accrued interest was repaid. The average income earner could repay his loan in approximately 20 years. The appropriate rate of repayment for the combined debt of a husband and wife would be applied to their combined incomes. Annual repayments could be deferred if the borrower's income falls below a minimum subsistence level, or during a maximum of three years when the borrower was engaged in national service. No cancellation or forgiveness is suggested for borrowers who enter particular professions, but upon the

[5] Maximum loan limits in the 1968 report were $2,500 per year for undergraduate students and $3,500 per year for graduate students without specification of any overall limit (December 1968, p. 29).

death of a borrower or at the end of 30 years from the date of the first payment, remaining indebtedness would be canceled.

If it proves infeasible to establish the National Student Loan Bank suggested by the Commission, it is recommended that the availability of funds for students be increased to establish a secondary market such as the proposed National Student Loan Association. But the Commission recommends that the original charter for such secondary market be broad enough to empower it to grant loans if further experience indicates the desirability of this course of action.[6]

Any loan program established should be a single comprehensive program covering all students—with the exception of medical students, for whom the Commission will make separate recommendations.

COST-OF-EDUCATION SUPPLEMENTS TO INSTITUTIONS

The proposed expansion of financial aid programs that enable more students to attend universities and colleges will add to the financial problems of these institutions. The full costs of education are not met by tuition payments. To relieve the institutions of some of the burden of such costs, the Commission recommends

. . . that the federal government grant cost-of-education supplements to colleges and universities based on the numbers and levels of students holding federal grants enrolled in the institutions (December 1968, p. 30; June 1970, p. 21)

Accredited colleges and universities, and institutions deemed potentially eligible for accreditation except for their recent date of establishment would receive the following amounts[7] for each federal grant holder enrolled (June 1970, p. 21):

	1970–71	1979–80
Undergraduate	$ 500	$1,000
First-level graduate	1,000	1,500
Doctoral	3,500	5,000

For the most part, these supplements would be used to meet general operating costs. They constitute, therefore, badly needed federal assistance to the institutions themselves.

[6]The Commission's recommendations for a National Student Loan Bank are based on the same general principles set forth in the Commission's 1968 report. That report included a recommendation for establishment of a federal contingent loan program but did not include detail on the operations of such programs. The 1970 recommendation of the Commission for a National Student Loan Bank does differ from some contingent repayment proposals in that it does not result in any redistribution of income among borrowers within the program (December 1968, p. 31).

[7]In the 1968 report the Commission had recommended that the higher level for cost of education supplements be reached by 1976–77 and had also recommended different levels of grants for lower-division and upper-division undergraduates: $525 for lower-division students in 1970–71, rising to $650; and $700 for upper-division students in 1970–71, rising to $1,000.

SUPPORT FOR MEDICAL EDUCATION

Although it subsequently devoted a full report to medical education, the Commission initially recognized the importance of giving federal support to medical education in *Quality and Equality.*

The federal government's increasing support of medical schools ($55 million for construction and $53 million for training in 1967–68) is recognized, but still higher levels are required.

The Commission recommends establishment of a substantial program of federal aid for medical education and health services for the purposes of:

■ Stimulating expansion of capacity at existing medical schools

■ Planning additional medical schools distributed on a geographical basis to provide needed service to areas not now served

■ Expanding educational facilities and developing new programs for the training of medical care support personnel

■ Increasing availability of health services in the community of the medical school and the quality of health care delivery (December 1968, pp. 33–34)

Adoption of a program to provide student grants on the basis of need in amounts up to $3,500 was suggested, and it was noted that medical students would have access to loan programs suggested by the Commission

The Commission also contemplated payments to institutions equal to the following amounts:

The institution's enrollment of students working toward the M.D. multiplied by $4,000.

That portion of the enrollment working toward the M.D. in excess of such enrollment in the fall of 1966 multiplied by $2,000.

The total number of residents and interns multiplied by $2,250, provided that no individual student shall be counted for more than four years, and provided further that the resident and intern program is conducted under the auspices of an accredited medical school either at its own or at an affiliated hospital.

In the Commission's report, *Higher Education and the Nation's Health,* many of the above recommendations were further detailed and some of them were modified.

CONSTRUCTION GRANTS

The great surge of enrollment in the 1950s and 1960s created a growing deficiency in facilities and the increased federal aid extended through the Higher Educational Facilities Act of 1963 came too late, and was inadequately funded to close the gap. The Commission recommends

1   That construction grants be made available to provide one-third[8] of total costs for construction and needed renovation of academic facilities

[8]In the 1968 report, this figure was one-half (December 1968, p. 37).

2   That funding levels for the academic facilities construction program be increased to provide sufficient loan funds for an additional one-third[9] of needed new construction costs (June 1970, pp. 21–22)

The Commission also recommends that start-up grants be provided for planning and nonconstruction costs for 230 to 280 new junior colleges and 50 urban institutions, not exceeding $10 million per institution but averaging more nearly $1 million per institution (December 1968, p. 38; June 1970, p. 22).

It is noted that if the Commission's recommendations were adopted, institutions could finance up to two-thirds of new construction through a combination of federal grants and loans.

RESEARCH

In recognition of the contributions of higher education to the advancement of knowledge, the federal government has played a substantial role in providing support for university-based research. By 1968, about three-fourths of all university research was federally financed.

There must be stability in the flow of federal support for university-based research; there should be enough growth in research funding to permit expansion of research in relatively neglected research fields— in the arts and humanities, social science, and environmental research, for instance; and research funds should be dispersed for projects that will yield the most needed results and be allocated to institutions best suited to achieve those results.

With these factors in mind, the Commission recommends

. . . that federal grants for university-based research (not including federal contract research centers), regardless of changing priorities for defense and space research, be increased annually (using grants in 1967–68 as a base) at a rate equal to the five-year moving average annual rate of growth in the gross national product[10] (June 1970, p. 16).

The Commission also recommends

. . . that a grant amounting to 10 percent of the total research grants received annually by an institution be made to that institution to be used at its discretion. The sum required for this purpose is to be included within the levels noted . . . above (June 1970, p. 26).

SPECIAL PROGRAMS

The federal government has been sensitive to many particular needs in higher education, but funding has often been inadequate. Since 1965,

[9] In the 1968 report, this figure was one-quarter (December 1968, p. 38).

[10] In the 1968 report the Commission had recommended that the level of federal funding for university and college research be increased at an annual rate of increase declining from 15 percent in 1970–71 to 10 percent in 1976–77 (December 1968, p. 40).

the Office of Education has given financial aid to colleges that have failed to reach their full capability because of limitation of resources. The level of funding for these developing colleges increased to $30 million in 1967. More such assistance is still needed. The federal government is also committed to support for college and research libraries, but although $50 million for this purpose was authorized in 1966, only $10 million was appropriated. In 1967 and 1968, the appropriation increased to $25 million. The International Education Act for 1966 authorized grant programs to support international studies. No funds have as yet been appropriated.

The Commission particularly recommends

. . . increased funding for the following three programs: aid to developing institutions ($100 million in 1970–71), library support ($100 million in 1970–71), and international studies ($25 million in 1970–71).[11] In addition, to stimulate cooperative programs among community colleges and universities for the preparation and reeducation of community college teachers and counselors, the Commission recommends $25 million in 1970–71 for an expanded special program of federal training grants (June 1970, p. 23).

NATIONAL FOUNDATION FOR THE DEVELOPMENT
OF HIGHER EDUCATION

Existing facilities must be developed to their greatest potential and new methods and techniques for improving operational efficiency and quality must be tried. To facilitate this the Commission recommends

. . . establishment of a National Foundation for the Development of Higher Education whose functions would be to encourage, advise, review, and provide financial support for institutional programs designed to give new directions in curricula, to strengthen essential areas that have fallen behind or never been adequately developed because of inadequate funding, and to develop programs for improvement of educational processes and techniques (December 1968, pp. 45–46).

Initial areas of concern for the Foundation would include:

1 Improvement of undergraduate education, and the development and evaluation of college and university activities designed to serve the needs of elementary and secondary schools

2 Aid in planning regional liberal arts centers to be established by groups of colleges for the purpose of increasing the quality, scope, and diversity of undergraduate education, of stimulating more economical and effective use of administrative and teaching personnel, and of sharing library and computer facilities

3 Effective use of modern technology

4 Development of new curricular programs and new concepts of public service for the purpose of seeking solutions to the problems of the inner city

[11] In the 1968 report this figure was $100 million (December 1968, p. 43).

TABLE 1 Estimate of federal expenditures* for Commission proposals (in millions of constant dollars)

	QUALITY AND EQUALITY, 1970–71	REVISED PROPOSALS, 1970–71	QUALITY AND EQUALITY, 1976–77	REVISED PROPOSALS, 1976–77	REVISED PROPOSALS, 1979–80
Student-aid programs	$1,905	$2,420	$ 3,560	$ 4,335	$ 4,984
Educational opportunity grants	(1,100)	(1,265)	(2,140)	(2,325)	(2,714)
Work-study program	(510)	(900)	(870)	(1,560)	(1,800)
Counseling program	(30)	(30)	(40)	(40)	(50)
Graduate talent search	(25)	(15)	(100)	(40)	(50)
Doctoral fellowships	(110)	(80)	(160)	(120)	(120)
Loan program	(130)	(130)	(250)	(250)	(250)
Cost-of-education supplements	1,130	950	2,710	2,600	3,610
Construction	1,150	900	925	725	700
Research	1,900	1,650	3,210	2,090	2,350
Foundation for the development of higher education	100	200	200	200	200
Special programs	300	250	800	600	800
Total	$6,585	$6,370	$11,405	$10,550	$12,644

* Does not include costs for veterans' educational benefits, or for Peace Corps or VISTA educational benefits or extension of any of the programs to vocational and technical students taking courses in institutions other than community colleges.

The Commission recommends that funding for the Foundation be provided in the amount of $200 million annually beginning in 1970–71[12]
including

... that ... $50 million be granted to the Foundation to be allocated to states and
regions which would, working with the advice and assistance of the Foundation,
make further plans for the effective growth of the states' postsecondary educational system. In the development of these plans the Foundation and the states
should give particular attention to creation of an adequate system of community
colleges and to stimulation and coordination of the states' occupational and technical educational resources (June 1970, pp. 27–28).

CONSOLIDATION OF FEDERAL ACTIVITY
It is doubtful that federal review of quality and programs in higher education can be adequately achieved through present fragmented organization of federal educational responsibility or through sporadic task-force
recommendations. It seems necessary to place federal responsibility for
such activities in a cabinet-level officer.

LEVELS OF FINANCIAL SUPPORT
Both in December 1968 and June 1970, the Carnegie Commission estimated the required levels of funding for each of its proposals for federal
support of higher education. In the December 1968 report, the funding
levels were projected to 1976–77. In June 1970, the projections (using
a different treatment of inflationary components and medical education
recommendations) were made to 1979–80, with the total federal aid suggested in that year approximately the same as that proposed earlier for
1976–77.

A summary of the projected levels in the two reports (with discrepan-
cies attributable to differences noted above) is provided in the table
above.

CONCLUSION
Higher education is today a basic national resource. The nation has a
great stake in a dynamic, healthy, and flexible system of higher education, and our recommendations are intended to add to the strength and
the progress of the system as well as to make possible greater service to
society.

---

[12]In its 1968 report the Commission had recommended an original level of funding of $100
million per year for the Foundation in 1970–71 rising to $200 million in 1976 (December 1968,
p. 46).

A CHANCE TO LEARN

AN ACTION AGENDA
FOR EQUAL
OPPORTUNITY IN
HIGHER EDUCATION
(MARCH 1970)

In 1900, 4 percent of the 18- to 21-year olds in the United States were enrolled in higher education. In 1970, that figure was 40 percent. But for many Americans there are still barriers. The five most relevant barriers are:

1 *Family income*—In 1968, a family with an income over $15,000 and one or more college-age (18 to 24 years old) children was five times as likely to include a full-time college student as a similar family with an income under $3,000.

2 *Ethnic grouping*—The proportion of black youths enrolled in college from the 18- to 24-year age group in 1968 was only half that of white persons. Young persons from other minority groups—Native Americans, Mexican-Americans, Puerto Ricans—were even less well represented.

3 *Geographic location*—Young people in the Deep South attend college at half the rate of those in the Pacific Southwest. Researchers have found that establishing a college within commuting distance raises attendance from one-third of college-age youths to one-half.

4 *Age*—Many persons beyond what has been traditionally considered "college age" could still benefit from further education but do not have it available to them.

5 *Quality of early schooling*—The quality of elementary and secondary schools varies substantially from district to district and even from neighborhood to neighborhood, resulting in poor educational foundations for many people.

LOWERING THE BARRIERS TO HIGHER EDUCATION

IMPROVEMENT OF EARLIER SCHOOLING
There can be no adequate increase in college enrollments for ethnic minority and low-income students unless there is an increase in the quality of education represented by a high school diploma and in the number of students who graduate from high school.

The Commission recommends that the first priority in the nation's commitment to equal educational opportunity be increased effectiveness of preelementary, elementary, and secondary school programs (p. 5).

ELIMINATION OF SEGREGATION
The harmful effects of racial and socioeconomic segregation on academic achievement are widely recognized, but the most effective ways of restructuring our precollege educational systems to eliminate de facto segregation are not clear. Institutions of higher education have an important responsibility to contribute to the solution of this problem.

In communities where effective desegregation of local school systems has not been achieved, institutions of higher education should offer their resources of research and consultation to local school administrators and other community leaders (p. 6).

TEACHER TRAINING FOR INNER-CITY AND RURAL SCHOOLS
As school systems are effectively desegregated, universities and colleges must concentrate greater resources in the development of new curricular materials and teaching techniques to reach more heterogeneous classroom populations. We need to know much more than we do now about what to teach and how to teach it, and about how to train those who do the teaching.

The Commission recommends the allocation of state and federal funds to colleges and universities for specific programs to meet the present needs of inner-city schools, and of desegregated schools with heterogeneous classroom enrollments . . . and endorses an intensive research and experimental undertaking in education such as was made possible in medical practice through the National Institutes of Health (p. 6).

In many parts of the country, educationally disadvantaged children are concentrated in rural areas. Indian reservations are often far from urban centers, 40 percent of black children in the South live in rural areas, and large numbers of white children live in isolated areas such as Appalachia and the Ozarks.

The Commission also recommends an allocation of funds for meeting the present needs of rural schools in disadvantaged areas (p. 7).

EDUCATIONAL OPPORTUNITY CENTERS
For some students, academic support from community agencies outside the formal classroom structure may prove effective. Educational opportunity centers combining the features of tutorial work and advice could:

Provide study space and tutorial help

Clarify vocational and educational goals

Conduct complementary testing for levels of achievement, aptitude, and interests

Provide information concerning financial and academic support available at local colleges

Prepare detailed documentation for use by admissions and financial aid officers

The Commission recommends that institutions of higher education, alone or in conjunction with local school districts, establish educational opportunity centers to serve areas with major concentrations of low-income populations (pp. 7–8).

RECRUITMENT OF DISADVANTAGED STUDENTS

The active recruiting of disadvantaged students is an important means of bringing more of them into higher education. To make recruiting programs fully effective, there is an urgent need for institutions to coordinate planning and combine resources.

The Commission recommends the establishment of recruiting and counseling pools among neighboring colleges and universities to coordinate resources and staff efforts for admitting educationally disadvantaged candidates (p. 8).

The same considerations apply to recruitment for graduate and professional schools. In this case, however, cooperative effort would be most effective at the department level.

The Commission recommends that graduate and professional departments coordinate recruiting of disadvantaged graduate students (p. 8).

CAMPUS AS A SUMMER CAMP

Making facilities of college campuses available during the summer months for organized activities for neighborhood and rural children would help break down distrust, create a sense of affiliation, and combat some of the academic and environmental factors of educational disadvantage. Dormitories, museums, cafeterias, classrooms, and recreation areas could be used for such activities. Counselors and tutors could be employed under an institution's work-study program.

The Commission recommends that institutions of higher education devote a portion of their summer schedule and facilities to camps for educationally disadvantaged children (p. 9).

PROGRAMS TO HELP DEVELOP VERBAL SKILLS

Because of environmental and other factors associated with low socioeconomic status, some students find it extremely difficult to develop the verbal skills required for college entrance and for completion of courses. Although academic success is also determined by mathematical skills, these, too, require verbal skills for proper development.

The Commission recommends establishment of experimental programs for the early development of verbal skills—to be sponsored and administered by institutions of higher education with active participation from members of the community, and establishment of programs for remedying verbal skill deficiencies at the secondary and higher levels of education (p. 9).

ACCESS TO HIGHER EDUCATION

We do not believe that every young person should attend college. We do favor universal *access* for those who want to enter institutions of higher education, are able to make reasonable progress after enrollment, and can benefit from enrollment. The provision of universal access and transfer opportunities is of importance to all students, but particularly to those coming from currently disadvantaged groups, since their numbers are growing proportionately the most rapidly. The Commission recommends that

1   Each state plan to provide universal access to its total system, but not necessarily to each of its institutions, since they vary greatly in nature and purpose

2   Community colleges or equivalent facilities be established within commuting range of potential students in all populous areas

3   Four-year colleges generally be prepared to accept qualified transfer students and give them appropriate credit for the work they have already completed

4   All institutions accept responsibility to serve the disadvantaged minorities at each of the levels at which they provide training, and that universities accept a special responsibility to serve a substantially greater representation of currently disadvantaged minorities in their graduate programs

5   Each institution issue an annual report on its present and potential contributions to equality of opportunity (p. 13)

ACADEMIC SUPPORT FOR THE STUDENT IN HIGHER EDUCATION

Students arrive on campus with varied backgrounds and interests. If a college were to structure the first-year course work for each student according to his own preparation, maturation, work schedule, and educational objectives, with the help of precollege examinations and individual faculty advisors, then no group—as a group—would be identified as special or disadvantaged, and all could be better served educationally.

The Commission recommends the initiation of programs for an individualized "foundation year", available on an option basis to all interested students (p. 14).

Some students will need to complete compensatory ("remedial") work that ideally should be completed at the high school level. Before any student is admitted to a college whose standard entrance requirements he cannot meet, the college should estimate how far below the minimum standard the student is, and ensure that the degree of its commitment to him, in compensatory resources, is potentially equivalent to the degree to which he falls below these standards.

The Commission recommends that every student accepted into a program requiring compensatory education receive the necessary commitment of resources to allow his engagement in an appropriate level of course work by the end of no more than two years (p. 14).

NATIONAL PLANNING AND COORDINATION

Many of the proposed programs and experiments for removing the educational consequences of economic and social inequities would benefit from national overview and coordination. Several groups have suggested the need for one agency or council to study, recommend upon, and monitor policy and strategy; to devise measures of progress and issue annual evaluation reports; to serve as a clearinghouse for materials and consultation; to propose further means to articulate the efforts at all educational levels; and to coordinate and oversee the activities within each regional area.

A unit within the U.S. Office of Education, with an appropriate advisory committee reporting to the Commissioner of Education, would seem to be the best device for serving these objectives (p. 25).

National policy for equal educational opportunity must be based on the most recent and significant data. High school graduation rates, the flow through undergraduate education to graduate and professional schools, the choice of majors and occupations constitute part of the educational data relating to black students, low-income white students, Mexican-American students, and other groups, that require constant research. Independent researchers are preparing important manuscripts, and the U.S. Office of Education is conducting several relevant studies: but these efforts should be coordinated, interpreted, and distributed.

The Commission urges institutions to keep detailed records on all their activities related to the expansion of educational opportunity and recommends that the Commissioner of Education designate a unit within the Office of Education to develop standard definitions and methods of reporting to ensure the coordination, evaluation, and dissemination of available data (p. 26).

GUIDELINES FOR INSTITUTIONAL CHANGE

The Commission has offered a series of recommendations and suggestions that would enable higher education to serve better a broader cross section of students. If results are to be equally beneficial to all groups, then the nation's campuses must be not only totally committed to the goals—and we believe that most of them are today—but also fully aware of the needs imposed by these programs—and it is apparent that some campuses are not. In fact, the campus is sometimes more unprepared for the educationally disadvantaged student than the student is unprepared for the campus.

To indicate the scope of institutional change that is being required, the Commission has compiled from its research and from reports and observations of experiences on campuses across the country an equal opportunity checklist for the academic community. The checklist is intended not to discourage colleges and universities from initiating equal opportunity programs, but rather to help assure the success of the programs that higher education must establish and expand.

AN EQUAL OPPORTUNITY CHECKLIST FOR THE ACADEMIC COMMUNITY

☐ Have other programs at institutions with similar selectivity, academic environments, and educational objectives been studied for strengths and weaknesses?

☐ Are considerable numbers of students, faculty, and administrators willing to reexamine and restructure traditional institutional and individual procedures and priorities?

☐ Have local and state government officials been informed of the plans and asked for their cooperation, ideas, understanding, and financial support?

☐ Are recruiters encouraged to present a realistic appraisal of the campus situation, including the scope and nature of the institution's objectives and resources? Are minority students used as recruiters?

☐ Have the requirements for additional educational, financial, and psychological support for a portion of the educationally disadvantaged students been discussed and met?

☐ Will each student with an educational disadvantage receive the commitment of compensatory resources necessary to enable him to engage in standard course work within two years?

☐ Can the community be involved in contributing financial resources and providing nonacademic support mechanisms for minority students on the campus?

☐ Has the institution examined its employment policies to identify and begin to eliminate those that are de facto discriminatory against minority persons within or outside of the campus?

☐ Will there be programs, facilities, resource persons, and funds available for the recognition of the particular ethnic heritages of minority groups?

☐ Have the campus and the local community been prepared for the language, dress, and social customs of new ethnic groups—just as these new students have been (or should have been) prepared for the values and customs of what has been the dominant academic culture?

☐ Are there administrators with the training and flexibility to provide adequate assistance? Will they be able to modify attitudes and increase understanding on the campus and in the community? Can they encourage and develop in themselves and in the students an ability to work out reasonable solutions?

☐ Are there faculty members sufficiently versed in the problems and needs of students from new ethnic groups to serve as faculty advisers? Are others willing to learn?

☐ Will persons from diverse ethnic backgrounds be available in the community and on the staff as "role models"?

☐ Are there persons either of the ethnic minorities or well accepted by them already on campus who can and will serve as resource persons or as coordinators of programs?

☐ Are these persons aware of, and in touch with, the variety of ethnic experiences?

☐ Will health, food, recreation, and living facilities be available that acknowledge and are appropriate to the needs and habits of diverse social groups?

☐ Are places of worship for the denominations or religious heritages of minority groups readily accessible, or will transportation be provided if these places are available only at some distance?

☐ Are a number of persons trained, prepared, or willing to learn how to handle ethnic conflicts that may arise, either from a sense of the part of the majority that they are being neglected because of special attention to the minority, or from a sense on the part of the minorities that they are being submerged in the life of the majority?

Use of this checklist may well reveal imbalances of which an academic community has not been fully aware, and may alert the community to the risks for both the disadvantaged students and the institution. As institutions move increasingly toward providing an excellent education to a diverse student population, the campus discovers how great a distance is yet to be covered. Too many campuses in the United States have started out with the assumption that the only problem was one of admissions. For most campuses, major changes, not just a new policy for admissions, are involved.

CONCLUSION

By 1976, the two-hundredth anniversary of the Declaration of Independence, the Commission proposes:

■ That all economic barriers to educational opportunity be eliminated, thus closing the present probability differentials for college access and completion, and graduate school access and completion, among groups of equal academic ability but unequal family income level.

■ That the curriculum and the environment of the college campus not remain a source of educational disadvantage or inequity; that questions of cultural balance no longer be a source of eruptions.

■ That substantial progress be made toward improvement of educational quality at levels prior to higher education, and toward provision of universal access to higher education where it is not available.

By the year 2000, the Commission believes that educational opportunities can and must be totally free of the last vestiges of limitations imposed by ethnic grouping, or geographic location, or age, or quality of prior schooling. It should not be necessary for colleges and universities in the year 2000 to provide compensatory educational programs or to struggle over flexible criteria for admissions and grading.

By the year 2000, there should be no barriers to prevent any individual from achieving the occupational level that his talents warrant and that his interest leads him to seek. Equalizing educational opportunity for the individual citizen could lead to a percentage of minority persons at the higher occupational and professional levels generally roughly equivalent to their percentage of the population. Such a situation would be an important signal that society was meeting its commitment to equality, and that education was fulfilling its functions.

THE OPEN-DOOR COLLEGES

POLICIES FOR COMMUNITY COLLEGES (JUNE 1970)

At the beginning of the present century, there were only a few students in two-year colleges. By 1969, there were almost 2 million, including full- and part-time students, accounting for nearly 30 percent of all undergraduates in the nation. Among the reasons for the rapid advance of community colleges are their open-admissions policies, their geographic distribution across the country, and their usually low tuition policies. They also offer more varied programs for a greater variety of students than any other segment of higher education, provide a chance for postsecondary education for many who are not fully committed to a four-year college career, and appeal to students who are undecided about their future careers and unprepared to choose a field of specialization. In addition, they provide an opportunity for working adults to upgrade their skills and training. There are now over 1,000 two-year colleges in the United States and there is no doubt that community college enrollment will continue to grow rapidly in the 1970s. As growth continues, there will be unsettled issues and problems relating to community colleges. Satisfactory resolution of these unsettled issues and problems is of importance and urgency for the future of higher education in the United States.

THE IMPORTANCE OF THE TWO-YEAR COLLEGE
OPEN ACCESS

The Commission believes that there should be an opportunity within the total system of higher education in each state for each high school graduate or otherwise qualified person to enter higher education. This does not mean that every young person should attend college—many will not want to attend and there will be others who would not benefit sufficiently to justify the time and expense involved. Community colleges should follow an open-enrollment policy, while access to four-year institutions should generally be more selective. Thus, community colleges will play a crucial role in the provision of universal access.

The Commission recommends that all states enact legislation providing for admission to public community colleges of all applicants who are high school graduates or persons over 18 years of age who are capable of benefiting from continuing education (p. 15).

PRESERVING THE TWO-YEAR INSTITUTION

Two years of higher education will meet the needs of many students. Moreover, if our two-year colleges become four-year colleges, they might place less emphasis on occupational programs and leave an unmet need in the local community.

The Commission believes that the two-year public community college has a unique and important role to play in higher education and should be actively discouraged by state planning and financing policies from converting to four-year institutions (p. 16).

GOALS FOR THE DEVELOPMENT OF COMPREHENSIVE COLLEGES
Public two-year colleges should provide meaningful options for students who have not yet made firm career choices, provide a chance to return to higher education for students who have dropped out of four-year colleges, and provide continuing education for adults.

The Commission recommends that all state plans for the development of two-year institutions of higher education should provide for comprehensive community colleges, which will offer meaningful options for college-age students and adults among a variety of educational programs, including transfer education, general education, remedial courses, occupational programs, continuing education for adults, and cultural programs designed to enrich the community environment. Within this general framework, there should be opportunities for varying patterns of development and for the provision of particularly strong specialties in selected colleges (p. 17).

OPPORTUNITIES FOR DEGREES
The Commission recommends

. . . that all two-year colleges should award an associate in arts or associate in applied science degree to students who satisfactorily complete a two-year pre-scribed curriculum and that students who enter with adequate advanced standing should have the option of earning the associate's degree in less than two years. Non-degree-credit courses should be confined to short-term courses and to train-ing of the skilled craftsman type, for which certificates should be provided, and to remedial work (p. 18).

TRANSFER PROGRAMS
About two-thirds of the students in two-year colleges are enrolled in transfer programs, and about one-third of entering freshmen do in fact transfer to four-year institutions after completing the community college program.

The Commission recommends that policies be developed in all states to facilitate the transfer of students from community colleges to public four-year institutions. Whenever public four-year institutions are forced, because of inadequacies of budgets, to reject students who meet their admission requirements, top priority should be given to qualified students transferring from community colleges within the state. Private colleges and universities should also develop policies encourag-ing admission of community college graduates. In addition, there should be no discrimination against students transferring from community colleges in the alloca-tion of student aid (pp. 18–19).

OCCUPATIONAL PROGRAMS
Although enrollment in transfer programs was predominant throughout the 1960s, there was an increase in the proportion of students enrolled in the occupational programs in the same period—from slightly more than a quarter of all students to perhaps one-third or more. Technological change is likely to be as rapid in the next few decades as it was in the 1960s. To adapt to this change, the average adult may have to shift his

occupation three or four times during his life and undertake continuing education at various intervals to protect himself against educational and occupational obsolescence.

The Commission recommends coordinated efforts at the federal, state, and local levels to stimulate the expansion of occupational education in community colleges and to make it responsive to changing manpower requirements. Continuing education for adults, as well as occupational education for college-age students, should be provided (p. 21).

GUIDANCE
Many students who attend community colleges have not developed clear educational or vocational goals, and they are unusually vulnerable to interrelated financial, academic, and personal pressures.

The Commission recommends that all community colleges should provide adequate resources for effective guidance, including not only provision for an adequate professional counseling staff but also provision for involvement of the entire faculty in guidance of students enrolled in their courses. The Commission also recommends that all community college districts provide for effective coordination of their guidance services with those of local high schools and for coordination of both counseling and placement services with those of the public employment offices and other appropriate agencies (p. 22).

REMEDIAL EDUCATION
Many of the community colleges find it necessary to offer remedial education for students who enter with inadequate preparation. This need is likely to continue until greater progress is made in overcoming deficiencies of elementary and secondary education in the United States. However, traditional approaches to remedial education frequently are not successful.

The Commission recommends that community colleges provide remedial education that is flexible and responsive to the individual student's needs, that such programs be subject to continual study and evaluation, and that community colleges seek the cooperation of other educational institutions in providing for remedial education. In addition, the Commission reaffirms its recommendation that an individual "foundation year" be made available on an optional basis to all interested students (pp. 22–23).[1]

OTHER TWO-YEAR INSTITUTIONS
Two-year branches of universities are found chiefly in Alaska, Connecticut, Hawaii, Indiana, Kentucky, Ohio, Pennsylvania, South Carolina, and Wisconsin, although 11 other states also have a few of them. In addition to two-year branch campuses and public community colleges, there are approximately 70 public two-year technical institutes, more than half of which are in North and South Carolina.

[1] See *A Chance to Learn*, p. 18 of this *Digest*.

The Commission recommends that state plans for two-year institutions should not provide for new two-year strictly academic branches of universities or new specialized two-year technical institutes, although it recognizes that there may be a case for exceptions under special circumstances prevailing in some of the states. Where such institutions now exist, they should be urged to broaden their programs as rapidly as possible so that they may fulfill the general purposes of comprehensive community colleges. The continuing existence of specialized two-year institutions, if the decision is to continue them in their narrow specialization, should not stand in the way of the establishment of comprehensive community colleges in the same areas. We also recommend that state plans should place major emphasis on the allocation of vocational education funds to comprehensive community colleges rather than to post-high school area vocational schools or other noncollegiate institutions (pp. 26–27).

THE SIZE OF TWO-YEAR INSTITUTIONS

In 1968 the enrollment at public community colleges ranged from fewer than 200 students to 10,000 or more students. However, in the majority of colleges, enrollment ranged from 500 to 5,000 students. Private two-year institutions tended to be much smaller; only about 13 percent reported enrollment of 1,000 students or more, while nearly two-thirds had fewer than 500 students.

. . . for the sake of quality of program, economy of operation, and easy availability, state plans should provide for community colleges generally ranging in size from about 2,000 to 5,000 daytime students, except in sparsely populated areas where institutions may have to be somewhat smaller, and in very large cities, where they may have to be somewhat larger (p. 31).

NEW COMMUNITY COLLEGES

The commission believes that there should be a community college within commuting distance of every potential student, except in sparsely populated areas where residential community colleges should be developed. More than one-half of all high school graduates tend to go to college if there is a public junior college in the community, whereas one-third or less do so if there is no college in the community.

. . . through the coordinated efforts of federal, state, and local governments, the goal of providing a community college within commuting distance of every potential student should be attained by 1980. In sparsely populated areas where it is not feasible to provide institutions within commuting distance of every student, residential community colleges are needed. State plans should also designate selected urban community colleges to provide housing arrangements for students from smaller communities and rural areas in order to encourage maximum access to specialized occupational programs. The Commission estimates that, to achieve this goal, about 230 to 280 new, carefully planned community colleges will be needed by 1980 (p. 39).[2]

[2] Because of the establishment of many new colleges and the availability of new information, the Commission revised its estimate of new community colleges needed by 1980. In *New Students and New Places* (October 1971) it estimates a need for 175 to 235 new community colleges.

THE NEED FOR BROADER FINANCIAL SUPPORT

THE FEDERAL GOVERNMENT

The Commission believes that, in order to stimulate the development of community colleges in all the states, as well as to bring about more equitable distribution of the burden of financial support for community colleges, federal provisions for institutional support to the community colleges should be expanded. Moreover, through an expanded federal program of student grants and student loans, financial barriers to access should be eliminated.

The Commission recommends that the federal government assist community colleges by providing (1) funds for state planning; (2) start-up grants for new campuses; (3) construction funds; (4) cost-of-education allowances for low-income students attending the colleges; (5) grants, work-study opportunities, and loans for students; and (6) an expanded program of federal training grants to stimulate expansion and improvement of graduate education programs for community college teachers, counselors, administrators (p. 44; see also *Quality and Equality,* p. 3 of this *Digest*).

The Commission believes that present procedures for reporting statistics of students enrolled in occupational programs are highly unsatisfactory. Non-degree-credit enrollment is not always equivalent to enrollment in an occupational program, and the regularly published statistics of the U.S. Office of Education shed no light on numbers enrolled in occupational programs in specific fields.

The Commission recommends that the U.S. Office of Education develop a more accurate definition of enrollment in occupational programs and expand its statistics to include changes in enrollment by field of study (p. 44).

THE STATES

Community college development will continue to lag in many of the states unless more adequate state financial support for community colleges is provided. Wherever state support is inadequate, the burden of financial support for community colleges falls on the local property taxpayer, and, in the face of rapidly rising tax burdens, there has been resistance in many areas to providing for the establishment or expansion of community colleges. Moreover, it is generally agreed that the property tax is inequitable and, to some degree, regressive in its impact.

The Commission recommends that states should expand their contributions to the financing of community colleges so that the state's share amounts, in general, to one-half or two-thirds of the total state and local financial burden, including operational and capital outlay costs. The Commission opposes the elimination of any local share on the ground that, if local policy-making responsibility is to be meaningful, it should be accompanied by some substantial degree of financial responsibility. In addition, the Commission believes that, in providing its share, the state should ensure that total appropriations for operating expenses are large enough to permit the institution to follow a policy of either no tuition or very low tuition (p. 45).

If the goal of universal access to the system of higher education is to be achieved, it seems imperative that tuition charges at community colleges be held to a minimum.

The Commission recommends that states revise their legislation, wherever necessary, to provide for uniform low tuition or no tuition charges at public two-year colleges (p. 46).

THE NEED FOR EVALUATION

There have been few careful studies evaluating community college policies, programs, and experiences. Very little is known about what happens to the students who hope to transfer but fail to achieve that objective, about the degree of success or failure in remedial education programs, and about the subsequent employment experience of students trained in occupational programs.

The Commission recommends that all states with community colleges undertake continuing evaluation studies of the experiences of these colleges, with particular reference to student achievement during the two-year educational period and their subsequent education and employment (p. 46).

THE GOVERNANCE OF COMMUNITY COLLEGES

Not only is it important to provide for a meaningful degree of local autonomy for community college government, but building community support for local community colleges without impairing their autonomy will be difficult. The state government has assumed complete control of the community colleges in about a dozen states and there appears to be a trend in that direction. The Carnegie Commission believes this trend should be reversed.

The Commission recommends that state legislation should provide for the formation of local community colleges within K–12 local school districts. In every local community college district there should be an elected or appointed board of directors with substantial powers relating to the development and administration of community colleges within the district. The Commission also recommends that local boards delegate substantial responsibility to the administration and faculty and provide for student participation in decisions relating to educational policy and student affairs. When community colleges are part of the state university system, there should be local advisory boards with substantial influence (p. 48).

ACCREDITATION

Two-year colleges are accredited, along with other institutions of higher education, on a general institutional basis by various regional accrediting bodies and on a specialized basis for particular programs by professional associations or specialized accrediting agencies. This dual basis of accreditation has created problems for the two-year colleges, with their specialized vocational and technical training programs.

The Carnegie Commission recommends a single program of institutional accreditation for two-year colleges and the elimination of accreditation specialties. The contribution of professional associations in the evaluation of specialized programs should be made through cooperation with the regional accrediting bodies (p. 49).

GOALS AND EXPECTATIONS FOR THE FUTURE

The Carnegie Commission envisions the following expectations and sets the following goals:

■ By 1976

Open access to all public community colleges

Removal of all barriers to enrollment

A state plan for the development of community colleges in every state

Comprehensive programs that provide meaningful learning options in all public two-year institutions of higher education

Achievement of the goal of a community college within commuting distance of every potential student, except in sparsely populated areas where residential colleges are needed—plans for 230 to 280 new community colleges[3] initiated by 1976

Low tuition or no tuition in community colleges

Adaptation of occupational programs to changing manpower requirements and full opportunities for continuing adult education

■ By 1980

230 to 280 new community colleges in operation[3]

35 to 40 percent of all undergraduate students enrolled in community colleges

■ By 2000

Establishment of the additional community colleges needed to provide for the increased enrollment in the final decade of this century

40 to 45 percent of all undergraduate students enrolled in community colleges

Continuing adaptation of the community colleges to the changing educational and occupational needs of our society as we approach the twenty-first century.

[3]See footnote, p. 26.

HIGHER EDUCATION AND THE NATION'S HEALTH

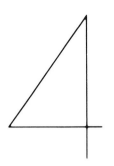

POLICIES FOR MEDICAL AND DENTAL EDUCATION (OCTOBER 1970)

The shortage of professional personnel is more serious in the health services than in any major occupation group in the United States. Thus, one of the greatest challenges to higher education in the 1970s is to mobilize its resources to meet the need for expanding the education of professional health manpower. To accomplish this task, the nation's medical and dental schools, along with educational institutions training allied health personnel, will need greatly augmented public financial support, and will also need to give sustained attention to restructuring their educational and service programs to meet the nation's need for a more adequate system of health care delivery. But no matter how many health professionals are trained, and no matter how adequately medical education facilities are distributed throughout the nation, Americans will not receive adequate health care unless a system is developed to deliver health care to those who need it, regardless of income, geographic location, age, or race. Health education efforts must, therefore, be coordinated with changes in the existing pattern of delivery of health care or recommendations of the Commission will not have maximum impact upon the actual health of Americans.

This report is concerned primarily with the education of physicians and dentists and with the programs for training physician's and dentist's associates and assistants that are being developed in several university health science centers.

THE FUTURE OF HEALTH MANPOWER EDUCATION

The Commission believes that vigorous efforts should be made in the 1970s to induce expansion of student places for M.D. and D.D.S. candidates in university health science centers and that these centers should also develop and expand programs for the training of physicians' and dentists' associates and assistants.

The Commission recommends that the number of medical school entrants should be increased to 15,300 by 1976 and to 16,400 by 1978. Toward the end of the 1970s, the question of whether the number of entrant places should continue to be increased will need to be reappraised. The expansion in the number of medical school entrants should be accomplished through an average expansion of about 39 to 44 percent in existing and developing schools by 1978, with nine new schools accounting for about 900 to 1,350 entrant places, adding another 8 to 13 percent. The number of dental school entrants should be increased at least to 5,000 by 1976 and to 5,400 by 1980 (pp. 44–45).

. . . all university health science centers should consider the development of programs for the training of physicians' and dentists' associates and assistants, where they do not exist, and that, wherever feasible, such programs be initiated forthwith. The Commission recommends, also, that in developing their plans for expansion, university health science centers should adopt programs designed to recruit more women and members of minority groups as medical and dental students (p. 45).

In addition, the Commission recommends the conversion of schools of osteopathy to schools of medicine, wherever feasible (p. 45).

THE ROLE OF UNIVERSITY HEALTH SCIENCE CENTERS
The Commission believes that university health science centers should be responsible for the education of health care personnel and for cooperation with other community agencies in improving the organization of health care delivery.

The Commission recommends that university health science centers should be responsible, in their respective geographic areas, for coordinating the education of health care personnel and for cooperation with other community agencies in improving the organization of health care delivery. Their educational and research programs should become more concerned with problems of health care delivery and the social and economic environment of health care. All new medical and dental schools should be parts of university health science centers, and, wherever feasible, existing separate medical and dental schools should likewise become parts of university health science centers (p. 47).

CURRICULAR REFORM

ACCELERATION OF MEDICAL AND DENTAL EDUCATION
The entire period of education, especially for medical students, is much too long. Several schools have already undertaken programs to shorten the amount of time required between the B.A. and M.D. and D.D.S. degrees. The Commission believes that acceleration is essential, and that it can be accomplished without loss of quality in instruction.

The Commission recommends that all universities with health science centers develop plans for accelerating premedical and medical education. The Commission also recommends that plans be developed for shortening the total duration of predental and dental education where it is unnecessarily prolonged. The Commission particularly favors a program calling for three years (instead of four) after the B.A. to obtain the M.D. or D.D.S. and a three-year residency (instead of the typical four years of internship and residency) (p. 49).

INTEGRATION OF THE CURRICULUM
A number of universities have adopted or are developing plans for restructuring preprofessional education in the health sciences. The plans differ somewhat in their objectives, but several of them would result in acceleration of premedical and medical education as well as in consolidation of all instruction in the basic sciences on main university campuses.

The Commission recommends that all universities with health science centers, and especially those developing new centers, consider plans for (1) greater integration of preprofessional and professional curricula, (2) increasing the student's options so that basic training in health-related sciences can lead on to training for a variety of health-related professions as well as medicine and dentistry, (3) awarding a master's degree at the end of this basic training period, and (4) integrating instruction in the basic sciences on main university campuses if this can be accomplished without major costs associated with the shift, without interfering with integration of basic science and clinical science instruction, and without delaying . . . early contact with patients (p. 52).

In addition, the Commission recommends that existing two-year medical schools that do not lead on to M.D.-candidate education within the same university system be converted to provide full M.D.-candidate education as soon as possible and that no new two-year schools of this type be established (pp. 52–53).

The Commission also recommends that new public health schools be made part of university health science centers and that existing public health schools become part of such centers as soon as possible (p. 53).

. . . new university health science centers should consider providing clinical instruction in selected hospitals on the British model (p. 53).

OTHER CURRICULUM REFORMS

The Commission believes that many of the reforms in medical and dental education being sought by students deserve serious consideration. In addition, the Commission believes that medical students should be given more training than they now receive in the problem of alcoholism and in the growing problem of drug addiction. The Commission also believes that, along with abolition of the internship, many changes are needed in graduate medical education.

The Commission recommends that all university health science centers give serious consideration to curriculum reforms. Their admission policies should be made more flexible and their programs more responsive to the expressed needs of students. Greater emphasis should be placed on comprehensive medicine in both the M.D.-candidate program and in graduate medical education. In all phases of medical and dental education, including residency programs, there should be more careful integration of abstract theory and clinical experience. Residency programs should be planned and reviewed by the entire faculty, and residency training should include experience in community hospitals, neighborhood clinics, etc., as well as in teaching hospitals (p. 54).

LOCATION OF NEW UNIVERSITY HEALTH SCIENCE CENTERS

The Commission believes that there should be a university health science center in every metropolitan area with a population of 350,000 or more, except for those areas which can benefit from the impact of centers that already exist in other geographically convenient communities.

The Commission recommends the development of nine new university health science centers (p. 55).

(To be in operation by 1980, the new centers would serve these metropolitan areas: Phoenix, Arizona; Norfolk-Portsmouth, Virginia; Springfield-Chicopee-Holyoke, Massachusetts; Jacksonville, Florida; Wilmington, Del.–N.J.–Md.; Tulsa, Oklahoma; Fresno, California; Wichita, Kansas; and Duluth-Superior, Minn.–Wis.)

ROLE OF AREA HEALTH EDUCATION CENTERS

In some parts of the country (such as the sparsely populated mountain states) the distance between university health science centers is likely to be great. Elsewhere, concentration of people in congested urban areas would overwhelm the facilities of even the largest health science center. In both types of areas there should be "area health education centers," which, in essence, would be satellites of university health science centers.

The Commission recommends the development of area health education centers in areas at some distance from university health science centers which do not have sufficiently large populations to support university health science centers of their own, and in a few metropolitan areas needing additional training facilities but not full health science centers. These area centers would be affiliated with the nearest appropriate university health science center and would perform somewhat the same functions recommended for university health science centers, except that the education of M.D. and D.D.S. candidates would be restricted to a limited amount of clinical education on a rotational basis, and research programs would be largely restricted to the evaluation of local experiments in health care delivery systems (p. 58).

LOCATION OF AREA HEALTH EDUCATION CENTERS

In developing its suggestions for the location of area health education centers, the Commission carefully considered these criteria: (1) distance from an existing university health science center, a developing center, or a recommended new health science center; (2) the population of the community and its surrounding area; and (3) the objective of providing for enough area centers so that no portion of a state or region would be remote from such a center. Final selection of locations for area health education centers should be based on careful regional planning. However, the number of centers indicated by the Commission's analysis is probably quite close to the number needed to provide adequate geographic distribution for such centers.

The Commission recommends the development of 126 new area health education centers, to be located on the basis of careful regional planning (see Table 1, Appendix B of the original report, p. 59).

FINANCIAL SUPPORT AND THE FEDERAL GOVERNMENT

STUDENT GRANTS

In view of the high cost of medical and dental education, there is a particularly critical need for grants for students from low-income families who wish to undertake such education. The case for providing medical and dental education to students from low-income families also rests on the need to provide equal opportunity to students who are members of minority groups, since there are indications that reluctance to incur indebtedness for the financing of education may be particularly prevalent among such groups.

The Commission recommends a federal program of grants in amounts up to $4000 a year for medical and dental students from low-income families and for students from low-income families enrolled in associate and assistant programs in medical and dental schools (p. 65).

STUDENT LOANS

Because medical and dental education are expensive, and because medical education is exceptionally prolonged, only students from upper-income families are likely to be in a position to meet all of the expenses of medical or dental education without the assistance of either grants or loans, and many students who are eligible for grants will also need to borrow funds. Indeed, a substantial percentage of all medical students now receive both grants and loans. The Commission believes that the proposal for an Educational Opportunity Bank, as proposed by the Panel on Educational Innovation to the U.S. Commissioner of Education and other federal officials and by several independent economists, is particularly well suited to the financing of costs of medical and dental students.

The Commission recommends an Educational Opportunity Bank for medical and dental students, including house officers, with repayment excused during periods of house officer training and during two years of military service (p. 66).

A NATIONAL HEALTH SERVICE CORPS

The Commission believes that the time is right for development of a national health service corps to bring improved health care service to low-income and rural areas of the nation. Medical students and other students in the health professions are increasingly interested in problems of delivery of health care to the poor, and many are motivated to participate in neighborhood clinics or other facilities in low-income areas. Normal periods of service in the health service corps would be two years.

The Commission recommends the development of a voluntary national health service corps. As an incentive for participation in the corps, an M.D. or D.D.S. would be excused from loan repayments during periods of service, and 25 percent of the maximum indebtedness he is eligible to incur would be forgiven (p. 66).

TUITION POLICY

At present there are wide variations in tuition charges from institution to institution, but tuition tends to be quite high, particularly at private medical and dental schools. The Commission believes a uniform tuition charge should be established. The charge would be adjusted from time to time to reflect changes in costs of education per student.

The Commission recommends a relatively low uniform national tuition policy for institutions providing medical and dental education (p. 68).

COST-OF-INSTRUCTION SUPPLEMENTS TO INSTITUTIONS

To ensure not only maintenance of current effort but also expansion and change in health education, the Commission believes that a substantial program of cost-of-instruction supplements per student should be under-taken by the federal government. This approach to financial assistance to institutions to aid in meeting instructional costs is dependent upon the concept that *separate* national funding will continue to be provided for research programs of these institutions and that patient care costs will be met, to a greater extent than at present in many teaching hospitals, by insurance or by such programs as Medicare and Medicaid.

Institutions would not receive instructional supplements automatically, but federal payments would be available to them in the following amounts:

1 An amount equal to the institution's enrollment of students work-ing toward the M.D. or D.D.S. or enrolled in a physicians' associate or assistant program, multiplied by $4,000. This amount is not intended to cover the full instructional costs per student, however.

2 In addition, an amount equal to that portion of the enrollment of stu-dents in the above programs in excess of enrollment in the fall of 1970, multiplied by $4,000. These bonuses would be available for eight years following initiation of a substantial program of expansion by an institu-tion, designed to achieve an increase of at least 20 percent in first-year student places within four years. Every institution should be expected to increase its average class size to at least 100.

The amounts in 1 and 2 above should be adjusted for medical and dental schools with three-year programs to enable those schools to receive the same amount of institutional aid as they would if they were four-year schools. This adjustment should be made until about 1980 but then should be reviewed (p. 70).

3 An amount equal to the total number of house officers in university health science centers and in university-affiliated hospitals or area health education centers, multiplied by $2,250, provided that no individual house officer shall be counted for more than three years, and provided that a policy is in effect to encourage specialization in fields in which a shortage exists and discourage it in fields in which there is a surplus. These supplements would also be paid under the condition that the in-stitution make an effort to reduce the duration of house officer education and make it more effective.

4 As an incentive for major curriculum reform, additional cost-of-in-struction supplements of $2,000 a year per student enrolled in M.D.- or D.D.S.-candidate programs, in physicians' or dentists' associate or assis-

tant programs, and, under specified conditions, in the last year of pre-medical or predental programs for up to three years.

All cost-of-instruction supplements recommended above would be based on the number of full-time-equivalent students rather than on the number of full-time students, as under the Health Manpower Act of 1968.

The Commission recommends (1) cost-of-instruction supplements to university health science centers for each medical and dental student enrolled; (2) bonuses for expansion of enrollment; (3) cost-of-instruction supplements to university health science centers and their affiliated hospitals for each house officer; and (4) bonuses for curriculum reform. The supplements and bonuses would also be available for each student enrolled in physician's and dentist's associate and assistant programs as well as . . . in the last year of premedical or predental education if curriculum reform is designed to achieve a reduction in the total duration of pre-professional and professional education (pp. 71–72).

CONSTRUCTION GRANTS AND LOANS

Construction funds should be allocated for new and expanding university health science and area health education centers and for renovation and replacement of existing buildings, with the federal government providing up to 75 percent of the total cost of construction in the form of grants and making 25 percent in the form of loans.

START-UP GRANTS

In view of the high costs associated with the developmental stage of a new university health science center and with the acquisition of land, especially in central city areas, the Commission believes that start-up grants should be made available for nonconstruction costs of new university health science centers. Funds would be made available from the time of issuance of a "certificate of reasonable assurance." As in the case of construction grants and loans, the start-up grants should be allocated on a competitive basis to ensure maximum effectiveness and efficiency in the curriculum.

The Commission recommends (1) construction grants for university health science centers and area health education centers in amounts up to 75 percent of total construction costs, with the remaining 25 percent available in . . . loans and (2) start-up grants for new university health science centers in amounts not exceeding $10 million per center (p. 73).

SUPPORT OF RESEARCH

The Commission believes that a vigorous biomedical research program is essential for continued progress in combating disease and that it is an integral component of the process of medical and dental education. The above recommendations for cost-of-instruction supplements are predicated on the continuation of federal support for biomedical research and for studies of the needed changes in health manpower education and in the delivery of health care.

The Commission recommends that federal financial support of research in university health science centers be maintained at its present percentage of the GNP, that funds should be made available to support research on methods of achieving greater efficiency in health manpower education and in the delivery of health care as well as for biomedical research, that federal allocations should cover the total cost of research projects, and that not less than 10 percent and not more than 25 percent of the research grants to any university health science center should take the form of institutional grants rather than grants for specific research projects (pp. 73–74).

EVALUATION AND PLANNING

NATIONAL AND REGIONAL PLANNING

The Commission believes that existing federal legislation providing for regional, state, and local planning of health services should be strengthened and expanded. The goal should be the adequate and effective delivery of health care in all parts of the nation as well as broad geographic distribution of health manpower educational institutions.

The Commission recommends strengthening existing federal legislation for regional, state, and local planning to encompass regional planning for all health manpower education and health care facilities. The university health science centers, along with their affiliated area health education centers, should have central responsibility for the planning of health manpower education, while the central responsibility for planning changes in the delivery of health care should be in the hands of regional agencies, in cooperation with state and local agencies, as well as appropriate private institutions. Continuing education of health manpower should be a major concern of the university health science centers and area health education centers with federal funds providing 50 percent of the financial support of such programs (p. 76).

RECERTIFICATION

In view of the rapid rate of progress of medical and dental knowledge and the associated problem of educational obsolescence of practicing physicians and dentists, the Commission recommends the development of national requirements for periodic reexamination and recertification of physicians and dentists. These functions should be carried out by specialty boards and other appropriate bodies, such as the Board of Family Physicians, which has adopted requirements for periodic reexamination and recertification.

The Commission recommends national requirements for periodic reexamination and recertification of all physicians and dentists by specialty boards and other appropriate bodies (p. 76).

STUDIES OF HEALTH MANPOWER

The Commission believes that there is a critical need for continuous studies of growth and change in health manpower, analyses of future supply. and demand and of the productivity of health manpower, and research on the development of new allied health specialties.

We recommend expansion and strengthening of the health manpower research programs in the Department of Health, Education and Welfare, in cooperation with the Department of Labor, to encompass broad continuous studies of health manpower supply and demand. Research funds should be made available for specialized studies of these problems in university health science centers and appropriate university research institutes (p. 77).

A NATIONAL HEALTH MANPOWER COMMISSION

The Commission believes that the time has come for appointment of a

. . . National Health Manpower Commission to make a thorough study of changing patterns of education and utilization of health manpower, with particular reference to new types of allied health workers, of changing patterns of health care delivery, and of the feasibility of national licensing requirements for all health manpower (p. 78).

THE ROLE OF THE STATES

Financial support by the states is of critical importance to the continued development and expansion of institutions providing education for physicians and dentists. The federal support recommended by the Commission will not by any means cover the full operational costs of medical and dental education, nor will it cover full construction or start-up costs. Moreover, the states have a crucial role to play in the support of house officer education and educational programs for allied health manpower.

The Commission recommends that states should continue to provide substantial support for medical and dental education and that states that have lagged in the past should plan for significant increases in expenditures for this purpose. The Commission also recommends that the states should provide financial support for medical and dental education in private institutions. In addition, the states should provide major financial support for house officer training and for the education of allied health personnel. The states, in cooperation with universities and with regional and local planning bodies, should also play a major role in the development of plans for the location of university health science centers, area health education centers, and comprehensive colleges and community colleges providing training for allied health personnel (pp. 89–90).

THE ROLE OF THE UNIVERSITIES

Universities with affiliated health science centers should encourage these institutions to orient themselves toward assuming a central role in devising and supervising more coordinated and integrated health personnel education systems. They should also cooperate with other community bodies in the development of more effective systems of health care delivery. This will require major internal changes within the universities and their schools to enable them to increase greatly their public service role, develop new and more inclusive educational programs for health care personnel, and emphasize research on health delivery systems and medical sociology.

The Commission recommends that university administrations appoint appropriate officers to develop plans for the expansion of university health science centers and for their transformation to perform the broad educational, research, and community service functions recommended in this report. University administrations should also be actively involved in the planning of area health education centers. To accomplish these objectives will often require administrative changes in the university and in the health science center as well. Careful integration of instruction in the biomedical sciences and social sciences between university health science centers and departments on major university campuses should be achieved (p. 93).

THE ROLE OF THE COMPREHENSIVE COLLEGES AND COMMUNITY COLLEGES

The rapid expansion of demand for workers in the allied health professions is creating an increasing need for curricula designed to prepare young people for these professions in both four-year comprehensive colleges and two-year public community colleges. Some of these institutions have responded to the need by expanding existing programs and introducing well-planned curricula designed to provide training for the many new technical specialties in the health field.

The Commission recommends that comprehensive colleges and community colleges develop and expand their curricula in the allied health professions where this has not been done and that they also seek and accept guidance from university health science centers in the planning and evaluation of these educational programs (pp. 95–96).

THE ROLE OF THE FOUNDATIONS

It is often more feasible for foundations than for government to support studies or projects that are innovative or experimental.

The Commission recommends that private foundations that have traditionally provided support for health manpower education and research should continue to do so and that foundations that have not provided such support in the past should consider expanding their programs to include it. The Commission also recommends that foundations expand their support for research on the delivery of health care (p. 97).

GOALS TO BE ACHIEVED BY 1980

■ Expansion of the functions of university health science centers so that they can play a central role in coordinating and guiding health manpower education and cooperating with other agencies in the development of improved health care delivery systems in their regions

- Development and expansion of programs for physicians' and dentists' associates and assistants

- Acceleration of medical and dental education, thereby achieving greater efficiency

- Integration of the curriculum, including such changes as consolidation of instruction in the basic sciences on main university campuses, integration of preprofessional and professional education, and more carefully integrated and coordinated programs of postgraduate training

- Changes in medical and dental education so that they are more responsive to the expressed needs of students and more concerned with problems of delivery of health care

- A 50 percent increase in medical school entrant places

- Initiation of nine new university health science centers

- Positive policies to encourage the admission of women and members of minority groups to professional training in medicine and dentistry

- A 20 percent increase in dental school entrant places

- Development of approximately 126 area health education centers, affiliated with university health science centers

LESS TIME, MORE OPTIONS

EDUCATION BEYOND
THE HIGH SCHOOL
(JANUARY 1971)

Several new developments have substantial impact on the structure of American higher education:

■ Many more young people attend college—In 1900, 4 percent of the college-age group went to college; in 1970, 40 percent attended. Young people today are of many more levels of academic ability and academic preparation than in earlier times, are from many more cultural backgrounds, and have more diverse career goals.

■ Much more of education takes place before college, outside of college, and after college than ever before—The schools, including high schools, have improved their quality since World War II and can improve still more —much of the last year of high school is wasted for those already admitted to college. Many students are one year further advanced, academically, than their age group was at the end of World War II. The first year of college is often largely wasted for students with a better general background than that to which the colleges earlier adjusted and for students with clear academic or occupational goals who want to get started toward their careers.

■ Jobs have changed—Rather than long-extended formal education in advance, more jobs require some basic skills and knowledge and then a willingness to keep on learning and an availability of opportunities to learn. Thus it would seem wise to space formal education over one's lifetime, reducing the amount of time spent on it early in life, and spending additional time on formal education later in life as desired and needed.

■ Young people have changed—They reach physiological and social maturity at an earlier age—perhaps by about one year, yet more are kept longer in the dependent status of student. Many students would like more options to try alternatives as they select lifestyles and more chances to try their productive skills in real-life situations.

POSSIBILITIES FOR IMPROVEMENT

The pace and organization of the college experience in the United States has become needlessly rigid and has limited the flexibility with which institutions of higher learning can adapt to the needs of their students and the society they serve.

The Carnegie Commission believes that improvements in the approach, content, and structure of higher education can make the post-high school experience more advantageous to many individuals and more useful to society. In this report we propose modifications in the structure of postsecondary education in these directions:

■ To shorten the length of time in formal education

- To provide more options

- To make educational opportunities more appropriate to lifetime interests

- To make certain degrees more appropriate to the positions to which they lead

- To make educational opportunities more available to more people, including women, employed persons, older people, and persons from the lower income levels

With these goals in mind, we suggest several changes designed to make postsecondary education more forward looking and more adaptable to individual situations than it now is. The proposed changes are not, of course, equally needed in all situations. But the greater range of options proposed should be available somewhere within the system to persons seeking them.

SERVICE AND WORK EXPERIENCE

We believe that *all* colleges should encourage prospective and continuing students to obtain service and work experience, and that *some* colleges may wish to require it before admission or at some point during matriculation. Where such experience is required, colleges might grant credit for it toward completion of degree requirements.

The Commission recommends that service and other employment opportunities be created for students between high school and college and at stop-out points in college through national, state, and municipal youth programs, through short-term jobs with private and public employers, and through apprenticeship programs in the student's field of interest; and that students be actively encouraged to participate (p. 13).

EXPANDED OPPORTUNITIES FOR POSTSECONDARY EDUCATION

As part of their provision for postsecondary education, the states should encourage and actively plan for

. . . the expansion of postsecondary educational opportunities outside the formal college in apprenticeship programs, proprietary schools, in-service training in industry, and in military programs; appropriate educational credit should be given for the training received, and participants should be eligible, where appropriate, for federal and state assistance available to students in formal colleges (p. 13).

HIRING AND PROMOTION BY EMPLOYERS

Employers should do more of their own screening for talent and rely less on the instrumentalities of the college. Greater reliance by employers on tests developed to screen applicants for positions would be vastly less costly to society than using the B.A. degree as a screening device.

The Commission recommends that employers, both private and public, hire and promote on the basis of talent as well as on prior certification (p. 14).

ALTERNATIVE ROUTES TO PROFESSIONS

We believe that more careers should be opened up to demonstrated talent, regardless of formal degrees, so that, for example, nurses should be able to become medical assistants and that technicians should be able to become engineers. We recommend

. . . that professions, wherever possible, create alternate routes of entry other than full-time college attendance, and reduce the number of narrow, one-level professions that do not afford opportunities for advancement (p. 14).

INNOVATIONS IN THE DEGREE STRUCTURE

MORE LEVELS IN THE DEGREE STRUCTURE

There is now essentially a two-level degree structure (B.A. and Ph.D.). We suggest a four-level structure (A.A., B.A., M.Phil., D.A. or Ph.D.) under which

. . . a degree (or other form of credit) would be made available to students at least every two years in their careers (and in some cases every year) (p. 15).

LESS TIME FOR DEGREES

High schools could be accredited by state university systems and by consortia of private colleges to give the equivalent of the first year of work in college. The first year in college could be made more challenging and useful. Thus, the lower division in college could soon become a one-year program except for those needing remedial work. The additional one or two years saved on the way to the Ph.D. and to M.D. practice can be offset by the constant opportunities for additional acquisition of knowledge during careers.

The Commission recommends that the time to get a degree be shortened by one year to the B.A. and by one or two years to the Ph.D. and to M.D. practice (p. 15).

NEW DEGREES

The *master of philosophy* now in effect at the University of Toronto calls for two years after the B.A. It is useful for persons intending to teach in high schools, community colleges, and in the lower division of colleges. The *doctor of arts,* now in effect at Carnegie-Mellon and the University of Washington, is also being offered, developed, or taken under consideration by at least 75 other institutions. We favor a doctor of arts degree for the nonresearch teacher.

The Commission recommends that these new degrees be widely accepted (p. 16).

ADULT AND CONTINUING EDUCATION

OPPORTUNITIES FOR OLDER STUDENTS

Higher education is now prejudiced against older students. To help correct this situation the Commission recommends

. . . that opportunities be created for persons to reenter higher education throughout their active careers in regular daytime classes, nighttime classes, summer courses, and special short-term programs, with degrees and certificates available as appropriate (p. 19).

ALTERNATE WORK AND STUDY

Programs at American colleges that combine work experience and formal study are increasing in number and should be encouraged.

The Commission recommends that opportunities be expanded for students to alternate employment and study, such as the "sandwich" programs in Great Britain and the programs at some American colleges (p. 19).

FLEXIBILITY OF ACCESS

Recent developments in the United States and in other countries point to increased flexibility in the routes open to persons seeking college degrees.

The Commission recommends that alternative avenues by which students can earn degrees or complete a major portion of their work for a degree be expanded to increase accessibility of higher education for those to whom it is now unavailable because of work schedules, geographic location, or responsibilities in the home (p. 20).

POSTSECONDARY EDUCATION AT THE INDIVIDUAL'S CONVENIENCE

To reduce the pressure to enter college directly out of high school or forgo the opportunity forever,

The Commision recommends that all persons, after high school graduation, have two years of postsecondary education placed "in the bank" for them, to be withdrawn at any time in their lives when it best suits them (p. 20).

This can be accomplished by (1) providing no- or low-tuition community colleges within commuting distance of nearly every American, or (2) by adding to social security a program for "educational security" to be paid through payroll taxes on employers and employees, with the benefits to be available on application after a period of sustained employment, or (3) by making grants, work-study opportunities, and loans available at any time during life, or (4) by providing through employers and unions the opportunity for educational leaves, or (5) by providing educational grants to persons following military and other service activity; or by some combination of the above.

GOALS FOR THE FUTURE

- By 1980

Community colleges spread across the nation

Associate in arts degrees generally available in all colleges

"Youth service" programs widely established

State planning includes all postsecondary education

The average length of time to a B.A. degree shortened initially to 3½ years on the average, and then to 3 years

The average length of time to a Ph.D. degree shortened to 4 years after the B.A.

The standard length of time to an M.D. degree shortened to 3 years and of a residency to 3 years

The master of philosophy and doctor of arts degrees generally accepted

"Sandwich" programs introduced at more institutions

Experiments undertaken with "open universities"

An "educational security" program in advanced planning stages

Tests fully developed and accepted in lieu of formal course work and in lieu of college credit

■ By 2000

"Open universities" well established

An "educational security" program in full operation

These reforms, if accomplished, would be the most significant undertaken since the modern system of higher education emerged from the classical college beginning a century ago. Formal higher education would absorb less of the time of students and less of the resources of society, and it would, at the same time, serve better both the interests of the students and the needs of society. We need more paths and more rates of progress to individual self-fulfillment and to service to society.

FROM ISOLATION TO MAINSTREAM

PROBLEMS OF
THE COLLEGES
FOUNDED
FOR NEGROES
(FEBRUARY 1971)

The colleges and universities founded for black Americans face most of the problems that confront all institutions of higher education. They also face special problems that arise from their unique history, from racial discrimination and, within the past two decades, from abrupt changes in their relationships to their traditional constituents and to other colleges and universities. They realize the gravity of the problems they face as they enter into wider competition for students and faculty, and some of them are taking bold actions to meet these problems. American society must respond to their needs with greater commitment and financial support—particularly during the coming decade when major efforts must be made to transform these colleges into fully viable institutions within the mainstream of American higher education.

MISSIONS OF THE COLLEGES FOUNDED FOR NEGROES

Some of the missions of colleges founded for Negroes are shared with other institutions of higher learning. One shared mission is to provide higher education for 1,100,000 black Americans by the year 2000. Colleges founded for Negroes will accommodate decreasing proportions of the total number of black students in American colleges, but, particularly with adequate financial assistance, they could increase their combined enrollments from about 150,000 to at least 300,000 by the end of the century and perhaps as early as 1980.

The Commission recommends that governing boards, administrations, and faculties of most colleges founded for Negroes plan to accommodate enrollments which may double on the average, certainly by the year 2000 and possibly by 1980 (p. 18).

EDUCATIONAL PROGRAMS

Three of the colleges founded for Negroes—Atlanta University, the Interdenominational Theological Center, and Meharry Medical College—enroll only graduate students. Only Howard University and Atlanta University grant Ph.D. degrees. In 1966–67, 9 of the 68 historically Negro institutions described in *American Univerisites and Colleges* (tenth edition) awarded professional degrees other than the Ph.D.; the remainder are undergraduate colleges. A review of data for those 68 colleges reveals their instruction to be heavily concentrated on liberal arts subjects. This emphasis reflects the career orientation of many black students toward the teaching professions and the reliance of these colleges on models provided by white liberal arts colleges that existed when they were founded. Black colleges now have an opportunity to reevaluate their structure and to consider curriculum innovations and enrichment designed to prepare their students for life in a society that is more competitive as well as more open than it has been in the past. To play a full part in that society, students at black colleges will need access to more of the natural and behavioral sciences, more of such subjects as economics and business administration, and more communication and quantification skills. Black colleges also should not neglect the international perspective in their curriculum, and should experiment with new calendars and new formats for teaching and learning.

The Commission recommends that colleges founded for Negroes utilize the present period of transition for curriculum innovation and enrichment and that most of them concentrate on developing, in addition to general arts courses, strong comprehensive undergraduate programs in preprofessional subjects and in subjects that prepare students for advanced education and high-demand occupations (p. 29).

COMPENSATORY EDUCATION

Because the problem of compensatory (also called *remedial* or *transitional*) education is so closely related to the past isolation and future aspirations of the black community, vigorous efforts to improve it should be made by the colleges founded for Negroes. Among short-range efforts that might be made is the establishment (preferably through consortia arrangements involving both black and white schools of education) of two or more regional centers for specialized training of teachers to work with students subject to prior educational deprivation. Financial support should be sought from the federal government, or foundations, or both for initial development. Estimated cost of operating such a center is about $350,000 annually during the first years of operation.

The Commission recommends the establishment of two or more regional centers for research on the academically disadvantaged and for training teachers for work with students thus defined. Such centers should be developed, wherever possible, with the cooperation of both predominantly black and predominantly white schools of education (p. 30).

Schools of education should continue to seek ways to counteract underpreparation of students. Encouragement should be given to the efforts of individual black colleges to extend the findings and experiences of the regional centers, as well as those of their own faculty members, in their immediate localities. Such efforts should be coordinated with those of other institutions to avoid duplication of effort in any given area.

The Commission recommends that colleges founded for Negroes initiate proposals to state coordinating councils, boards of education, and other educational agencies for the support and development of seminars, special training institutes, and classes to improve the skills of elementary and secondary schoolteachers (pp. 30–31).

PROFESSIONAL AND GRADUATE EDUCATION

Blacks are underrepresented in all the higher professions. Studies of the Ford Foundation in 1968, drawing data from one-third of all American institutions granting the doctoral degree, reported that 1.72 percent of their graduate enrollment in arts and sciences was black and that only 0.78 percent of the Ph.D.'s they granted between 1964 and 1968 went to black Americans. Adequate places already exist or are being provided in the nation's graduate and professional schools so that black graduate enrollments can be accommodated without establishing new graduate and professional departments at colleges founded for Negroes. The greatest deterrents to black entrance and persistence in professional and graduate schools are the length of time and high costs required to complete studies at this level.

. . . graduate and professional schools [should] give special consideration to the graduates of Negro colleges who are candidates for admission, and we reaffirm our recommendations that federal grants and loans be provided to assist students from low-income families who enroll in graduate and professional schools (p. 33).

AFRO-AMERICAN STUDIES

The movements for college-based study of the role of black Americans in the social, political, cultural, and economic development of the United States has special relevance to the college founded for Negroes. A few already have developed strong library and archival resources in this field.

The Commission recommends that those Negro colleges with strong resources and successful operating programs of Afro-American instruction and research be encouraged to seek special financial support for the further development of such endeavors and that foundations and government favorably consider requests for such support (p. 33).

ADULT AND CONTINUING EDUCATION

Few black colleges are now engaged in education programs for adults. This deficiency must be corrected as soon as possible. As more occupational fields open to black Americans, there will be increasing need to prepare older adults as well as youth to enter them.

The Commission recommends that more colleges founded for Negroes provide education for adult members of the black community and that the federal government and foundations give favorable consideration to requests for the support of such activities (p. 34).

GROWING TO MORE EFFECTIVE SIZE

In all comparable groups of institutions except one, the average enrollment at black colleges is considerably smaller than that of their white counterparts. The exception is in public liberal arts colleges, a category that includes 3 of the 32 public institutions founded for Negroes. In both public and private two-year institutions, enrollments at predominantly white colleges are more than 2½ times larger than colleges founded for Negroes. In general, guidelines for effective size applied to other institutions of higher education in the United States are equally applicable to colleges founded for Negroes.

The Commission recommends that, by the year 2000, colleges founded for Negroes have enrollments in keeping with the guidelines suggested for all institutions of higher education of comparable types. Comprehensive colleges should have 5,000 students. Liberal arts colleges should have at least 1,000 students. Public community colleges should have at least 2,000 students. Colleges with very low enrollments and with little prospect of meeting these goals should consider relocation or merging with other institutions which have complementing programs and facilities (p. 36).

IMPROVEMENT AND RECRUITMENT OF FACULTY

FACULTY SALARIES

Building faculties is especially difficult for black colleges because of their low faculty salary levels. A recent report of faculty salaries at 41 black colleges (21 private, 20 public) revealed the following: The highest average salary for all ranks was $13,770; the lowest was $8,241. The average for all institutions reporting was $11,170. If the salaries of faculty members in the black colleges are compared with salaries of faculty members at all colleges nationwide, it is found that salaries at black colleges were lower at all ranks, although the difference tended to narrow in dollar and percentage terms with descending rank.

The Commission recommends that coordinating agencies and boards of education in the states where there are black colleges make studies of compensation paid to faculty members in comparable ranks at all state-supported institutions and advise legislative bodies of inadequacies where they exist. The Commission also recommends that states give careful consideration to providing aid for private institutions of higher education (p. 46).

FACULTY RESOURCES

The best hope of black colleges for recruiting and holding faculty members lies in enlarging the pool of black faculty members available to all institutions of higher learning. Only 26.8 percent of the faculty members of black colleges have doctoral degrees. Increasing the number of black faculty members who have appropriate academic qualifications should alleviate some of the staffing problems of black colleges.

The Commission recommends that all colleges and universities make a special effort to identify and support, at all levels of their college and graduate preparation, young Negro men and women who show promise of becoming college teachers. We also suggest that black colleges seek assistance from state governments and foundations that will pay the salaries of their faculty members while they complete work for their doctorates at other institutions. We recommend further that, until qualified scholars and teachers become more plentiful, exchanges of visiting professors, joint appointments, and other arrangements that enable talented people to serve more than one institution be attempted as a means of expanding the pool of teaching available to black colleges (pp. 62–63).

FINANCIAL CONSIDERATIONS

STATE SUPPORT

For the public black colleges, as for public white colleges, state government support is by far the most significant source of revenue for educational expenditures. The present position of public black colleges in comparison with other public institutions in their states reflects serious efforts to overcome imbalances of the past. For example, between 1967 and 1972, North Carolina's Board of Higher Education, with the approval of the Advisory Budget Commission, will allocate $2,300,000 in "special financial assistance" to black colleges in the state. The funds are earmarked for admissions, student recruitment and counseling, faculty improvement and recruitment, special instructional programs, and library books and services.

The Commission recommends that the examples of special effort made by North Carolina and certain other states to overcome the historical disadvantages of black colleges be followed by other states where such institutions are located (p. 50).

RECOMMENDED FEDERAL ASSISTANCE

In our report *Quality and Equality: New Levels of Federal Responsibility for Higher Education,* as revised in June 1970 (see page 3 of this *Digest*), we recommended several programs that, if adopted, would provide substantial improvement in the financial status of all colleges and universities, particularly black colleges, and aid them in moving toward a more effective size. We believe the black colleges would be eligible in the 1970s for federal construction grants averaging $25 million annually and approximately the same amount in construction loans. They could also qualify for $4 million to $5 million annually in library funds. On the basis of the present pattern of income distribution for students at colleges founded for Negroes, approximately 57 percent of their students would be eligible for full educational opportunity grants, and another 23 percent would be eligible for grants averaging half the maximum grant, totaling about $100 million in basic opportunity grants and perhaps another $75 million in supplementary matching grants and work-study payments. Recommendations in the Commission's report *Higher Education and the Nation's Health* (see p. 35) calling for $4,000 annual grants to needy medical and dental students and $4,000 cost-of-education supplements to medical schools would add a total of about $5 million to the federal funds channeled to colleges founded for Negroes in 1970–71. Of the $100 million recommended in *Quality and Equality* for The Developing Institutions Program, we recommend that $40 million be channeled annually over the next decade to black colleges during their present transition.

FEDERAL AGENCY FOR DEVELOPMENT OF BLACK COLLEGES

In *Quality and Equality* we recommended establishment of a National Foundation for the Development of Higher Education whose major functions would be to encourage, advise, review, and provide financial support for institutional programs designed to give new directions in curricula, to strengthen essential areas that have fallen behind or have never been adequately developed because of inadequate funding, and to develop programs for improvement of educational processes and techniques. As black colleges move more fully toward integration, they will have to correct specific deficiencies and embark on new programs— some of which are highly experimental.

. . . the Commission recommends that a special subdivision for their [black colleges'] development be created within the National Foundation for Development of Higher Education proposed in *Quality and Equality* [see page 3]. This division, in which Negroes should have a vital role in advisory and management capacities, would aid black colleges in developing and implementing new programs and activities that respond to the challenges confronting them as institutions in transition. To fund this division, the Commission recommends that an average of $40 million annually in the 1970s from the proposed funding to The Developing Institutions Program be channeled through the division for allocation to those black colleges working with the division toward the development and implementation of specific proposals for modification and expansion of the range of curricular offerings at the institution, or for the development of consortia to facilitate such changes, or to effect mergers among institutions to enable the desirable transition. The Commission further recommends that $1 million annually be earmarked from planning funds assigned to the National Foundation for Higher Education to aid states and black colleges to plan for their growth and transition. If the Foundation is not established at an early date, thus delaying the creation of the subdivision within it, the Commission recommends that the above-described responsibilities be assigned to a special commission appointed by the President of the United States in consultation with representatives of institutions founded for Negroes, and that the funds which would have been channeled through the subdivision be assigned to this special commission (pp. 57–58).

THE BUSINESS COMMUNITY

Business and industry have an important stake in the development of black colleges. Increasingly, employers are awakening to these institutions as "new" sources of educated employees. More of them need to be awakened also to the opportunities for business and industry to assist these institutions in their further development.

We recommend that business and industry, on a nationwide basis, be fully informed about the rapid transitions occurring in colleges founded for Negroes. Representatives of business and industry should be invited to serve on advisory boards for the development programs of these colleges and should be asked to assist in planning effective communications between these institutions and the industrial community (p. 58).

ADMINISTRATIVE LEADERSHIP

The reluctance of white institutions and government agencies to accord full recognition to black colleges has historically required the black college president to be an ambassador to the white educational community. He is chief fund raiser in contacts with white philanthropy and government and, even more than his white counterpart, must divide his attention between school and community and needs extraordinarily able support in his administration. However, the lack of executive experience in the black community has meant that most administrators of black colleges must "learn on the job."

The Commission recommends that historically white colleges, in the North and South, consider appointing blacks to some of the administrative positions open at their institutions. Organization of advanced management seminars and short courses for administrators at black colleges, supported at least partially by foundations and business firms, is also recommended. We also suggest that colleges and universities develop programs and prepare proposals to the government and foundations for support of administrative intern programs for black students (p. 64).

CONCLUSIONS

The colleges and universities founded for Negroes constitute a valuable resource in knowledge and facilities needed to accommodate the still rising demands of young Americans of all races for higher education.

By the end of the present decade, the following objectives should be achieved:

■ Black colleges should expand to accommodate enrollments that might double by the year 1980 and almost certainly will double by the year 2000.

■ Salary levels for faculty in black colleges should be more nearly equal to those in white colleges than they are now.

■ Colleges founded for Negroes should have more comprehensive curricula and should provide instruction in more of the fields in which careers are opening up to black Americans.

■ Some of the black colleges should build upon available resources to create national centers for the study of Afro-American history, tradition, arts, and literature.

There are roles for state governments, the federal government, foundations, business and industry, and other colleges in helping achieve these goals. Black colleges are a national asset. They should be encouraged and assisted along with all other colleges to the extent that their problems are similar, and they should be given additional encouragement and assistance to the extent that they have special problems resulting from the position in which they have been placed by history.

THE CAPITOL AND THE CAMPUS

STATE RESPONSIBILITY FOR POST-SECONDARY EDUCATION (APRIL 1971)

Historically, the primary responsibility for the development of higher education in the United States has resided in the states. In the chartering of colonial private colleges, in the subsequent creation of state colleges and universities, in the more recent support of the community college movement, and in planning and overall coordinating, state governments have provided initiative and funds, and have exercised some control over postsecondary educational institutions of their states. The mix of funding, initiative, and control has changed over time and has varied with the geographic, economic, political, and cultural circumstances of the individual states.

The central aim of each state has remained the same: to meet, in one way or another, the goals of its citizens for training beyond the high school. The goals have been achieved with considerable success in the past. But needs continue to expand and evolve:

- For educating greater proportions of the population
- For educating citizens over more of their lifetimes
- For broader ranges and alternative choices in types of training
- For higher levels of training
- For expertise that aids in solving today's social problems
- For manpower training geared to the state's changing employment patterns

The states should continue to carry primary governmental responsibility for higher education. But to successfully meet these expanding needs, each state will have to make even greater efforts than it has in the past.

State governments should broaden their focus on higher education. As it is usually defined, higher education encompasses only public and private two-year and four-year colleges and universities—some 2,500 institutions and about 8 million students. *Postsecondary education* more broadly defined also includes private profit and nonprofit trade and technical schools, public adult and area vocational schools, and various trade union apprenticeship programs. Under this definition, postsecondary education includes not only 2,500 colleges and universities but also approximately 7,000 private trade and technical schools, and at least 500 apprenticeship programs, adult public schools, and correspondence schools, bringing the number of institutions to about 10,000 and the total enrollment to about 10 million.

NATURE OF STATE RESPONSIBILITY

The state responsibility is both residual and pivotal. The state need not and should not directly supply all the resources necessary, nor should it exercise complete control over the system of postsecondary education—but it must assure that such a system exists through a multiplicity of public and private resources and institutions of various types. The state role in assuring such a system is shaped in large part by the educational policies of the governor and his staff and of the legislature.

Enrollment in public two-year colleges increased fivefold in the 1960s. These institutions were often established, controlled, and partially financed by local governments. In those states in which community colleges were created by local initiative and rely heavily on local support, state responsibility for postsecondary education has been significantly modified. Massive expansion of locally controlled two-year institutions has caused problems of articulation between the community colleges and other state institutions, of shifts in patterns of public support, and of expanded needs for financial aid for students who transfer to four-year colleges.

The Commission recommends that state governments continue to exercise major responsibility, in cooperation with local governments and private institutions, for maintaining, improving, and expanding systems of postsecondary education adequate to meet the needs of the American people (p. 16).

THE GOVERNOR, THE LEGISLATURE, AND HIGHER EDUCATION

Governors can profoundly affect higher education in their states. The Commission believes that in the relationship between governors and higher education, the checks and balances and avoidance of conflict of interest that prevail throughout the American political system should be observed.

The Commission recommends

■ That governors not serve as chairmen or voting members of state coordinating agencies or governing boards of colleges and universities; and

■ That appointments by the governor to governing boards of state colleges and universities, and to state coordinating and/or planning agencies, be made with the advice and consent of the senate (p. 20).

Apart from its budget appropriation functions, the most significant power of the legislature over a state's colleges and universities is in coordination. It is the legislature that creates the structure for coordination in a state and provides the impetus and mechanisms for planning.

COORDINATION AND PLANNING

By 1969, 27 states had formal coordinating boards for higher education and 19 states had consolidated control of public institutions under single governing boards. Coordination agencies are created to:

Avoid wasteful duplication in programs and harmful competition for resources

Work toward greater efficiency in the use of resources

Aid orderly growth

Assist in developing admissions policies

Collect data needed for policy determination

Encourage diversity within the state's system of higher education

Serve as communications agencies

Foster excellence in the development of the programs of the expanding postsecondary education network

STATEWIDE COORDINATION

While recognizing the need for more effective coordination of postsecondary education at the state level, the Commission recommends that states strongly resist:

Investing coordinating agencies with administrative authority, particularly over budget matters, or

Establishing single governing boards, except in those states in which a special combination of historical factors and present circumstances make such agencies more feasible than other types of coordinating agencies (pp. 28–29).

The Commission further recommends that:

1   If an existing state agency such as the budget office or finance office undertakes budget review for higher education, the coordinating agency should not be given the responsibility for an independent budget review, but should instead be involved in the budget review process of the other state agency. This involvement should include, at the very minimum, the availability of the budget analyst's data, including the institutions' presentations and the budget department's analysis, and representatives of the coordinating agencies should attend and participate in all hearings on the appropriation request. In some instances, it may also be possible for members of the coordinating agency staff to work with the budget analyst's staff in a consultative capacity in making the budget review.

2   If there is no existing state agency which does or can undertake budget review for higher education, budget review, as opposed to budget control, could be assigned to the coordinating agency.

3   Although the Commission recommends against investing coordinating agencies with authority to control institutional budgets, it does recommend that states grant to coordinating agencies some funds which the agency itself can grant to institutions to encourage quality improvement, and experimentation and innovation consistent with the state's long-range educational goals. Agencies allocating funds for these purposes should regularly evaluate the programs developed with such funds.

4   Coordinating agencies should be assigned program review responsibilities and authority consistent with their educational planning functions.

5   Coordinating agencies should act in an advisory capacity on matters such as:

Effective use of resources

Educational quality

Access to postsecondary education

Appropriate functions for the various types of institutions

Articulation among the various elements within postsecondary education

6   Coordinating agencies should serve as buffer and communicator:

Explaining the above matters to agencies of the state government and to the public

Developing mutual understanding of common goals among the elements of postsecondary education

Protecting the institutions, when necessary, from legislative, executive, or public interference in carrying out their educational functions (pp. 29–30).

It is often proposed that coordinating agencies be granted more authority in order to improve their performance. But the quality of performance may not be as clearly related to the authorities which they possess as to the nature of their staffs and the levels at which they are funded.

The Commission recommends:

1   That states review the funding levels of their coordinating agencies to determine if the levels permit attention to the broader functions of coordination or only to those minimal duties legally required of the agencies.

2   That states take steps to attract staff members of the ability, stature, and sensitivity required to carry out the complex tasks of the agencies (e.g., salary level increases, opportunities for educational and research leaves, and adoption of certain other fringe benefits usually available to members of the academic community).

3   That states with heavy institutional representation in the composition of their boards take steps to increase the proportion of lay members and to introduce appropriate nominating techniques for appointment of outstanding noninstitutional members, regardless of who has the final appointing authority.

4   That boards seek to increase acceptance by the institutions through:

More effective consultation with the entire range of postsecondary institutions

Experimentation with a program of limited term exchanges of personnel between agency and institutional staffs

Establishment of joint board staff and institutional staff seminars or workshops focused on state educational concerns

5   That institutions examine their own levels of cooperativeness to determine whether failures to respond to advisory agencies might lead more surely and quickly to establishment of regulatory agencies (pp. 30–31).

STATEWIDE PLANNING

The exact nature and content of statewide planning and the emphasis placed on various aspects of that content will depend upon the particular circumstances in each state.

As minimum elements in any state planning effort, the Commission recommends attention be given to:

■ Present and future access to postsecondary education, including need for student spaces, student financial aid programs, geographic availability of institutions, and admissions standards for types of institutions

■ Appropriate functions for the various types of institutions within postsecondary education, including degrees to be granted, research activities, and public service functions

■ Orderly growth of postsecondary education—including location of new campuses, development of new schools, and optimum size of institutions

■ Articulation among the various elements of postsecondary education and within secondary education

In setting the parameters for these planning functions, the Commission recommends that state agencies:

■ Take into account the present and potential contributions to state needs of all types of postsecondary institutions including universities, colleges, private trade and technical schools, area vocational schools, industry, and unions and other agencies providing various forms of postsecondary education

■ Encompass the entire timespan of a person's postsecondary education needs from immediately after high school throughout life

The Commission further recommends that states, in developing both their short- and longer-range plans, give greater attention to institutional diversity, and to building sufficient flexibility into both institutional and systemwide plans to permit adaptation as educational processes and needs change (p. 34).

STATEWIDE PLANNING—RESPONSIBILITY There is substantial variation among the states in the type of agency assigned responsibility for planning. The Commission recommends

. . . that a state's initial development of a broad postsecondary educational plan be undertaken by a commission appointed for that purpose with a small staff augmented by special task forces as needed, selected so as to assure participation by both public representatives and leaders of educational constituencies (p. 36).

STATEWIDE PLANNING—PERIODIC REVIEW OF PLANS A plan once developed is in danger of being considered more or less final and unchangeable. The Commission recommends

. . . that a basic reassessment of a state's postsecondary educational plan be undertaken by the advisory coordinating board, if such exists, or by a commission appointed for that purpose every five or ten years or whenever it becomes apparent that such a reassessment is essential to reflect adequately the totality and interaction of changing conditions and educational needs (p. 36).

IMPLEMENTATION OF PLANS Once established, plans must be implemented and be subject to short-run modification. Implementation can be carried out by whatever coordinating mechanism exists, whether advisory or regulatory or governing.

The Commission recommends that coordinating agencies be given the following authorities to be exercised within the context of long-range plans or guidelines established for the state:

1 To approve or disapprove new institutions, branches or centers, and, where appropriate, to take active steps toward the establishment of new institutions

2   To approve all new degree programs at the doctoral level, and new master's and baccalaureate programs in general fields not previously offered, and in high-cost fields

3   To allocate funds under state-administered federal programs (pp. 36–37)

COMPARISONS OF STATE EFFORT

The Commission believes that every state should strive to create an open-access system of postsecondary education—one in which admissions requirements for various segments of postsecondary education within the state are such that every young American who can benefit from further education will not be barred from doing so because of past educational disadvantages or because admissions requirements are not properly related to educational function. Effective educational opportunity requires adequate provision of student places, through appropriate geographic distribution of institutions, and through combinations of tuition and student-aid policies designed to overcome economic barriers. Because of differences in educational systems from state to state, it is not possible to make precise comparisons of state efforts to achieve these goals. However, the Commission has been able to obtain an approximation of comparative success through examination of (1) undergraduate enrollment of state residents as a percentage of the college-age population (18 to 21), and (2) first-time undergraduate enrollment as a percentage of current-year high school graduates.

The Commission recommends that:

▪ All states, but particularly those with ratios below 70 percent, take steps to increase the percent of high school students who remain in high school and successfully complete the high school program.

▪ States that rank low in terms of the proportion of students going on to higher education substantially increase their financial commitment to higher education.

▪ State and local communities implement the Commission's recommendations for establishing 230 to 280 additional open-door community colleges as set forth in the Commission's report *The Open-Door Colleges.*[1]

▪ States showing a low proportion of their students within commuting distance of free-access colleges immediately undertake an evaluation of their higher education system to determine if, in fact, it lacks open access as a system and, if so, what steps need be taken to achieve reasonably open access (p. 56).

THE STATE AND THE NONRESIDENT STUDENT

RESIDENCY CRITERIA

To alleviate some of the problems and inequities resulting from current policies of some states concerning nonresident students, the Commission recommends that:

[1] This recommendation was later revised. See pp. 85–87 of this *Digest.*

■ States, possibly working through the Education Commission of the States, carefully review their residence requirements and modify them if necessary for the purpose of granting immediate residence status to students whose families came to the state for other than educational reasons.

■ States, possibly working through the Education Commission of the States, cooperate for the purpose of developing relatively standard residence criteria and that each state review the implementation of requirements of its own institutions to ensure similar application of the criteria among public institutions (p. 59).

INTERSTATE COOPERATION

A much higher degree of interstate cooperation is required if states are to take advantage of the opportunities afforded by interstate student migration. These opportunities are most evident at the graduate level.

To encourage the continued development of quality in graduate education at public institutions by permitting students of high ability to attend public institutions without reference to their residency the Commission recommends that:

■ The cost-of-education supplements accompanying the doctoral fellowships recommended in the Commission's first report be available only to those institutions that charge the doctoral recipient a fee that is not affected by his residency status.

■ States consider carefully the adverse affects of enrollment limits at the graduate level for out-of-state students (p. 60).

To take advantage of the opportunities afforded by interstate mobility of students, the Commission recommends that states enter into reciprocity agreements for the exchange of both undergraduates and graduate students in those situations where the educational systems of each of the states will be enhanced by such an exchange agreement (p. 60).

THE STATE AND PRIVATE INSTITUTIONS

The Commission believes there is a continued need for a strong private sector in American higher education. The presence of the private sector extends diversity, provides valuable competition for public institutions in developing quality, aids in protecting autonomy for all higher education, and fosters the type of institution that gives individual treatment to individual students.

The Commission recommends that states that do not presently have a strong private sector consider the desirability of making the equivalent of land grants to responsible groups who can demonstrate financial ability to operate new private institutions. Such grants should encourage groups to start new institutions or to open branches of existing well-established private institutions in the granting state (p. 66).

PUBLIC AND PRIVATE TUITION LEVELS

Present average tuitions at four-year public institutions are almost three times as high as those at two-year public institutions. This differential is apparently based on the generally held assumption that quality—and therefore costs—are higher at four-year institutions, and thus tuition should also be higher. In states with both a university system and a college system, the same assumption about relative costs at different educational levels leads to higher tuition levels at the university. This tuition practice results in greater inequality of educational opportunity for those students who are financially disadvantaged.

The Commission recommends that states and public institutions that find it necessary to increase tuition and other required instructional fees, not increase such fees at a rate higher than the rate at which per capita personal disposable income rises, except that institutions which have kept their fees unusually low for many years may find it necessary to exceed this rate in initial increases (p. 85).

If private institutions held their tuition increases to a rate somewhat less than the rate of increase in personal disposable income, the present gap in public and private tuition could be narrowed at least to the historic rate of about 1:3. Appropriation of some state funds to aid private colleges would make the slower rise of tuition possible.

The Commission recommends that states establish a program of tuition grants for both public and private institutions to be awarded to students on the basis of financial need. Only after establishment of a tuition grants program should states consider raising tuition levels at public institutions. To avoid upward pressures on private tuition from such grants, states would need to set a maximum tuition grant (p. 86).

A basic goal for any long-range policy should be that a student's selection of an institution depend upon the academic ability and talents of the student, rather than upon his economic ability to pay.

The Commission recommends that no tuition or very low tuition be charged for the first two years in public institutions including community colleges, state colleges, and universities (p. 86).

PUBLIC FUNDS FOR PRIVATE HIGHER EDUCATION

The Commission is aware that if public aid is to be granted to private institutions, careful consideration must be given to the constitutional and political problems inherent in grants to private institutions. However, we believe that many private institutions are experiencing real financial difficulties and that many of these difficulties could be alleviated by adoption of Commission proposals set forth in *Quality and Equality,* as revised in June 1970. Further, we have found that many of the state studies on higher education have stressed the great need for both public and private colleges and universities to improve their management practices and to make better use of present and potential resources.

The Commission recommends that foundations, government agencies, and higher education associations give special attention to funding studies and projects concerned with management problems of universities and colleges with effective utilization of available and potential resources (p. 97).

The Commission also recommends that states enter into agreements, or make grants, for the purpose of continuing certain educational programs at private institutions (for example, Florida and Wisconsin grants to private medical schools). These should be selected after consideration of special manpower needs, evaluation of existing student places for these programs in public institutions, and the relative costs of expanding public capacity or supporting and expanding private programs (p. 97).

The Commission also recommends that those states that do not already have programs enabling private institutions to borrow construction funds through a state-created bond-issuing corporation take steps to develop such agencies if the private institutions can demonstrate the need for them (p. 97).

For those few states in which the above recommendations prove inadequate, and this might be the situation in states that rely heavily on private universities and colleges, the Commission recommends that each resident student be given cost-of-education vouchers which would entitle any private institution selected by the student to receive a state payment increasing gradually each year up to one-third of the subsidy granted by the state for students at the same levels attending comparable public institutions (p. 99).

PUBLIC ACCOUNTABILITY AND INSTITUTIONAL INDEPENDENCE

Colleges and universities that enjoy the support and protection of the states also need, on occasion, to be protected from intrusion by the state into academic and other matters that should be the province of the institutions.

It is difficult to indentify an agency that is in a sufficiently independent position to censure a state. However, it is possible to reduce the potential for encroachments upon institutional independence by assuring a composition of public institution governing boards and state coordinating councils that militates against too early an involvement of the state in key educational policy matters and in the administration of the institution.

The Commission recommends that:

■ Public and private institutions seek to establish guidelines clearly defining the limitations on state concern and state regulation or control

■ A special commission on institutional independence be established within the American Council on Education; this commission, which should consist of both ACE members and public members, would be assigned responsibility for reviewing external interference with institutional independence and issuing findings after such reviews

■ Elected officials (unless elected for that specific purpose) not serve as members of governing boards of public institutions or coordinating agencies

■ A system be developed to assure adequate screening and consultation prior to appointments to governing boards, regardless of who has the final authority to appoint (p. 107).

CONCLUSION

If American higher education is to retain its present quality, states must make a further vigorous effort to provide their fair share of the resources needed to accommodate the additional 3 million students expected in the seventies. One measure of whether a state is carrying its share of the national burden of providing places for students is the state's ratio of total public and private student places to the number of 18- to 21-year-olds in the state.

The Commission recommends that states having a ratio of less than 30 places in both public and private education in the state for every 100 eighteen- to twenty-one-year-olds in the state should take emergency measures to increase the availability of higher education in the state (p. 113).

In 1966–67 approximately 0.7 percent of per capita personal income was spent through state and local taxes for higher education. To accommodate the expanded enrollment expected in the next decade, the amount spent will have to increase to approximately 1 percent of personal per capita income, taking into account the slight relative decline expected in the state's share of financing higher education.

The Commission recommends that states with a present expenditure of less than 0.6 percent of per capita personal income spent through state and local taxes for higher education should take immediate steps to increase their financial support of higher education (p. 114).

The tests mentioned above (in addition to the two on p. 62) are especially relevant for the immediate future. However, the long-range objectives can be met only if the state has also broadened its concern to include the entire range of postsecondary education, and has educational opportunities available to meet the various educational needs and qualifications of its citizens throughout their lives and to develop the leadership, professional, and technical skills needed by the society.

DISSENT AND DISRUPTION

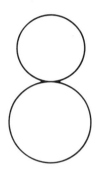

PROPOSALS FOR CONSIDERATION BY THE CAMPUS (JUNE 1971)

Dissatisfaction and disaffection on our college and university campuses reflect many current problems of American society—achieving equality of opportunity for all citizens, ending the war in Vietnam, eliminating poverty, preserving and restoring our physical environment, assessing and controlling the impacts of technology, and making our institutions responsive to the needs of the people. Attitudes of unrest also reflect problems on our campuses—including disagreements over forms of governance and over the substance of academic programs. It is likely that dissatisfaction and disaffection will persist for some time, rising and falling periodically in the extent and intensity of their expression.

The Carnegie Commission generally endorses the report of the President's Commission on Campus Unrest (Scranton Commission). Our concern is that dissatisfaction and disaffection be expressed on campus in constructive ways and in accord with the principles of a free society.

Public expressions of dissatisfaction by students and faculty members take two broad forms: dissent and disruption. Dissent must be protected; disruption must be ended. In achieving these goals, repression must be prevented and unnecessary harshness by law enforcement officers must be avoided. There is great diversity among colleges and universities and among students within institutions, and procedures should take such diversity into account.

Most students and most faculty members oppose disruption. Solutions to disruption, therefore, must be aimed at the disrupters in particular and not at higher education or its component parts in general.

DISSENT VERSUS DISRUPTION

Dissent respects the rights of one's fellow citizens; it relies on persuasion. Disruption is activity that is not protected by the First Amendment and interferes with the rights of others. It relies on coercion in one form and violence in another. Dissent is essential in a free society. Disruption is destructive of legitimate democratic processes.

The Commission recommends that evaluation of and response to events on a campus be based upon the distinction between dissent and disruption (p. 13).

The Commission also recommends that dissent be protected as a democratic right and a major means of renewal for society; that repression be rejected (p. 13).

The Commission further recommends that disruption be met by the full efforts of the campus to end it and, where necessary, by the general law, while guarding against excessive force by law enforcement personnel (p. 14).

MANY PROBLEMS, MANY INDIVIDUALS, MANY CAMPUSES

MANY PROBLEMS

An examination of the factors contributing to protest activities on the campuses suggests that dissent and disruption reflect many changes, controversies, and problems in American society and in colleges and universities. We conclude

. . .that dissatisfactions on campuses and their public expression should be viewed as the reflection of many problems and conditions both in society and on the campuses. Both campus and society share responsibility. Dissenters are also responsible for their choice of tactics in advancing their goals—for some of their tactics are the source of the dissatisfactions and negative reactions of the public at large (p. 16).

MANY INDIVIDUALS
Many students are dissatisfied about many things, but it is also important to recognize that the dissatisfaction is not uniform. It has many different sources, participants of varying points of view, and a variety of forms of public expression. We conclude

. . . that students and faculty members are divided, as is American society, about means and ends; but they stand predominantly, as does American society, against disruption and violence and for ordered change (p. 20).

MANY CAMPUSES
Of the more than 2,500 diverse campuses in the United States, about one-half have experienced some organized dissent, but only 5 percent have experienced violence or terrorism in any recent year.

We conclude that actions by society in response to coercion and violence should be undertaken only with reference to those specific individuals and groups who engage in it. A campus as a whole, or a system as a whole, or higher education as a whole, should not be penalized (p. 21).

GUIDELINES FOR RIGHTS AND RESPONSIBILITIES
Campuses, historically, have had few explicit guidelines for the rights and responsibilities of all their members. They have operated, instead, on the basis of certain principles and relationships affecting separately each of their constituent groups. Increasingly, these traditional arrangements are no longer effective in some places.

The Commission believes that each campus, if it has not already done so, should develop its own bill of rights and responsibilities. The Commission has prepared a model of such a bill that is intended as a working document. Because of the great diversity in higher education in the United States, the principles set forth are necessarily general, and individual institutions would need to adapt them according to their particular circumstances. However, we see at least three merits in the general approach of our model bill: (1) it treats rights and responsibilities simultaneously; (2) it approaches a total campus community as a single entity; and (3) it establishes the principle that the greater the privileges of members of the institution, the more responsible they should be for maintenance of high standards of conduct and an environment conducive to extending, sharing, and examining knowledge and values.

A BILL OF RIGHTS AND RESPONSIBILITIES FOR MEMBERS OF THE INSTITUTION: FACULTY, STUDENTS, ADMINISTRATORS, STAFF, AND TRUSTEES

PREAMBLE

Members of the campus have an obligation to fulfill the responsibilities incumbent upon all citizens, as well as the responsibilities of their particular roles within the academic community. All members share the obligation to respect:

The fundamental rights of others as citizens

The rights of others based upon the nature of the educational process

The rights of the institution

The rights of members to fair and equitable procedures for determining when and upon whom penalties for violation of campus regulations should be imposed.

As citizens, members of the campus enjoy the same basic rights and are bound by the same responsibilities to respect the rights of others, as are all citizens.

■ Among the basic rights are freedom of speech; freedom of press; freedom of peaceful assembly and association; freedom of political beliefs; and freedom from personal force and violence, threats of violence, and personal abuse.

Freedom of press implies the right to freedom from censorship in campus newspapers and other media, and the concomitant obligation to adhere to the canons of responsible journalism.

It should be made clear in writings or broadcasts that editorial opinions are not necessarily those of the institution or its members.

■ The campus is not a sanctuary from the general law.

■ The campus does not stand *in loco parentis* for its members.

Each member of the campus has the right to organize his or her own personal life and behavior, so long as it does not violate the law or agreements voluntarily entered into, and does not interfere with the rights of others or the educational process.

■ Admission to, employment by, and promotion within the campus shall accord with the provisions against discrimination in the general law.

All members of the campus have other responsibilities and rights based upon the nature of the educational process and the requirements of the

search for truth and its free presentation. These rights and responsibilities include:

■ Obligation to respect the freedom to teach, to learn, and to conduct research and publish findings in the spirit of free inquiry.

Institutional censorship and individual or group intolerance of the opinions of others are inconsistent with this freedom.

Freedom to teach and to learn implies that the teacher has the right to determine the specific content of his course, within the established course definition, and the responsibility not to depart significantly from his area of competence or to divert significant time to material extraneous to the subject matter of his course.

Free inquiry implies that (except under conditions of national emergency) no research, the results of which are secret, is to be conducted on a campus.

■ Obligation not to interfere with the freedom of members of a campus to pursue normal academic and administrative activities, including freedom of movement.

■ Obligation not to infringe upon the right of all members of a campus to privacy in offices, laboratories, and dormitory rooms and in the keeping of personal papers, confidential records and effects, subject only to the general law and to conditions voluntarily entered into.

Campus records on its members should contain only information which is reasonably related to the educational purposes or safety of the campus.

■ Obligation not to interfere with any member's freedom to hear and to study unpopular and controversial views on intellectual and public issues.

■ Right to identify oneself as a member of the campus and a concurrent obligation not to speak or act on behalf of the institution without authorization.

■ Right to hold public meetings in which members participate, to post notices, and to engage in peaceful, orderly demonstrations.

Reasonable and impartially applied rules designed to reflect the educational purposes of the institution and to protect the safety of the campus shall be established regulating time, place, and manner of such activities and allocating the use of facilities.

■ Right to recourse if another member of the campus is negligent or irresponsible in performance of his or her responsibilities or if another member of the campus represents the work of others as his or her own.

■ Right to be heard and considered at appropriate levels of the decision-making process about basic policy matters of direct concern.

■ Members of the campus who have a continuing association with the institution and who have substantial authority and security have an especially strong obligation to maintain an environment conducive to respect for the rights of others and fulfillment of academic responsibilities.

Tenured faculty should maintain the highest standards in performance of their academic responsibilities.

Trustees have a particular responsibility to protect the integrity of the academic process from external and internal attacks and to prevent the political or financial exploitation of the campus by any individual or group.

The institution, and any division or agency which exercises direct or delegated authority for the institution, has rights and responsibilities of its own. The rights and responsibilities of the institution include:

■ Right and obligation to provide an open forum for members of the campus to present and debate public issues.

■ Right to prohibit members of the campus from using its name, its finances, or its physical and operating facilities for commercial activities.

■ Right and obligation to provide for members of the campus the use of meeting rooms under the rules of the campus, including use for political purposes such as meetings of political clubs; to prohibit use of its rooms on a regular or prolonged basis by individual members or groups of members as free headquarters for political campaigns; and to prohibit use of its name, its finances, and its office equipment and supplies for any political purpose at any time.

■ Right and obligation not to take a position, as an institution, in electoral politics or on public issues, except on those issues which directly affect its autonomy, the freedom of its members, its financial support, and its academic functions.

■ Right and obligation to protect the members of the campus and visitors to it from physical harm, threats of harm, or abuse; its property from damage and unauthorized use; and its academic and administrative processes from interruption.

■ Right to require that persons on the campus be willing to identify themselves by name and address, and state what connection, if any, they have with the campus.

■ Right to set reasonable standards of conduct in order to safeguard the educational process and to provide for the safety of members of the campus and the institution's property.

■ Right to deny pay and academic credit to members of the campus who are on strike,[1] and the concomitant obligation to accept legal strikes legally conducted without recourse to dismissal of participants.

---

[1] In case of total or partial closures due to strikes, we suggest immediate cessation of pay and of academic credit for those directly participating. The campus should not make claim to be the only area of society where strikes are cost-free to their participants. Workers uniformly forgo their pay as they withdraw their services. They are subject to the costs of strikes as well as the potential benefits. Persons on campus can hardly expect the one and only "free ride." A cost-free strike, also, is not an effective means of demonstrating moral convictions.

All members of the campus have a right to fair and equitable procedures which shall determine the validity of charges of violation of campus regulations.

■ The procedures shall be structured so as to facilitate a reliable determination of the truth or falsity of charges, to provide fundamental fairness to the parties, and to be an effective instrument for the maintenance of order.

■ All members of the campus have a right to know in advance the range of penalties for violations of campus regulations. Definition of adequate cause for separation from the campus should be clearly formulated and made public.

■ Charges of minor infractions of regulations, penalized by small fines or reprimands which do not become part of permanent records, may be handled expeditiously by the appropriate individual or committee. Persons so penalized have the right to appeal.

■ In the case of charges of infractions of regulations which may lead to notation in permanent records, or to more serious penalties such as suspension or expulsion, members of the campus have a right to formal procedures with adequate due process, including the right of appeal.

■ Members of the campus charged or convicted of violations under general law may be subject to campus sanctions for the same conduct, in accord with campus policies and procedures, when the conduct is in violation of a campus rule essential to the continuing protection of other campus members or to safeguarding the educational process.

CONSULTATION AND CONTINGENCY PLANNING
To handle grievances directed at the campus itself, every campus should have a well-publicized procedure.

. . . we recommend that regular procedures and channels for hearing grievances and suggestions be established and well publicized; that decisions be based on wide consultation with those segments of the campus affected by them; and that decisions and the rationale behind them be made widely known (p. 64).

Organized protest activity has become a frequent form of dissent on many campuses. In order to help assure that protest actions will be peaceful and to discourage disruptive interference with the educational process

. . . The Commission recommends that campus rules be formulated which regulate the time, place, and manner of peaceful assemblies. . . . On campuses where organized protest does occur, faculty and student marshals might be made available to monitor these events and to report on violations of campus rules and excessive actions by law enforcement officers. The marshals should be organized so that they are available on a regular, ongoing basis (p. 65).

The president must have the full power to deal with crisis situations, and

... we recommend that presidents be given this authority, and that they seek advice from preexisting consultative groups drawn from the campus community (p. 67).

We also recommend that the administration keep the campus and its trustees informed of the decisions it makes and the rationale behind them (p. 68).

THE RANGE OF ALTERNATIVES

If and when disruption does occur on a campus, the administration should consider the whole range of responses open to it.

The Commission recommends that in cases of nonviolent disruption, to the extent possible, procedures internal to a campus be used initially and nonviolent actions be met by responses which do not use force. . . . Violent actions, involving injury to persons or more than incidental damage to property, should be met immediately by enforcement of the law, using internal and external personnel to the full extent necessary (p. 68).

The Scranton Commission enumerated successive options through which an administration should move in preventing or ending disruptive interference. We endorse these suggestions:

1 Negotiation
2 Wait out a nonviolent incident to see if it dissipates on its own
3 The use of injunctions, particularly in static situations like building occupations
4 Disciplinary and judicial procedures
5 Closing the campus in the face of continued violence or unrelenting and potentially dangerous nonviolent disruption (p. 68)

Although the First Amendment expressly protects the freedoms of speech, press, assembly, and petition, no federal statute yet provides effective remedies against private acts which violate these rights.

We recommend that it should be unlawful to interfere in any way with any person's exercise of his constitutional rights. Aggrieved persons should be able to bring civil action for appropriate relief, and United States district courts should be given original jurisdiction to grant permanent or temporary injunctions, temporary restraining orders, or any other orders, and to award damages (p. 75).

A CAMPUS IS NOT A SANCTUARY

A campus is not and should not be a sanctuary from the law, a place where the outside police may under no circumstances enter.

We recommend that the view that a campus is a sanctuary from the processes of the law and law enforcement be totally rejected (p. 81).

POLICE RELATIONS

On campuses, reason is enthroned and violence is abhorred; some of their members are especially sensitive to involvement by the police and even enraged by their presence. Thus, it is wise for campuses to spell out in advance the situations in which they would want and need outside law enforcement assistance.

We generally endorse the recommendations of the Scranton Commission in their chapter on "The Law Enforcement Response," while noting the variety of situations on different campuses and on the same campus at different moments of time (p. 82).

The Carnegie Commission also recommends that whereas a campus should initially respond internally and peacefully to nonviolent coercive interference, as noted above, it should have immediate recourse to the assistance of outside law enforcement authorities in situations of potential violence, violence, and terrorism unless its own security force is fully competent to handle the situation.

Campus personnel chosen to communicate with law enforcement agencies should consist of persons who not only can achieve rapport, but also can effectively present the views of the campus community.

Representatives of the administration, the faculty, and the students should participate in establishing guidelines and procedures for relations between a campus and law enforcement authorities. These guidelines should be made public (pp. 82–83).

PROCEDURES FOR DETERMINING VIOLATIONS OF CAMPUS REGULATIONS AND ASSESSING PENALTIES

Serious, violent actions such as physical assault, rape, bombings, and arson have always been handled by the outside courts. However, other actions that are in violation of campus rules and which could also be construed as violations of general law have frequently been handled only by the campus. There is no strong argument for the campus to handle cases that involve the general law.

We recommend that significant actions which could be construed as violations of the general law be handled by the outside courts. A corollary to this is that campus authorities have an obligation to report significant violations of the general law that come to their attention (p. 96).

Regarding what alleged campus violations should be handled by the campus, we agree with the Scranton Commission that members of the campus ". . . should be held legally accountable only for conduct that they had reason to know was prohibited. The absence of clear, enforceable, and enforced rules of conduct can produce confusion and turmoil."

We recommend that members of a campus should be tried or punished only for alleged violations of existing codes or regulations; therefore, these should be regularly reexamined. Such regulations should be consistent with the bill of rights and responsibilities adopted by a campus (p. 96).

The campus needs its own procedures to handle violations of its codes and regulations. These procedures should be structured so as to facilitate a reliable determination of the truth or falsity of charges, to provide fundamental fairness to the parties, and to be effective instruments for the maintenance of order.

We recommend that careful consideration be given to use of (1) ombudsmen, (2) hearing officers, and (3) campus attorneys (p. 98).

We also recommend that in serious cases involving "rights and responsibilities" of members of the campus community and possible campus penalties beyond those for violation of the external law, campus judicial tribunals be composed partially or wholly of external persons, defined as persons drawn from outside the particular school or college or campus whose members are involved in the dispute (p. 100).

CONCLUDING NOTE

New directions are now being required of, and chosen by, both the nation and colleges and universities. It is of the greatest importance that these new directions be charted through democratic processes in an atmosphere of reason. The campus has an essential role to play in this period of historical transition. To be fully effective, for the sake of the nation and for its own welfare, it must protect the expression of dissent, however vigorous, while eliminating disruption, however insistently it may be pursued. This requires, in our judgment, new agreements over the norms governing academic life, new methods to handle emergency situations, and new judicial procedures to assure justice.

(*An Important Note:* Many exhibits are inserted in the original report to illustrate or to amplify textual material and to suggest the many different approaches to the complex problems discussed.)

NEW STUDENTS AND NEW PLACES

POLICIES FOR THE FUTURE GROWTH AND DEVELOPMENT OF AMERICAN HIGHER EDUCATION (OCTOBER 1971)

Higher education in the United States has been a rapid growth segment of the nation for more than three centuries. During that time, enrollments have increased at a rate faster than the expansion of American society generally. Over the past century, in particular, enrollments have doubled regularly every 14 or 15 years. Now, a new period is beginning. It is marked by two features: (1) *Go-Stop-Go in the short run*—enrollments will increase by one-half in the 1970s, remain steady through the 1980s, and increase again by one-third during the 1990s and (2) *Reduced growth rate in the long run*—the percentage of college-age youth actually in college (which increased from about 2 percent in 1870 to about 35 percent in 1970) will probably level out at about 50 percent in the year 2000.

The Commission has made two enrollment projections. One is based on past and current trends; the other is based on prospective trends reflecting new policies and developments.

PAST AND CURRENT TRENDS

YEAR	TOTAL ENROLLMENTS
1970	8,500,000
1980	13,500,000
1990	13,300,000
2000	17,400,000

PROSPECTIVE TRENDS

YEAR	TOTAL ENROLLMENTS
1970	8,500,000
1980	12,500,000
1990	12,300,000
2000	16,000,000

The "prospective trends" are those that could develop if the Carnegie Commission's recommendations, past and present, are adopted. The net effect of these changes would be a reduction of estimates of students in 1980 based on past trends in the general order of about 1 million. The Commission believes that higher education would be healthier in 1980 with 1 million fewer students than current trends indicate, and that these fewer students would be more equitably drawn from the total population if our policy recommendations become effective practice.

Regardless of which projections are used, in the year 2000 enrollment in higher education will be roughly 10 times larger than it was in 1940. The additional new students could be mostly absorbed in 1980 (and thus also in 1990) within the existing 2,800 campuses in the United States without either forcing undue size or unduly rapid growth on these campuses—with one very major qualification: these campuses are not uniformly well located. There is a major deficit of two types of institutions—community colleges and comprehensive colleges—particularly in metropolitan areas, and especially in those with over 500,000 population. Thus we recommend 175 to 235 additional community colleges and 80 to 105 additional comprehensive colleges by 1980. We find no need in the foreseeable future for more research-type universities granting the Ph.D. Available resources should be concentrated on those that now exist.

The nation is clearly moving toward universal-access education. This presents problems. It also creates opportunities for more nearly equal treatment of all our citizens, for more nearly adequate services to all localities, for more varied responses to the increasingly varied composition of the enrollments in higher education, for new methods and new types of institutions, for a more thoughtful consideration of the future role of each of the major components of our universe of higher education, for a more careful look at the essential nature of each of our institutions, and for a more systematic examination of the effective use of resources.

THE FUTURE OF HIGHER EDUCATION: ASSUMPTION A—LARGELY UNINHIBITED GROWTH

ENROLLMENT INCREASES

The outlook for smooth absorption of the increased numbers of students in the 1970s is at present very uncertain. Assuming, however, that these uncertainties are resolved in a way not inhibitive to growth, enrollment trends in the 1970s and the following two decades will be determined by (1) changes in the rate of growth of the college-age population and (2) a continuation of the long-run upward trend in enrollment rates, which in turn reflects primarily the influence of three interrelated and overlapping factors: *(a)* the upward trend in high school graduation rates, *(b)* the rise in real per capita income, and *(c)* changes in the occupational structure that result in an increased demand for persons holding academic degrees.

The Carnegie Commission staff has developed projections of enrollment based on U.S. Bureau of the Census population projections and on extrapolations of trends in enrollment rates for men and women separately from 1947 to 1970. The undergraduate projection is a single series, but we have developed three alternative projections of postbaccalaureate enrollment, based on the following assumptions:

■ Projection A: That the first-time baccalaureate enrollment rate for men, which declined from 1965 to 1969, will return to its 1965 level (58.5 percent of the weighted average number of male recipients of bachelor's degrees in the preceding five years) as draft calls decrease and the number of returning veterans increases, and thereafter will gradually rise at a decreasing rate, reaching 70 percent by the year 2000; and that the first-time enrollment rate for women will rise gradually from its current level of 47 percent to 60 percent by 2000.

■ Projection B: That first-time postbaccalaureate enrollment rates will rise at one-half the rate assumed under Projection A.

■ Projection C: That first-time postbaccalaureate enrollment rates will remain unchanged from 1969 on.

The *number* of students added to enrollment in higher education in the 1970s is likely actually to be slightly larger (5.0 million) than the number added in the 1960s (4.7 million). But the *rate* of increase over the decade as a whole (59 percent) will be markedly lower than the exceptionally high rate of increase in the 1960s (124 percent). The picture in the 1980s will be very different because those entering college will have largely been born from 1962–63 to 1972–73, a period of generally declining absolute numbers of births as well as of a decline in the birthrate. In the 1990s, on the other hand, we are likely to see a sizable increase in the numbers enrolled in higher education. But the percentage rate of increase for the decade as a whole (about 30 percent) is likely to be far below that of the 1960s and considerably lower than that of the 1970s.

ENROLLMENT RANGES BY TYPE OF INSTITUTION
If changes in the 1970s reflect the shifts that occurred from 1963 to 1970, the most rapid growth of enrollment to 1980 is likely to occur in two-year institutions. Their enrollment will increase 70 percent and may increase these institutions' share of total enrollment from 28 to 31 percent. Most of this growth will occur in public two-year colleges, which are likely to account for 96 percent of all enrollment in two-year institutions in 1980, as compared with 94 percent in 1970.

Comprehensive colleges are expected to experience rapid growth—a 58 percent increase in the 10-year period. However, their share of the total is expected to rise only from 31 to 32 percent.

The most slowly growing group of institutions will be the doctoral-granting institutions, although they will experience a substantial 37 percent increase in enrollment. Their share of the total is likely to fall from 30 to about 27 percent.

The rate of growth of enrollment in liberal arts colleges is likely to be roughly comparable to that of the doctoral-granting institutions—32 percent. Specialized institutions are likely to experience substantial enrollment increases, averaging 54 percent by 1980. But their share of total enrollment is likely to remain fairly constant.

The Commission's projections assume that there will be no change in

shares of types of institutions in enrollment during the stationary enrollment years of the 1980s, but that from 1990 to 2000, changes in enrollment shares will once again occur at the 1963 to 1970 rate. The projections also indicate a continued rise in the share of public institutions in
total enrollment, from 75 percent in 1970 to 79 percent in 1980 and to 81
percent in the year 2000. In fact, if the stationary trend in enrollment in
private institutions that has characterized the last few years were to continue, the rise in the share of public institutions in total enrollment would
be even sharper than our projections indicate. The Commission believes,
however, that policies should be developed to preserve and strengthen
the financial condition of the private institutions, so that they will be able
to maintain a reasonably stable share of total enrollment.

The Commission recommends that the federal and state governments develop and
implement policies to preserve and strengthen private institutions of higher education. The federal aid which we have recommended in *Quality and Equality: Revised Recommendations, New Levels of Federal Responsibility for Higher Education* would be available for public and private institutions alike. Policies for state
aid to private higher education, with emphasis on student aid as the major approach, were recommended in *The Capitol and the Campus.* We reiterate those
recommendations (p. 48).

THE FUTURE OF HIGHER EDUCATION: ASSUMPTION B—THE CARNEGIE COMMISSION GOALS AND OTHER INFLUENCES

CONSTRUCTIVE CHANGE
Recommendations made in this and earlier reports that would have the
most significant effects on future patterns of enrollment and needs for
new institutions may be summarized as follows:

■ Tending to increase enrollment

Increased student grants for low-income students, cost-of-education supplements to institutions enrolling these students, and a liberalized student loan program *(Quality and Equality)*

Involvement of institutions of higher education in programs to improve
the quality of education in ghetto and rural schools, to bring about more
effective recruitment of minority-group students, and to provide additional opportunities for disadvantaged students to overcome any handicaps with which they may have entered during their first two years in college *(A Chance to Learn)*

Open access to public two-year colleges *(The Open-Door Colleges)*

175 to 235 new community colleges by 1980; 80 to 125 of these to be in
large metropolitan areas *(New Students and New Places,* Section 7)

85 to 105 new comprehensive colleges by 1980; 60 to 70 of these to be
in large metropolitan areas *(New Students and New Places,* Section 7)

■ Tending to reduce enrollment

A three-year bachelor of arts program for qualified students *(Less Time, More Options)*

A 1- to 1½-year associate in arts program for qualified students *(Less Time, More Options)*

■ Tending to strengthen the capacity of private institutions to retain their existing share of total enrollment

Federal cost-of-education supplements to institutions, public and private, admitting students holding federal grants *(Quality and Equality)*

State aid to private institutions *(The Capitol and the Campus)*

Expanded federal aid to black colleges, one-third of which are public and two-thirds of which are private *(From Isolation to Mainstream)*

■ Tending to broaden the age distribution of students enrolled in higher education

Encouraging stop-outs *(Less Time, More Options)*

Increased emphasis on adult education, especially in the 1980s, when institutions will be in a particularly favorable position to expand adult programs because of stationary college-age enrollment *(New Students and New Places,* Sections 5 and 8)

An education security program *(Less Time, More Options)*

External degree systems and open universities *(Less Time, More Options* and *New Students and New Places,* Section 8)

■ Tending to equalize educational opportunity among the states

Expanded federal aid to higher education *(Quality and Equality)*

Increased state effort in states that have lagged in supporting higher education *(The Capitol and the Campus)*

■ Tending to reduce inequality in the size of institutions, to achieve more effective use of resources, and to preserve and encourage diversity

Optimum size ranges for universities, comprehensive colleges, liberal arts colleges, and community colleges *(New Students and New Places,* Section 6)

Recommendations relating to cluster colleges and consortia *(New Students and New Places,* Section 6)

■ Tending to improve the quality of instruction in higher education through increased emphasis on a two-year master of philosophy (M.Phil.) degree and a four-year doctor of arts (D.A.) degree, both designed specifically to prepare candidates for college and university teaching

The M.Phil. degree *(Less Time, More Options)*

The D.A. degree *(Less Time, More Options)*

■ Tending to reduce the length of time required to obtain a doctor's degree and other advanced degrees

Recommendations for a four-year D.A. and for a four-year Ph.D. *(Less Time, More Options)*

Recommendations for a three-year M.D. and a three-year D.D.S. degree *(Higher Education and the Nation's Health)*

ALTERNATIVE ENROLLMENT ESTIMATES
We have developed alternative estimates of future enrollment that reflect the influence not only of implementation of Carnegie Commission recommendations, but also of changes in the labor market for college graduates and holders of advanced degrees, possible shifts in attitudes toward participation in graduate education, and other factors.

FACTORS TENDING TO INCREASE ENROLLMENT   The major influences that would tend to increase enrollment above the future levels discussed in the previous section are the Commission's recommendations (1) for greatly increased student aid, (2) for new comprehensive colleges, and (3) for new community colleges. We have recommended a substantial increase in federal support for student aid, with federal expenditures for this purpose estimated to rise (if the Commission's recommendations are adopted) from $3,614 million in 1971–72 to $4,984 million in 1979–80 in constant dollars. We estimate that the combined impact of this increased federal student aid and of our recommendations for new public nondoctoral institutions and community colleges would be to raise total enrollment in 1980 above our Projection A by about 600,000 to 900,000 students. However, this increase may be more than offset by other factors, making for a decrease in total enrollment.

FACTORS TENDING TO REDUCE UNDERGRADUATE ENROLLMENT   We estimate that implementation of our recommendation for a three-year bachelor of arts degree would result in a reduction in the number of undergraduates enrolled in higher education by about 10 to 15 percent by 1980, allowing for a possible increase in retention rates and for the fact that some students entering college with less than adequate preparation would require four years to complete the work for the B.A. degree. This would mean a reduction of about 1.0 to 1.5 million in total undergraduate enrollment by 1980. The recommendation for a 1-year to 1½-year associate in arts degree would probably not have an appreciable *additional* impact on enrollment, because many students who could complete the work for an A.A. degree in 1 to 1½ years would probably go on for a B.A. degree.

THE IMPACT OF INCREASED ADULT ENROLLMENT   A figure of 250,000 to 350,000 would be a reasonable estimate of the "extra" adults enrolled in higher education over and above our Projection A by 1980.

FACTORS TENDING TO REDUCE GRADUATE ENROLLMENT   The Commission has made several recommendations that would affect graduate enrollment and expects to make additional recommendations in forthcoming reports. Labor market changes, especially the deteriorating market for Ph.D.'s, are also having an impact on patterns of graduate enrollment. Moreover, recent surveys in several institutions indicate that the proportion of undergraduates planning to go on to graduate work has dropped substantially in the last few years. A more critical factor, particularly if financial stringency in higher education continues, may be decisions by institutions of higher education to cut back on admissions to graduate education.

We believe that these influences are likely to depress graduate enrollment by 280,000 to 500,000 below that of Projection A by 1980. The combined impact of all these influences would reduce total enrollment about 680,000 to 1,750,000.

In view of the expectation of an essentially stationary college-age population and enrollment in the 1980s, and the fact that we do not anticipate that the shares of various types of institutions in enrollment will change significantly during that decade, the effects of the influences we have been examining here on projected enrollment by 1990 will not be greatly different from their effects in 1980. However, we anticipate that adult participation in higher education will go on increasing in the 1980s and that the reduction in graduate enrollment, as compared with our Projection A, will range from 380,000 to 680,000. The net impact of all factors incorporated in the estimate will be a reduction of 410,000 to 1,580,000 or 630,000 to 1,440,000.

COST ESTIMATES
The combined impact of the Carnegie Commission recommendations and other influences would also produce major savings in construction costs of higher education institutions. Total construction costs would be reduced by about $5.6 billion over the decade from 1971–72 to 1980–81. If the Commission's recommendation, in *Quality and Equality: Revised Recommendations, New Levels of Federal Responsibility for Higher Education,* for federal construction grants is implemented, one-third of this saving, or $1.9 billion, would accrue to the federal government and two-thirds, or $3.7 billion, to other levels of government and to private sources of financing.

With respect to estimating impact of these influences on current educational costs, we have developed three alternative estimates of the total educational costs of institutions of higher education associated with enrollment increases in 1971–72 and 1980–81. By our estimates, the savings by 1980–81 would be from $2 billion to $4 billion per year.

THE GROWTH OF INSTITUTIONS

OPTIMUM SIZE

American institutions of higher education range in size from colleges with fewer than 100 students to campuses of major universities with 40,000 or 50,000 students. The Commission believes, with some qualifications, that there is an optimum size range for each major type of institution of higher education. Colleges and universities that are too small cannot operate economically, while, beyond a given size, there may be minimal additional economies of scale, and the institutions may become too large to provide an intellectually challenging environment for many students. In addition, the Commission believes that a state plan for higher education will provide more adequate geographical distribution of institutions if it sets a reasonable maximum on the size of existing campuses of various types and plans on new campuses to absorb enrollment increases beyond that point.

The Commission recommends that state plans for the growth and development of public institutions of higher education should, in general, incorporate minimum FTE enrollment objectives of (1) 5,000 students for doctoral-granting institutions; (2) 5,000 students for comprehensive colleges; (3) 1,000 students for liberal arts colleges; and (4) 2,000 students for two-year (community) colleges (p. 85).

Similarly, the Commission recommends that state plans should, in general, incorporate maximum FTE enrollment objectives of (1) about 20,000 students for doctoral-granting institutions; (2) about 10,000 students for comprehensive colleges; (3) about 2,500 students for liberal arts colleges; and (4) about 5,000 students for two-year (community) colleges (p. 85).

The Commission also recommends that, in developing their policies for state aid to private institutions, states should study and adopt policies providing financial incentives for expansion in those cases in which private institutions are clearly much too small for efficient operation, but that state policies should not be designed to force growth on private institutions of demonstrably high quality which are desirous of retaining unique characteristics associated with their comparatively small size. In some states it may be desirable, also, to study and adopt policies providing financial assistance for merger of very small private institutions in appropriate cases. The federal government should also encourage small institutions to grow by giving them priority in the awarding of construction grants and by aiding them through its "developing institutions" program (p. 86).

CLUSTER COLLEGES

In a search for ways of retaining some of the advantages of small size within a larger institution, a growing number of American colleges and universities are experimenting with a cluster of semi-autonomous colleges within the overall framework of a large university. There appear to be many advantages to cluster colleges and the Commission favors their further development.

The Commission recommends that universities, colleges, and state planning agencies carefully study and adopt plans for the development of cluster colleges. The Commission also recommends that the federal government, the states, and private foundations make funds available for research evaluating the comparative experience of these colleges (p. 89).

FEDERATIONS AND CONSORTIA

Some of the advantages of cluster colleges can be achieved through federation or consortium arrangements among existing institutions. Consortia typically are arrangements under which two or more institutions enter into agreements to sponsor specialized programs, to share computer or library facilities, or to offer students a broader range of courses. Only a few existing consortia bear much resemblance to cluster colleges, but many more could come to have some of the features of cluster colleges through more extensive arrangements for sharing courses and facilities.

The Commission recommends that colleges and universities continue to seek ways of sharing facilities, courses, and specialized programs through cooperative arrangements, that existing consortia make continuous efforts toward increasing the effectiveness of their cooperative programs, and that institutions—especially small colleges—that are not now members of consortia carefully consider forming consortia with neighboring institutions (pp. 93, 94).

The Commission reiterates its recommendations in *Quality and Equality* that the proposed National Foundation for the Development of Higher Education aid in planning liberal arts centers to be established by groups of colleges for the purpose of increasing quality, scope, and diversity of undergraduate education, of stimulating more economical and effective use of administrative and teaching personnel, and of sharing library and computer facilities.

PRESERVING AND ENCOURAGING DIVERSITY

Despite the pressures for conformity in American higher education, the strong tendency for comprehensive colleges and emerging universities to want to model their programs after those of the leading research universities, and evidence that institutions of higher education are growing more alike, there are also encouraging developments that may play an important role in preserving and encouraging diversity.

In framing its proposals both for federal aid and state aid to private institutions, the Commission has placed its major emphasis on grants for students, with accompanying cost-of-education supplements to the institutions they choose to attend. One of the important reasons for preferring this approach is that we believe it will help to preserve diversity.

NEEDS FOR NEW INSTITUTIONS

In *The Open-Door Colleges: Policies for the Community Colleges,* the Commission recommended the establishment of 230 to 280 new public community colleges by 1980. Between 1968 and 1970, however, about 80 new institutions were added to the nation's supply of public two-year colleges. But only 25 of these were in large metropolitan areas. After reviewing needs of a state-by-state and metropolitan area basis, we have revised our nationwide estimate of needs for new community colleges to 175 to 235.

In estimating needs for new urban institutions, the Commission assembled data on the supply of existing institutions in the central cities and outer rings of large metropolitan areas, along with data on their enrollment, control, and selectivity. The analysis was carried out for all metropolitan areas with populations of 500,000 or more in 1970. Data were also compiled on the supply of institutions in smaller metropolitan areas and in nonmetropolitan areas. An important caveat that must be expressed in connection with our estimate of needs for new urban institutions is that if external degree programs and open universities now being initiated prove to be popular with students, there may be less need for urban institutions of the traditional type.

The Commission recommends that state and local planning bodies develop plans for the establishment by 1980 of about 60 to 70 new comprehensive colleges and 80 to 125 new community colleges in large metropolitan areas with populations of about 500,000 or more. In determining the location of these new institutions within metropolitan areas, particular emphasis should be placed on the provision of adequate open-access places for students in inner-city areas.

The Commission also recommends that a special effort be made to develop new institutions in those metropolitan areas which have comparatively low ratios of enrollment to population. Especially deficient ratios are found in the following metropolitan areas:

Paterson-Clifton-Passaic, N.J.	Fort Lauderdale-Hollywood, Fla.
Gary-Hammond-East Chicago, Ind.	Jacksonville, Fla.
Indianapolis, Ind.	Louisville (Ky-Ind.)
Kansas City (Mo.-Kans.)	

However, in view of the very recent movement to establish external degree programs and open universities, the Commission recommends that state and local planning bodies continuously study the impact of these innovations on patterns of enrollment and modify estimates of needs for new institutions accordingly (p. 104).

We estimate that 60 to 70 new comprehensive colleges are needed in metropolitan areas with populations of 500,000 or more. There is also a need for about 20 to 35 additional comprehensive colleges in somewhat smaller areas, generally those with populations of 200,000 to 500,000 in 1968. This brings our estimate of total needs for new comprehensive colleges by 1980 to about 80 to 105.

The Commission recommends that state and local planning agencies develop plans for about 80 to 105 new comprehensive colleges, including those already recommended for large metropolitan areas, by 1980 (p. 107).

In addition to the 80 to 125 new community colleges recommended for metropolitan areas with populations of 500,000 or more, we believe that an additional 95 to 110 new community colleges should be established by 1980. In determining the location of these new community colleges, particular attention should be paid to the needs of metropolitan areas with populations from 200,000 to 500,000.

The Commission recommends that state and local planning agencies develop plans for the establishment of about 175 to 235 new community colleges in all, including those already recommended for large metropolitan areas, by 1980 (p. 109).

TOWARD MORE FLEXIBLE PATTERNS OF PARTICIPATION IN HIGHER EDUCATION

If students are to be encouraged to stop out for a few years after high school or after several years of college and complete their higher education at a later stage, and if their participation in higher education is to increasingly take the form of part-time study as adults, it is imperative that existing weaknesses in the organization and structure of adult higher education in the United States be overcome.

A number of innovative programs are now being tried. The Commission believes that they should be encouraged.

The Commission reiterates the recommendations in its report *Less Time, More Options* to encourage more flexible patterns of participation in higher education.

The Commission also recommends that state and federal government agencies, as well as private foundations, expand programs of support for the development of external degree systems and open universities along the lines of programs initiated within the last year or so. It will also be important for governmental bodies and foundations to provide funds for evaluation of these innovative programs as they develop (p. 117).

SUMMARY

As we look forward to the growth and development of American higher education in the last three decades of the twentieth century, we believe that a major goal should be the preservation and enhancement of both diversity and flexibility, along with the greater equality of opportunity we have stressed as a goal in earlier reports. To the recommendations we have made in earlier reports, the present report adds, and in some cases reiterates, recommendations directed to the following goals:

■ Preserving and enhancing quality

Avoiding either excessively large or uneconomically small campuses through state plans that incorporate optimum enrollment ranges

Encouraging innovation and experimentation in undergraduate education through expansion of the cluster college movement

Encouraging institutions to achieve more effective use of resources and a broader selection of programs for their students by participation in consortia

Reiteration of recommendations designed to aid and preserve private institutions of higher education

■ Increasing opportunities for students to attend relatively open-access institutions, especially in inner-city areas, by 1980

Locating about 60 to 70 new comprehensive colleges in metropolitan areas with populations of 500,000 or more

Establishing 80 to 125 new community colleges in metropolitan areas with populations of 500,000 or more

In determining the location of new community colleges and new comprehensive colleges in these large metropolitan areas, placing particular emphasis on the needs for new institutions in inner-city areas

Establishing about 20 to 35 new comprehensive colleges in smaller metropolitan areas, generally those with populations of 200,000 to 500,000

Establishing 95 to 110 new community colleges in smaller metropolitan and nonmetropolitan areas

■ Increasing opportunities for more flexible patterns of participation in higher education

Developing external degree programs and open universities

Implementing other recommendations included in the Commission's report *Less Time, More Options,* designed to encourage more flexible patterns of participation

Revising plans for establishing new nondoctoral institutions and community colleges if external degree systems and open universities alter patterns of participation extensively

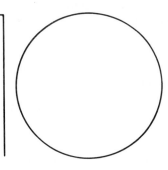

INSTITU-
TIONAL AID

FEDERAL SUPPORT
TO COLLEGES AND
UNIVERSITIES
(FEBRUARY 1972)

Higher education in the post-Sputnik era expanded rapidly, putting severe strains on its traditional sources of revenue—state and local governments, tuitions, and private donations. Higher education thus began to rely more heavily on federal support. The National Defense Education Act, enacted in 1958, provided loans for college students and grants for graduate students, and some categorical aid to higher education. In 1963, the Higher Education Facilities Act provided matching grants and loans for the construction of facilities. And in 1965, the Higher Education Act provided new programs of aid to students as well as financial assistance for a number of specifically designated college-based programs.

While the federal contribution to higher education has risen sharply —from $700 million to $3.5 billion between 1957 and 1967—the relative contribution of other sources of revenue has declined. State and local support has fallen from 33 percent of the total to 27 percent. Public institutions dependent on state and local revenue are facing growing legislative reluctance to increase its support in proportion to increased enrollment. Taxpayers are resisting increased support for capital projects needed to accommodate expanded enrollment. And the proportion of private support to higher education has also dropped. Between 1957 and 1967 the share of private support to higher education, including tuition, gifts, and income from endowments, dropped from 54 percent to 52 percent. The private share would have fallen even more had not private institutions substantially increased their tuition charges during this period.

While we can reasonably hope for continued increases in the total dollar amount of higher education expenditures from private, state, and local sources, it seems unlikely that the private share will constitute more than 50 percent of the total, and in view of the nature of local and state tax structures, it is likely that the share of these sources will continue to decline to a level of 25 percent by 1980. Thus, under our present general pattern of support for higher education, the only major source of support capable of offsetting the decline in the percentage of funds from these sources is the federal government. Because of the nature of its tax base, the federal government is able to raise its general revenue faster than the rise in the gross national product.

It is largely these realities that have led to Carnegie Commission (and many major higher education associations and several other commissions) to call upon the federal government for increased levels of support for higher education and for programs that provide direct institutional grants to be used by institutions for general educational expenses. The Carnegie Commission has recommended in earlier reports (*Quality and Equality,* 1968 and 1970) a full program of federal aid to higher education. Federal institutional aid is an essential element of that program. This report examines many of the possible alternative formulas for institutional aid, and attempts to outline their major implications for United States colleges, universities, the states, and the federal government.

PRINCIPLES OF INSTITUTIONAL AID

The Commission believes that any federal program of institutional aid should be based on these basic principles (pp. 2–3):

1 The basic support of and responsibility for higher education should remain with the states and with private initiative.

2 The highest single priority for higher education in the 1970s is to help fulfill the two-century-old American dream of social justice.

3 Students should be given the maximum freedom of choice in choosing the institutions they wish to attend.

4 Federal aid should be given in a manner which does not encourage the states and private sources to reduce their support.

5 The form of federal aid should minimize constitutional aid problems and hopefully eliminate them altogether.

6 The automony of institutions should be preserved.

FORMULA VARIATIONS

All formulas for federal institutional grants have two principles in common: (1) public and private institutions are treated alike and (2) the institutional allocation is based upon some quantitative dimension of the institution. The distribution of funds to institutions will depend upon which major components are included in allocation formulas, and on how the components are defined.

COMPONENTS

The components suggested by various institutional aid proposals include:

■ Allocation tied to general input, e.g., some measure of enrollment

■ Allocation tied to general output, e.g., degrees awarded

■ Special increments for small colleges

■ Formula tied to specified groups of students such as returning GIs, low-income students, or highly able doctoral students, or related to particular educational programs such as science or research

■ Allocation based on growth factors or cost increases

ALTERNATIVE ENROLLMENT DEFINITIONS

The Carnegie Commission research shows that:

■ Public colleges and universities as a whole would receive a somewhat larger proportionate share of the total institutional grants distribution if the formula defines *enrollment* as all students rather than degree-credit students.

■ Among public institutions, a shift from an "all student" definition to "degree-credit" students would lead to a loss in proportion of allocation for two-year colleges and a gain for leading research universities.

■ Inclusion in the definition of only full-time students rather than full-time and part-time students has little effect on the division of institutional funds between all public institutions and all private institutions.

■ Among public institutions, leading research universities fare relatively better if only full-time students are included in the definition, while two-year colleges fare relatively less well.

■ Among private institutions, comprehensive universities and colleges are somewhat better off if the formula counts full-time-equivalent students, while liberal arts colleges fare better if only full-time students are included in enrollment.

WEIGHTING OF INSTRUCTIONAL LEVELS
The Commission finds that:

■ Private institutions would gain a larger share of institutional grants as greater weight is given to graduate students.

■ Public and private two-year colleges, of necessity, would receive less aid as greater weight is assigned to upper-division and to graduate students.

■ Leading research universities, with their heavy concentration of graduate students, obtain the greatest relative improvement in their allocation as greater weights are assigned to graduate students.

WEIGHTING OF DEGREES
The Commission also finds that:

■ Public two-year colleges do about as well under the most favorable degrees-awarded formula as under the least favorable.

■ The distribution of funds would be markedly different if the associate in arts degree were in general use in four-year as well as two-year institutions.

■ Public and private comprehensive colleges and universities and private liberal arts colleges fare best under a single $100 per bachelor's degree-awarded formula.

EQUALITY OF OPPORTUNITY
Cost-of-education supplements, often referred to as "equality-of-opportunity" components, are based on the number of students receiving

one or more forms of federal financial aid or on the percentage of funds received under such programs.

■ Private institutions as a whole fare better under an equality-of-opportunity formula than under either the enrollment or degrees-awarded formulas described thus far.

■ Public comprehensive colleges and universities and two-year colleges receive a larger share if the grant is based on number of total EOG payments at the institution rather than on the percentage of EOG payments.

■ The share received by private liberal arts colleges varies from 16.3 percent for a specified percentage of all total EOG, NDSL, and work-study payments to 21.2 percent for a specified amount per EOG recipient. This share is greater than under any of the previously discussed enrollment or degrees-awarded formulas.

SMALL COLLEGES

Many proposals for institutional aid provide bonuses for small colleges: for example, $500 for each baccalaureate degree awarded if the number of degrees awarded does not exceed 200, the amount decreasing with the number of degrees up to 2,000 degrees per year. An under-300 enrollment restriction on special benefits would be an unfortunate cut-off point if the intention is to provide special aid for private liberal arts colleges—92 percent of all private liberal arts colleges exceed this enrollment. If the intent is to aid liberal arts colleges generally, the special benefits should be targeted on colleges of less than 1,500 enrollment as this would include over 80 percent of all private liberal arts colleges.

An institutional grants formula based on degrees awarded (instead of enrollment) and on bonuses to small colleges tends to favor the private sector; it would channel almost half of the total institutional grants to private colleges and universities, though such colleges and universities account for less than one-third of the total enrollment. The Commission, in *New Students and New Places,* has indicated that some private colleges are too small in size to make effective use of resources. Subsidizing them in this fashion might encourage them to perpetuate this small size.

DISTRIBUTION PATTERNS OF SELECTED FORMULAS

The distribution patterns of six selected formulas is shown in Table 2. Each formula would have a different impact on each type of institution, illustrating the difficulty of achieving any formula that will be equally satisfactory to all institutions and to all legislators.

TABLE 2   Distribution of institutional grants under six formulas

CARNEGIE CLASSIFICATION*	PERCENTAGE OF ENROLLMENT†	PERCENTAGE OF EXPENDITURES	FORMULAS					
			(1)	(2)	(3)	(4)	(5)	(6)
Public								
Research and doctoral universities I	9.6%	16.2%	9.4%	8.3%	10.2%	10.1%	3.4%	14.2%
Research and doctoral universities II	2.8	6.2	7.3	6.5	6.1	6.7	2.8	7.3
Doctoral-granting universities I	3.5	4.2	3.3	3.1	2.9	3.2	1.4	2.5
Doctoral-granting universities II	3.3	2.8	3.5	3.7	2.6	2.8	1.6	2.2
Comprehensive universities and colleges I	20.5	13.6	21.7	20.8	18.8	18.7	11.0	16.0
Comprehensive universities and colleges II	5.2	3.5	7.5	6.2	6.5	5.8	5.2	5.6
Liberal arts colleges II	0.4	0.4	0.3	0.3	1.2	0.9	0.9	1.1
Specialized colleges	1.3	4.5	0.3	0.3	0.7	1.0	1.5	0.6
Two-year colleges	22.5	12.3	7.7	7.3	9.0	12.8	23.8	7.2
Total public	69.1%	63.7%	61.0%	56.5%	58.0%	62.0%	51.6%	56.7%
Private								
Research and doctoral universities I	7.2%	10.8%	1.8%	2.4%	5.9%	4.7%	1.0%	11.7%
Research and doctoral universities II	1.9	3.7	1.6	1.8	3.2	2.7	0.8	4.1
Doctoral-granting universities I	1.6	2.0	1.1	1.5	1.3	1.4	0.7	1.1
Doctoral-granting universities II	1.3	1.5	1.0	1.3	1.1	1.2	0.7	0.9
Comprehensive universities and colleges I	5.2	4.2	5.6	5.8	5.9	5.5	4.1	5.1
Comprehensive universities and colleges II	1.5	1.2	2.6	2.7	2.5	2.2	2.7	2.2
Liberal arts colleges I	2.0	2.6	3.2	3.8	3.6	3.3	4.5	3.2
Liberal arts colleges II	6.2	5.2	18.6	21.2	14.4	12.3	20.5	12.5
Specialized colleges	2.3	3.7	1.6	1.5	2.1	2.4	7.0	1.8
Two-year colleges	1.7	1.3	2.1	1.9	2.0	2.3	6.3	1.8
Total private	30.9%	36.2%	39.2%	43.9%	42.0%	38.0%	48.3%	44.4%

* See Appendix A of original report for explanations of the criteria used in classifying institutions.
† FTE enrollment

Formulas: (1) Equality of opportunity—payments based on number of EOG recipients. (2) Equality of opportunity—payments based on amount of EOG recipients. (3) Two-thirds equality of opportunity—(2 above) and one-third based on enrollment with larger grants for first 300 students. (4) One-third equality of opportunity—(2 above) and two-thirds enrollment (3 above). (5) Dual choice—alternative of payments based on $600 per EOG or $100 each for the first 1,000 FTE students. (6) Three-factor formula—60 percent EOG (2 above), 25 percent enrollment (3 above), and 15 percent in proportion to the amount of federal research funds received by institutions for the prior fiscal year.

FEDERAL AND STATE RESPONSIBILITY FOR HIGHER EDUCATION

Historically, states have functioned as educational entrepreneurs, financiers, and planners. The federal government has been primarily a purchaser of services; for example, it has supported research and, through its student-aid program, has encouraged others to become consumers of higher education. State aid has typically been for general support, federal aid for special programs, or particular purposes.

The present distinction between federal and state responsibility has resulted in *supplemental* funding for higher education from the federal government. Across-the-board institutional aid formulas could substitute for some portion of state funding. There is an inherent danger in this: it may be the first step to a single national system of higher education as, first, the states would reduce their sense of basic responsibility, and second, federal controls would inevitably follow the lump sum.

DIVERSITY IN ACADEMIC PROGRAMS

Certain proposals for federal institutional aid could discourage reform and development of postsecondary education through excessive reinforcement of the status quo. If the federal government wishes affirmatively to encourage innovation, educational reform, and improvements in quality, it would be ill-advised to channel funds to institutions solely through an across-the-board institutional formula. Such grants could conceivably be used to improve quality, but if improvement in quality and implementation of educational reform requires any change in faculty function or attitude—as it usually does—there is nothing in a general institutional grants formula that would prompt the college to utilize the funds in this way. The grant could just as easily be used to raise all faculty salaries, or to enhance existing programs and procedures.

Therefore, the Carnegie Commission's recommendations for federal aid intended to improve quality and foster academic reform are, in general, based on the *project grant technique* rather than on any general formula.

RESPONSIVENESS TO THE FINANCIAL CRISIS

The serious financial distress of higher education in the seventies has often been used as a justification for federal institutional grants programs. A general across-the-board formula response to the financial crisis is inherently inadequate in that:

■ Since the degree of financial distress varies from institution to institution, a uniformly applied general formula will result in windfalls to some institutions; on the other hand, it is difficult to develop exact measures of financial distress that could eliminate these windfalls.

■ Without an effective "maintenance of effort" clause, a federal, general formula institutional grants program could be an open invitation to other revenue suppliers to adjust their grants accordingly.

SPECIFIC AID FOR SPECIFIC FINANCIAL PROBLEMS

The evidence reveals that the financial crisis is not a single crisis with a single cause. It is doubtful that any single solution would bring more than a brief respite. It seems far better to provide federal aid for those programs that have been identified as contributing significantly to institutional financial distress and *at the same time* relate to areas in which the federal government has a substantial national interest and/or responsibility. Thus, to support equality of opportunity in higher education the Commission has recommended in a previous report that

. . . institutions providing grants for students on the basis of demonstrated financial need from funds obtained by the institution from private sources, shall be paid an institutional grant amounting to 10 percent of the total amount of such student grants for the preceding fiscal year (*Quality and Equality,* 1968, p. 22).

And to maintain research excellence at leading research universities despite overall cuts in the rate of federal research spending, the Commission has recommended that

. . . a grant be made to the institution totaling 10 percent of all federal research funds received by the institution the prior fiscal year (*Quality and Equality,* 1968, p. 40; 1970, p. 26).

FAIR AND EQUITABLE FORMULAS

Though there is general agreement that any formula for allocating federal funds must be fair and equitable, the problem is finding a suitable criterion for "fair and equitable." Across-the-board general formulas attempt to meet the test of fairness through equality of treatment, but this type of uniformity is likely to lead to fair and equitable results only when it is applied to units with relatively homogeneous financial characteristics. No uniformly applied across-the-board formula would take into account the different levels of current state responsibility, yet the burden on the individual taxpayer in each state varies greatly. Secondly, a general formula institutional grant would lead to very uneven monetary impacts on institutions because of the wide institutional differences in per-student costs.

THE RESOURCE AND TUITION GAP

A resource gap in favor of private institutions now exists in higher education. In 1967–68, private institutions received about 40 percent of current fund income for all higher education institutions, but enrolled only 30 percent of the total number of students. Thus institutional grant formulas which differently favor private institutions require special justification. The resource gap now places them in an advantageous position.

The dollar gap between tuition at public and private institutions has widened sharply in the last two decades, and private institutions frequently cite this growing gap as the reason for their falling enrollment and worsening financial condition. General formula institutional grants, however, would permit both public and private institutions to keep tuition levels down, leaving the dollar gap between them at about the same level.

The two gaps point in different directions—the first toward more support for public institutions since their resources from students are lower, and the second toward more support for private institutions to help them survive without increasing their tuition even higher above public institutions. Closing the first gap creates pressures for the second gap to be closed also; closing the second gap creates pressure for the first gap to be closed. Different interests are concerned with which gap should be closed. There are important complications. Whatever policy seeks to close one gap should be concerned with the impact on the other gap as well; certainly there will be repercussions if the other gap is widened as a result.

FEDERAL PRIORITIES

The Commission believes it would be unwise to put into effect a program of institutional aid that has no more well-defined purpose than making more funds available to all institutions, regardless of need or additional social contribution. Such a program would constitute a substantial shift in basic financing responsibilities, and in the long-run might lead in the direction of a national system of higher education.

Increased federal funding for higher education can be accomplished without any major relocation of funding responsibilities. Federal funds can be assigned for those programs and concerns which already constitute major national priorities.

EQUALITY OF EDUCATIONAL OPPORTUNITY

The first priority for any program of federal aid to higher education should be to establish equality of educational opportunity. We have recommended in prior reports (*Quality and Equality,* 1968; 1970) an integrated financial aid package for students. One of our recommendations, greater federal student aid, would raise institutional costs by increasing the enrollment of persons that would otherwise not attend college or university. It would also raise costs by requiring greater inputs of educational resources to help students from culturally or educationally deprived backgrounds obtain the maximum benefit from their college experiences. For these reasons the Commission recommends that

. . . the federal government establish a program of cost-of-education supplements to colleges and universities based on the numbers of students enrolled in the institutions who hold grants awarded on the basis of financial need. Under this program, it is recommended that any college or university officially recognized as being eligible for participation in this program by the Office of Education, be paid $500 for each undergraduate student at the institution that is a recipient of a grant from the federal government which was made to the student because of his financial need. Proportionate cost-of-education supplements would be paid to institutions for any part-time students who are enrolled at that institution and who hold such grants (p. 81).

Students from families with income of $10,000 to $15,000 often face economic barriers to higher education. Under existing and proposed federal student financial assistance programs, these students would be eligible for subsidized loans. So as not to curtail educational opportunity for this income group, the Commission recommends that

. . . colleges and universities officially recognized as eligible for participation in this program by the Office of Education shall receive a grant of $200 for each student who receives a subsidized loan provided, however, that no such payment shall be made for students who hold federal grants or for students who borrow less than $200 during the fiscal year (p. 81).

GRADUATE EDUCATION

We believe that the need for top-level experts in many fields is a matter of national concern which transcends state boundaries, and, that support for institutions selected by highly able students completing advanced graduate education should be a federal responsibility. To aid institutions in meeting the high instructional costs in programs for Ph.D.'s and D.A.'s, the Commission suggests that:

■ The level of continued support for graduate programs should be influenced by our estimated needs for high-quality Ph.D.'s and D.A.'s in the immediate future.

■ Institutions be paid a cost-of-education supplement amounting to $5,000 for each federal doctoral fellow enrolled at that institution (p. 83).

HEALTH EDUCATION

A shortage of health manpower now exists in the United States. In keeping with the principle of federal support for national priorities, the Commission has recommended (in *Higher Education and the Nation's Health*) increased federal aid to colleges and universities for the training of more health care personnel.

CONSTITUTIONALITY

A general formula institutional grant is relatively easy to administer at the federal level and at the institutional level. But it runs a greater risk than special purpose grants of being unconstitutional. Lump-sum grants to institutions with strong religious affiliations may violate the First Amendment. The cost-of-education supplements to institutions may also run into constitutional difficulties, but long experience with the GI Bill and institutional grants in doctoral fellowship programs suggest they may be less subject to serious constitutional questions.

CONCLUSION

The Commission cautions against the possible *substitution* effects of some proposed formulas for federal institutional aid upon state contributions to higher education and upon existing programs of aid to students and institutions. Unless the federal government is willing to increase its total support sufficiently to add new programs while retaining and expanding existing programs, new forms of direct aid to the institutions may be gained at the expense of present aid to the institutions and students.

The principle of selective support for federal grants to institutions, as distinguished from across-the-board lump sums to colleges and universities, permits the retention by the federal government of federal initiative. With selective support, the federal government can use its initiative to increase equality of opportunity, expand the supply of health manpower, and encourage desirable innovation and reform. Selective aid at the federal level has been, and can be, a major force for drawing higher education into high-priority social endeavors.

THE FOURTH REVOLUTION

11

INSTRUCTIONAL
TECHNOLOGY IN
HIGHER EDUCATION
(JUNE 1972)

Higher education is on the brink of the first great technological revolution in five centuries—the revolution of the new electronics. New technology has already transformed research techniques in many fields and administrative methods on many campuses. It is now affecting large libraries and is entering into the instructional process. The new technology may provide the single greatest opportunity to introduce academic change on and off campus.

New technologies can bring education to the sick, the handicapped, the aged, the imprisoned—to members of the armed forces, to persons in remote areas, and to many adults who might prefer instruction at home. For students, the expanding technology has some major advantages: properly applied, it increases opportunities for independent study and it provides students with a richer variety of courses and methods of instruction; also, the new technology is infinitely patient with the slow learner. For faculty members, the new technology can lessen routine instructional responsibilities and may reduce the need for teaching assistants and for additional new faculty members.

WHEN SHOULD TECHNOLOGY BE USED?

The Commission believes that technology should not be adopted merely because it exists. These two tests should be applied in deciding whether any technology should be used:

1 The teaching-learning task to be performed by technology should be essential to the course of instruction to which it is applied.

2 The task to be performed could not be performed as well without it.

THE NEED FOR SOFTWARE

The use of instructional technology at colleges is faltering, largely because of a deficiency in the supply of computer programs, video- and audiotapes, printed learning modules, films, and other "software" of instructional technology. The deficiency exists for important reasons:

■ Instructional technology is not uniformly welcomed by the academic community.

■ Faculty members who are interested in designing learning materials for the new instructional technology are usually not rewarded for their efforts.

■ There is little compatibility of components in mediaware made by different manufacturers, tending to fragment the educational market.

■ Uncertainty as to where to develop instructional programs: on the campus or at a national center.

■ Few faculty members have the combined interests and expertise in subject matter, media development, and learning theory that the design of high-quality instructional materials requires.

■ Faculty have been disenchanted by persistent findings in many studies that the effectiveness of instruction provided by technology is not significantly different from that of good professors and teachers using conventional modes of instruction.

TODAY'S TECHNOLOGY

Many examples of educational technology are so familiar they are taken for granted—for example, books and films. Other kinds of instructional technology in use today at many colleges and universities are:

Multimedia classrooms

Self-instruction units—language laboratories, audiolistening centers

Instructional radio

Instructional TV

Computer-assisted instruction

Computer-as-control instruction

DEVELOPMENTS ABROAD

Technology has figured prominently in the efforts of several countries to extend higher educational opportunities to persons who have been unable to take advantage of them in the past. Sweden's Television-Radio University, Japan's University of the Air, Great Britain's Open University, and West Germany's extramural television courses all make wide use of instructional technology, mainly to bring higher education to that part of the population that in the past has had to forgo college or university attendance in order to devote full time to earning a living.

LIBRARIES

Colleges, universities, and their libraries are facing an information explosion: there is more printed material to catalog and store, more nonprinted information to assimilate into collections, more clients to serve as the community and campus get bigger, and more complexity in the interrelations of concepts and ideas and in the ways different people approach the search for information. Libraries have responded mainly through miniaturization techniques and by automating their operations and services. They are also turning to computers to do more and more library operations.

The Carnegie Commission believes that the college library should become a central instructional resource on the campus—housing print and nonprint information, illustrations, and instructional software components cataloged and stored in ways that facilitate convenient retrieval as needed. The Commission also believes that the movement by some public and college libraries to form regional library networks is a logical answer to many of the problems that they face. The move to regional organization will give colleges, universities, and the libraries a stronger, united voice in claims for rights of access to communications media controlled by government. It will also give them increased capability to adopt advanced information and communications technologies.

PENETRATION OF INSTRUCTIONAL TECHNOLOGY

On the whole, the use of various instructional media in American higher education is still a largely ad hoc enterprise, advancing unsystematically in response to the enthusiasms and achievements of certain devoted practitioners and the occasional emergence of promising new devices. Site visits by Commission staff indicate that the new technologies are now in use at small as well as large colleges. According to one survey, faculty members predict that routine audiovisual technology and student-initiated access to audiovisual materials will be routinely used by undergraduates by 1980. Programmed instruction, routine computer-assisted instruction, computer simulation, and routine classroom broadcasting with electronic student feedback will be routinely used for undergraduates by 1990. The faculty in this survey also predict that advanced computer-assisted instruction, computer-managed instruction, and computer-aided course design would be routinely used in undergraduate instruction by the year 2000. In general, faculty in business and education are the most optimistic about future use of technology in their fields, followed closely by faculty in engineering and science. The greatest pessimism is expressed by teachers in the liberal and fine arts.

RECOMMENDATIONS FOR FUTURE EXPANSION

Colleges and universities, industry, governments, and foundations concerned with educational endeavors should make an effort to advance the time when technology will be fully utilized for the instruction of our youth and the continuing education of our citizens because:

■ Technology can provide greater flexibility and variety in the organization of instruction, and give students a more self-reliant role in their own education.

■ An enormous investment has already been made in experimentation and research with instructional technology in the United States. Prudence dictates making an early effort to begin to capitalize on the investments we have made already.

■ Expanding technology has the potential economic effect of spreading the benefit of investment in a single unit of instruction among very large numbers of students. The earlier efforts are made to develop the expanding instructional technology fully, the earlier this increased productivity will be realized.

■ College enrollments are now declining and are expected to stabilize in the 1980s; the current abundance of faculty should be utilized in the development and introduction of expanded technologies so that higher education can accommodate the rising enrollments in the 1990s with minimal expansion of physical facilities and faculties.

■ Coordination and planning will be easier now, when considerable flexibility still exists in the development and organization of new technologies, than later, when current divergent directions of development become rigidly fixed.

The Carnegie Commission recommends that

. . . because expanding technology will extend higher learning to larger numbers of people who have been unable to take advantage of it in the past, because it will provide instruction in forms that will be more effective than conventional instruction for some learners in some subjects, because it will be more effective for all learners and many teachers under many circumstances, and because it will significantly reduce costs of higher education in the long run, its early advancement should be encouraged by the adequate commitment of colleges and universities to its utilization and development and by adequate support from governmental and other agencies concerned with the advancement of higher learning (p. 46).

MORE LEARNING MATERIALS
One of the great disappointments of the national effort to date is that for all of the funds and effort thus far expended for the advancement of instructional technology, penetration of new learning materials and media into higher education has thus far been shallow. Though existing technology is far from perfect, a remarkable amount of operational technology is available for use today. What is needed is less financial support for invention of equipment and more for the development and utilization of what we have already. High priority must be placed, during the next two decades, upon the design and utilization of high-quality instructional programs suitable for use or adaptation by more than one institution. The Commission therefore recommends that

. . . since a grossly inadequate supply of good-quality instructional materials now exists, a major thrust of financial support and effort on behalf of instructional technology for the next decade should be toward the development and utilization of outstanding instructional programs and materials. The academic disciplines should follow the examples of physics and mathematics in playing a significant role in such efforts (p. 48).

INSTITUTIONAL COMMITMENT

No one segment of our society—industry, government, or higher education—will be able to bring about the full and effective use of instructional technology alone. But the Commission feels the greatest single obstacle to higher education's accepting a leadership role is the lack of institutional commitment. On too many campuses a handful of instructors, and occasionally an isolated department, develop enthusiasms for specific media or devices. Their successes are inadequately communicated to the rest of the campuses; their failures are ignored.

The responsibility for improving this situation rests with the top academic administrators. Such administrators should mobilize their institution's instructional resources to make effective use of technology. Under their auspices, information about instructional technology should be maintained and made available to faculty members. They should arrange training sessions. They should serve as campus liaison with government foundations and other sources of financial support for the expanding technology. They should assume responsibility for identifying effective uses of technology on campus and, when appropriate, for calling it to the attention of the total faculty and of regional, national, or professional organizations.

Institutions should make the new technologies available for use on campus. They should make certain that new buildings are fully adaptive for the use of technologies, and they should see to it that faculty members engaged in the development of instructional technology have adequate professional assistance. The Commission thus recommends that

. . . institutions of higher education should contribute to the advancement of instructional technology not only by giving favorable consideration to expanding its use, whenever such use is appropriate, but also by placing responsibility for its introduction and utilization at the highest possible level of academic administration (p. 51).

LIBRARIES

The Commission notes the significant progress that libraries have made in utilizing the new technologies. It therefore regards libraries as promising catalysts of continuing innovation and development for the expanded use of technology by colleges and universities, and as the information centers of campuses. Thus the Commission recommends that

. . . the introduction of new technologies to help libraries continue to improve their services to increasing numbers of users should be given first priority in the efforts of colleges and universities, government agencies, and other agencies seeking to achieve more rapid progress in the development of instructional technology (p. 51).

EXTRAMURAL EDUCATION

A realistic appraisal of current progress in the use and development of instructional technology suggests that the most significant advances, in the coming decade at least, will be generated by emerging institutions and extramural educational systems. These institutions will have a considerable tolerance for innovation and will need instructional materials of some variety. The Commission recommends that

. . . major funding sources, including states, the federal government, and foundations, recognize not only the potential of new and developing extramural education systems for expanding learning opportunities, but also the crucial role such systems should play in the ultimate development of instructional technologies. Requests of these systems for funds with which to introduce and use new instructional programs, materials, and media should be given favorable consideration (p. 53).

COOPERATIVE LEARNING-TECHNOLOGY CENTERS

To prevent undue centralization of effort by the federal government while promoting coordinated multi-institutional efforts in developing instructional materials, and spreading the major costs of constructing and acquiring expensive mediaware and facilities among many users, the Commission recommends that

. . . by 1992, at least seven cooperative learning-technology centers, voluntarily organized on a regional basis by participating higher educational institutions and systems, should be established for the purpose of sharing costs and facilities for the accelerated development and utilization of instructional technology in higher education (p. 54).

The regional cooperative learning-technology centers would be primarily service units for participating institutions. They could engage in research and development activity, but would be required to devote most of their efforts to the identification, production, and distribution of already-developed teaching and learning materials.

The Commission believes that

. . . the federal government should assume full financial responsibility for the capital expenditures required initially to establish one cooperative learning-technology center every three years between 1973 and 1992 (p. 58).

and that

. . . the federal government should provide at least one-third of the funds required for the operation of cooperative learning-technology centers for the first ten years of their operation (p. 58).

Participating institutions should share the cost of development and operation of these centers, and the centers should be encouraged to seek short-term project support from governments, foundations, and industry. To qualify for federal assistance, the Commission believes that cooperative learning-technology centers should plan to serve at least 200,000 students and show efforts to organize one or more regional library systems, one or more operating computer time-sharing programs, and one or more extramural educational systems.

THE FEDERAL GOVERNMENT
The Commission believes that financial initiative for the development and application of the new technologies remains mainly with the federal government, probably through the year 2000. Of all the possible funding agencies, the federal government has the largest resources to draw upon. Moreover, the development of instructional technology promises qualitative and financial benefits to all of education, not just to certain kinds of institutions or only to institutions in certain areas of the country.

Therefore, the Commission recommends that

. . . the federal government should continue to provide a major share of expenditures required for research and development in instructional technology and for introduction of new technologies more extensively into higher education at least until the end of the century. The total level of federal government support for these purposes should be at least $100 million in 1973 and should rise to 1 percent of the total expenditures of the nation on higher education by 1980 (p. 62).

To administer federal support to instructional technology, the Commission further recommends that

. . . the proposed National Foundation for Postsecondary Education and the proposed National Institute of Education should be established and the proposed National Foundation for Postsecondary Education should be assigned the responsibility for administering loans and the provision of capital investment funds and grants for the utilization of instructional technology. Grants to support research and development activities in the field of instructional technology for higher education should be made by the proposed National Institute of Education (p. 63).

FACULTY
The basic objective of technology is to make better and fuller use of faculty capabilities. The new technology should save faculty time and reduce some of the routine teaching load. But the design, development, and revision of instructional materials take a good deal of faculty time.

Colleges and universities should provide incentives to faculty members who contribute to the advancement of instructional technology. Released time for the development of instructional materials and promotions and salary improvement for successful achievement in such endeavors should be part of that encouragement (p. 66).

Widespread utilization of technology at colleges and secondary schools will change the role of teachers and professors. To prepare future teachers for their roles, the Commission believes that

. . . colleges and universities that are responsible for the training of prospective university, college, and high school teachers should begin now to incorporate in their curricula instruction on the development of teaching-learning segments that appropriately utilize the expanding technologies of instruction (p. 68).

NEW PROFESSIONALS

As the variety of instructional alternatives for each lesson and course increases, the planning of instruction will require more differentiated knowledge and skills than most individual professors are likely to have. Technologists and specialists will need to join the staffs of colleges and universities. *Instructional technologists* can aid faculty in defining objectives of courses of instruction, in plotting learning strategies, and in evaluating results. *Media technologists* can organize the technological resources needed for effective instruction. *Information specialists* can guide their colleagues to information essential for the preparation of instructional materials. His or her job will be to know where the needed data, illustrations, films, slides, audiotapes, and other instructional "software" that might be used for a course are to be found.

It is reasonable to expect that the specialist members of an instructional planning team could work in a concentrated way with perhaps 10 professors in an academic year, and might reasonably be able to serve 50 faculty members over a five-year period. To provide at least three specialists to assist every 50 professors will require employment of as many as 45,000 new instructional professionals in higher education by 1980 and 54,000 by 2000.

Colleges and universities should supplement their instructional staffs with qualified technologists and specialists to assist instructors in the design, planning, and evaluation of teaching-learning units that can be used with the expanding instructional technologies. Institutions of higher education at all levels should develop their potentials for training specialists and professionals needed to perform the new functions that are associated with the increasing utilization of instructional technology on the nation's college and university campuses (p. 73).

IMPACTS ON STUDENTS

The new technology holds two major promises for students: they will become more active agents in their own education; they will have more flexibility and variety in their education. Instructional technology allows students to initiate the learning experience. It can give a student access to presentations by exceptionally talented and knowledgeable teachers who live and work at great distances from the student's campus. It can enrich and supplement classroom instruction that is already available. It can give a student alternative modes of instruction for the same subject. And it can give students access to instructional programs designed with bigger budgets, more expertise, and greater talent than can be found on a single campus.

Students will have to be trained in the use of the new instructional media, especially in the use of the computer. It is important that colleges begin now to train more prospective high school instructors in the use of computers and that high schools instruct their pupils in computer operation so that entering college students will be trained adequately in their use.

High schools that do not already do so should offer instruction in basic concepts and uses of computers and should encourage their students to obtain, as early as possible, other skills that will be helpful in the use of new media for learning (p. 78).

PRODUCTIVITY AND COSTS

The costs of introducing more of the new technology into higher education are going to be high in the short-run; just how high is virtually impossible to estimate. For most institutions, initial expenditures for introducing the new instructional technologies onto campuses will be in the form of add-on costs. But in return for such expenditures the new technologies will enrich instructional content, will provide more flexibility in class scheduling, and will generate more variety in instructional modes.

In the long run, the new technology can help increase productivity in the following ways:

■ By decreasing the time required by students to learn specified modules of information

■ By taking advantage of the capabilities of available technological capacity

■ By reducing faculty time required for a given instructional objective

■ By prolonging the time during which instruction is available

■ By utilizing quality instructional materials produced off the campus

■ By sharing high-quality instructional programs and learning materials with other institutions

■ By a conscientious integration of available technologies to produce desired objectives

■ By enlarging the market for instructional materials and instructional media

Instructional technology may provide the best means to educate growing numbers of students of all ages within a budget the American people can afford. But enthusiasm should be tempered by caution. At least for the coming three decades the Commission believes that efforts to utilize and improve the new instructional technology should be accompanied by periodic review of progress and results.

An independent commission, supported either by an appropriate agency of the U.S. Department of Health, Education and Welfare or by one or more private foundations should be created to make assessments of the instructional effectiveness and cost benefits of currently available instructional technology. Findings of the commission should be published and appropriately disseminated for the advice of institutions of higher education, such cooperative learning-technology centers as may be established, and governments and foundations supporting the advancement of instructional technology (p. 87).

GOALS

By 1980

The Commission suggests that the following goals be reached:

1   Institutions of higher learning will have accepted a broad definition of instructional technology such as: The enrichment and improvement of the conditions in which human beings learn and teach achieved through the creative and systematic organization of resources, physical arrangements, media, and methods.

2   Most colleges and universities will have devised adequate administrative and academic authority and procedures for the encouragement and appropriate utilization of instructional technology.

3   Colleges and universities that are responsible for training prospective teachers for high schools and colleges will have incorporated instruction in the design of courses and in the effective utilization of instructional technology (as broadly defined in this report) in their curricula.

4   A concerted federal government effort, utilizing the resources of the nation's finest libraries and museums as well as the resources of the nation's campuses, will have been made to design and produce courses of instruction of good quality for presentation using advanced electronic media.

5   At least three cooperative learning-technology centers, combining the instructional technology capabilities of many member institutions within a geographic region, and originating and directing centralized instructional services through information, communications, and computing networks will be in operation.

6   The level of federal support for development and application of instructional technologies should have reached a figure equal to 1 percent of the total national expenditure for higher education.

7   Extramural higher education programs should be available to most Americans through Open University–type programs initiated by existing

colleges and universities, states, or cooperative learning-technology centers.

8   Legal restraints upon the duplication of educational materials should have been thoroughly reviewed by Congress with special attention given to their impacts on the capabilities and advantages of instruction provided by the new instructional technology.

9   Manufacturers of equipment for uses in teaching and learning at colleges and universities will have made a greater effort to adapt their designs so that compatible instructional components can be produced for use on a wide variety of makes and models.

10   Systems for identifying promising instructional materials will have been developed and procedures for encouraging their development and utilization will be operable.

11   New professions for persons engaged in creating and developing instructional materials on the nation's campuses will have emerged (pp. 89–93).

By 1990

1   Most colleges in the country will have introduced sufficient technologies so that: savings of at least 15 percent of a professor's time per course will be realized; a wide variety of learning modes will be available; students will have considerable logistical flexibility in that certain amounts of their instruction will be at times and places most convenient to them.

2   Six of the seven proposed cooperative learning-technology centers will be in operation (p. 93).

By 2000

1   All instructional technology identifiable in 1972 will be in general use on college and university campuses.

2   The availability of education through independent study within and without traditional institutions will have become widespread through applications of the expanding technology (p. 93).

THE MORE EFFECTIVE USE OF RESOURCES

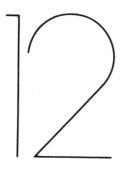

AN IMPERATIVE
FOR HIGHER
EDUCATION
(JUNE 1972)

Higher education in the United States has just completed its decade of greatest academic success. In the 1960s it more than doubled its enrollments (from over 3 million to over 6 million full-time-equivalent students) without reducing quality of instruction. It became the preeminent world center for research. Yet higher education in the early 1970s is experiencing its greatest financial crisis.

This anomalous juxtaposition of triumph and depression is a fact that must be accepted, and adjustments must be made to it. The central thrust of this report is that the total institutional expenditures of higher education must be, should be, and can be reduced by nearly $10 billion per year (in 1970 dollars) by 1980 as compared with the costs which would be incurred if the trends of the 1960s were to be continued; that expenditures should be held to a level of around $41.5 billion as against $51 billion per year. This is approximately a 20 percent reduction. Expenditures would rise to 2.7 percent of the GNP as compared with their present percentage of 2.5 and as compared with the possibility of 3.3 percent if the trends of the 1960s were to be continued and as against about 1.0 percent in the year 1960. The report sets out to show why a reduction of about 20 percent needs to take place and how it can be accomplished without any general deterioration in the quality of higher education.

THE FINANCIAL CRISIS

Higher education is facing a serious financial crisis. A growing imbalance between the rate of increase in income and the rate of increase in budgetary needs began about 1967–68. Expenditures on higher education were rising as a percentage of the gross national product—from about 1 percent at the beginning of the 1960s to more than 2 percent at the end of the decade—but appropriations for higher education were encountering increased competition with other needs. All the available evidence suggests that the financial problems of institutions of higher education are likely to continue to be serious, at least until the mid-1970s and most likely far beyond.

The financial crisis has forced many institutions to curb increases in expenditures. Some have taken great care to ensure that expenditures might be pruned in ways that would be least harmful to the quality of education, but too many institutions have resorted to across-the-board cost-cutting. These colleges and universities must turn to more carefully considered selective economies. But even if the financial crisis were to abate in the near future, the Commission believes that the effort to achieve more effective use of resources should continue to receive very substantial emphasis in institutions of higher education. It can bring positive benefits to higher education. Already many colleges and universities—especially those that are privately controlled—are coming together as never before to analyze their mutual situations, to seek increased federal and state aid, and to study ways in which they might achieve economies through interinstitutional cooperation.

BEHAVIOR OF COSTS

Higher education is a labor-intensive service sector of the economy in which it is difficult to achieve the gains in productivity that are experienced in goods-producing industries. In the 1960s, costs per FTE student in higher education rose at an annual average rate that was 3.3 percent higher than the rate of increase in the consumer price index. For private institutions the difference was 5.2 percent, and for public institutions it was 2.5 percent.

Expenditures among institutions (per FTE student) vary widely—graduate costs exceed those for undergraduate education, costs at research-oriented universities exceed those at non-research institutions, educational costs in large urban areas exceed those in other geographical areas. Higher education benefits from economies of scale, but the tendency for institutions to become more complex as they grow in size is an offsetting factor.

An important step in achieving more effective use of resources is a careful analysis of costs in relation to (1) appropriate measures of input such as FTE enrollment and (2) appropriate measures of output or quality such as credit hours completed, degrees awarded, and performance of graduates on the Graduate Record Examination.

The Commission recommends that all relatively large institutions of higher education maintain an office of institutional research or its equivalent and that relatively small institutions seek to enter into arrangements with nearby similar institutions to conduct jointly sponsored programs of institutional research (p. 46).

The Commission also recommends that all appropriate agencies—the U.S. Office of Education, the Southern Regional Education Board, the Western Interstate Commission on Higher Education, and similar bodies—give high priority to the development of more adequate data on the behavior of costs, income, and output in higher education (p. 47).

DEGREE-STRUCTURE REFORM

The most promising single avenue toward more effective use of resources in higher education is to shorten and reconstitute many of the prevailing degree structures. Recommendations for such changes were made in an earlier Commission report, *Less Time, More Options* (1970).

1   Incorporation of the last year of high school into the first year of college

2   Incorporation of the first year in college into the last year of high school

3   A change to the three-year, rather than a four-year, bachelor of arts degree either through reducing requirements or operation on a year-round basis

4   Credit given to students by examination for work accomplished outside the formal classroom

5   Integration of bachelor's and master's programs

6   Horizontal integration of overlapping or duplicating programs

7   Development of new types of master's programs that will provide more effective preparation for teaching in community colleges and, to some extent, in four-year colleges (e.g., the M.Phil. degree)

8   Placing greater emphasis on other two-year master's programs of a professional type, e.g., the master in human biology degree, which would prepare an individual to be a physician's assistant, to teach at an appropriate level, or to go on for an M.D., D.D.S., or a Ph.D.

9   Emphasizing development of a four-year doctor of arts degree as the standard degree for college teachers and for many positions in government, industry, and academic administration

10   Reducing the length of time required to complete the work for the Ph.D. and the M.D. degrees

The Commission reiterates the recommendations made in its report, *Less Time, More Options,* for changes in degree structures (p. 58).

The great number of degrees offered on American campuses contributes to ineffective use of resources in higher education. In *Less Time, More Options,* the Commission recommended the total number of degrees awarded be reduced to about 160.

The Commission reiterates its recommendation for greatly reducing the number of different types of degrees awarded in higher education (p. 58).

RETENTION RATES AND STUDENT COUNSELING

The Commission believes that each high school graduate or otherwise qualified person should have an opportunity to enroll at an institution of higher education. But we do not believe that colleges and universities should strive to hold the 5 to 15 percent of students—the "captive audience"—who are there because of social pressures only and are not really interested in continuing their education. Nor do we believe that efforts should be made to retain students who have been given ample opportunity but have shown that they cannot "make the grade" in higher education.

Nevertheless, we recognize that the dropout rate in American higher education is high. Improved counseling might prevent some students from dropping out—for example, those who cannot meet the expense of college, or those who are unhappy. An "exit interview" for students wishing to leave would also provide institutions with useful information about cases of ineffective teaching and indifferent or ineffective handling of student complaints.

The Commission recommends that institutions of higher education seek to increase their retention rates through improved counseling programs, where these are deficient, and through establishing the practice of conducting an "exit interview" with every student who plans to withdraw (p. 61).

The Commission believes that colleges and universities should seek to reduce the "captive audience." Admissions officers should attempt to identify students who are applying only because of social pressures and who might be better off in a job or in an occupational program or in a different type of college. Colleges and universities might also initiate a policy of annual interview with all students.

The main attack on this problem must be made long before the student enters college—through improved high school counseling.

The Commission recommends that colleges and universities inaugurate programs designed to discourage poorly motivated students from entering and from continuing once they have entered. These programs should be designed to include appropriate counseling of applicants, generally through the admissions office, as well as counseling of all undergraduate students, perhaps through the medium of a regular annual interview (p. 62).

We also recommend that high school counseling programs be strengthened and improved, not only for the purpose of guiding students to appropriate colleges or to appropriate jobs or occupational programs, but also to dissuade poorly motivated students from entering college (p. 62).

FACULTY

Salaries of faculty members represent a major item of expense in higher education, accounting, on average, for about one-third of educational and general expenditures (less organized research).

STUDENT-FACULTY RATIOS

Achieving a significant increase in the student-faculty ratio is a major avenue to effective use of resources in a college or university, provided it can be accomplished without sacrificing quality. A number of studies show wide variations in student faculty ratios among institutions that are similar in type and quality, though it has also been shown that there is a significant positive relationship between ratios of faculty to students and institutional quality. However, in the 1960s student-faculty ratios in most types of institutions rose with no apparent adverse effect on quality.

The Commission recommends that all colleges and universities examine their utilization of faculty time and in particular that they do so if their student-faculty ratios fall below the following median levels for their categories (p. 85).

CARNEGIE CLASSIFICATION*	PUBLIC	PRIVATE
Research universities	22.0 *(weighted)*	16.0 *(weighted)*
Other doctoral-granting universities	21.6 *(weighted)*	22.0 *(weighted)*
Comprehensive universities and colleges I	19.7 *(weighted)*	18.6 *(weighted)*
Comprehensive universities and colleges II	17.9 *(weighted)*	16.5 *(weighted)*
Liberal arts colleges I	†	12.2 *(unweighted)*
Liberal arts colleges II	†	14.3 *(unweighted)*
Two-year colleges	19.2 *(unweighted)*	15.4 *(unweighted)*

*See *Institutional Aid,* Appendix A, for explanations of the criteria used in classifying institutions.

†There are no public liberal arts colleges I, and data have not been included on public liberal arts colleges II, because the number of these colleges reporting the necessary information was very small.

NOTE: The weight for graduate as against undergraduate students used here is 3 to 1 for universities and 2 to 1 for comprehensive universities and colleges.

We believe that a careful examination of student-faculty ratios, department by department and campus by campus, can result in an overall average increase in the ratio from an unweighted 16 to an unweighted 17 without impairing education quality.

FACULTY TIME

The goal of effective use of faculty time is more likely to be accomplished through sustained attention to the many facets of the problem than through any single, sweeping change.

We recommend consideration of the following:

■ Carefully studying and adopting a varied mixture of class sizes at the different levels of instruction and establishing appropriate average class sizes that different departments may be expected to meet

■ Seeking to prevent undue proliferation of courses by periodic review of the totality of course offerings in a department

■ Involving the faculty in developing policies directed toward achieving appropriate and equitable teaching loads

■ Establishing standards relating to a reasonable maximum amount of time to be spent in consulting activities

■ Maintaining reasonable and equitable policies relating to sabbatical leaves for all career members of the faculty, including assistant professors

■ Analyzing costs of support personnel, in comparison with those of other similar institutions, with a view to identifying possible excessive costs in some aspects of support functions, but also of making certain that these functions are being conducted efficiently and that highly paid faculty members are not performing functions that could be delegated to lower-paid support personnel (p. 86).

SALARIES

The deterioration in the job market for faculty members is likely to mean that faculty salaries will not rise as rapidly, relative to other wages and salaries, in the 1970s and 1980s as they did in the 1960s. Faculty salaries are more likely to rise with professional salaries generally in the decade ahead, and these may rise at a slower level than all wages and salaries. The faculty response to a slow-down in the rate of salary increase may well be toward greater unionization. Administrators in many institutions of higher education—especially in large public systems of higher education—will need to establish successful collective bargaining relationships. The results will not necessarily be adverse to efforts to achieve effective use of resources. The union contract can be a means by which some costs are made more certain. It may also be possible for "management" to achieve provisions designed to increase faculty productivity, e.g., modest increases in teaching loads in return for increases in salaries and fringe benefits.

The Commission recommends that institutions of higher education engaged with faculty unionism employ staff members or consultants who are experienced in collective bargaining negotiations and consider the possibility of agreements that will induce increases in the productivity of faculty members and other academic employees without impairing educational effectiveness (p. 89).

BUDGET FLEXIBILITY

When both enrollment and income were growing rapidly, as was the case throughout the 1960s, the budget could adapt to changing needs with relative ease. With budgetary stringency such as we have today, flexibility is much more difficult to achieve. Funds must be found to develop new programs or expand existing ones; this may well necessitate curtailing or dropping programs for which demand has declined or in which the institution has not developed great strength.

The need for budgetary flexibility will be especially important in the next two decades. In the 1970s the job market for highly trained manpower will change radically. There is expected to be a surplus of teachers and Ph.D.'s, for example, and a shortage of professional personnel in health sciences, counseling, urban planning, and social work. Students are showing a growing interest in areas of special concern like ecology and the urban crisis. In the 1980s, total enrollment in higher education is expected to become essentially stationary, increasing the difficulty of obtaining funds for new programs.

SELECTIVE CUTBACKS

One means of achieving budgetary flexibility is to cut back some programs in order to release funds for new or developing ones. Though general cutbacks in graduate programs at leading research universities are undesirable, carefully considered cutbacks of developing doctoral programs may be desirable in some cases. The proliferation of doctoral-granting institutions may result in increased overall costs per student and in deterioration of quality.

The Commission recommends that leading research universities refrain from cutbacks in graduate programs except on a carefully considered, selective basis. We also recommend that institutions with less emphasis on research consider curtailment or elimination, on a selective basis, of Ph.D. programs that are not of high quality or that are too small to be operated economically. We urge great caution in the development of new Ph.D. programs in particular fields at existing doctoral-granting institutions and do not believe that there is a need for any new Ph.D.-granting institutions, although some or even many institutions will be introducing the D.A. degree (p. 97).

American colleges and universities are turning to other approaches to achieve budgetary flexibility: *across-the-board* cuts (in some cases with a view to releasing funds for programs that need to be expanded), *readapting programs* to meet new needs, and *reallocating vacated positions* to the central administration which will determine where the need for reassignment is greatest. Harvard University achieves considerable budgetary flexibility through its longstanding policy—"every tub on its own bottom"—in which every school or college develops its own resources.

The Commission recommends that all institutions of higher education place emphasis on policies that will ensure budgetary flexibility. Combinations of policies that will achieve this goal will vary from institution to institution but may well include elements of (1) selective cutbacks, (2) across-the-board budgetary cuts, (3) consolidation of existing programs, (4) readaptation of existing programs, (5) "every tub on its own bottom," and (6) central reassignment of positions vacated due to resignation, retirement, or death (p. 103).

During the greater part of the 1960s, when both enrollment and expenditures were rising rapidly in higher education, new programs were frequently adopted without careful evaluation of their long-run costs. Colleges and universities should exercise more caution in adopting new programs. There is a strong case for periodic or continuous review of programs, especially in large colleges and universities, and multicampus institutions. Considerable savings can be achieved by confining costly or specialized degree programs to one or two campuses within the system. Some state coordinating councils or boards with regulatory functions already have powers to prevent the establishment of new programs and

to require discontinuation of existing programs. The Commission therefore recommends that

. . . colleges and universities use great caution in adopting new degree programs
and conduct periodic reviews of existing degree programs, with a view to eliminating those in which very few degrees are awarded, whether or not they are required
to do so by state coordinating bodies. Coordinating bodies may also need to conduct such review if the institutions fail in their responsibilities. In multicampus
institutions, there is a strong case for confining highly specialized degree programs to only one or two campuses within the system (p. 104).

The Commission further recommends that institutions of higher education consider the establishment of committees, including faculty, students, and administrators, to serve in an advisory capacity in relation to the preparation of the budget
when severe cuts must be made. Where it is not considered feasible or desirable
to establish such committees, the more traditional practice of holding hearings
on major budgetary decisions can provide faculty and students with opportunities
to express their views (p. 105).

We consider it essential that some existing funds each year be made
available for new or expanded endeavors. Thus, the Commission recommends that

. . . colleges and universities develop a "self-renewal" fund of 1 to 3 percent each
year taken from existing allocations (p. 105).

INCENTIVES

One obstacle to the achievement of effective use of resources in higher
education is that compensation and budgetary procedures are typically
not structured in such a way as to induce change.

The Commission recommends that institutions of higher education seek to alter
their budgetary procedures in such a way as to induce cost-saving change, giving
special attention to the possibilities of permitting departments and schools to carry
over from year to year significant proportions of unspent balances in their budgets
and of permitting them to retain a portion of the budgetary savings resulting from
innovation or investment in more efficient equipment. Ways and means of providing monetary compensation, probably principally in the form of special awards, for
employees who make constructive suggestions for innovations that result in
economies, should be developed (p. 109).

Because changes in budgetary procedures in public institutions of higher education will often require changes in state legislation or administrative regulations,
it may be necessary for institutions to seek permission to carry out pilot projects
designed to demonstrate that changes in procedures will yield economies. The
Commission recommends that state coordinating councils and boards seek to encourage such projects (p. 110).

THE IMPACT OF DECLINING GROWTH

The rate of higher education's enrollment growth will decline over the
next two decades. Colleges and universities must take measures to en-

sure continued flexibility in the use of faculty despite probable reductions in funds for new and expanding academic programs.

We recommend that campuses consider the following special policies for increasing their flexibility to adjust to a period of declining rate of growth:

■ Recapturing certain vacated positions for central reassignment, as recommended earlier

■ Hiring temporary and part-time faculty members

■ Providing that tenure does not necessarily apply only to the specific original assignment of specialized field and location

■ Employing persons with subject-matter flexibility, as made easier in the training for the doctor of arts degree, and by encouraging persons to shift fields where this is desirable and possible

■ Providing opportunities for early retirements on a full-time or part-time basis (pp. 116–117).

CAPITAL COSTS

PLANNING
Institutions of higher education must overcome certain weaknesses in their long-term planning of capital expenditures to achieve more effective use of resources. Less selective private institutions that are having difficulty maintaining their enrollments will have more difficulty predicting future enrollment than highly selective private universities or colleges. Large state systems cannot predict instate migration with high precision. Capital expansion programs have frequently made inadequate allowance for increased maintenance costs. Estimates of debt service and maintenance costs often take little account of possible fluctuations in income. And most institutional planning separates capital and operating budgets. Consolidating the two provides greater resource flexibility; if needs for capital expansion decline, accumulated funds from a capital budget might be transferred to an operating budget.

The Commission recommends (1) that long-range plans for capital expansion be continually revised to meet changing circumstances, (2) that adequate allowance be made for meeting increased debt service and maintenance costs on the basis of several alternative and relatively conservative estimates of the behavior of future income, and (3) that capital and operating budgets be consolidated (with the capital budget converted to a rental-cost basis), so that shifts can be made from one allocation to the other at the discretion of the board of trustees (p. 120).

The Commission believes that departments, research units, libraries, and other users of space should have budgets that include total user costs. Groups reviewing budgets should be able to see the total cost of an endeavor, including rental charges, against the total output.

The Commission recommends that institutions of higher education develop plans for gradually shifting to a practice of requiring budgets of departments and other units to include a rental charge for the space they occupy and the equipment they use (p. 121).

Accelerated degree programs will allow the same number of students to move through the system more rapidly and thus have the potential for saving on construction costs. Construction expenditures in the 1970s will also be reduced if students who might otherwise have enrolled in conventional institutions decide instead to enroll in open universities or other nontraditional study programs.

The Commission recommends that all capital investment plans give full advance consideration to the possible impact of accelerated degree programs (p. 122).

YEAR-ROUND OPERATION
The savings in capital costs can be appreciable with year-round operation of institutions of higher education, but whether there will be overall net savings depends upon whether or not increases in operating costs exceed savings in capital costs. The argument for year-round operation is particularly strong for those institutions with residence halls.

The Commission recommends that institutions of higher education carefully consider programs of year-round operation, but also recognize that the conditions that determine whether net savings will be achieved through year-round operation are complex and require careful study and planning (p. 124).

Effective utilization of classrooms is a more complex issue than some authors imply. The traditional view of space utilization can be misleading because it focuses on capital costs only. Often attempts to increase the number of weekly hours of classroom utilization lead to smaller classes which, in turn, lead to increases in teaching costs.

The Commission recommends careful study of space utilization standards and their reasonable application (p. 125).

OTHER AVENUES TO EFFECTIVE USE OF RESOURCES

CONSORTIA AND INTERINSTITUTIONAL COOPERATION
Significant economies can be achieved through consortium agreements and other forms of interinstitutional cooperation, particularly in graduate education. The number of effective consortia is increasing, and in the last few years financial stringency has led institutions to seek forms of cooperation that probably would not otherwise have developed.

The Commission recommends the development and strengthening of consortia in higher education. It also welcomes developments that are occurring in several states in the direction of increased cooperation and sharing of facilities by public and private institutions of higher education, and urges that such collaboration be considered in all states (pp. 128, 129).

MANAGEMENT DEVELOPMENT

The Commission believes that presidents, chancellors, deans, and other top administrative officials should continue to be drawn from the ranks of the faculty. College and university faculty tend to feel that an individual who has experienced the intellectual discipline of study and who has engaged in scholarly teaching and research will be a more effective defender of academic standards and academic freedom than someone who is chosen because he has been a successful leader in business, government, or military service. Perhaps the most promising approach to more effective management in higher education is the training and development of a middle-level administrative staff to assume some of the more mundane responsibilities of department chairmen, deans, and other administrators.

The Commission recommends that increased emphasis should be placed on the development and training of a staff of middle-managers who could assume many of the day-to-day functions of department chairmen, deans, and top administrators, thereby (1) reducing the amount of released faculty time required for administration; (2) providing more efficient and consistent administrative policies and practices; and (3) providing experienced and informed professional assistance to faculty members assuming new administrative responsibilities. There should likewise be emphasis on providing specialized training for nonacademic administrators.

The Commission also recommends that the president of the institution be given adequate assistance from a highly capable staff (p. 132).

ADMINISTRATIVE COSTS

Administrative costs per FTE student vary even among similar institutions. Such costs tend to be higher among private institutions, mainly because they devote far more attention to functions associated with the recruitment and selection of students. Colleges and universities will be in a far better position to identify excessive administrative costs or poorly handled administrative activities due to inadequate or inefficient administrative staff if they conduct thorough studies of administrative costs.

The Commission recommends that all institutions of higher education, especially those with relatively high administrative costs, conduct analyses of these costs with a view to identifying functions or parts of the institution in which these costs may be excessive or in which there is evidence of administrative inefficiency (pp. 134, 135).

COMPUTER COSTS

Computers are now in use at most colleges and universities—in research, computerized instruction, and for administrative tasks such as handling payrolls, accounting, student records, and in developing management information systems. A study of costs at 10 major private universities showed that computer expenditures in these institutions increased at an annual average rate of 41 percent from 1961–62 to 1965–66. Colleges and universities should seek ways to bring computer expenditures under more effective control.

The Commission recommends that all institutions of higher education seek economies in computer expenditures by (1) contracting for computer services where this is found to be advantageous, (2) charging the full costs of computer services used in extramurally financed research against the relevant research budgets, and (4) sharing computer facilities with nearby institutions of higher education where this appears to be a more advantageous solution than contracting out (p. 136).

MEDICAL AND DENTAL SCHOOL DEFICITS
One of the sources of financial difficulty for some universities is medical and dental school deficits. Although the Comprehensive Health Manpower Training Act of 1971 provided for a substantial increase in federal financial support of medical and dental education, appropriations have been below authorizations. And state support of medical and dental education is very uneven. Moreover, the financial difficulties of teaching hospitals will not be fully overcome until there are more adequate sources and mechanisms for reimbursement of patient-service activities. The problems of administering medical and dental schools are complex, and the Commission therefore recommends that

. . . all universities with university health science centers seek to ensure that management of these centers is organized in such a way as to enable the centers to meet the greatly increased responsibilities they are now being asked to fulfill. Among the policies that are likely to contribute to effective management are (1) separate, but coordinated, administration of health science centers and teaching hospitals and, where feasible, reliance on agreements with affiliated hospitals rather than ownership of a teaching hospital, and (2) development of an able core of middle-managers to assume responsibility for the more routine administrative functions (pp. 138, 139).

AUXILIARY ENTERPRISES
To achieve maximum economies in the running of certain auxiliary enterprises, the Commission recommends that

. . . all colleges and universities seek maximum economies in the operation of auxiliary services. These may be achieved through (1) contracting out, especially in small colleges and universities, (2) the development of student cooperative housing, and (3) employing students in food and room service activities. Students should be charged for services on a full-cost basis, and those who cannot afford these charges should be assisted through student aid or jobs.

STUDENT-AID POLICIES
Student-aid expenditures for low-income and lower-middle income students account for much of the deficit at some colleges and universities,

especially private institutions. Colleges and universities will continue to face difficulties in providing adequate student aid until federal student-aid expenditures are brought up to approximately the level recommended by the Commission in *Quality and Equality* (1968, 1970). In the meantime, student-aid funds can often be "stretched" by increasing loans and work opportunities in place of grants.

The Commission recommends that colleges and universities seek maximum effectiveness in the allocation of student-aid funds through limiting aid given exclusively in the form of grants to the neediest and most disadvantaged students, while providing combinations of grants, loans, and work opportunities to less needy students (p. 141).

FINANCING STUDENT SERVICES

During the postwar period, colleges and universities tended to increase the scope and variety of student services provided. They introduced or expanded counseling and placement services, initiated or improved student health services, and established cultural centers.

The Commission recommends that colleges and universities review their student services, with particular reference to reducing the extent of subsidization of these services where it seems justified. However, in view of the critical need for counseling services for disadvantaged students, the changes that are occurring in patterns of participation in higher education, and the complex shifts that are taking place in the labor market for college graduates, we believe that counseling services will need to be expanded rather than contracted in many colleges and universities (p. 142).

MANAGEMENT OF INCOME AND ENDOWMENT

Institutions of higher education should aim to maximize their income as part of plan for achieving effective use of resources.

RECRUITMENT

As the rate of increase in enrollment begins to level off, colleges and universities will need to devote more attention to recruitment in order to maintain adequate enrollments. This will be particularly true of less selective colleges located in areas characterized by net out-migration.

The Commission recommends that all colleges and universities give careful attention to recruitment policies designed not only to maintain adequate enrollments, but also to achieve such objectives as equality of opportunity, broad geographical distribution wherever feasible, and diversity in the student body. As we approach a period of stationary enrollment, many public institutions of higher education will need to place greater emphasis than they have in the past on recruitment programs aimed at maintaining adequate enrollments (p. 146).

CASH BALANCES AND INVENTORIES

To maximize interest yielded by an institution's liquid assets, the Commission recommends that

. . . colleges and universities minimize cash balances held in checking accounts and make certain, especially in large institutions, that purchasing functions and inventory management are handled by persons with adequate special training (p. 147).

ENDOWMENT FUNDS

Traditionally, colleges and universities tend to be conservative in the investment and use of endowment funds. Stocks are regarded as risky, and many institutions invest mainly in bonds. Typically, they avoid spending any of the principal of endowment funds. Experts on the management of endowment funds now regard such policies as excessively cautious.

The Commission recommends that colleges and universities should (1) aim to maximize long-term total return in the investment of endowment funds, (2) delegate responsibility for portfolio management to an able professional, and (3) generally follow modern principles of endowment management (p. 148).

Endowment funds are a larger source of income for well-established, selective private universities and colleges than for less selective, poorly financed institutions and for most public institutions. The Commission believes that public colleges and universities must place more emphasis on raising endowment funds.

The Commission recommends that public institutions of higher education, as well as private institutions, pursue systematic and vigorous policies aimed at attracting additions to their endowment funds (p. 149).

CONCLUSION

The Commission proposes that institutions of higher education can save about $10 billion (1970–71 dollars) by 1980–81, as compared with the total sum that would be spent if the trends of the 1960s continued. Creating shorter time options for students at all degree levels and reducing the ranks of reluctant attenders will save them half this $10 billion. The other half will come from those reforms that reduce the cost per student per year from 3.3 percent to 2.4 percent above general rise in the cost of living.

About two-thirds of the total reductions will require hard policy choices within higher education. Plowing back 1 to 3 percent of existing funds per year will always require hard policy choices and actions. If wise actions are taken, higher education will gain greater academic strength and more vitality, particularly as it seeks internal self-renewal. But higher education must take the initiative to make better use of its resources and not rely alone on the pressures and policies of society.

Our final recommendation is:

That higher education should undertake internally the constructive actions necessary to get more effective use of resources and not wait for less constructive (and sometimes destructive) actions to be required because of external initiative (p. 152).

REFORM ON CAMPUS

13

CHANGING
STUDENTS,
CHANGING
ACADEMIC
PROGRAMS
(JUNE 1972)

Academic reform has been frequently discussed and occasionally undertaken for over two centuries in American higher education. It reached a peak about a century ago when the transformation from a classical curriculum to the elective system was being made. Another high plateau of interest is now manifesting itself on campus and in society. This time, however, the alternatives are more varied and the situation is more complex.

In this report the Commission makes an effort to constructively contribute to the contemporary discussion, focusing its attention on reforms that will increase the opportunities for each student to find the academic environment, academic program, and instructional situations that will best help him improve the quality of his or her life.

A century ago, higher education in the United States was "modernized" to reflect the new role of science, the rapid industrial advance of the nation, and the surging populism of the people. The Commission believes that that period is over and that a new emphasis is needed. That emphasis should be on fully developing individual human capabilities in order to enhance the quality of life in all its aspects. In this report, the Commission focuses on the kinds of reforms that will bring about this strengthened humanizing orientation in higher education.

REPORT CARD ON THE PERFORMANCE OF HIGHER EDUCATION

In 1969–70, the Carnegie Commission sponsored the largest survey of academic opinion ever made (70,000 undergraduates; 30,000 graduate students; 60,000 faculty members). This survey was concerned with, among other things, the current attitudes of the direct participants toward academic life. In general, the responses show general satisfaction with academic life today; but they also show areas of strong specific dissatisfactions.

Three areas of substantial agreement, two of partial agreement, and two of more substantial disagreement between students and faculty members were revealed by this Commission survey.

■ Faculty and students agree:

That teaching effectiveness, not research, should be the primary criterion for faculty promotion

That course work should be more relevant to contemporary life and problems

That more attention should be paid to the "emotional growth of students"

■ They partially agree:

That a compulsory community-service requirement should be created

That more emphasis should be placed on broad liberal education and less on specialized training

■ Faculty and students disagree:

On whether all grades should be abolished

On whether all courses should be elective

Based on these and other survey responses, the Commission concludes that:

1   No revolutionary transformation in academic life need now be undertaken as a result of widespread dissatisfaction by students and faculty.

2   Either widespread or selective support can now be given to such major reforms as greater emphasis on teaching, more concern for relevance in the curriculum, more attention to students' emotional growth, and more outlets for creative activities.

3   Other reforms might be undertaken in certain specific situations.

OBSERVATIONS ON THE ACADEMIC CONDITION

Based on the data from the Commission survey and other sources, and on the Commission members' experience and judgment, the Commission concludes that dissatisfaction with academic life is not a major source of dissent and disruption. Dissent and disruption has been concentrated in "high-quality" institutions not because students are more unhappy with their academic life there—in fact, the opposite is true—but because more of the students attracted to that kind of campus are likely to engage in protest and disruption. Basically, participation in demonstrations springs more from the nature of the student and his or her reaction to external events, and from an environment that facilitates protest endeavors, than from dissatisfaction with academic life. Since political activism and academic life are separate entities, academic reform should not be undertaken as a response to the recent history of disruption. Reforms should be made on their own merits.

The Commission also believes that some dissatisfaction is a prerequisite for improvement and usually accompanies both individual growth and institutional change.

FORCES FOR CHANGE

The coming academic changes, as the Commission views them, relate to much more than reducing the dissatisfactions—general and specific—of the current campus participants. Other forces at work in the direction of new developments include:

TABLE 3   Undergraduate and graduate student satisfaction

UNDERGRADUATES	
"What is your overall evaluation of your college?"	
"Very satisfied with my college"	19%
"Satisfied with my college"	47
"On the fence"	22
"Dissatisfied with my college"	9
"Very dissatisfied with my college"	3
Total	100%
GRADUATE STUDENTS	
"I am basically satisfied with the education I am getting."	
"Strongly agree"	23%
"Agree with reservations"	54
"Disagree with reservations"	17
"Strongly disagree"	6
Total	100%

■ A much more diverse student population, which demands more diverse academic courses and programs

■ A student population that is much better prepared when it enters college and much more likely to continue its education after graduation

■ The enormous increase in new knowledge and the accelerated pace at which old knowledge is becoming obsolete

■ A changing and more dynamic labor market situation for college-trained people in which new occupations are being born and the demand for old occupations is declining

■ The transformation of the world of knowledge caused by the dominance of science and the scientific viewpoint

■ The extension of the problems of society into the university

■ A cultural revolution that emphasizes the politicalization of life and more attention to the sensate

■ An increase in tension between the campus and major parts of the surrounding society

THE CHANGE OF ACADEMIC LIFE
Change in the academic world has always been unsettling, but though this fact must be taken into account and the long-term gains measured against the short-term costs, constructive change must be undertaken.

That change is best accomplished if it is based on broad discussion and consent: it is better that reforms come about through negotiation rather than by imposition.

Current changes should be viewed as a part of a continuing flow and not the end of a process. Ten years from now, the emphases in reform will undoubtedly be different from what they are today. Alternative approaches should be kept alive.

Can reform be accomplished? Some argue that it cannot, but the Commission does not agree. Higher education is not frozen in its ways and reform is urgently needed in a number of major directions. That is not to say that there is a deep crisis in higher education now—but it may occur in the future if needed reforms do not occur now. Internal interest in, and incentives for, reform are today at extremely high levels. The reforms may not be easy to accomplish, but the Commission believes they are possible. If enacted, they are capable of making fundamental improvements in the intellectual and social life on campus.

THE UNWRITTEN ACADEMIC CONSTITUTION—PRINCIPLES AND LIMITATIONS

For two important reasons, it is essential today to reach a clear definition of basic academic principles. First of all, some current efforts to change higher education would draw it away from its primary academic purposes as the Commission views them. Secondly, if, as the Commission recommends, a greater diversity of programs becomes the order of the day, it will become more essential to be clear about limits.

Academic life, as it has developed over many years in many countries, has come to place supreme emphasis on cultivation of the intellect, on rationality, on attempted objectivity based on facts and logical argument. The campus has become preeminently a place of learning through use of the mind. The principal test of academic achievement is the quality of intellectual performance—not politics, not creed, not power. This emphasis must remain if some of the special purposes of the university, particularly the search for new knowledge and the independent criticism of society by its members, are to be preserved. No other institution in a progressive and democratic society provides so well for the performance of these special tasks. They, in particular, are protected by the academic constitution.

The intellectual approach includes not only logic in search for truth, but also aesthetics in the appreciation of beauty in art and nature, and ethics in the pursuit of a definition of the virtues that define what is good. It excludes, however, concentration on the solely emotional that appeals only to the immediate and direct stimulation of the senses, and on the solely ideological that seeks to exclude fair consideration of alternatives.

The campus is a multipurpose institution, but it is not an all-purpose institution. Many other institutions and arrangements exist in a pluralistic society to serve nonacademic purposes.

Much of the current agony of the campus comes not only from the need to make more clear where it should be going but also to make more certain that it will not abandon its central convictions. Consequently, to guide academic reform, the Commission suggests these missions and boundaries.

■ Emphasis on the intellect and avoidance of the anti-intellectual and the nonintellectual

■ Emphasis on the society's wealth of alternative views and its component parts and avoidance of compulsory single-minded religious or political indoctrination on campus

■ Emphasis on academic competence and avoidance of political tests in determining preferment among faculty members and students

■ Emphasis on persuasion through facts and analysis and principles, and avoidance of coercion to prevent free expression of opinions or require acceptance of unwelcome opinions

■ Emphasis on the advancement in knowledge and skill under conditions of equality of opportunity, and avoidance of a doctrine of equality of results regardless of ability and effort

Within these broad missions and boundaries, the Commission urges that greater attention be paid to the wishes of the students. They are not always right but they are reasonably well-informed consumers, and it is both unwise and inherently wrong to be unconcerned about their reactions and wishes.

RECOMMENDATIONS—MANY AVENUES TO EXPLORE

DIVERSITY

Higher education in America has been marked by a diversity that has been one of the system's greatest strengths and a major source of much of its dynamism. Recently, this diversity, which increased steadily over the long sweep of history, began to be reversed by a trend toward homogenization. The major direction of this homogenization has been toward science, research, and graduate study, and, for the individual faculty member, toward identification with a single discipline.

The Commission believes that this process of homogenization should be halted and that there should be a renewed emphasis on diversity. The need for more diversity, rather than less, flows from the more varied interests of college students, from new occupations constantly being created and the new training necessary for them, from the new, or at least newly visible, problems of society, from the new emphasis on quality of life and on independent choice of lifestyles.

Differentiation is especially important, the Commission believes, for the private liberal arts colleges and the comprehensive colleges. Both are searching for new educational approaches. Diversity and innovation will also come from new kinds of institutions and from differentiation that occurs within the larger institutions. Selectivity of effort, the composition of the student body, the kinds of policies an institution makes, and the way money is given to an institution all influence diversification. No one campus need to be exactly like any other. Many new developments are now taking place; many more are possible.

The Commission recommends that

Diversity among institutions and within them should be a major goal of higher education, and one test of institutions and of their major segments should be how successful they have been in defining their special characters and how successful they are in achieving them.

Cluster and theme colleges within large institutions provide particularly good opportunities for diversity.

State plans and multicampus plans should provide for specialization by field and for differentiation of general functions among campuses and groups of campuses.

Admissions policies should be examined to assure that they serve both the cause of diversity within higher education and also the possibilities for diversity at the high school level (p. 40).

THE "BROAD LEARNING EXPERIENCE"

One of the hallmarks of higher education, historically, in the United States has been its emphasis on what has been called a "liberal" or "general" education, on preparing the student for citizenship and for the noncareer aspects of life. But general education is now in trouble. What was once our greatest success is now becoming our greatest failure. A tendency is now developing that urges that general education be abandoned altogether and that students be allowed to take anything they want—provided they take one or two years in doing so. The Commission regrets this new tendency to relinquish concern for general education.

While preferring to drop the nomenclature of general education and liberal education, the Commission believes that a concept of a broad learning experience should be maintained. "General education" emphasized preselected content. The Commission believes that, instead of that concept, emphasis should be placed on a "broad learning experience" that would help students confront large bodies of knowledge and large issues. The essence of this approach would be to create several options from among which students may choose. Each option would follow some internal logic that would give it coherence.

At a time when students desire and times require a better understanding of society and the place of the individual within it, it seems particularly unwise to abandon the purposes of broad learning.

The Commission recommends that consideration should be given to establishing campus by campus a series of coherent options for a broad learning experience among which students may choose (p. 45)

THE "RELEVANT" CURRICULUM

A good working definition of relevance might be: courses that relate directly to actual personal interests of students and to current societal problems. Relevance includes special programs as, for example, those that relate to ethnic groups, to the new emphasis on creative arts, to the establishment of more problem-oriented courses, to new concerns for the environment, and to the student's understanding of himself and his place in society.

The Commission recommends that students should be added more generally as voting members to curriculum committees in the departments and the group majors and the professional schools where they are majors, and on committees concerned with broad learning experiences, or be given some other forum for the expression of their opinions.

Greater attention in the curriculum should be given to (1) the creative arts and (2) world cultures.

The curriculum as a whole should be reviewed, campus by campus, in consultation with high school leaders, to assess its broad relevance not only to appropriate student interests but also to prior and subsequent learning experiences (p. 47).

TEACHING

During the quarter century after World War II, the dominant new emphasis of the academic world came to be concentrated around organized basic research. Now, however, the pendulum is swinging back toward teaching. This reemphasis depends, in part, upon the evaluation placed on the importance of teaching, although admittedly teaching is notoriously difficult to evaluate. Beyond the standard methods, the Commission makes six suggestions:

1   Students should be incorporated into the evaluation process

2   Teaching loads in universities should be differentiated

3   Policies should be adopted that allow superior teachers to rise more nearly to as high salary levels as superior research persons

4   Doctor of arts and master of philosophy degrees be established

5   A greater emphasis be placed on awards to honor outstanding teachers

6   "Teaching funds" be created to parallel research funds

The Commission also suggests that the ratio of spending on lower-division and upper-division courses be almost one to one. On the basis of these suggestions the Commission makes the following recommendations:

Teaching performance should be the basic criterion for rewards to faculty members, except in research universities where research, of necessity, is of equal or greater importance.

Students should be associated with the evaluation of teaching performance.

More faculty attention and more funds, on a comparative basis, should be devoted to lower-division students (p. 50).

THE LIBRARY AS A LEARNING CENTER

Libraries are usually looked upon as rather passive centers on the campus. But libraries can play a more active role if, for example, the library staff is viewed as part of the instructional staff and libraries are developed as centers for the new instructional technology.

The Commission recommends that the library should become a more active participant in the instructional process with an added proportion of funds, perhaps as much as a doubling (p. 50).

RELUCTANT ATTENDERS

About 30 percent of all enrolled undergraduates appear to be less than fully committed to college attendance. Because these students are apt to be among those who are particularly likely to be dissatisfied, their presence can cause a deterioration in campus atmosphere. Since reluctant attenders remain in college for a variety of reasons, the solutions to the problems caused by their presence are not easy.

The Commission recommends that reasonable efforts should be made to reduce the ranks of the reluctant attender (p. 53).

ADVISING

The educational process involves essentially three aspects: advising, instructing, and testing. Historically, and quite properly, more attention has been paid to the second than to the first or third. Testing, however, now needs to be improved and more widely used in academic, vocational, and personal counseling, and in granting credit for achievement outside instruction in the classroom. Moreover, mass higher education has brought into the colleges new types of students, many of whom lack any prior family background in college attendance. These new students bring with them new problems. For these or other reasons, students, as noted earlier, are asking for more attention to their emotional growth, more personal contact with faculty members, and more advice and guidance from faculty and staff.

Advising falls into several major categories: academic, financial, vocational, and personal. In the Commission's opinion, advising is not now a well-performed aspect of higher education in any of these categories. To improve it, the Commission suggests:

- Raising advising to a higher order of importance

- Making advising a more recognized assignment for faculty members

- Relying on well-trained and carefully selected professional personnel for financial, vocational, and psychological advising

- Designating a dean or an associate dean to be concerned with the quality of advising services on campus

Recognizing that a student's intellectual development bears an intricate relationship to his affective, interpersonal, and ethical development, and thus, that the latter is potentially a proper concern for an academic institution, the Commission recommends that

Enhanced emphasis should be placed on advising as a increasingly important aspect of higher education (p. 57).

REASSESSMENT OF GRADUATE EDUCATION

Although according to the Carnegie Commission survey most graduate students in liberal arts colleges are particularly well disposed toward the education they are getting, 23 percent of these students are nonetheless dissatisfied with that education. Some of this dissatisfaction is endemic, but some is subject to amelioration. The status of women graduate students and teaching assistants and the intensely competitive and often ambiguous character of graduate work all need to be thoroughly reviewed. The Commission, therefore, makes the following recommendations:

Existing graduate education warrants a thorough review.

Any further general expansion of graduate education should proceed only after the most careful consideration (p. 59).

COMMUNITY SERVICE

Two substantial problems must be dealt with in this area of higher education: how to finance community service programs and how to set standards for awarding credit to students enrolled in these programs. The Commission believes that these problems can be solved and recommends that:

More opportunities should be created for students to gain community service and work experience (p. 59).

FACILITATING THE PROCESS OF CHANGE

The process of change is as important or even more important than the specific content of change. New endeavors—creating new campuses and new segments of campuses—provide an unusual opportunity for innovative action. Moreover, the Commission believes that faculty members now have a favorable attitude toward innovation and change. The basic question is how to make this attitude more effective in practice. The Commission makes the following suggestions:

1   More latitude for innovation should be given to departments and schools and cluster and theme colleges, subject only to minimum standards in advance and careful review subsequently.

2   Leadership for innovation should be strengthened by appointing deans of undergraduate instruction and councils or boards of undergraduate studies to parallel the dean of the graduate division and the graduate council. The principal leadership for innovation at the macro level, however, should come from the presidents of institutions.

3   Special funds at both the state and federal government levels should be earmarked to assist innovation.

4   Coordinating councils, state legislative committees, and trustees should, through inquiry, continue to encourage such major innovations as the three-year B.A. degree, the creation of the doctor of arts degree, and the inauguration of "open universities."

5   Students should be assured a reasonable range of educational options from among which to choose and should be given opportunities to make proposals and participate appropriately in the decision-making process.

6   A "Code of Teaching Responsibility" for faculty members and a statement of the "Rights of Students to Receive Instruction" should be established for each campus.

7   Relatively unstructured academic areas should be created on each campus to accommodate students who do not fit well into the more structured programs.

Based on these suggestions the Commission makes the following recommendations:

The process of change in each institution should be examined to assure (1) that innovations can be initiated without unnecessary impediments, (2) that all innovations of significance are subject to subsequent evaluation and review; and (3) that all experimental programs include a specific time plan for their termination or for their incorporation into the mainstream of the academic program.

One to three percent of all funds should be taken each year from existing programs and set aside as a self-renewal fund for new or expanded programs.

Higher education should take responsibility and undertake needed reforms internally rather than wait for them to be imposed externally (pp. 64–65).

CONCLUDING REMARKS

While the learning process is still something of a mystery, it clearly is a process that centers on people—on the special interactions between individual students, individual teachers, and individual subject matters at particular moments of time.

The Commission believes that the period just ahead may be, and certainly can be, one of the two most experimental, innovative, and progressive periods in the history of American higher education. The main direction of development in this period will be an effort to create a more diverse series of optimal learning environments to meet more precisely the needs of each person. If this development is successful, each person will have an equality of opportunity, through one form of education or another, to maximize the quality of his or her life. This is the Commission's basic vision of where higher education should be moving, a vision that sees higher education becoming a more humane system as part of the further humanizing of American society.

THE CAMPUS AND THE CITY

14

The university was born in the city—Salerno, Bologna, Paris, Prague. But American practice generally has been to establish campuses in small towns and rural areas—this practice reflected the models of Oxford and Cambridge, the Puritan aversion to the "evils" of the city, the "booster" inclinations of small towns, and the choice of agriculturally oriented state legislatures in placing state colleges and universities outside big cities.

The campuses accepted the practice because they were oriented toward their middle-class students and toward national and world—not local—problems. And the university has been able to prosper in Göttingen as well as in Berlin, in Cambridge as well as in London, and thus also in Iowa City as well as in Chicago.

This dominant American practice has resulted (1) in a deficit in student places in some metropolitan centers and (2) in a lack of widespread campus experience in dealing with city problems until very recent years. But American society is now irretrievably an urban civilization, and some of its most pressing problems involve the quality of life in the city.

HIGHER EDUCATION AND THE CITY

The troubles that beset American higher education today are sharpened by the crisis of American cities. Pressures created by urban problems reinforce the demands from within our colleges and universities for reassessment of higher education's priorities and functions. The challenge is to forge a new relationship between the campus and the city that will both aid the city and revitalize urban higher education. Moreover, it is not a single relationship between two clearly identified entities but rather a whole series of relationships with the identity of the participants shifting somewhat from one relationship to another, and from time to time.

Certain of these relationships carry obligations which higher education has not yet adequately met and opportunities it has not yet fully realized.

URBAN COLLEGES AND UNIVERSITIES

There are many types of institutions of higher education which could be considered, in varying degrees, "urban colleges or universities" under different definitions of that term. An institution that is fully oriented toward urban concerns would have developed its educational, research, and service programs to be responsive to urban needs, would have organized its decision-making mechanisms to work well with those of the metropolitan area, and would conduct itself in its corporate role in a way that makes its presence in the city an asset rather than a potential liability.

It is doubtful that any institution has such a total urban orientation. But an institution that takes its responsibility to urban society in general and to its own urban locale in particular as a dominant force in determining institutional objectives and allocating institutional funds, can be considered an urban university or college even though its particular combination of urban activities includes only a portion of those activities generally identified as urban activities. No one institution can respond to the total range of needs of a major metropolitan area. But each institution must define and examine its own urban activities in the context of the combined activities of colleges and universities in the metropolitan area, the special needs of the area, and its own general institutional mission.

ROLE AS EDUCATOR

The most traditional and central of higher education's many functions is education of an enrolled student body. In developing their educational programs, urban-oriented colleges and universities should consider the special educational needs of an urban population including:

■ The availability of student spaces for residents of metropolitan areas

■ The creation of programs designed to provide skilled and professional manpower needed for urban management and development

■ The development of curricula and institutional support activities responsive to the needs of urban students

■ Effective use of the rich educational resources (museums, theaters, parks, etc.) of the city in their own educational activities

■ The cooperative use of city agencies and industry to provide effective education and service

ACCESS TO HIGHER EDUCATION

There is no good substitute for intensive study of each metropolitan area, but it is possible from examination of gross comparative data of higher education resources in metropolitan areas to make preliminary and tentative findings of deficiencies, thus identifying those areas that have the greatest need for further careful and detailed analysis.

TOTAL HIGHER EDUCATION PLACES

Access to higher education by residents of different metropolitan areas will be affected by the availability of student spaces. We believe, in the absence of unusual circumstances, that any metropolitan area that has fewer than 2.5 student spaces per 100 population is unlikely to be able to meet the educational needs of its residents. Those areas that have a ratio of student places to population between 2.5 and 3.5 might be considered as having a marginal deficiency in total available resources.

We recommend that appropriate state and local agencies take steps to improve availability of student places in colleges and universities in those areas which now have less than 2.5 places available per 100 population, and to evaluate the adequacy of the number of higher education student places in those areas which have between 2.5 and 3.5 places available per 100 population (pp. 28–29).

Several metropolitan regions have a high proportion of out-of-state enrollment, and variations in these proportions must be considered along with total student places in estimating potential deficiencies in total higher education resources in the various areas. With modifications on the basis of 1968 student migration data, the ratio of student spaces to 100 population would decline significantly for a number of metropolitan areas.

We recommend that careful studies be made in these areas to determine whether present patterns of nonresident enrollment correspond closely with those of 1968 and, if so, to take whatever steps are necessary to expand facilities for higher education (p. 34).

BALANCE WITHIN METROPOLITAN AREAS
Growth in population in metropolitan areas is occurring primarily in suburban regions rather than in the central cities. But the resources for higher education are largely concentrated in the central cities. In addition, most of the unfilled freshmen places are in private colleges and universities. Thus, while it would seem that there would be an inadequacy of student spaces in some metropolitan areas, there might at the same time be a surplus of student spaces of a type for which students do not have effective demand. Both economic and ability barriers could prevent students from utilizing available student spaces.

Lack of adequate financial resources and the necessity of living at home or working while in school force many high school graduates either to seek their higher education experience in their cities of residence or to forgo it. For at least a considerable portion of the high school graduates within the central city, this requires that there be available, as a part of the higher education resources of the city, open-admissions institutions. We believe that at least one-third of the spaces in the central city's colleges should be available on an open-admissions basis.

In our report *New Students and New Places,* based on enrollment estimates to 1980, we called for establishment of some 175 to 235 additional two-year community colleges with from 80 to 125 of these colleges to be established in metropolitan areas with populations in excess of 500,000. We have recently revised certain of the estimates based on more recent data. Based on the analysis for the present report, we also believe that 15 to 20 more two-year colleges should be established in those metropolitan areas of 100,000 to 500,000 population identified as currently deficient in both total and open-access student places.

In metropolitan areas with a currently satisfactory ratio of student places to population but a deficiency of open-admission places, any need for new facilities resulting from expected growth in total enrollment should probably be met first with the development of open-admissions institutions. A more desirable first step in these areas, however, would be to reevaluate admissions policies at existing institutions in the area and to consider granting public subsidies to private institutions which could expand availability of open-admissions places.

We add here the recommendation that private colleges reexamine their admission policies to determine whether expansion of open-admission or flexible-admission student places in their institutions would be compatible with their particular educational missions (p. 43).

In our report *New Students and New Places,* we estimated that 80 to 105 comprehensive colleges would be needed by 1980, with 60 to 70 in urban areas with population in excess of 500,000.

On the basis of our analysis for this present report, we estimate that another 9 of the 80 to 105 comprehensive colleges should be located in metropolitan areas with populations between 100,000 and 500,000 even after fuller utilization of the resources of private institutions.

ACCESS IS NOT ENOUGH

Making adequate numbers of student spaces available and removing barriers to enrollment are necessary first steps to providing for the educational needs of residents of the metropolitan areas. They are not, however, sufficient by themselves.

While the subtle changes in ambience, image, and interrelationships that must accompany an institution's determination to serve the educational needs of significant portions of the urban clientele are not fully known, it is clear that colleges that seek to serve large numbers of lower-income minority students and part-time working students must:

■ Provide highly individualized educational programs at least for a "foundation" year

■ Make available a greater range of student services including adequate financial-aid counseling, educational and vocational counseling, health services, and, at least, initial or emergency personal counseling and health services

■ Devote a greater portion of their resources to the entry-level students

■ Modify their institutional reward structure to provide adequate rewards for commitment and excellence in teaching

The Commission recommends that colleges enrolling large numbers of disadvantaged or minority students review their institutional programs in each of the above four areas to determine if they are designed to meet the educational needs of the students involved (pp. 47–48).

While four-year colleges have enrolled low-income and minority students, the major burden has fallen on community colleges. Unfortunately, community colleges have often been given inadequate resources to provide appropriate student services and adequate developmental programs for these students.

The Commission recommends that state financing authorities and local agencies review their policies for funding community colleges to determine whether adequate funds are being made available for this segment of higher education with its difficult and important tasks (p. 48).

NEW DIRECTIONS FOR PLACE AND TIME

Colleges and universities are increasingly recognizing that not all instruction must take place on the campus. They can serve more students and at greater convenience to the students by dispersing certain types of educational programs throughout the metropolitan area. Classes can be held in industrial plants, in schoolrooms, in residential areas, or in libraries.

Patterns of work and residence in urban areas, transportation concerns, and the need for better utilization of physical facilities all underline the growing desirability of dispersing some of the university's educational programs throughout the urban area. New technological developments will aid greatly in accomplishing this dispersal.

The Commission recommends that urban campuses, in appropriate instances, offer certain portions of their programs in off-campus facilities—at industrial plants, in business and government offices, and at public libraries and schoolrooms in residential areas (p. 50).

LEARNING PAVILIONS

While geographic dispersion will make education more readily accessible to many, there are also substantial benefits to bringing learners to the campus, to make the campuses visible and attractive educational resources for residents of the community.

For this purpose we recommend consideration of the establishment of *learning pavilions* at community colleges and comprehensive colleges located in central cities (p. 50).

Learning pavilions would provide a home base for adult learners, technological aids for independent study, basic-education programs, and general-education discussion groups. Many colleges are already providing these educational services through extension or continuing-education programs. But we believe that coordination and expansion of such programs under the aegis of a new vehicle, such as the proposed learning pavilions, will increase their visibility and communicate a new sense of educational mission.

COMMUNITY COLLEGES AND COMMUTER COLLEGES

Community colleges hold great promise for urban areas. In fact, in terms of education and service, they might well be considered the urban parallel to the land-grant institutions. While a community college in a rural area may serve primarily as a feeder institution offering the first two years of a baccalaureate program, we believe that the urban setting and an urban student body will encourage and permit urban community colleges to develop truly distinctive educational missions and to use educational process particularly suited to those missions.

We recommend that urban community colleges, in order to serve more fully their urban clientele, give careful consideration to the following:

1   Establishment of multiple campuses in a metropolitan area rather than concentration of all students on one campus, and the development of some specialization of educational missions among the various campuses

2   Systematic experimentation and evaluation of remedial and developmental programs

3   Possible early admission of urban high school students requiring remedial work or seeking immediate entry into vocational training programs (p. 53).

The community colleges and some four-year colleges in urban areas are commuter colleges. But many of these colleges are not designed physically or educationally with the particular needs of the commuter in mind.

The Commission recommends that commuter institutions make available lockers, study and lounge areas, and other physical facilities designed to meet the special needs of commuters, and that scheduling of educational programs and activities be undertaken with the commuter in mind (p. 54).

NEW TYPES OF URBAN INSTITUTIONS

Urban educational needs will be met in part by the creation of some additional community colleges and comprehensive four-year colleges, and by the expansion and modification of existing urban institutions. But the need to provide flexibility in postsecondary educational experiences will undoubtedly require establishment of alternative avenues by which students can pursue postsecondary education. Some of these avenues, such as certain types of external degree programs could as easily be established in nonurban as in urban areas. Other new institutional types are, however, particularly well adapted to utilize the resources of the city and to meet the needs of city students:

▪ The Minnesota Metropolitan State College has a program especially designed for adults in an urban area. Using the city as the campus, each student establishes his own educational goals and is awarded a degree on the basis of demonstrated competencies rather than on accumulation of credits.

▪ The University Without Walls is a consortium of institutions which seeks to build highly individualized and flexible programs of learning, making use of new and largely untapped resources for teaching and learning, and redefining the role of the instructor as facilitator and coparticipant in the planning and design of the student's learning experience.

■ The College for Human Services in New York has developed a new kind of professional curriculum in the human services, emphasizing the closest possible relationship between classroom and field work, and creating an interdisciplinary college-level curriculum based on concepts in the social sciences and humanities.

We recommend that both planning agencies and urban-located institutions review and analyze the educational resources in their areas and the educational needs of urban students to determine whether use of such experimental approaches as those described above, or others that may be developed are desirable to expand effective options for postsecondary educational opportunities in the metropolitan areas (p. 60).

URBAN STUDIES
One of the major educational responses of a university or college to the problems of the metropolitan area is the inclusion within its curriculum of courses designed to teach students about such problems and to train the technicians, professionals, and leaders who will work toward the solution of these problems.

It is not always necessary to add new colleges or even degree programs to make the curriculum of an institution more responsive to the problems of the city. Many students feel that faculty members should make greater efforts to develop an urban emphasis in educational programs result in a few specialized programs rather than a pervasive point of departure in many programs. The latter is certainly more difficult to obtain and requires the active participation of a much larger proportion of any given faculty.

RESEARCH ON URBAN PROBLEMS
Universities have traditionally considered research activities as their major contribution toward the development of solutions to urban problems. This contribution ordinarily is manifested in one of two forms:

■ University research centers place a multidisciplinary emphasis on applied or service research. In most instances, attempts have been made to achieve interaction between the research activities and policy makers in urban areas.

■ The network of urban observatories carries out two types of research activities—network or national research projects and local projects. National programs are undertaken by all observatories on a coordinated basis, while local projects are of particular interest to the individual city.

Research on urban matters is complicated by the fact that no satisfactory methodology for basic social science research, parallel to that for physical or biological science research, has yet been devised. As a result, much of the social science research falls in the uncomfortable category of neither qualifying as basic research nor being sufficiently practical to qualify as good applied research. Good applied research is undoubtedly facilitated by an organization such as the urban observatories in which the research client is a prime mover in defining the research needed.

PUBLIC SERVICE

The American university is usually described as having three major and complementary functions—teaching, research, and public service. These three are often spoken of as equally important with each essential to the strength of the other two. Yet the distinctions among institutional types and determinations of levels of quality are almost always made today on the basis of teaching and research without reference to the scope and quality of the institution's public service programs. We believe, however, that higher education must respond to the problems of the city not only through its formal educational programs and research activities, but also through renewed emphasis on public service. This will entail action by individuals within the institution as well as by the institution itself.

STUDENT SERVICES TO THE COMMUNITY

The ideal student service activity would seem to be a service which was also treated as a learning experience by the university or college. While the student is supplying needed services such as tutoring and professional assistance in the community, the community serves as a learning resource. The Urban Corps is one example of such programs.

We believe that the Urban Corps provides an excellent mechanism for giving opportunities to students to have experience in city government and recommend that cities that do not now have such programs seriously consider developing them (p. 72).

SERVICE BY FACULTY MEMBERS

Suggestions to provide services to the city by stimulating activities of individual faculty members through increased rewards to faculty have never adequately addressed some of the inherent problems. If community service is to be rewarded by the promotion criteria of the university, must it be free to the community? Should a minimum of community service time be required before the faculty member has a right to charge for consulting services? Questions such as these will be sharpened as the faculty work-load question is subjected to increased public scrutiny.

INSTITUTIONAL SERVICES

Urban institutions have responded in a variety of ways to community demands for increased services. Differentiation of educational missions among institutional types would suggest that certain categories of urban service would be more appropriate for some types of institutions than for others. But no such pattern emerges from a review of which institutions have undertaken which services. The decision to provide a particular service seems to be much less a deliberate decision that the service is consistent with both the goals and resources in the institution than it is a result of the interests of some within the institution or a reaction to specific pressures and demands on the institution.

We recommend that institutions of higher education undertake those community service activities which:

■ Revitalize educational functions and constitute an integral part of educational programs

■ Are within the institutional capacity both in terms of personnel and resources

■ Are not duplicative of the services of other urban institutions

We further recommend that quasi-university agencies be established through which faculty members and/or students could provide services, even on controversial matters, without directly involving the university or college in its corporate capacity (p. 77).

IMPACTS ON THE LIFE OF THE CITY
The university located in an urban setting is not only an educational institution that happens to be in a city—it is a physical entity and a corporate force that has diverse and major impacts on the life and environment of the city. It is in the context of the growing urban crisis, however, that these impacts have taken on new significance requiring more conscious efforts on the part of the institution to maximize positive aspects and control potentially negative effects.

ENVIRONMENTAL IMPACTS
It is clear that some cities have a hostile reaction toward institutions within their boundaries. There are many reasons:

■ Uncertain expansion plans of a university can adversely affect maintenance standards of neighboring areas as well as real estate values in such areas.

■ Requirement for parking facilities and the increased traffic burdens in the vicinities of the campus may place an excessive burden on the city.

■ Particularly recently, the tendency of "street people and hippies" to congregate around college and university campuses has accentuated further some of the problems created by the physical presence of the campus.

■ Student housing patterns, from the viewpoint of some inhabitants of the neighborhood, may have undesirable effects on otherwise attractive residential areas.

■ Many institutions have become involved in urban renewal projects, and some have themselves become, in a sense, developers, using endowment funds for rehabilitation or construction not only for university housing but also for low- and moderate-income housing for their immediate environs.

The Commission believes that colleges and universities do have responsibility for their impacts on their surrounding environs.

We therefore recommend:

1   That universities and colleges develop long-range plans which give adequate attention to the interaction between the campus and the neighborhood in which it is located

2   That, where appropriate, colleges and universities participate actively in urban-renewal activities, but that only in unusual circumstances should this participation extend to investment of scarce institutional resources in housing development for the general community

3   That institutions limit their need for expansion into scarce urban space by better use of existing space (p. 84)

ECONOMIC IMPACTS

There are many ways in which colleges and universities, particularly large universities, affect the economics of the city. Among the most important are the following considerations:

■ As employer and purchaser, universities and colleges have not always been aware of their influence upon either the employment patterns of the city or upon the vitality of various city businesses. Personnel policies for nonacademic employees in many major universities have often been far behind the policies of industrial corporations.

■ The tax-exempt status of college and university property has often been a source of friction between the city and campus. This is particularly true today when city revenue is quite inadequate to meet the growing demands for city funds. Increasingly, colleges and universities, even though tax exempt, are making some payments for services received from the city.

We recommend that:

1   Colleges and universities seek to assist the surrounding areas through the operation of their employment and purchasing policies

2   Regardless of rights given them by charter, colleges and universities pay the usual taxes on any property held by them for noneducational purposes, and when expanding their campuses, should make every effort to develop the property in such a way as to permit its continuation on the tax rolls (p. 88)

CULTURAL IMPACTS

Cultural enrichment made possible directly or indirectly by the presence of a college or university is rarely singled out as a major service by higher

education to the community. Yet it may afford one of the most successful interactions between a campus and its neighbors.

We recommend that the National Foundation on the Arts and Humanities provide
grants for university-based cultural activities available to both the campus and its
neighbors and for cooperative endeavors involving higher education and city
museums and performing arts centers (p. 89).

POLITICAL IMPACTS
Higher education's political impact on cities, particularly small- or medi-
um-sized cities with large universities or colleges, is now gaining new
importance. Increasing political awareness of students combined with the
newly gained right of 18-year-olds to vote has resulted in new discussions
of the political role of students. Just as higher education discovered in its
efforts to respond to the community that the community was not a single
entity, so too are cities becoming aware that student bodies are not
homogeneous groups with single sets of interests and responses.

INSTITUTIONAL ORGANIZATION
The ability of most urban-located universities and colleges to respond to
urban needs is severely handicapped by failure to reflect this important
function in their organizational structure. On most campuses neither
those within the university nor those within the community had a visible
office or unit to which they could turn for information on urban activities.
In addition, few institutions have developed overall policies to guide
the development of institutional urban-related activities. The Commission recommends:

■ that large universities located in urban areas appoint a vice-president or vice-
chancellor for urban affairs who would be concerned with the university-urban
interface in terms of the urban impact of the university's educational, service, research, and corporate functions (pp. 92–93)

■ that an *urban affairs advisory council* including faculty, administration, and student representatives be appointed to consult with the vice-president or vice-chancellor of urban affairs (p. 93)

■ that colleges and universities develop overall policies concerning appropriate
urban activities for their institutions to avoid response to new proposals on an ad-
hoc basis without reference to consistency with the educational mission of the
institution (p. 94)

TOWARD AN URBAN COMMITMENT
While some have argued that it is almost impossible for a university to be
great and also to have a clear urban commitment, there are examples of
universities that have gone far to accomplish both. Unfortunately, many
institutions are seriously handicapped in such endeavors by lack of adequate funding. In a period of financial stringency it is difficult to obtain
risk capital from traditional support channels for the purpose of making
sweeping changes in educational missions. We believe that the federal

government is, however, in a position to provide this risk capital to carefully selected universities that wish to undertake a reorganization of their institutional program in terms of a comprehensive urban commitment.

We recommend that an Urban-Grant program be established which would provide 10 grants to carefully selected institutions for the purpose of undertaking a comprehensive urban commitment for their institution. These grants should not exceed $10 million each for a ten-year period with reviews every two years (p. 101).

ORGANIZATION FOR POSTSECONDARY EDUCATION IN THE CITY

Metropolitan areas have wide arrays of postsecondary public and private educational institutions, including universities, four-year colleges, two-year colleges, and usually some public vocational schools and many private trade and technical schools. While the student is offered a rich selection of educational opportunities, he rarely has adequate information or guidance to use these wisely to meet his educational goals. The institutions themselves may not know enough about their neighboring institutions to consider ways of cooperating to make their own operations more effective.

In each metropolitan area with population in excess of one million, we recommend establishment of:

1   a *metropolitan higher education council*
2   a *metropolitan educational opportunity counseling center* (p. 113)

The *Metropolitan Higher Education Council* would:

■ Act as primary market-research agency for educational needs in the metropolitan area and as central focus for planning for higher education in that area

■ Create a vital, working system of interaction between industry and education in the city

■ Develop a cooperative working relationship between appropriate metropolitan colleges and universities and the public school system

■ Serve as the coordinating agency for student service projects in the community

The *Metropolitan Educational Opportunity Counseling Center* would:

■ Act as educational and vocational adviser to the citizens in the metropolitan area, regardless of their age or past educational preparation

■ Act as adviser to the higher education council on the need for new facilities and on any discernable shifts in student educational demands

Few cities have anyone on the city staff with special responsibility for liaison with higher education in the city. We believe that such an assignment of responsibility would be desirable.

We recommend that mayors of major cities assign someone on their staff primary responsibility for liaison with higher education in the city (p. 113).

FUNDING FOR HIGHER EDUCATION IN THE CITY

At the present time, the property tax base of the cities is not expanding rapidly enough to meet the growing demands on the cities' revenues. Colleges and universities have increasingly looked elsewhere for financial support.

In our report, *Quality and Equality,* issued in December 1968 with *Revised Recommendations* issued in June 1970, we recommended that the federal government provide start-up grants for planning and non-construction costs for urban institutions, not to exceed $1 million per institution. We reiterate that recommendation and urge that these funds be made available for the types of educational activities and programs described in this report. We also believe that the effective use of existing facilities within metropolitan areas will reduce the need for construction of new facilities.

We further recommend that:

1 Within the level of research funding which we recommended in *Quality and Equality,* high priority be given both basic and applied social science research

2 The network of urban observatories be continued and that each observatory be funded at approximately $100,000 per year

3 The new National Institute of Education make grants available to those institutions that are conducting systematic experiments with remedial education

4 From funds allocated to the Secretary of Health, Education and Welfare for innovation and reform in higher education, grants be made available for development and testing of new techniques for assessing individual competencies

5 States recognize the public-service demands made on public institutions and provide funds for such services (pp. 116–117)

We also recommended, in *Quality and Equality,* that $30 million be made available from federal funds for counseling programs. Assuming that experimentation in early programs is successful, we would urge that a very substantial part of this funding for counseling be channeled through the proposed *metropolitan educational opportunity counseling centers.*

The opportunity centers will require funding beyond that amount.

We recommend that the centers be funded one-half from local sources and one-half from state and federal sources.

We also recommend that funding for administrative expenses of the metropolitan councils be similarly shared, with one-half from local sources and one-half from state and federal sources (p. 117).

We recognize that local revenue sources have many competing demands, but we believe that these two agencies can do much to aid residents of the area and to use educational resources in the area more effectively. Effective coordination and counseling might well reduce the demands for extensive local investment in new resources.

CONCLUSION

Improving higher education in the nation's urban areas and improving the capabilities of our colleges and universities to serve urban needs are tasks of highest priority. And they are tasks which must be accomplished within a very short time frame. Their accomplishment will require the active cooperation of the many agencies concerned with higher education.

The land-grant college movement was one of the most revolutionary ideas in the history of higher education both in the United States and in the world. It provided the momentum for the development of colleges with a new sense of direction to the needs of a dominant force in American society—at that time, rural America. Today we need a similar commitment to direct the attention of our colleges and universities to the concerns of urban America.

COLLEGE GRADUATES AND JOBS

ADJUSTING TO A
NEW LABOR
MARKET
SITUATION
(APRIL 1973)

Historically, the labor market has not been a continuing source of concern for higher education. Except in times of depression, it has absorbed all the college and university graduates and has been taken for granted as a generally adequate outlet for highly trained talent. This has now changed and has probably changed for the foreseeable future.

This report seeks to set forth this new situation as realistically as possible. Its central themes are (1) that many adjustments will and should be made to alleviate the negative consequences inherent in some of the broad statistical prophecies about the future and (2) the good as well as the bad consequences that may flow from the new situation in the market for college graduates.

BASIC ISSUES

Foremost among the historically accepted advantages of a college education has been access of the college graduate to a relatively remunerative and high-status job. Thus, there is a danger, in a less favorable job market, that colleges may respond by restricting enrollment.

However, preparation for the labor market is only one of the functions of higher education. The Commission does not believe that colleges and universities should tighten their undergraduate entrance requirements because the job market for college graduates is likely to be less favorable in the future than it has been in the recent past. Nor should they restrict the flow of student aid for this reason. The Commission recommends that:

Institutions of higher education and governments at all levels should not restrict undergraduate opportunities to enroll in college or to receive student aid because of less-favorable trends in the job market for college graduates than have prevailed in the recent past (p. 21).

Nevertheless, shifts are clearly taking place in demand and supply relationships in many occupations in which college graduates are employed. Students are changing their career choices, and institutions of higher education are facing many adjustments as a result. Therefore, the Commission recommends:

Individual institutions of higher education and state planning agencies should place high priority in the 1970s and 1980s on adjusting their programs to changing student choices of fields that will occur in response both to pronounced occupational shifts in the labor market and to changing student interests and concerns. High priority should also be placed on continued flexibility in the use of resources in order to facilitate such adjustments (p. 21).

CHANGES IN THE JOB MARKET FOR COLLEGE GRADUATES, 1900–1970

College graduates are employed primarily as professional and managerial workers, and the enormous increase in demand for the services of college-educated workers since the beginning of the present century has been closely associated with the rise in the relative importance of these two major occupation groups in the labor force. Despite the enormous increase in enrollment in higher education and in the number of college graduates since World War II, the demand for college graduates was also rising rapidly. In some occupations such as engineering, demand was rising more rapidly than supply in certain short-run periods.

PATTERNS OF OCCUPATIONAL CHANGE

The capacity of our economy to employ steadily increasing numbers of college graduates, especially in professional and managerial occupations, can be understood by examining certain patterns of occupational change:

■ Among men, the most significant development in the first half of the present century was a rise in the number of occupation groups in which most workers tend to be college graduates.

■ Since 1950, there have been relatively high percentage increases in the employment of professional and technical occupation groups, due to a sharp increase in expenditures on research and development and a pronounced increase in elementary and secondary school enrollment.

■ The overriding factor in the history of employment patterns of female college graduates has been the predominance of elementary and secondary school teaching among their career destinations.

■ When classified by industry rather than occupation, college graduates tend to account for a considerably larger proportion of all workers in the rapidly growing services sector of the economy than in production sectors.

EMPLOYMENT PATTERNS OF PERSONS WITH ONE TO THREE YEARS OF COLLEGE

A large and rapidly growing segment of the labor force consists of persons who have had some college education but have not completed a four-year program. Some of them have dropped out of a four-year program, but an increasing number are graduates of two-year colleges. We believe that the labor market conditions of the 1970s are likely to encourage an acceleration of the rise in the relative importance of enrollment in occupational programs in two-year colleges that occurred in the 1960s. Although the data on employment patterns of college graduates are far from ideal, the dearth of good data on graduates of community colleges and on dropouts is far more serious. Accordingly, the Commission recommends:

Federal government agencies should develop more adequate data on occupational and industrial employment patterns of graduates of two-year colleges and of dropouts from institutions of higher education. In addition, community college districts should conduct follow-up studies that would provide information on employment patterns of their former students by occupation and industry (p. 47).

EDUCATIONAL UPGRADING

Throughout the last hundred years the average level of educational attainment of the American labor force has steadily risen. And, for many professional and managerial occupations, educational requirements imposed by employers, state licensing agencies, and professional certifying boards have tended to call for increasingly extended periods of higher education.

With the pronounced increase in the rate of college graduation in the 1960s, the percentages of workers who were college graduates rose. There has also been a tendency for the proportions of employed professional workers holding master's and doctor's degrees to rise. Yet most of the increase in employment of college graduates in the 1950s and 1960s was attributable to occupational growth rather than to educational upgrading.

RELATIVE INCOME OF COLLEGE GRADUATES

Ratios of median income of college graduates to median income of high school graduates and of all persons aged 25 and over rose between 1949 and 1959. In the next ten years these ratios continued to rise in relation to high school graduates but fell somewhat in relation to all persons. The 1950s and 1960s were a period of exceptional increases in demand as well as in supply in the job market for college graduates and holders of professional and advanced degrees. The improvement in the relative income position of highly educated workers during this period appears to be contrary to the secular trend and may be reversed under the less favorable job market conditions in prospect for the 1970s, at least for some of these professions.

THE OUTLOOK FOR THE1970s

Despite reports early in 1973 that the job prospects of college graduates were considerably more favorable than in the several preceding years, most predictions indicate that they are unlikely to return to anything resembling the situation that prevailed during a large part of the 1960s, when recruiters were besieging college placement officers and prospective graduates could pick and choose among attractive job offers. The U.S. Bureau of Labor Statistics estimates that 9.8 million college-educated persons will enter the labor force during the 1970s and that the demand for college-educated workers will amount to 9.6 million.

Looking ahead in the 1970s, we cannot be certain whether or not some new development—not anticipated at present—might provide a new stimulus to the demand for college graduates that would restore the generally favorable conditions of the 1960s. In the meantime, adjustments to the changing situation are clearly discernible:

■ The poor job market may be affecting enrollment patterns. In 1971, there were reports that unusual shifts were occurring in enrollment from traditional academic programs into vocational programs of all types. In both 1971 and 1972, prebaccalaureate degree-credit enrollment declined in four-year colleges and universities.

■ Students are changing their choices of fields in response to the changing job market.

TEACHERS

The occupations in which surpluses of college-educated jobseekers are likely to be most serious in the 1970s are elementary and secondary school teaching and college-level instruction. In each of these occupations the reason for the current and future surpluses are primarily demographic.

The children entering elementary school in the fall of 1971 were born in 1965 or 1966, when the number of live births was declining significantly. Instead of facing a situation in which elementary and secondary school enrollment was rapidly increasing, as had been the case in the 1950s and the early 1960s, the college graduate or holder of a master's degree in education seeking a teaching position in the public schools faced a situation in which the rate of increase in enrollment was falling off and would eventually be replaced by a period of absolute decline. By 1971, a surplus of persons seeking teaching jobs existed in all sections of the country.

However, we believe that there is a danger of overreaction to the changing job market for teachers. To avoid this situation the Commission recommends that:

State planning agencies should give very high priority in the next few years to careful adaptation of teacher education to the changing needs of a period of shrinking job opportunities for elementary and secondary school teachers. We believe that consolidation of teacher education into a more limited number of institutions that can offer high-quality training would be generally preferable to a cutting back of teacher education on an across-the-board basis. States should encourage the participation of private as well as public colleges and universities in such planning. We also recognize that many state colleges that have largely concentrated on teacher education will need to develop more comprehensive programs if they are to serve students effectively, and that in sparsely populated states this will require division of labor among such state colleges in adding new fields or in some cases a merger of two or more such state colleges into a single location (p. 79).

High priority should be given to adaptation of teacher-training programs to changing needs. There should be increased emphasis on specialized training to prepare teachers for service in ghetto schools, in programs for mentally retarded or physically handicapped children, in early child development programs and day-care centers, and in vocational education programs (pp. 79–80).

The U.S. Bureau of Labor Statistics and the U.S. Office of Education should develop revised estimates of the future demand for teachers that take account, as existing projections do not, of the growing demand for teachers in preelementary education and in such other settings as adult education programs. There is also a need for revised estimates of supply that take account of the declining enrollment in undergraduate education programs and of a possible future decline in enrollment in master's degree in education programs (p. 80).

We also believe that there is a strong case for lowering the age of permissible entrance into the public schools, so that four-year-olds will be encouraged to attend. The Commission recommends that:

States should give careful consideration to the adoption of policies encouraging a lower age of entrance into the public schools, specifically at the age of four (p. 80).

HEALTH PROFESSIONS

The most serious shortages of professional personnel are in the health field. The Medicare and Medicaid programs, adopted in 1965, tended to exacerbate these shortages by channeling substantially increased funds into the health care system without embodying appropriate and decisive policies for accompanying increases in the supply of health manpower and facilities.

However, the indications of recent increases in supply of personnel and of shifts in enrollment into nursing and allied health training programs suggest that we may be beginning to move out of a period of chronic general shortages in these fields, even though problems of geographic maldistribution are likely to continue.

With regard to the health professions, the Commission includes a number of recommendations:

Vigorous efforts should be made at the state level to develop training programs in nursing and allied health professions in state colleges and community colleges in those states that have lagged in the past (p. 96).

There should be increased emphasis on basic programs of education in the health sciences—in curricula leading to associate's, bachelor's, and master's degrees—to provide a uniform core of training for nurses, allied health workers, physicians, dentists, and persons preparing themselves for administrative, educational, and research careers in the health field (p. 96).

There should be increased emphasis in educational programs on providing experience in working with other health care personnel as a team (p. 96).

Federal government agencies involved in studies of health manpower should continuously review projections of supply and demand during the 1970s. Meanwhile, as long as shortages continue, federal funds to support the training of health personnel should not be cut back, as under the proposed federal budget for 1973–74 (p. 96).

University health science centers and area health education centers should provide leadership in encouraging the development and expansion of continuing education programs for nurses and allied health workers in appropriate educational institutions (p. 96).

There should be increased emphasis on encouraging research on alternative ways of utilizing health manpower. There is a need for studies evaluating innovations in health care delivery, and there is also a need for comparative studies on differing patterns of utilization of health manpower in selected countries, especially with a view to determining how a number of other industrial countries have achieved lower infant mortality rates and higher life expectancy rates than the United States, despite lower physician-population ratios (p. 97).

OTHER SELECTED PROFESSIONS

The various professional fields have many problems in common as they face the shifting and uncertain job market trends of the 1970s and as they consider various proposals for innovation and reform in their educational programs. In certain fields, particular trends emerge:

■ Law schools have been experiencing a sharp rise in applications for admission in the last few years due to a less-favorable market for Ph.D.'s and the increased interest of students in careers that would contribute to the solution of society's problems. But law schools have been cautious about increasing enrollments in response to rising applications. The market for lawyers is also changing: consumer legislation, the development of legal insurance groups, and the spread of no-fault automobile insurance will have an impact on demand; reforms in law schools such as specialization, paralegal studies, and clinical training will have an impact on supply.

■ Business schools have been among the relatively rapidly developing sectors of higher education, especially in the 1960s. Increased emphasis on organizational problems in business, a recent upsurge of college graduates' interest in starting small business enterprises, and the rising demand for salaried managers are likely to be major factors in continued growth in the employment of M.B.A.'s and holders of other appropriate degrees in the 1970s.

■ A leading characteristic of engineering is that the growth of employment of engineers has been very irregular, reflecting fluctuations in the demand for engineers in the economy. Enrollment in engineering is highly sensitive to shifts in the job market for engineers which fluctuates with federal expenditures on research and development. Recent declines in enrollments, along with the indications of improvement in the job prospects of engineering graduates in the spring of 1972, suggest that there may well be a reappearance of a shortage of engineers before many more years have passed.

■ Natural and social scientists experienced very pronounced percentage increases in employment in the 1960s but are expected to experience less rapid growth in the 1970s. Those with master's degrees were slightly more likely to be unemployed than those with bachelor's degrees, and considerably more likely to be unemployed than holders of doctor's degrees toward the end of the 1960s. If the proportion of college-age young people entering the natural sciences is actually relatively stable, then shortages in at least some of these fields are virtually certain to reappear because of the long-run upward trend in demand for services of these professionals associated with the advance of knowledge and technology. In view of this, there is clearly a need for increased emphasis on research and data gathering on college-educated manpower.

Associations of professional schools and professional societies should undertake the responsibility for careful studies of manpower supply and demand for graduates in their respective fields (p. 138).

Although we oppose the creation and assignment of student places in accordance with an overall manpower plan, we recognize that situations exist in which institutions and governmental agencies must plan for the allocation of places and resources on the basis of more than immediate student choices. For the institutional decisions to be made well, field-by-field manpower studies can be helpful.

The federal government should give high priority to the development of more adequate, sophisticated, and coordinated programs of data gathering and analysis relating to highly educated manpower. Because professional associations can be particularly helpful in these efforts, we also believe that federal government agencies should develop programs designed to elicit and support the efforts of these associations (p. 138).

Associations of professional schools should collect annual data on enrollment of women and minority-group students and should stimulate programs designed to encourage and assist them. Within arts and science fields there should be similar efforts (pp. 138-139).

Professional schools in universities and colleges should undertake the responsibility for cooperating with and providing guidance for comprehensive colleges and community colleges in the development of paraprofessional training programs, as we have earlier recommended in the case of university health science centers (p. 139).

Such guidance will be especially needed where paraprofessional training has not existed in the past, as in the field of law.

Professional schools in universities and colleges should also undertake the responsibility for providing guidance and advice in connection with programs of

continuing education for members of their professions, whether these are provided under the auspices of extension divisions, evening school programs of the
professional schools, or in other ways (p. 139).

There is now widespread recognition of the problem of educational
obsolescence in all fields as the pace of technological advance quickens
and as society's needs for specialized services increase, as in the fields
of medicine and law. We anticipate rapid expansion of programs of adult
and continuing education in response to these needs in the 1970s.

Associations of professional schools, as well as individual professional schools
in universities and comprehensive colleges, should undertake leadership and
responsibility in more carefully planned integration of preprofessional and professional education (p. 140).

Integration of premedical and medical education programs is eliminating overlapping and duplication between premedical and medical education and is shortening the time between high school graduation and
receipt of the M.D. degree. Similar developments are now being proposed in law and in other professional fields.

In virtually all professional fields, increased attention should be devoted to providing students with opportunities to proceed along carefully planned and at the
same time flexible career training ladders (p. 140).

In all professional fields, careful and sustained attention needs to be given to adaptation of educational programs to the advancement of knowledge and technological change, and to society's changing problems and needs (p. 140).

There is also a need to encourage faculty members to engage in periodic
retraining or retooling efforts in response to shifting needs for particular
specialties.

All programs of professional education involving human services should seek to
incorporate clinical or operational experience in the student's training, but we
would also warn that successful clinical training requires careful planning, evaluation, and adaptation to changing needs (pp. 140–141).

Such training may also require increased faculty-student ratios, as
some law schools are discovering.

Most professional schools and academic departments should be actively involved,
along with their institutions, in developing policies that encourage students to
stop out between high school and college, or after several years of undergraduate
education, or between undergraduate and graduate work, and that assist those
students to gain relevant work experience during periods away from school. Of
equal importance are policies that facilitate part-time study for the working student
(p. 141).

However, there are exceptions to this general principal. Stopping out
is probably least desirable for the medical student. Stopping out is especially desirable in the field of business administration.

In recent years, there has been a trend toward the development of joint degrees between professional schools and departments—for example, law and sociology or law and city planning. This trend has been associated with the emergence of societal problems that are essentially interdisciplinary in character, for example, urban and evironmental problems.

Professional schools and academic departments should cooperate in the development of joint degree programs in response to emerging societal problems and in response to the advancement of knowledge or technogical change (p. 141).

However, such programs are more likely to be successful if the student receives thorough training in the basic principles and analytical methods involved in at least one of the two disciplines, and preferably in both, than if his training in one or both of the fields is superficial.

The federal government should not only stabilize its support of graduate training and research, but should attempt to stabilize the scope of activities, like the space program, that have in the past involved sudden and sharp shifts in demand for scientists and engineers (p. 142).

THE CHANGING MARKET FOR Ph.D.'s AND ITS IMPLICATIONS
Whereas the market for Ph.D.'s was exceptionally favorable during the greater part of the 1950s and 1960s—until 1968 or 1969—it is likely to be increasingly unfavorable during the 1970s. There are at least three underlying causes for this growing imbalance:

1   Not only has the propensity of college graduates to go on for graduate work been rising, but the number completing the work for the doctorate has increased very rapidly.

2   The marked reduction in the rate of growth of research and development expenditures toward the late 1960s was an early adverse influence on the market for Ph.D.'s, and, although such expenditures are likely to increase in the 1970s, they will probably not increase more rapidly than the gross national product.

3   The major factor depressing the job market for Ph.D.'s in the 1970s and on into the 1980s will be the expected slowing down in the rate of increase and the subsequent leveling off of enrollment in higher education.

SUPPORT OF GRADUATE EDUCATION
Cutbacks on enrollments in leading graduate schools have been strongly influenced by a decline in federal government support of graduate fellowships and the discontinuation or phasing out of certain private foundation fellowship programs. There is a case for consistent and sustained federal government support of graduate education, geared to continuous studies of the supply of, and demand for, highly educated scientists and other

scholars. However, stop and go policies are extremely undesirable because of their disruptive nature. Moreover, the rights of qualified students to pursue graduate education should not be curtailed.

THE DURATION OF DOCTORAL EDUCATION

One of the hazards associated with the appearance of a less-favorable job market for Ph.D.'s is the probability that the number of years spent in obtaining the degree will rise. We believe that any further prolongment would be a most unfortunate development, and we urge doctoral-granting institutions to take vigorous steps to prevent it.

DOCTORAL-GRANTING INSTITUTIONS

One of the most disturbing trends in graduate education is the proliferation of doctoral-granting institutions, many of which are small and of low-quality. The inefficiencies associated with small doctoral programs impose a heavy burden on the taxpayers of states permitting the extension of doctoral-granting programs to public colleges that have not previously had them. We believe that federal and state government policies should be designed to confine comprehensive doctoral programs to a relatively limited number of universities that have high-quality programs in many disciplines. Other existing doctoral-granting institutions should be encouraged to develop selective Ph.D. and D.A. programs on the basis of regional or multicampus plans.

In relation to the changing market for Ph.D.'s, the Commission recommends that:

State coordinating councils and similar agencies should develop strong policies (where these do not now exist) for preventing the spread of Ph.D. programs to institutions that do not now have them. In addition, every effort should be made to prevent the establishment of new Ph.D. programs in particular fields of study in institutions that now have Ph.D. programs unless an exceptionally strong case can be made for them. We also strongly recommend the continuous review of existing degree programs with a view to eliminating those that are very costly or of low quality and the concentration of highly specialized degree programs on only one or two campuses of multicampus institutions (p. 160).

Regional plans for the development of Ph.D. programs along the lines of those of the New England Board of Higher Education and the Southern Regional Education Board should be strengthened and extended to regions that do not now have them. We also recommend far more extensive use of consortium arrangements that involve planning for concentration of development of Ph.D. programs in particular fields in individual members of the consortium as well as the rights of students to cross-register for individual courses or fields of concentration. Such plans should call for developing the strength of an individual institution in a group of related fields, such as the physical sciences or the social sciences (p. 160).

The continued development of doctor of arts programs should be encouraged. We consider the doctor of arts a more suitable degree than the Ph.D. for many types of employment (p. 160).

Agencies and individuals that have been conducting studies of future supply and demand for Ph.D.'s should continue to review and update their work. We are impressed by the differences in outlook among fields and believe that the time has come for increased emphasis on projections relating to individual fields or groups of fields and less reliance on broad aggregative studies (p. 160).

We have also been impressed by the almost complete lack of analysis of the implications of the changing job market for holders of master's degrees and for master's programs in colleges and universities. Some of the fields that will be most affected by the changing job market, such as education, include a very large proportion of candidates for master's degrees.

Federal and state government agencies and other appropriate bodies should undertake studies of the implications of the changing job market for holders of master's degrees and for enrollment in master's programs (p. 161).

POTENTIAL ADJUSTMENTS IN DEMAND AND SUPPLY
An unfavorable job market for college graduates and other influences may depress future enrollment rates below those indicated by projections based on past trends. If this tendency were to persist through the 1970s, its effect in alleviating a potential imbalance in the job market for college graduates could be appreciable, but the evidence on this point is far from clear as yet. In addition, a number of other types of probable demand-supply adjustments may well contribute to a more satisfactory job market for college graduates:

SHIFTS IN ENROLLMENT PATTERNS BY FIELD
On net balance, the evidence seems to reveal a considerable degree of student responsiveness to changes in relative job opportunities, but within a framework of rather substantial stability in overall patterns of student tastes and abilities. Although college graduates with liberal arts majors have had relatively severe difficulty in obtaining jobs in recent years, training in narrow specialities may make it more difficult for college graduates to make desirable occupational shifts in the course of their adult lives. We believe that, in view of the pronounced changes that are occurring in the job market for college graduates, institutions of higher education should place considerably greater emphasis on vocational counseling:

Colleges and universities should take immediate steps to strengthen occupational counseling programs available to their students. We also recommend that college placement services be strengthened where they have not been well developed. Professional schools should maintain their own placement programs for those receiving master's, first-professional, and doctor's degrees, while arts and science departments should have their own placement programs for students at the doctoral level (p. 167).

EDUCATIONAL UPGRADING AND CREDENTIALISM

The imposition by employers of educational requirements that are not clearly indicated by the requirements of particular jobs is a rising trend. The less-favorable job market anticipated for the 1970s will probably exacerbate this tendency. So will the increasing complexity of managerial decision making, which will lead to increased preference for trained managers. Civil rights pressure and recent court decisions will serve as a partially counteracting force.

Employers should not raise educational requirements in response to changes in the job market for college graduates. We strongly recommend that educational requirements should not be imposed except where they are clearly indicated by job requirements (p. 170).

ALTERNATIVE LIFESTYLES AND NONTRADITIONAL CAREERS

One of the great imponderables in looking ahead is the question of how far the choice of alternative lifestyles among young people will go and what its long-run effect on the job market will be. Communal living, sidewalk vending, and street musicians are a few examples of the emerging youth subculture. But the important point is that significant proportions of young people are rejecting conventional careers, and perhaps especially those careers that are most closely identified with corporate capitalism.

THE STRUCTURING OF DEMAND

Since World War II, government policies have become a far more important determinant of the demand for college graduates and holders of advanced degrees than they were in earlier decades. Apart from the need to overcome the deficiencies in elementary and secondary education, to which the Commission attaches high priority, we should move forward to meet the other critical unresolved problems of our society.

As debates inevitably proceed in the coming years over the reordering of national goals, the goal of fulfilling the aspirations of many young people for more useful roles in our society should be given high priority, along with the more widely recognized goal of overcoming critical human, urban, and environmental problems (p. 179).

LABOR MARKET RULES AND POLICIES

In higher education circles, there has been increasing interest in the past few years in encouraging students to "stop out" for a year or more either immediately after high school or during the course of their college careers. However, there is little evidence as yet of much interest in this concept in employer circles.

A REVERSAL OF THE BRAIN DRAIN?

The immigration of scientists, engineers, physicians, and nurses was an important source of supply in these occupations during the 1950s and

1960s. Meanwhile, there have been some interesting recent reports of emigration of school teachers. It does not seem likely that employment openings for United States college graduates abroad will be an appreciable factor in the overall demand for college graduates in the coming years, but in particular fields a reduced rate of immigration to this country seems probable.

The international migration of students and professional personnel should be explicitly incorporated into analyses of changes in demand and supply, and opportunities for student places and student aid for foreign students in the United States should not be curtailed (p. 183).

CONCLUSION

We explicitly reject a "manpower planning" requirements model as the basic general criterion for the development of higher education. Our rejection of such a model is based on three main considerations:

1 We believe that individuals should enjoy maximum freedom in the choice of their career objectives.

2 We have found that students' choices of fields of study are highly sensitive to shifts in the job market and can be relied upon to be a major factor in the process of adjustment to occupational shifts.

3 Adequate long-range manpower forecasting—especially when it is concerned with the outlook in particular professions—is an exceedingly intricate affair, and, in varying degrees, the methods used in many recent projections have been deficient.

We have made recommendations relating to the need for improved counseling and for improved projections relating to the various professions. We also need to improve the flow of current occupational information.

Federal government agencies should take steps to improve the flow of current occupational information and to make it available more promptly (p. 187).

For the remainder of the present century, college graduates more than ever will have to be prepared to adapt to shifts of specialty within a given occupation and in some cases to shifts from one occupation to another during the course of their lifetime careers.

GOVER-
NANCE OF
HIGHER
EDUCATION

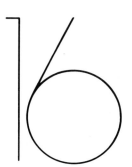

SIX PRIORITY
PROBLEMS
(APRIL 1973)

The governance of higher education in the United States is currently more subject to challenge than it has been in most earlier historical periods. This development reflects the pressures of conflict and change now affecting academic life, because both conflict and change make the processes of decision making more important to those who participate in, or are substantially affected by, higher education. Central issues have been raised. Basic principles are at stake.

THE GOVERNANCE OF HIGHER EDUCATION IN THE AMERICAN CONTEXT

One of the unique features of the governance of higher education in the United States is the great diversity of forms among institutions. Our system also has been especially characterized by these general features:

1   Absence of centralized control by the national government—essential authority has rested with state governments and with boards of trustees.

2   Concurrent existence of strong public and private segments.

3   Trustee responsibility—basic responsibility to provide for governance of individual institutions has been in the hands of lay boards in both public and private institutions.

4   Presidential authority—the president has had substantial executive authority delegated by the lay board.

5   Departmental authority—within the faculty, the department has been the key unit of academic organization over most of the past century.

Great and inconsistent pressures in recent years, however, have been placed on this historically effective overall structure. Not only are these pressures greater than ever before in American history, but they tend to be more at cross-purposes with one another. As we seek solutions to these problems, we believe that certain features of governance of higher education merit preservation and enlargement:

- A reasonable degree of independence from state and federal control
- Institutional separation from partisan political activity
- Academic freedom for faculty members and students
- Faculty influence over academic affairs
- Availability of many options from among which students may choose in selecting their campuses, their periods of attendance, their fields of study, and their courses
- Diversity among institutions
- Adaptability to changing circumstances
- A reasonable degree of consent within the campus
- A reasonable degree of public support externally

GENERAL CONSIDERATIONS AFFECTING GOVERNANCE

Recognizing the variety of situations and the absence of any single organizing principle, we call attention to the following considerations affecting governance and the suggested directions for improvement:

- Size of an institution adds to complexity and formality. In our report, *New Students and New Places,* we recommend "points of reassessment" in relation to size.

- Excessive aggregation of functions also adds complexity and can compound problems. Some activities can be eliminated or turned over to semi-independent agencies. Also, differentiation of functions among institutions reduces the tendency toward undue aggregation of functions in any single institution.

- Strong centralization of authority can delay decisions and make them less responsive to specific problems. Reasonable decentralization within systems and large campuses can accelerate and personalize the making of many decisions.

- Freedom of choice and expansion of individual options reduces the burden that is placed on the organized decision-making process.

- Open hearings on codes of conduct and on other major matters of policy can give expression to diverse points of view and inform the decision-making process.

- The more attention that is given to the needs of individuals and of special minority groups, the fewer are the complaints that are likely to be directed against the processes of governance in the longer run.

- It is important to clarify who has what authority and what policies are to be followed, and to set forth for all to see where answers can be obtained.

- Statements of rights and responsibilities can be helpful in clarifying relationships.

- Faculty members and students should have a full measure of academic freedom, and faculty senates and councils should have essential authority, substantially as defined by the American Association of University Professors.

- Staff members who are at the counters, across the desks, and on the phone with students, faculty members, and the public are of key importance in handling problems with clarity, accuracy, and a spirit of helpfulness.

- Adequate grievance machinery, ending in full impartial tribunals, is essential.

CAMPUS INDEPENDENCE

The independence of the campus from external authority has declined significantly since World War II and particularly over the past decade—more coordinating councils and superboards at the state level, more gubernatorial and legislative investigation and intrusion into once internal affairs, more federal regulations and supervision. This decline has affected both public and private institutions. A crisis of substantial importance has developed.

It is customary to speak of campus "autonomy" but there is no such thing in any full sense of the word. Full autonomy is always limited by the general law and often also by the charter of the institution. Increasingly it is also limited by state and federal influence and control. Thus complete autonomy is generally neither sought by higher education nor can it be given by public authority. Higher education, however, should be substantially self-governing in its intellectual conduct, its academic affairs, and its administrative arrangements. We distinguish these three areas where a substantial degree of independence is essential, and we assert that selective independence—not autonomy—is the issue. We also distinguish between external influence, which recognizes freedom of action, and external control, which limits it. To the extent that public authority relies upon influence and not control, institutions of higher education must rely upon their own wisdom in selecting among whatever alternatives are made available.

WHY INDEPENDENCE?

No natural law confers upon higher education escape from public surveillance. The case for independence largely rests on the professional nature of many of the decisions that must be made, on the need to elicit the devotion and sense of responsibility of the major groups internally involved, on the wisdom of drawing advice and support from interested private citizens, on the costs of partisan political and bureaucratic intrusions, on the desirability of having the campus community as one of the checks-and-balances in our pluralistic society, and on the experience of history of what works best both academically and politically.

EARNING INDEPENDENCE

Control usually follows money, and more money is now coming from public sources. How then may independence be earned? We suggest that it may be earned by:

■ Performing, at a high level of quality, functions that are important to the people in the larger society

■ Demonstrating capacity for effective self-governance

- Making effective use of resources provided by society
- Abiding by the law on campus
- Assuring institutional neutrality in partisan politics and in public controversies external to the institution
- Preserving intellectual integrity from attacks from within as well as from without
- Giving full and honest explanations—to the public in general, and to legislators and elected administrators in particular—about all matters of broad public concern

DISTRIBUTION OF AUTHORITY

To achieve balance between public control and influence versus institutional independence, the Commission favors the careful distribution of authority in matters related to governance, financial and business affairs, academic and intellectual affairs, and innovation:

PUBLIC CONTROL	INSTITUTIONAL INDEPENDENCE
Governance	
Basic responsibility for law enforcement	
Right to insist on political neutrality of *institutions* of higher education	Right to refuse oaths not required of all citizens in similar circumstances
Duty to appoint trustees of public institutions of higher education (or to select them through popular election)	Right to independent trustees: No ex officio regents with subsequent budgetary authority
	Right to nonpartisan trustees as recommended by some impartial screening agency, or as confirmed by some branch of the state legislature, or both; or as elected by the public
Right to reports and accountability on matters of public interest	
Duty of courts to hear cases alleging denial of general rights of a citizen and of unfair procedures	
Financial and Business Affairs	
Appropriation of public funds on basis of general formulas that reflect quantity and quality of output	Assignment of all funds to specific purposes
Postaudit, rather than preaudit, of expenditures, of purchases, of personnel actions	Freedom to make expenditures within budget, to make purchases, and to take personnel actions subject only to postaudit

PUBLIC CONTROL	INSTITUTIONAL INDEPENDENCE

Financial and Business Affairs

PUBLIC CONTROL	INSTITUTIONAL INDEPENDENCE
Examination of effective use of resources on a postaudit basis	Determination of individual work loads and of specific assignments to faculty and staff members
Standards for accounting practices and postaudit of them	
General level of salaries	Determination of specific salaries
Appropriation of public funds for buildings on basis of general formulas for building requirements	Design of buildings and assignment of space

Academic and Intellectual Affairs

PUBLIC CONTROL	INSTITUTIONAL INDEPENDENCE

General policies on student admissions:
  Number of places
  Equality of access
  Academic level of general eligibility among types of institutions
  General distribution of students by level of division
	Selection of individual students

Policies for equal access to employment for women and for members of minority groups	Academic policies for, and actual selection and promotion of, faculty members
Policies on differentiation of functions among systems of higher education and on specialization by major fields of endeavor among institutions	Approval of individual courses and course content
No right to expect secret research or service from members of institutions of higher education; and no right to prior review before publication of research results; but right to patents where appropriate	Policies on and administration of research and service activities
	Determination of grades and issuance of individual degrees
	Selection of academic and administrative leadership
Enforcement of the national Bill of Rights	Policies on academic freedom
Policies on size and rate of growth of campuses	Policies on size and rate of growth of departments and schools and colleges within budgetary limitations
Establishment of new campuses and other major new endeavors, such as a medical school, and definition of scope	Academic programs for new campuses and other major new endeavors within general authorization

INFLUENCE BUT NOT PUBLIC CONTROL	INSTITUTIONAL INDEPENDENCE
Academic Affairs—Innovation	
Encouragement of innovation through inquiry, recommendation, allocation of special funds, application of general budgetary formulas, starting new institutions	Development of and detailed planning for innovation

An effort to assure essential institutional independence is now necessary. But in this effort, the academic community should realize that public initiative has had, and can have, good as well as bad results, and that it may be needed in the future to protect the campus from internal attacks on academic freedom even though public interference once was and may again be a major source of threat to academic freedom.

The Commission makes several recommendations with regard to independence:

State grants to institutions for general support should be based on broad formulas and not line-item control (p. 29).

Academic policies set by state agencies should be of a broad nature and should not interfere with the more specific professional academic judgments about faculty appointments, courses of study, admission of individual students, grades and degrees for individual students, specific research projects, appointment of academic and administrative staff and leadership, and protection of academic freedom (p. 29).

Innovations in programs and in policies should be encouraged by public authorities by influence and not by control (p. 29).

Coordinating agencies at the state level should seek to establish, in cooperation with public and private institutions of higher education, guidelines defining areas of state concern and areas of institutional independence that avoid detailed control (p. 29).

The American Council on Education may wish to consider establishing a Commission on Institutional Independence to be concerned with policies affecting independence and the review of cases of alleged undue external influence. Such a Commission should include members drawn from the public at large (p. 29).

THE ROLE OF THE BOARD AND OF THE PRESIDENT
The board of trustees is an essential institution in higher education. It is not just the best of several unsatisfactory alternatives. At its best, it serves these functions:

■ It holds and interprets the "trust"—the responsibility for the long-run welfare of the total institution.

■ It acts as a "buffer" between society and the campus, resisting improper external interference and introducing a necessary contact with the changing realities of the surrounding society.

■ It is the final arbiter of internal disputes involving the administration, the faculty, and the students.

■ It is an "agent of change," in what is historically a conservative institution, deciding what changes should be encouraged and when.

■ It has the basic responsibility for the financial welfare of the campus.

■ Above all, it provides for the governance of the institution.

These roles are important at any time; they are more than usually important under current circumstances, when purposes are being re-examined, when the essential independence of the campus is being eroded, when conflict on campus has intensified, when change is more than normally necessary, and when governance has become so much more difficult. The role of the board of trustees is due for a renaissance. The Commission recommends that:

Elected officials with the power of budgetary review should not serve as members of governing boards of public institutions over which they exercise such review because of the conflict of interest and the resulting double access to control, and because of the partisan nature of their positions (pp. 34–35).

Members of governing boards of public institutions (where the governor makes the appointments) should be subject to appropriate mechanisms for nominating and screening individuals before appointment by the governor to assure consideration of properly qualified individuals, or to subsequent legislative confirmation to reduce the likelihood of purely politically partisan appointments, or to both (p. 35).

Faculty members, students, and alumni should be associated with the process of nominating at least some board members in private and public institutions, but faculty members and students should not serve on the boards of institutions where they are enrolled or employed (p. 35).

Board membership should reflect the different age, sex, and racial groups that are involved in the concerns of the institution. Faculty members from other institutions and young alumni should be considered for board memberships (p. 35).

Boards should consider faculty and student membership on appropriate board committees, or the establishment of parallel committees with arrangements for joint consultation (p. 35).

Boards periodically should review the arrangements for governance—perhaps every four or five years—to be certain that they fit the current needs of the institutions and are appropriate to the various functions being performed (p. 35).

THE PRESIDENCY
Under the general direction of the board, the president holds the key administrative position. He must extend leadership in relation to faculty members and other staff, students, alumni, government agencies, and the

public more generally. We believe that the present period calls for substantial changes on campus and in the relationships of the campus to society. This, in turn, will require greater presidential influence to initiate and guide the changes. Accordingly, the Commission recommends that:

Boards should seek active presidents and give them the authority and the staff they need to provide leadership in a period of change and conflict (p. 38).

Boards may wish to consider the establishment of stated review periods for presidents so that withdrawal by the president or reaffirmation of the president may be managed in a more effective manner than is often now the actual situation. Faculty members and students should be associated in an advisory capacity with the process of review as they are in the initial appointment (p. 38).

COLLECTIVE BARGAINING AND FACULTY POWER

The 1960s were marked by student dissent and student organization. The 1970s may equally be marked by faculty dissent and faculty organization. The decade of the student may be followed by the decade of the faculty. Faculty members, at least in the more prestigious academic institutions, have long engaged in informal and discrete bargaining with administrators, individually or through their faculty committees. But in many colleges, particularly in community colleges and some former teachers colleges, faculty members never have had much influence through committees and senates. The Commission recommends, as a high priority, that:

Faculties should be granted, where they do not already have it, the general level of authority as recommended by the American Association of University Professors (p. 41).

We believe that faculty members should have the right to organize and to bargain collectively, if they so desire, in both public and private institutions. We, therefore, recommend that:

State laws, where they do not now permit it, should provide faculty members in public institutions the opportunity of obtaining collective bargaining rights. One alternative under such laws should be choice of no bargaining unit (p. 43).

There are several routes to power, but they cannot all be followed simultaneously. The basic choice at the present time is among (1) codetermination and (2) collective bargaining, or (3) some combination between the two where codetermination is effective in some subject-matter areas (such as curriculum) and collective bargaining in others (such as salaries). But it should be clearly understood that faculty members cannot have it both ways—they cannot engage in codetermination and in collective bargaining on the same issues at the same time.

Faculties in each institution should undertake the most careful analysis of the implications of collective bargaining and, more broadly, of which of the alternative forms of governance they prefer (p. 48).

Much confusion now exists over bargaining units and contract coverage—some decisions have gone one way and others another way—and even over the right of faculty members to bargain at all in many states. In general, we oppose broad bargaining units and broad contract coverage. In addition, given the special nature of institutions of higher education, we favor special laws to cover bargaining by faculty members, or, if this is not possible, then special sections of laws, or at least, special administrative interpretations to reflect the special circumstances.

Representation and bargaining units should be composed of faculty members, including department chairmen (p. 49).

The approach to contract coverage should be one of restraint, with the contract covering economic benefits and with academic affairs left (or put) in the hands of the faculty senate or equivalent council (p. 49).

A separate federal law and separate state laws should be enacted governing collective bargaining by faculty members in both private and public institutions and should be responsive to the special circumstances that surround their employment. If this is not possible, then separate provisions should be made in more general laws, or leeway should be provided for special administrative interpretations (p. 50).

Our general view is that collective bargaining, to the extent that it enters higher education, should not now become the new system of governance. Rather, it should be an amendment, in certain areas, to the existing forms of governance.

PRINCIPLES AND PRACTICES OF ACADEMIC TENURE
Granting tenure is a long-established practice in most of the leading colleges and universities in the United States. Recently, however, it has met a widespread attack:

■ Many students now question tenure, charging that some faculty members are incompetent to teach and that many are too little concerned with teaching as compared with their other activities.

■ Some members of the public at large, as in times past, attack tenure as an artificial protection for incompetent or politically unpopular professors.

■ Some women and members of minority groups are increasingly doubtful about tenure practices, as expansion slows down, for fear that the practices may reduce their opportunities to move up the ladder.

■ Administrators are concerned that tenure practices will lead to a rise in fixed costs, thereby reducing institutional flexibility.

Tenure, however, has several major advantages to the academic world and to society. Greater assurance of academic freedom for faculty members to express unpopular opinions, greater protection for the public in its access to the full and free views of faculty members, greater opportunity for a more serious review of the quality of faculty members, and a fuller feeling of partnership in the campus enterprise by senior faculty members are the basic reasons for tenure. They are, we believe, quite persuasive.

To make tenure both more effective in achieving its positive benefits and to avoid its deterioration through abuses:

■ Appointments and promotions to tenure should be made only after the most careful review.

■ "Merit" increases after tenure should be made on the basis of merit and not seniority.

■ A statement of rights and responsibilities should guide the conduct of both faculty and students.

■ A broader interpretation than has been customary should be made of the requirements of institutional welfare as a basis for ceasing the employment of tenured faculty members.

■ In cases related to dismissal and termination, clear and reasonable rules should be in force, and independent tribunals should be available.

■ Some reasonable percentage needs to be set well in advance to indicate a "peril point" where the percentage of tenured faculty members may be deemed excessive.

Provided these policies and practices are in effect, it is our conviction that the principle of tenure has clear advantages both for academic institutions and for American society.

The principle of tenure should be retained and extended to campuses where it does not now apply (p. 58).

Tenure systems should be so administered in practice (1) that advancements to tenure and after tenure are based on merit, (2) that the criteria to be used in tenure decisions are made clear at the time of employment, (3) that codes of conduct specify the obligations of tenured faculty members, (4) that adjustments in the size and in the assignments of staff in accord with institutional welfare be possible when there is a fully justifiable case for them, (5) that fair internal procedures be available to hear any cases that may arise, and (6) that the percentage of faculty members with tenure does not become excessive (p. 58).

Persons on a part-time basis have a particularly difficult time accumulating a record that merits tenure over the same elapsed period as for full-time persons.

Persons on a 50-percent time basis or more should be eligible for tenure, but the time elapsed before a decision on tenure must be made should be counted on a full-time-equivalent basis (p. 59).

Tenure, in its derivation from land tenure, means not the ownership of a position but rather the right to hold it under certain conditions. Ownership implies the right to use, or not to use, or even to misuse. Tenure implies the right to make good use. It is the definition of "good use" that warrants reconsideration, not the concept of tenure itself.

STUDENT INFLUENCE ON CAMPUS AND OFF

Dissent against society and participation within the academic affairs of the campus are the new manifestations of the intermittent three-century-old drive of students for a position of greater influence, and the use of TV and political lobbying are among the new tactics. This drive seems, at the moment, to be in low gear. We do not believe, however, that this signals an end to all further attempts at forward motion.

The Commission is generally sympathetic to greater student participation in those areas of governance where they have substantial interest and adequate competence, and where they will assume responsibility. We believe that in such areas, students can inform the decision-making agencies about their experiences and desires, give good advice, exercise good judgment, and support innovation. Some of the most valuable contributions of student participation can be at the departmental level, which is the most active working level of the campus. Students are often a large and heterogeneous group, but within their major fields they are less numerous and more homogeneous.

We believe that majority student wishes for more participation can generally be accommodated within the governance arrangements of colleges and universities while adding to the information available and to the quality of the judgments exercised in making decisions.

Governance arrangements should provide (1) adequate academic options from among which students may choose and (2) the right to be heard on important campus issues (p. 71).

Students should serve on joint faculty-student (or trustee-student or administrative-student) committees with the right to vote or should have their own parallel student committees with the right to meet with faculty, trustee, and administrative committees in areas of special interest and competence such as educational policy and student affairs. Students serving on such committees should be given staff assistance (p. 71).

Students should be given the opportunity to evaluate the teaching performance of faculty members, and students should be involved in periodic reviews of the performance of departments (p. 71).

Conduct codes should be prepared with student involvement in the process of their preparation, ombudsmen or their equivalent should be appointed, and formal grievance machinery should be available and should end in impartial judicial tribunals (p. 71).

EMERGENCY OR UNPROGRAMMED DECISION MAKING

Many new stresses have developed on campus; many new strains have been introduced into the groves of academe; many mistakes have been made. The old mechanisms of governance have not been equal to the new institution. The new context is more dynamic, and more of the decisions now have to be handled on an unprogrammed basis—quicker responses are needed and are undertaken in a more complex setting.

In our report, *Dissent and Disruption,* we set forth our views on how to be prepared for contingencies.

RETURN TO CONSENSUS OR ADJUSTMENT TO CONFLICT?

A consensus over governance depends, in part, on a consensus about purposes. Rules governing independence, for example are not so important when there is general agreement between society and the campus about purposes as when there is disagreement. Should conflict continue, however, it will then need to be institutionalized within more specific rules, will need to be adjudicated by more effective mechanisms, will need to be guided in constructive directions. The basic test of governance, as we see it, is whether the decisions actually made do or do not enhance the long-run welfare of higher education and of society, and the quality of the individual campus, and whether the solutions are appropriate to and commensurate with the problems.

In conclusion, acknowledging the importance of structures and processes and the need for their improvement, we note that the quality of governance depends in the end, and above all else, on the people who participate in it.

THE PURPOSES AND THE PERFORMANCE OF HIGHER EDUCATION IN THE UNITED STATES

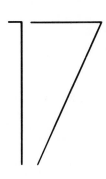

APPROACHING THE YEAR 2000 (JUNE 1973)

Conflicts over purposes exist in higher education in the United States today. These conflicts affect both internal conduct of institutions and external relations between institutions and society. A period for reexamination of purposes, somewhat comparable to—but less intense than—that of a century ago is at hand.

FORCES FOR A REEVALUATION OF PURPOSES

One century ago, the United States was undergoing great change and so also was higher education within it. The "classical" college devoted to *in loco parentis,* to the Bible, and to European culture gave way to the "modern" college and university open to scientific research, to training for new professions and occupations, to service to society, and to a more welcoming approach to students from all income strata. Once again, great forces are at work, including:

A further extension of educational opportunity to members of minority groups, to women, and to adults. Higher education has moved from its elite stage to its mass stage, and is now moving to the stage of universal access.

New knowledge is more central to the conduct of society. It has taken its place along with land, labor, capital and management as a great factor influencing production.

Intellectuals, trained within higher education and often clustered around it, are both more numerous within society and more essential to its performance.

Society is in the process of reexamining values and lifestyles, with the campus heavily involved in the process of this examination.

Students are changing. They come out of more permissive environments, and they are more oriented in college toward their developmental process in its totality.

PURPOSES AND PERFORMANCE

It is no longer sufficient to say that higher education has the purposes of "teaching, research, and service." Teaching to what ends? Research for what reasons? Service to whom? We are particularly concerned with purposes for this time—the last quarter of the twentieth century, and for this place—the United States, while recognizing that some purposes of higher education should be both universal and eternal. We next set forth five major purposes, toward which we believe that higher education in the United States should now be directed, our evaluation of the performance of higher education in each of these areas, and our suggestions for improvements.

PURPOSE 1: THE EDUCATION OF THE INDIVIDUAL STUDENT AND THE
PROVISION OF A CONSTRUCTIVE ENVIRONMENT FOR
DEVELOPMENTAL GROWTH

The campus has a basic responsibility to provide good educational opportunities for its students (1) to develop an understanding of society, (2)
to obtain academic and technical competence in selected fields, (3) to
fulfill appropriate standards of academic conduct, and (4) to explore cultural interests and enhance cultural skills. The campus has a subsidiary
concern to provide an environment that enhances the "emotional growth"
of students, but it need not assume accountability for such growth.

Performance is very hard to measure in this area because millions of
students, hundreds of campuses, and several quite imprecise criteria
are involved. Our own evaluation is that, in terms of prodividing opportunities for academic competence, higher education in the United States
is generally adequate and sometimes superb. For meeting standards of
academic conduct, it is generally adequate. For exploring cultural interests and enhancing cultural skills, it is improving, but the adequacy of
programs varies greatly from campus to campus. And for obtaining a
good general understanding of society, it is often poor and may be deteriorating.

The college environment, we believe, is often a quite artificial "hot-
house", too far removed from work and service, and too age-stratified
to youth alone. More work and service opportunities can be provided
by work-study jobs on campus and off, by facilitating off-campus service
work, and by encouraging part-time employment opportunities for students by outside employers and providing contact with part-time jobs
more generally. The Commission recommends that:

More broad learning experiences should be made available to students, and more
opportunities for creative activity should be provided as through independent
study and the creative arts (p. 21).

More work and service opportunities should be created for students by government and industry and nonprofit agencies, and students should be encouraged
to pursue these opportunities, including through "stop-outs" (p. 21).

More attention should be paid to the occupational training interests of students,
and to occupational counseling and guidance as students and adults seek to adjust to changing labor market conditions (p. 21).

There should be a greater mixing of age groups on campus through providing
more opportunities for older persons to take classes and to obtain needed financial
support (pp. 21–22).

PURPOSE 2: ADVANCING HUMAN CAPABILITY IN
SOCIETY AT LARGE

Higher education has a great responsibility for (1) developing and making
available new ideas and new technology, (2) finding and training talent

and guiding it to greater usefulness, and (3) generally enhancing the information, the understanding, and the cultural appreciation and opportunities of the public at large.

In the area of enhancing human capability throughout society, we believe that the performance of higher education, particularly in the century since the land-grant movement, has been at a comparatively superior level among industrial nations. On the other hand, service by higher education in the distribution of information and advice has been directed more toward power and toward money than an even-handed policy would warrant. Agriculture, industry, the professions, and the federal government have all been able to obtain substantial service, in the form of applied research and consulting advice, from faculty members. Trade unions were for a long time neglected; so were the cities; so, now, are many voluntary agencies and groups.

The value of a more educated and better informed human society is great, but incalculable, and we believe that many individuals would be willing to pay a high price for the advantages of living in a society where many, if not most, persons are well-educated, or well-informed, or both.

Federal research funds expended within higher education should be maintained steadily at a level of about 0.3 percent of the gross national product (p. 27).

Funds for basic research should be concentrated on highly productive centers and individuals, and money for applied research should be subject to periodic reassignment to reflect the decline of old and the rise of new potentialities (p. 27).

Service should be extended on a more even-handed basis to groups and persons in connection with problems where it may be helpful, subject to the major limitation that any service should be appropriate to the educational functions of higher education (p. 27).

The training of health care personnel should be substantially expanded for the immediate future to eliminate the one remaining major deficit in highly trained manpower (p. 27).

Cultural and "life-long learning" facilities and opportunities should be made available to the general public on an expanded basis (p. 27).

PURPOSE 3: EDUCATIONAL JUSTICE FOR THE POSTSECONDARY AGE GROUP

Higher education has an obligation to join with and to assist other institutions in society in providing educational opportunities for all persons who seek them beyond the secondary level.

The chance of young persons going to college from families in the lower half of the income range and from racial and other less advantaged ethnic minority groups is substantially less than that of young persons from families in the upper half of the income range and from the historically dominant social group. Inadequate as it is, however, the United

States has a better record in providing opportunities for postsecondary education to persons drawn from throughout its population than does any other industrial nation for which data is available.

We believe, first, that concern should be spread from the college-attending group to the total postsecondary age group; second, that adequate provision should be made for several alternative channels into adult life; and third, that there should be equal opportunity of access regardless of family income and social background to each of these several channels, including college. The Commission recommends:

The total postsecondary age group should become more the subject of concern, and attention should be comparatively less concentrated on those who attend college (p. 37).

Public policy should be directed to improvement of existing channels into adult life and to the creation of new channels—college being only one of several preferred channels (p. 37).

Open-access opportunities should be provided into most and perhaps all of these channels and such access should be subject to public financial support where and as appropriate and not restricted to college attendance alone (p. 37).

Admission standards should be relaxed for members of disadvantaged groups, provided that the chances are good that such students can meet graduation requirements in full (p. 38).

Special efforts should be made to find qualified members of minority groups and women for inclusion in the "pool" of candidates for consideration when faculty appointments are being made; and such persons should be given special consideration in employment for faculty positions, where their employment will lead to the creation of a more effective total academic environment for the entire student group that will be affected (p. 38).

Curricula should be examined to be certain they reflect the history, the culture, and the current roles of minority groups (p. 38).

PURPOSE 4: PURE LEARNING—SUPPORTING INTELLECTUAL AND ARTISTIC CREATIVITY

Higher education has a fundamental obligation to preserve, transmit, and illuminate the wisdom of the past; to find, preserve, and analyze the records of the past; to provide an environment for research and intellectual creativity in the present; and to assure for the future the trained mind and the continuing interest so that the store of human knowledge may keep on expanding—all this beyond reference to any current practical applications. We include here basic research in science and social science, humanistic scholarship, creative artistic activity, and speculative social thought.

In the area of pure scholarship, higher education in the United States ranks comparatively well on the world scene—superior in science and the social sciences, more than adequate in the humanities, but only now entering full-scale into the creative arts. To maintain and improve this record, it is important that funds for basic and applied research, particularly from federal sources, be available at a reasonable level, that this level be maintained steadily and not be subject to sharp changes which impede the conduct of individual projects and complicate institutional administration, and that funds be distributed increasingly into the areas of the social sciences, humanities, and creative arts. The continuation of academic freedom is also a prerequisite for creative scholarship. Freedom and money and trained curiosity are the basic resources for scholarship. We recommend:

Federal research funds should be substantially increased for the social sciences, humanities, and creative arts from their current level of about 7 percent of the amount for science (p. 41).

PURPOSE 5: EVALUATION OF SOCIETY FOR SELF-RENEWAL—
THROUGH INDIVIDUAL THOUGHT AND PERSUASION
Faculty members and students, as an integral part of their scholarly activities, should have both the freedom and the opportunity to engage in the evaluation of society through individual thought and persuasion.

In this area, we see two major problems: one is that the public does not fully understand or accept this purpose of higher education, and the other is that some elements on some campuses exploit the opportunity unwisely and even illegally. The answers to the first problem are more public discussion of the constructive possibilities and even urgent necessities inherent in this form of service. The second problem requires better rules and more self-restraint on campus. Critical evaluation should not be allowed to extend to disruption of the campus or of society, to the improper use of campus facilities to mount public campaigns for or against some idea or program or political candidate, to the indoctrination of students to some one point of view on threat of lower academic rewards, to use of political tests for preferment among faculty members, or to the commitment of the institution as such to any single program of social change.

The critical evaluation of society has been in good supply in recent years, even though often less constructive and effective than might ideally be desired. The Commission recommends:

The principles of academic freedom for faculty members should be preserved where they are now effective and extended into areas where they do not now prevail, and the essential institutional independence of the campus should be fully protected by society to assure the continuance of the possibilities of critical evaluation of society by individual faculty members and students (p. 51).

Each institution of higher education should establish a policy of self-restraint against disruptive activities, against improper use of campus facilities, against improper political indoctrination of students, against selection and promotion of faculty members in accordance with their political beliefs, and against commitment of the institution as such to the pursuit of specific external political and social changes; each institution should be prepared to defend its own integrity (pp. 51–52).

PURPOSES: APPROACHING THE YEAR 2000

The possible contributions by higher learning to the needs of society change both as higher learning accumulates more knowledge and new methodologies, and as society evolves and becomes a more intricate web of activities and relationships. Thus the purposes of higher education as seen from different cultural perspectives and as accumulated over the centuries should be reevaluated periodically. In total, the forces for re-evaluation will change the surrounding society substantially and thus will have indirect as well as direct impacts on the purposes of higher education.

The purposes of higher education in the United States are plural, the constituent institutions are diverse, and performance is subject to many interpretations. We expect that, in the future, higher education will demonstrate an equal or perhaps even greater willingness to accept the need for continuing reform and an equal or perhaps even greater capacity to help shape society—even more than it has since 1870.

FUNCTIONS

Higher education in North American began with the founding of Harvard in 1636. The college pattern was basically taken from Stuart England with some Scottish influence, and the purpose was to maintain the old culture brought from England into the middle of a wilderness. A broad general education was combined with a deep concern for the moral and religious development of youth, and out of this concern grew the many rules that stood *in loco parentis.* Thus an original purpose of American higher education was personal development through acculturation to the classics and to moral principles.

A second theme was also introduced early, and this was the economic one. Concerned with practical pursuits—crafts, vocations, industries—it was thought that through education, available to all in accord with their individual talents, would come a free and wealthy society. But like so many other features of American higher education, the economic purpose was principally developed in the late nineteenth century.

A third theme saw education as fulfilling a political role. This role was three-fold: to give all citizens an education so that they could be effective participants in a democracy; to find and to train the "natural aristocracy" of talent for positions of leadership; and to assure some equality of opportunity so that deprivations in one generation need not necessarily be passed on to members of succeeding generations.

A fourth purpose was added with the national endorsement of the land-grant movement, and this was service to the surrounding society. The logic of this service orientation was clear. More problems required more research for their solution, and the campus was the chosen—but not exclusive—national instrument for basic research. Also, the campus had ready-made audiences for cultural and entertainment events, and could readily accept members of the public at them as well as members of the campus.

ACCUMULATING PURPOSES

One purpose has been added to another—personal development, economic growth, political health, service to society—and each purpose has become more complex: thus the historical process of proliferating purposes. Further, these purposes may be partially translated into the five current and future purposes we set forth above as follows:

Personal development into the education of the individual student and the provision of an environment for developmental growth

Economic advancement into aspects of advancing human capability in society at large

Political health, in part, into educational justice and into evaluation of society

Service to society into aspects of advancing human capability

Pure scholarship has come along more as a companion to these four historical purposes than as a consciously chosen purpose by American society. We believe, however, that it should now be set forth formally as a central purpose, as we have done.

Functions actually performed within the system of higher education in addition to the purposes set forth above are a whole series of functions directly related to carrying them out. These direct functions are supplemented by support functions such as business services and by ancillary functions such as operation of a government laboratory. We shall be concerned here only with direct functions, and we set forth the major ones as follows:

Education of students and provision of a constructive environment for developmental growth:

(1) General education or what we have called "broad learning experiences"—the provision of opportunities to survey the cultural heritage of mankind, to understand man and society

(2) Specialized academic and occupational preparation—the offering of programs in depth that advance specialized academic and occupational interests

(3) Academic socialization—the establishment and application of a set of rules and standards which govern academic conduct

(4) Campus environment—provision of a series of activities, such as cultural, athletic, work, and service opportunities, and a set of personal relationships which provide an interesting and stimulating environment

(5) Personal support—making available informal and formal advisory and counseling services

(6) "Holding operation" or period of "moratorium"—providing for students a period to assess options and make choices before committing themselves to occupations, styles of life, and marriage partners; a period for maturation

Advancing human capability in society at large:

(7) Research—particularly research that adds directly or indirectly to human health, welfare, and wealth

(8) Service—advice and instruction to persons and organizations external to the campus

(9) Sorting talent—finding talent, guiding and rating it, and placing it in productive occupations

(10) Training in vocational, technical, preprofessional and professional occupations

(11) Cultural advancement—provision of cultural and informational facilities and personnel

Assistance with the provision of educational justice:

(12) Development of an adequate number of places—particularly of the open-access type

(13) Development of appropriate special programs—both remedial and cultural

(14) Financial support—making available funds to cover essential costs of students

Providing an effective locus for pure scholarship and artistic creativity:

(15) Provision of facilities and personnel and a favorable climate for the advancement of pure scholarship, in the sense of scholarship that is motivated by a desire to enhance the cultural heritage and respond to human curiosity and add to wisdom, and of artistic creativity

Providing an effective locus for evaluation of society:

(16) Provision of freedom, of opportunities, and of reasonable rules of conduct relating to such evaluation

These several functions relate back to purposes and ahead to such issues as governance and finance. Some functions, such as development of open-access places and conduct of research projects, by their very nature, tend to draw governmental control or influence; others, such as pure scholarship and professional training, inherently, lead to strong faculty influence and control; and still others, such as development of special remedial and ethnic-study programs, attract student attention. All this, in turn, leads to different governance patterns in different types of endeavors.

The accumulation of functions by an institution adds to its complexity, to greater size and thus to more levels of bureaucracy, to divided attention by top administrators, and to uncertain loyalties. It may also lead to contradictions in purposes, to inefficiencies in operation, and to inconsistences among activities. We believe the rule should be: only necessary and compatible functions—they have proved hard enough to handle. Higher education generally and each campus specifically should not overextend itself. We do not suggest an approach of substantial disaggregation but we do suggest that all functions now being performed should not necessarily be taken for granted; that each function should be subject to periodic scrutiny by each institution of higher education.

CONTRADICTIONS AND COMPARATIVE EFFECTIVENESS IN THE PERFORMANCE OF FUNCTIONS

The campus is primarily an academic institution. We consider it a contradiction when the campus takes on functions which are at odds with the inherent nature of academic life. We also consider it inefficient when an academic institution takes on nonacademic operations which can be performed as well or better by other institutions. We propose two tests: (1) is the activity, even if largely academic in method or content, compatible with the mores of academic life? and (2) is the activity, if not academic in method or content, better done by the campus than by any other alternate agency? If the answer is "no" in specific cases to either question, we believe there is a prima facie case for disengagement. Specifically, the Commission recommends:

Each institution of higher education should survey periodically the totality of the functions it performs to be sure that none of them contradicts the ethos of academic life, and that none of the nonacademic functions could be as well or better performed by some quasi-university or external agency (p. 72).

All secret research should be eliminated from all campuses as a matter of national policy, except under quite unusual circumstances (p. 72).

Campuses should not add and, where feasible, should eliminate, operational, custodial, and service functions that are not directly tied to academic and educational activities, and which can be performed as well or better by other agencies (p. 72).

COMPLEMENTARY COMBINATIONS OF THE FUNCTIONS PERFORMED ON A SINGLE CAMPUS   Certain functions may be appropriate for the totality of higher education but may not fit well together on a single campus. For example, the faculty mentality that goes along with highly specialized research institutes is often inconsistent with that of a liberal arts college devoted to the education of generalists; careful attention to remedial work is not likely to be forthcoming from a faculty engaged in pure scholarship; and vocational training calls for quite different faculty skills and interests than does Ph.D. training. The faculty members and students drawn to these contrasting activities have such different interests that they are not likely to mix well with each other, to develop a sincere concern for each other's welfare, and to make jointly effective policy concerning the disparate functions.

Functions may be viewed as "complementary" (and in the research university the complementary functions are comparatively numerous), as competitive for attention and resources, or as essentially independent of other functions. It is our view that complementary functions should be combined, that competitive functions should be disaggregated into separate institutions or into separate segments within the same institution, and that independent functions should be turned over to other agencies unless there are strong reasons to the contrary. We recommend:

Institutions of higher education should seek to avoid and eliminate noncomplementary functions (p. 74).

Coordinating councils, consortia, and multicampus systems should adopt policies of clear differentiation of functions among campuses and of assigned specializations among fields—such differentiation of functions should follow the logic of complementarity of interests (p. 75).

COHESION   There is still another criterion in determining the functions of a campus. This criterion is that nothing should be added if it does not make a contribution to the whole enterprise, and something should be subtracted if it would not be missed by the whole enterprise. This is the criterion of cohesiveness, and it goes beyond complementarity. We believe that many individual institutions of higher education in the United States would be in an improved situation if they were more uniformly concerned with cohesion, in the sense that each function adds to the welfare of the total enterprise. Each campus should be able to state what its functions are, why they are important, and how they fit together. It should be able to state why it is a cohesive enterprise.

CONFLICT
The period of great change in American society around 1870 became a period of great change in higher education; and a great philosophical debate about higher education then took place. To the extent that the period of 1970 turns out to be a period of great change for American society, we expect that it will be one also for higher education and that a major philosophical debate will again take place. A debate about purposes is always endemic in higher education. It is important, therefore, to understand how specific purposes may relate to overall doctrinal views about the central logic of higher education; of how people think about these matters rather than of how they have reacted and should react within actual situations and in response to actual problems.

CONTENDING PHILOSOPHICAL VIEWS ABOUT
PURPOSES AND FUNCTIONS
Three central philosophical views of the primary purposes of learning in general, and of higher education in particular, have animated men in planning and developing colleges and universities over the centuries. Much of the current intellectual debate about and the struggle over the purposes of higher education has roots, often unnoticed, in these three views:

SEARCHING FOR VALUES The essence of this view is that there are eternal truths in the universe or ultimate values which have been discovered or which can be discovered; that there is an eternal world behind the changing perceptions of the actual world.

PURSUING NEW KNOWLEDGE Truth, from this point of view, is more related to current facts, including facts about the physical universe, and is always being discovered and tested and applied anew. It will be found, in an expanding and changing universe, through analysis of current experience and through experimentation.

SUPPORTING A DESIGNATED SOCIAL STRUCTURE The starting point for this approach is one particular, envisioned, perfected society whether anarchy, or democracy, or the socialist state, or the "cultural revolution" triumphant, or whatever.

We set forth these three views as "ideal types," as abstractions from the full reality and complexity of views actually held. We do this in an effort to illuminate the essential philosophical orientations from which more balanced, or at least more mixed, positions are constructed, drawing, as they often do, on elements of two or even all three of these "pure" doctrines—but in quite differing proportions.

THE THREE VIEWS COMPARED AND CONTRASTED   It should quickly be noted that there are great tensions within each of these three points of view, as well as among them, that each is really an axis of thought with terminal points quite far apart. However, each of these three views shows up on campus. The first tends to find its greatest support in theology, in the humanities, and in the liberal arts college; the second, in the sciences and the professions, and in the land-grant university, the community college, and the comprehensive college; and the third, in some of the social sciences and in the "free universities." The first and the third are more nearly like each other in their inherent logic of a more stabilized orientation toward a set of values or a designated social structure than they are alike in the second which is more oriented to means and less to ends.

But all three views also have certain concerns in common. They all believe that the higher learning should be useful for some purpose or purposes; that the higher learning should be concerned with the "truth," though variously defined and variously discovered; and that higher education should lead to change in one direction or another and by one means or another. Thus education is seen by each as a high activity of man and as an instrument that can help shape a better world.

It is also important to set forth a second crosscut view of higher education. This crosscut is by the degree of emphasis placed upon societal control and interests as compared with decisions by individuals and the interests of individuals. Thus the first view can be expressed through authoritarian control or through "rugged individualism"; the second view, through centralized planning or individual initiative; and the third view, through anarchism or state socialism. With this crosscut added, it might then be better to say that there are six "ideal-type" approaches rather than three.

THE THREE VIEWS IN ACTUAL CONFLICT   Each view has experienced its periods of triumph. The first view generally ruled supreme in Western Europe at least until the end of the sixteenth century; the second view rose gradually to dominance, particularly in the nineteenth century; and the third view has been gaining in strength in the twentieth century. But there are at least two good reasons why contending theoretical schools have not had more of an impact on higher education in the contemporary United States. (1) To begin with, the United States is a pluralistic society, and adherence exclusively to the doctrines of any one school—particularly the first and the third—would cause higher education to be in great dissonance with society. (2) Additionally, it is not the nature of the intellectual world, without great external control, to agree totally on one cultural model, on one mentality, as against all others—and the external control to force such agreement is not present in American society. One mentality may be ascendant but not to the total exclusion of all others. American society is pluralistic, and the inherent nature of the intellectual world is such that it also is pluralistic. Thus all three views have been and will continue to be in contention as far as one can see ahead.

We also drew on each of the three philosophical views we have set forth. Our emphasis, for example, on the importance of "academic socialization" and on general education draws on values; our stress on "advancing human capability," on the approach of evolutionary knowledge; and our concern for effective "evaluation of society" through individual study and comment, on the philosophical concept of helping to shape a better future. Our main approach, however, has been that of the evolution of knowledge and how it can be advanced most successfully, of the application of free and trained thought and research to the great problems of the current age.

We have also considered the comparative emphasis to be placed on individuals and on society. We have placed reliance more on the free choice of individuals among alternatives available to them rather than on centralized collective determinations; we have declared faith in our respect for the decision-making capacity of individual persons.

THE FUTURE—A PERIOD OF CONFLICT ABOUT PURPOSES AND FUNCTIONS?

The always latent and long-standing debate about the purposes of higher education is now being invigorated. American society is once again changing rapidly. Public attitudes about higher education are less supportive, more questioning. New tensions exist on campus and between campus and society.

The broad alternatives for society are to dispense with much of higher societal conduct, to participate in society, or to fight society as now constituted. The course of effective participation, we believe, holds out the greater prospects both for higher education and for American society.

The broad alternatives for society are to dispense with much of higher education, to work along with it, or to control it in detail. The course of working along with higher education, we believe, also holds out the better prospects.

Higher education should serve society by serving the cause of knowledge; it should serve the cause of knowledge by protecting the freedom of its members and the essential independence of its institutions; and it should protect freedom and independence by responding with consideration to the needs of society, and by safeguarding its own universal values of free thought and expression.

HIGHER
EDUCATION:
WHO PAYS?
WHO
BENEFITS?
WHO
SHOULD
PAY?

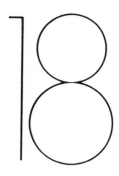

From the point of view of individual and national welfare, higher education is one of the most important services in the United States. Quantitatively, colleges and universities account for expenditures totaling about one-fortieth—2.5 percent—of our national production of goods and services. How higher education is financed is of substantial significance to millions of individuals and to society as a whole.

THE EDUCATIONAL ACCOUNTS
People pay the total bill for higher education—directly through charges to students and their parents, indirectly through tax assessments, through philanthropic gifts and bequests, and through contributions to other institutions that in turn support collegiate education. In these forms and through these agencies, the current burden is shared among users and nonusers, the well-to-do and the less well-to-do, older and younger generations.

"Who pays for college education?" cannot be answered without giving attention to several aspects of college costs. First, there is the "price" charged for attending college—that is, the basic tuition and fees charged to each student. Second, there is the "out-of-pocket cost" to the student or his family, which includes tuition and fees, room and board, books and supplies, travel and other living costs, and which may be partially offset by scholarship grants. Third, the cost of educational services in almost every institution of higher learning is partially subsidized from public funds, gifts, and endowments. Finally, there are forgone income opportunities for the student. In many cases these are decisive in whether a person can or should attend college.

It is useful to simplify the educational accounts, as usually reported, by eliminating items that do not reflect the educational mission of colleges and universities:

Federal research and services—About three-fourths of federal payments to colleges and universities for research and services are for activities that could have been performed by other contractors and which are not an integral part of the educational process.

Sale of services—Services provided for fees under this category primarily include services performed for nonstudent audiences.

Related activities—Income from this source generally includes fees for extension programs, athletic and artistic events, operation of real estate, and a variety of other income categories that are not essential to the main educational function of institutions.

Student-aid income—Student-aid funds pass through institutions, coming from public or philanthropic gifts or grants, and are passed on to students to enable them to pay for tuition and subsistence expenses. Thus to leave student-aid income in the educational income account would be to double count it as institutional income.

Auxiliary enterprises—Income from the operation of dormitories, cafeterias, and bookstores is almost evenly balanced off by expenditures, leaving the auxiliary accounts as essentially "wash" items in the institutional income and expense accounts.

After these adjustments, 30 percent of the burden of educational costs are borne by the family; 60 percent by the taxpayers; and 10 percent by philanthropy.

AN AGGREGATE VIEW OF COLLEGE FINANCING

Since World War II, the American economy has been devoting an increasing percentage of its total resources to higher education. The share of educational expenditures in the GNP has approximately tripled in the last 15 years, and it is likely to continue to increase until about 1975 and then remain relatively constant in real terms over the next decade as expected total college and university enrollments stabilize. Viewed in the aggregate, the costs of higher education are shared by individuals as "users" (students and their parents), by taxpayers, and by private philanthropy.

Over the last 30 years, the relative contribution by students and their families has declined significantly, and taxpayer support has risen dramatically. Philanthropy's relative share has dropped by one-fifth. However, the most striking fact is that, while dollar outlays for higher education on the part of the average student and family are three times as high today as they were 20 or more years ago, in real terms the average cost of attaining higher education has remained almost unchanged for the last 40 years. This surprising constancy on the part of the average outlay is accounted for by the increasing proportion of students over the years attending low-tuition public institutions and by the rapid growth of student assistance.

CAPITAL COSTS

Between 1957 and 1967 about 51 percent of plant income originated with state and local governments, 14 percent came from federal sources, 23 percent from private gifts and grants, and 12 percent from other institutional income (student fees, investments, and service fees). The effect of adding these annual capital costs is to raise total educational costs by about $1.7 billion for 1970–71, to raise the philanthropic contribution by 1.6 percentage points, and to increase the taxpayer share by 1.3 percentage points. The family share of the total cost burden declines from 30.2 percent to 27.3 percent.

CONSIDERATIONS OF EQUITY

More than two-thirds of all support funds subsidize the "price" of higher education. Because many students from upper-income families attend institutions with tuition charges that are far below costs, these educational subsidies are not distributed as effectively as might be desired if minimizing the financial barrier to attendance were the primary goal.

The Commission believes that both equity considerations and problems of retaining vitality in private higher education call for a serious reexamination at both the state and national levels of the distribution of the burden of college costs. State governments should be primarily concerned with pricing policy in public institutions and the possible partial subsidization of educational costs at private institutions. State governments should also be concerned with assistance to low-income students, even though we believe the federal government should assume the primary responsibility for student aid. Federal policy should concern itself not only with programs to aid the disadvantaged, but also with regional equalization of educational resources and the support of specific areas of study in which a vital national interest is involved.

THE TAX BURDEN

The taxpayer contribution to the support of higher education amounted to approximately $12 billion in 1970–71, or 54 percent of the total monetary outlay. Approximately 60 percent of tax funds supporting higher education come from state revenues, about 8 percent from local government taxes, and 32 percent from federal sources. Local tax structures are almost invariably regressive, depending chiefly upon real estate and sales tax sources. State tax burdens are, on balance, nearly proportional to income above the lowest income brackets. In some states, which rely heavily upon sales and excise levies, taxes have a regressive impact. The federal tax structure relies on the progressive personal income tax for about 60 percent of its revenues, and so its burden is moderately progressive throughout the range of taxable incomes.

Judged merely in relation to estimated tax contributions, the distribution of institutional subsidies appears to contribute to greater social equity. But if one contrasts the distribution of these subsidies with the family income distribution of the college-age population, one might arrive at the contrary conclusion. The lowest income groups have a larger share of college-age dependents (8.4 percent) than the share of higher educational benefits they receive (4.9 percent), while the over $15,000 group receives an estimated 27.6 percent of subsidy benefits for its 16.4 percent of the 18–24 age group.

Families without children make approximately the same tax contribution as those who benefit from public support by sending children to college; families with children not of college age share the burden at any moment in time with families who have children attending college; single taxpayers also contribute to the education of their neighbor's children through approximately the same tax contributions as do families who directly benefit from sending their children to college.

Families contribute taxes throughout their working lives but receive higher education benefits in a relatively concentrated period of time—when their children are of college age. If one looks at the total educational system from kindergarten through college, however, this unevenness in the balance of costs and benefits is sharply diminished, for parents receive substantial benefits from public education at the elementary and secondary school level in their working careers.

FORGONE INCOME

If a student gives up or postpones taking an income-producing job to go to, or return to college, he or she obviously has an additional cost of attending college over and above actual expense outlays. For some students this is a major factor in determining attendance, and it should be considered a cost of attending college.

Forgone income is not a major factor in the short-run calculation of costs for many students from relatively affluent families. In these cases, the alternative to entering college may not be an immediate job, but travel, public service, or the enjoyment of leisure time in the final years of maturing into adulthood. But for students from low-income or from lower-middle-income families, forgone earnings are likely to be viewed as a significant sacrifice. At public community colleges, where tuition tends to be low, forgone earnings are especially significant because young people from low-income families form a larger proportion of students in these colleges than in four-year institutions.

The average family share of the total monetary outlays for higher educational services has declined over the last 40 years from nearly two-thirds to nearly one-third; however, when forgone incomes are included, the family share of the total economic cost has remained relatively constant at about two-thirds of the total. Greatly expanded student-aid programs have diminished the monetary share paid by students and parents, but, simultaneously, incomes forgone by virtue of attending college instead of entering the work force have increased sufficiently to offset this and stabilize the overall private share of the cost burden.

TUITION AS INCOME TO INSTITUTIONS OF HIGHER EDUCATION

Despite increases in tuition charges, tuition income has declined from 34 percent of total educational income prior to World War II to about 30 percent. The reason is that state and local contributions have increased significantly during this period.

When tuition rates increase, there are always internal pressures to increase scholarship funds at least by an absolute amount equal to the tuition increase for students receiving grants-in-aid. Part of the problem facing insitutions of higher education in determining their tuition levels and student-aid policies is that the portion of total scholarship aid over which they have direct control is relatively small. The Commission believes that basic student funding may alter familiar attitudes toward tuition policies. It will be possible for colleges and universities—especially the traditionally low-cost public institutions—to impose somewhat higher tuitions without barring access to low-income students. However, we believe that any changes should be gradual, and that state legislatures should not attempt to "capture" these federal funds by a rapid escalation in public tuition charges.

USER COSTS FOR HIGHER EDUCATION
In periods of relatively stable prices and only modest growth in enrollments, tuition charges in the public and private sectors maintained a reasonably constant relationship to one another. Throughout the 1930s, tuition charges at private colleges were about three times as high as they were in the average public institution. In the immediate postwar period the gap narrowed and only returned to its prewar level in 1953. Over the last 15 years, however, tuition levels have drawn further apart. By 1971–72 average gross tuition and fees of private institutions were 4.9 times those at public institutions. This gap has contributed to the decline in the share of total degree-credit enrollment held by the private colleges and universities.

The Commission has consistently recommended low tuition levels in community colleges, and preferably a lower rate for lower-division students in public senior colleges than for juniors and seniors.

THE BENEFITS OF HIGHER EDUCATION
The benefits of higher education accrue both to individual users and to society as a whole. Throughout the history of advanced education it has been a doorway, although not an exclusive one, to a world of intellectual and aesthetic appreciation, and a path toward advantageous and sometimes privileged occupations. In the modern world of economic industrialization and political democracy, education has come to play a critically important role for society in helping to provide a source of inspiration, renewal, and innovation.

Some of the benefits are quantifiable. Other benefits are more subjective, having to do with the development of the human personality and intellect or with the creation of conditions that enhance the nature and organization of society. In asking "Who benefits from higher education?" each of these effects must be taken into account.

RATES OF RETURN ON THE INVESTMENT IN HUMAN CAPITAL

A human investment calculus can be made by taking the direct costs of education plus forgone income, and then comparing this sum with the discounted income stream that beneficiaries of education can expect throughout their lives. Comparing the average earnings associated with various levels of education in relation to the additional cost of obtaining that unit of education, one can estimate the rate of return for various segments of higher education.

A recent study estimated rates of return to society of 14 percent for one to three years of college, 10 percent for baccalaureate attainment, 7 percent for some graduate education, 8 percent for the master's degree, and 4 percent for the Ph.D. It concluded that the lower rates of return at the graduate level indicated diminishing returns to additional education, but we would suggest that they may reflect increasing components of nonpecuniary income for persons with advanced education.

We belive the attempts of economists to determine rates of return on various types and levels of higher education are useful for making intertemporal, and possibly international, comparisons. We do not believe, however, that such findings are particularly useful in determining whether individuals or societies are underinvesting or overinvesting in higher education. To the extent that higher education represents a value judgment on the part of the individual or a society about the kind of life and society one aspires to, a strict pecuniary calculus can do no more than suggest hazy guidelines for decision making.

USER BENEFITS VERSUS SOCIETAL BENEFITS

Although the benefits that society derives from having a well-educated populace are difficult to define unambiguously, and even more difficult to quantify, it does not follow that they are unimportant. No one would deny the importance in life of love, beauty, and happiness merely because they are impossible to quantify and are perceived somewhat differently by different individuals.

There are many opinions about the optimal pattern of financing higher education, based primarily upon the assumed distribution of personal and societal benefits. At the risk of oversimplification, three positions might be identified to orient the spectrum of opinion:

1   At one extreme are those who believe that the primary benefit of higher education is the enhanced earning power of those who are educated, and that since the "user" reaps the major return on this investment, he or she should pay for it.

2   At the other extreme are those who argue that the societal benefits of higher education are substantial, that anything approaching full-cost pricing would result in a significant underinvestment in higher education,

and that equity is best served by making higher education a free or near-free service to everyone.

3   In between these two points of view is a broad middle ground that might argue that the historical mix of public and private higher education makes a simplistic approach impossible, that the present system has worked reasonably well, and that the present division of the burden of costs is reasonably appropriate in view of the joint private and public benefits that are thought to accrue.

Two other points of view cut across these positions and focus on the intergenerational sharing of costs and benefits. One view holds that the financing of education at all levels is essentially an intergenerational transfer—adults fund the education of the young, whether they do so as parents or taxpayers. The other view is that students ought to be emancipated at the time they enter college, and should be encouraged to make independent decisions about their education. Thus, the user generation should bear the cost and should repay the funds advanced for their education through taxes on their later earnings. In this sense we might envisage each generation paying for its own education by funding the education of the succeeding generation. To the extent that college education raises one's lifetime earnings, it would also raise one's tax contribution in financing the next generation's education.

Considerable interest recently has been shown in income-contingent loan plans, chiefly because they are a form of "user tax," and would place more of the financial burden of paying for higher education on those who directly benefit from it. If it were clear that all the benefits of higher education accrued to the student, then some form of user tax would be a reasonable way of meeting the costs. But if one assumes that the primary benefits accrue to society in general, then a progressive income tax might be deemed the most equitable means of paying for higher education.

In fact, the benefits are neither all personal nor all societal. To the extent that the education and training of students is the essential purpose of colleges and universities, however, it would appear that the benefits of education both to the student and to society are similar in nature and extent whether a student attends a public or a private college or university. Yet, when we view the aggregate accounts, the educational funds of institutions derived from tax revenues are nearly 80 percent in public institutions and only 15 percent in the private colleges and universities. The Commission has urged that greater attention be given by the states to the needs of private colleges and universities, for these institutions serve many of the same public purposes and add to both the strength and diversity of educational offerings available to a state's citizens.

As one looks toward the 1980s, it seems increasingly likely that after the first two years of college, user charges will become a more substantial source of support for higher education. In fact, we believe that after the first two years of college, the emphasis in student-aid programs should gradually shift toward deferred payment or contingent loan plans. We conclude that although the portion of total educational costs borne by the average student and parent should remain approximately what it is today, a gradual redistribution of this burden in a manner that will ensure greater equity within the system will be necessary.

THE LEVEL AND QUALITY OF EDUCATION

College education is not undifferentiated. Most public systems are divided among community colleges, four-year colleges, and universities. And there are significant qualitative differences within and among states in both their private and public sectors. Students are not randomly distributed among institutions, and so attention must be paid to the sorting process in considerations of equity.

To the extent students are sorted out between two-year and four-year colleges on the basis of real ability, or to the extent the presence of a community college enables a capable student to attend college who might otherwise have been unable to do so for other than strictly financial reasons, the lower subsidy per student in the two-year college sector should not be a matter of major concern. This low subsidy is a means of conserving scarce resources to maximize the educational benefit to society. But every attempt should be made to ensure that two-year colleges, particularly in dense urban locations, do not become "educational ghettos" for low-income families who cannot afford to send their children to senior colleges. Adequate financial aid should be available to assist the bright student to attend the college that best fits his or her capabilities. We believe that differentiation by ability, with open doors to higher-level study, will effectively serve both equity and efficiency goals.

GRADUATE AND ADVANCED PROFESSIONAL EDUCATION

The financing of graduate-level education differs from that of undergraduate education. It is commonly much more costly to the institutions, particularly at the doctoral level. Graduate students are older and can no longer expect the same degree of parental support undergraduates receive. Since World War II, federal agencies have played a key role in the direct support of students, training programs, and related research activities.

Two different philosophies have been evident in the support of graduate students over the last two decades. Advanced professional students in such fields as law, medicine, and dentistry have been predominantly self-supporting—until the last several years fellowship funds have been relatively scarce—chiefly on the argument that the private returns to investment in professional education are high and that therefore students could be expected to borrow against future earnings. By contrast, in the arts and sciences a high proportion of doctoral students have been traditionally supported by fellowship funds or assistantships on the theory that societal returns have appeared to be significantly high and private returns relatively low in the academic disciplines.

Today, however, because manpower surpluses are developing in many fields and because the need for additional college teachers seems likely to decline as we move toward enrollment stabilization, the argument on behalf of the societal benefit of continuing high subsidies is weakened. Too great a reliance on manpower assessments in determining public funding, however, tends to overlook the delicate balance of institutional well-being; what may appear to be a rational policy in adjusting manpower flows may exact a penalty on the institutions whose continued vitality is essential to the public interest. The effective long-term stability of universities, which perform valuable services as national laboratories for research and renewal, should be an important consideration in public policy.

POLICY CONSIDERATIONS AND RECOMMENDATIONS

The public share of college costs has been rising. This increase is largely due to the growing proportion of students in low-tuition public institutions, and particularly to the expanding community college sector since World War II. As a steadily rising proportion of the nation's youth completes high school and chooses to go to college, the public costs of higher education grow at a much more rapid rate than does the national income.

POLICY CONSIDERATIONS

The Commission sets forth the following broad considerations for policy:

Access to higher education should be expanded so that, within the total system of higher education in each state, every high school graduate or otherwise qualified person will have an opportunity to pursue postsecondary studies.

Existing patterns of tuition charges should be modified only gradually, and the overall proportion of economic costs met by students and their families should not be substantially increased.

Changes in the future funding pattern of higher education should be made in such a way as to make the distribution of public support more selective—targeted to help those most in need of financial aid. We do not favor abrupt change; rather, we believe that a gradual shift in pricing policy and public support programs should be undertaken over the next decade.

We conclude that the overall division of economic costs that has evolved historically among families, taxpayers, and philanthropy should not be greatly altered.

SHARING THE COST BURDEN

In order to achieve equity in the distribution of the costs of higher education, the Commission recommends:

Over the next few years, the taxpayer share of monetary outlays in higher education should be increased modestly, as student-aid funds expand to assist students from low-income families (p. 104).

States with regressive tax structures should develop more progressive tax systems in the interests of greater equity and adequacy in the financing of education and other public services (p. 105).

The balance of public support for higher education must shift over the coming decade if the goal of universal access is to be achieved, and federal funds should partially relieve the states of added financial burdens resulting from the expected expansion in higher education. We recommend that federal support of higher education should gradually expand to about half of the total governmental contribution by the early 1980s (p. 105).

TUITION POLICY

With respect to tuition policy, we recommend:

Public institutions—and especially the community colleges—should maintain a relatively low-tuition policy for the first two years of higher education. Such tuition should be sufficiently low that no student, after receipt of whatever federal and state support he or she may be eligible for, is barred from access to some public institution by virtue of inadequate finances (p. 108).

Public colleges and universities should carefully study their educational costs per student and consider restructuring their tuition charges at upper-division and graduate levels to more nearly reflect the real differences in the cost of education per student, eventually reaching a general level equal to about one-third of educational costs (p. 109).

Private colleges and universities should increase their tuition charges at a rate that is no more rapid than the increase in per capita disposable income. The rate of increase in tuition should be less pronounced than this, if at all possible (p. 110).

Private colleges and universities also should carefully study their educational costs per student and consider restructuring their tuition charges, so that tuition is relatively low for lower-division students, somewhat higher for upper-division students, and considerably higher for graduate and professional students (p. 110).

BASIC OPPORTUNITY GRANTS

A number of actions should be taken by the federal administration and the Congress as soon as possible. We recommend:

The Basic Opportunity Grant program should be fully funded; this legislation, already on the books, is a major step in providing critically needed assistance to both students and institutions of higher education (p. 111).

In keeping with the principles elaborated under the recommendations above, the

50 percent of cost limitation for Basic Opportunity Grants for lower-division students should be raised, perhaps in steps, to 75 percent over the next few years (p. 111).

The Commission also recommends that in the future the $1,400 ceiling on Basic Opportunity Grants be raised gradually in line with increases in educational and subsistence costs (p. 111).

The federal government should appropriate full funding for state student incentive matching grants. We also recommend that the federal program be modified in the next several years to provide one-fourth of all state awards that meet the criterion of making up, for students with full need, the difference between federal Basic Opportunity Grants and the full cost of attending college in the first two years at public institutions, and a significant fraction of the difference in upper-division years. The awards would be reduced by appropriate amounts for students with less than full need (p. 112).

STATE POLICIES

We recognize that various states have different historic traditions, different current patterns in the balance of public and private higher education, and different constitutional, political, and financial factors that may affect the state's long-term policy goal and the speed with which it is implemented. Nevertheless, we recommend:

State governments should take positive steps toward a gradual narrowing of the tuition differential between public and private institutions in their jurisdictions. This can be accomplished through adjustments in tuition levels at public institutions with an accompanying statewide program of student aid that will minimize the cost to the low-income student, by a program of direct or indirect support to private institutions to enable them to keep tuition charges from rising unduly rapidly, or by a combination of both (p. 114).

LOAN POLICIES

Debates over the issue of tuition levels often confuse two questions: What can one afford to pay? When can one afford to pay? In light of our proposals for institutional pricing policy and public student-aid programs, significant numbers of students will need to borrow—or otherwise defer tuition and subsistence costs—to meet part of their educational needs. The Commission once again urges that:

The federal government charter a National Student Loan Bank as a nonprofit corporation financed by the sale of governmentally guaranteed securities, which would serve all eligible students regardless of need. The fund should be self-sustaining, except for catastrophic risks, and should permit borrowing up to a reasonable limit that would reflect both tuition charges and subsistence costs. Loan repayments should be based upon income currently earned, and up to 40 years should be permitted for repayment. Provision should be made for public subsidy of catastrophic risks (p. 121).

COST ESTIMATES

The estimated cost to the federal government of fully implementing the Basic Opportunity Grant program, with the modification that we have recommended in the cost limitation for lower-division students, ranges from about $1.7 to $2.3 billion, depending on how many "extra" students, who would not otherwise enroll, are induced to attend college because of the existence of the program. The total cost in current dollars might be expected to rise some 60 to 70 percent above these levels by 1980, depending on future increases in enrollment and in costs per FTE student, as well as on the willingness of Congress to adjust the maximum award to cost increases.

The estimated federal cost of the State Student Incentive matching grants, with the federal government contributing 25 percent of the state award, is about $120 million for fiscal year 1973–74. The cost to the states would be about $360 million, but this would represent an increase of only about $170 million over 1969–70 state expenditures for scholarship programs. As in the case of the Basic Opportunity Grants, these costs might be expected to rise 60 to 70 percent by 1980, depending on the behavior of enrollment and of the cost of education.

WHO DOES WHAT?

The adjustments that we envisage over the next ten years to make universal access a reality and to ensure greater equity will require the concerted action of federal and state governments, and of both public and private institutions. Our recommendations for the most part are in keeping with recent trends in the financing of higher education, and would provide an orderly path toward our national objectives.

THE FEDERAL GOVERNMENT

Over the course of the decade the priorities for federal action are:

Full funding of existing student-aid legislation, particularly the Basic Opportunity Grants Program

Increasing the Basic Opportunity Grants Program maximum award gradually in future years to reflect increases in student costs

The extension, as soon as practical, of the ceiling on Basic Opportunity Grants awards to 75 percent of the student cost for lower-division education

Extension of the federal matching provisions to state scholarship programs to 25 percent of expenditure, providing that state programs appropriately supplement federal Basic Opportunity Grant awards

Stabilization of federal support for graduate education at a reasonable long-term level, and the establishment of a comprehensive doctoral fellowship program with selection based upon demonstrated academic ability

Gradual increases in the funding of sponsored research approximately matching the growth in the GNP

Establishment of a national student loan bank to provide long-term student loans with repayment contingent upon income

STATE GOVERNMENTS

Our recommendations encourage the following state actions:

Assume greater responsibility for the well-being of all higher education within their boundaries, recognizing that private colleges and universities provide public benefits similar in nature and magnitude to that of state or municipal colleges and universities

Reform state tax systems to make them more progressive, thus providing greater equity in the financing of education and other public services

Provide adequate support to public institutions to maintain the quality of programs and to accommodate all students who can benefit from postsecondary education and training

Through funding formulae for public institutions, assure that tuition charges for the first two years of postsecondary education are not beyond the means of students from low-income families

Enable students of limited means to attend either public or private colleges by developing a comprehensive student-assistance program that adequately supplements federal programs

Support action to narrow gradually the tuition gap between public and private institutions through tuition adjustments in public colleges and universities

Provide modest direct institutional aid to private colleges and universities, and/or tuition grants that take into account higher tuition at private institutions

COLLEGES AND UNIVERSITIES

We have recommended that public institutions:

Carefully study their educational cost with an eye to adjusting their tuition charges to more nearly reflect real differences in cost by level of education, and particularly to make the charges for the first two years of college as low as is feasible

Cooperate in a gradual change in pricing philosophy which would permit tuition levels to rise gradually to about one-third of educational costs, assuming that federal, state, and institutional student-aid resources keep pace so that students in need of assistance are not barred from access to postsecondary education

Private colleges and universities are urged to:

Consider the advisability of charging differential tuitions by level of education, as in the case of public institutions, and use institutional student-aid funds so as to effectively offset a larger proportion of the costs of attending college for the first two years and assume increasing self-help on the part of students in upper-division and graduate studies

Insofar as is possible in keeping with the maintenance of quality of programs, to limit increases in tuition charges to not more (and preferably less) than the proportionate increase in per capita disposable income

In the case of all institutions, public and private, the Commission urges restraint in expenditures and redoubled efforts to assure the most effective use of resources consistent with the maintenance of quality.

STUDENTS AND PARENTS

Our recommendations do not propose any specific action on the part of students and their families, but the adjustments we envisage in tuition and student-assistance policies will gradually change the perceptions and expectations of individuals as "consumers" of education. Over the period of the next decade or so we anticipate that:

A larger proportion of college students will come from economically disadvantaged backgrounds

They will be enabled to attend college by a significant expansion of federal and state programs of student aid

Tuition charges in public institutions will rise more rapidly than in the past

Tuition charges in private institutions will rise at about the rate of increase in per capita disposable income (somewhat more slowly than in the recent past)

Students, and their parents, who can afford to pay will have to shoulder a larger proportion of educational costs, but low-income students will be enabled to meet subsistence as well as tuition costs

The principle of increasing self-help as one progresses through college will become more common, and beyond the lower-division years students may have to depend somewhat more heavily upon loan financing

Thus the net effect of our recommendations in the longer run is to maintain the proportion of total monetary outlays on higher education borne by students and their families at about one-third (two-thirds of total economic costs, including forgone incomes), but to aid students from low-income backgrounds by requiring a proportionate increase in the share borne by those from more affluent families. In addition, this effect has the added advantage of promoting an environment in which the private college or university has a better chance to achieve financial stability.

In conclusion, several cautionary notes concering implementation of our recommendations should be reiterated:

1   We have indicated the direction in which we believe public policy should move during the decade, but caution should be observed in the speed with which the shift in the funding patterns is effected.

2   Tuition increases in the public sector must be accompanied by compensating increases in student-aid and loan funds or ground will be lost in assuring universal access.

3   State policy must keep in step with federal action in funding basic student-aid programs.

4   Our recommendations, while perhaps adequate to the present and near future, may need further modification in light of the evolving social and legal milieu.

We have proposed a series of steps both for federal and state action that we believe will serve the nation's educational needs well in the 1970s and into the 1980s. Building on the start already made, a more equitable and more sensible system of financing higher education can be created to make better connections between those who benefit and those who pay.

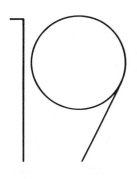

CONTINUITY AND DIS-CONTINUITY

19

HIGHER EDUCATION AND THE SCHOOLS (AUGUST 1973)

A majority of high school students, perhaps two out of three, enter some form of postsecondary education. New constituencies of postsecondary students come from the lower academic ranks of high school classes, older persons, women, part-time students, and minorities. At the same time, colleges become a smaller fraction of postsecondary education, as "further education" grows more rapidly in a whole series of institutions. Thus, the high schools become *one* stage in the educational process and not the *final* stage for most persons. They must now prepare their students for many alternative channels of postsecondary education, not college alone.

A CENTURY OF ACCOMMODATION: 1870–1970
Schools and colleges have often worked together to make adjustments to changing enrollments during the past century. The strains and tensions between them have never disappeared, largely because each sector has been engaged with its own problems and each has been somewhat out of phase with the other. There has been a discontinuity.

THE SEARCH FOR A SYSTEM, 1870 TO 1910
The rise of public secondary education after the Civil War triggered new problems in school-college relations. Because there were more secondary school students and more secondary schools than in previous times, it became necessary for colleges to systematize admissions (which in turn had curriculum implications for the schools), and to produce more teachers for secondary education.

In the nineteenth century, colleges developed and administered their own entrance examinations. These course-by-course examinations required preparation in particular texts. Since these examinations were by no means uniform from college to college, the schools had to provide college preparation in courses that were specifically geared to the examination requirements of dozens of colleges. Schools soon focused their attention on college preparatory curricula and standards for them that would be satisfactory to the colleges.

The definition of content for college preparatory courses required machinery for evaluation and enforcement, and two means were developed: accreditation and examination. These two approaches to systematic relationships between higher education and the schools—accreditation and examination—had some similar features. Both encouraged communication between schools and colleges, and both relieved the schools of conflicting pressures from idiosyncratic practices of individual universities. Both promoted an increasing geographic mobility among college-bound students by promulgating standards that were recognized beyond the boundaries of a single state. The two approaches also had one contrasting feature. The accreditation approach placed much of the responsibility for college admission on the school. As long as it remained accredited, a school could usually count on the admission of the students it recommended to college. The examination approach, on the other hand, introduced an outside appraisal of a student's performance that was independent of the school's judgment.

By 1910, 45 percent of the students who completed high school went on to college. The curriculum they had pursued in high school reflected a traditional view of education, and this view was firmly implanted in the schools by a systematized examining and accrediting mechanism dominated by the colleges.

THE SCHOOLS' RESPONSE TO INDUSTRIAL AMERICA, 1910 TO 1940
Only 15 percent of American youth were enrolled in secondary schools in 1910; by 1940 the figure was 75 percent. During this period, the American public high school became an institution serving the vast majority of American youth. College enrollments jumped from 4 percent of the college-age group in 1910 to 15 percent in 1940. Thus, it was not until 1940 that the colleges enrolled the same proportion of the age group as the high schools had enrolled in 1910. In short, school and college had moved out of phase with each other. Educators at both levels faced different sorts of problems and found communications and joint activity increasingly difficult.

During this era, the schools were transformed from institutions concerned with college preparation for the few to institutions concerned with terminal education for the many.

The march of industrialism, the growth of labor unions, the displacement of rural farm youth to the city, the need for skilled manpower to operate machines, the child-labor movement, the spread of compulsory school attendance laws—all this would have transformed secondary education in any case. Progressive education provided the direction.

Progressivism had many elements:

■ The drive for vocational education found significant expression in the passage of far-reaching federal legislation in 1917.

■ Social reform was directed at urban problems and lent support to the child-labor movement.

■ The intellectual foundations for the transformation of the secondary school were found in newly emerging fields in the social sciences.

■ The emerging science of psychological measurement led to the development of tests to measure mental capacity.

As the era of mass terminal education in secondary schools came to a close in 1940, teacher education enrolled more students than any other occupational or professional training program at the undergraduate level. Then, as now, roughly one-third of all bachelor's degrees in the United States went to graduates prepared to enter teaching careers.

MASS HIGHER EDUCATION, 1940 TO 1970

Higher education enrolled 15 percent of the college-age group in 1940 and 48 percent by 1970. The 30-year period before 1940 belonged to the schools; the next era was that of the colleges. They were forced to face the implications of mass higher education.

College enrollments began to grow immediately after World War II as veterans with GI Bill financial benefits flooded the campuses. Their success was one more step toward the democratization and extension of educational opportunity.

Meanwhile, progressive education came apart after World War II and rapidly disappeared as an organized movement. Much that had been advocated during the previous era had long since been incorporated into the schools; much that the early progressives had stood for was distorted and opened to caricature; and a cold-war psychology had gripped the nation. Academic intellectuals were saying that the schools had gone soft during the previous era and that, in their concern for terminal education, they were neglecting academically talented students. The first Sputnik in 1957 confirmed a suspicion that the Russians were providing better education, and the secondary schools of America found themselves barraged with criticism.

Most of the publicity, if not most of the students, went to the prestigious private colleges where "selective" admissions meant four or five qualified applicants for every available space. In many instances this competition strengthened the high school curriculum. But some students, once they reached college, found themselves duplicating work that they had already covered in high school, and were often taught by young graduate students who sometimes compared badly with high school teachers.

But in the mid-1960s dramatic new concerns arose at both school and college. And many of the problems since have been related in one way or another to curricular and admissions problems concerning minority youth. It is ironic that this should be the case after a century of progress toward what now appears to be a realizable goal—universal access to higher education.

UNIVERSAL ACCESS TO HIGHER EDUCATION

The Carnegie Commission has said that access to higher education should be expanded so that every high school graduate or otherwise qualified person would have an opportunity to attend college. There are two conditions. First, universal access does not mean universal attendance. Many high school graduates will not want to attend college, and others would not benefit sufficiently to justify their time and expense. Second, universal access does not mean open-admissions policies at all institutions. The Commission does believe that, within each state system of higher education, community colleges should follow open-enrollment policies and should, therefore, play a crucial role in providing universal access.

FREE-ACCESS INSTITUTIONS

In 1968, 45 percent of all first-time students were enrolled in 789 free-access colleges. These institutions charged no more than $400 tuition (5 percent of the United States median family income in 1967) and enrolled at least one-third of their students from the bottom half of their high school graduating class. Most were public two-year colleges. This supports the credibility of the recommendation that the community college should be the means by which universal access to higher education in the United States is achieved.

RESTRICTED-ACCESS INSTITUTIONS

Restricted access means high tuition or selective admissions, most often both. Of the first-time students in 1968, 55 percent were enrolled in 1,807 restricted-access institutions. Whereas the truly open-door college accepts all high school graduates (level 1) and the nonselective college generally requires a C average and accepts all but some in the bottom quarter of their high school class (level 2), the lowest level selective institution (level 3) generally requires about a C+ average and takes students from the top 50 percent of their graduating class. In short, there is an arbitrary distinction between the two free-access levels and the lowest level of the restricted-access colleges.

Both public and private four-year colleges moved in the same direction between 1958 and 1968: decreasing accessibility. There were two reasons. First was the academic revolution that produced a campus ethos in which academic excellence, research, and the pursuit of knowledge tended to replace older collegiate values. In recent years this ethos has also reached traditionally open-access public institutions. The second explanation has been, until recently, the seller's market in higher education. During the 1960s, the supply of college spaces tended to fall behind the demand for them. In addition, increased costs meant higher tuition at both public and private colleges and tended to restrict access even further.

Now the supply-demand relationship is reversing itself. The reasons are many: a restricted job market, high tuition costs, changing lifestyles, and the end of the draft. Colleges that had more applicants than spaces in the 1960s now find themselves with empty dormitory beds.

But many institutions are also looking toward new constituencies—in particular, the large adult population, including veterans, and transfers from two-year colleges. Other institutions are admitting larger numbers of students after their junior year of high school. This search for new constituencies is likely, in the long run, to be more useful to the college and to society than an increased competition through recruitment from a smaller pool of senior high school students.

THE DOCTOR OF ARTS DEGREE AND A NEW DEFINITION OF QUALITY
Most colleges in the United States are mildly selective in admissions, and 45 percent of all freshmen attend colleges that enroll at least one-third of their students from the bottom half of their high school graduating class. It is therefore questionable whether traditional Ph.D. training, which is essentially training for a career in research, is appropriate for many, if not most, college teaching jobs. The Carnegie Commission has recommended experimentation with the doctor of arts degree as a new teaching degree for college teachers.

The quality of an institution should be determined by what it does for the students it enrolls, not by the characteristics of its entering students or by the record of its graduates. Simple input or output measures are not sufficient.

The Commission recommends:

Both public and private institutions should give careful attention to admissions policies suitable to an era characterized by universal access to the total system of higher education and by a no-growth enrollment trend. Public agencies, including coordinating councils and state planning commissions, should determine general policies on student admissions within state systems, including policies with respect to number of places, equality of access by race, age, and sex, and the level of academic admissibility among types of institutions. Decisions on individual students should be left to each campus (p. 39).

Colleges should develop programs to serve new constituencies, especially adults and transfers from two-year colleges (p. 40).

To help maintain differentiation of function and to reduce excessive tension within state systems, two steps should be taken: (1) There should be experimentation on a large scale with doctor of arts degrees as a teaching alternative to the research Ph.D. and (2) there should be a redefinition of institutional quality to focus upon the value added by the college experience itself (p. 40).

Testing agencies through new testing techniques should aid colleges in developing appropriate criteria and measures of value added to reflect a diversity of institutional objectives and outcomes (p. 40).

REFORM IN THE ADMISSIONS PROCESS
Experimentation and new reform are called for to improve the mechanisms by which universal access to higher education will be achieved.

ADMISSIONS REQUIREMENTS

College programs must be sufficiently diverse to meet student needs. In turn, requirements for admission to different kinds of colleges serving different kinds of students will vary. This means that there can no longer be an agreed-upon "college preparatory curriculum."

Colleges should review their admissions requirements and, except for competence in the basic skills of reading, writing, and arithmetic, should not require or suggest particular courses of study at the secondary level unless such requirements or suggestions are tied explicitly to the colleges' own degree requirements, or to those of the system of which they are a part (p. 43).

High school students should be encouraged to study mathematics sequentially from grades 9 to 12 in order to keep options open to college programs, jobs, and careers requiring background in mathematics (p. 43).

TESTING

Today, tests are widely attacked because they are said to be unfair to minority youth, to measure relatively narrow aspects of human potential, to penalize creativity, and to restrict the curricula at both schools and colleges. Other criticisms, particularly of the College Board tests, are that they cost too much, take too much time, create extreme anxiety in students, and that colleges pay too much attention to test score results despite the efforts of testing agencies to play down their importance.

Colleges should closely examine their admissions policies with respect to sex, race, and age. They should then be certain that their admissions practices implement those policies that relate to social justice in higher education. Separate prediction equations for men and women, minority students, and adults should be developed and, where feasible, differential prediction by general field of study should be used (p. 46).

Testing agencies should initiate the development of a family of admissions and placement tests, with special versions prepared for individuals with particular educational and career aspirations (p. 46).

COUNSELING AND EXPERIMENTATION

At the school level, guidance services have been notoriously weak. There have been three areas of weakness: insufficient numbers of high school counselors, insufficient training for counselors, and a lack of easily accessible and useful materials for the students.

Colleges must share the blame for the lack of good guidance materials. Often more concerned with image than reality, college brochures and admissions materials are insufficiently descriptive of the college, its programs, faculty, and students. College counseling at the high school level cannot improve without a corresponding improvement in the quality of information provided by colleges.

A new information system should not be dependent upon a one-to-one relationship between student and counselor. A variety of resources—

counselors, community-based resource people, written materials, self-administered assessment batteries—should be available so that students can begin early in their secondary school careers to formulate ideas about their own potentialities and future. The Commission recommends:

College admissions officers should be appointed with great care because their work is intimately tied to the primary mission of the institution. If possible, they should have both faculty status and a prominent place in the administrative hierarchy (p. 49).

Schools, colleges, and testing agencies should work together in developing a complete and coherent information system that enables sound decision-making by both students and colleges. Colleges should prepare frank, accurate, and complete descriptive materials, so that students will know as much about colleges as the colleges know about students (p. 49).

Students in elementary and high school should be counseled through a variety of resources—counselors, written materials, community-based people, as well as college students—minority students and women, in particular (p. 49).

In those areas where multiple college applications are a problem, clearinghouse operations utilizing single application forms, transcripts, and school report forms should be developed. Concern for the small amount of college autonomy involved should be less important than better service to students (p. 52).

Experimentation with college admissions practices should be encouraged. In particular, more experimentation is needed to determine the quality of testing as a basis for admission and placement, the importance of student motivation and life experience as indicators of promise, and the feasibility of deferred admissions as a means of providing educational flexibility for students (p. 52).

IMPROVEMENT IN POSTSECONDARY EDUCATION
In a broad prospective, American high school students appear to compare favorably with their counterparts in other countries. For example, the brightest American students rank first in reading comprehension when compared to the brightest students elsewhere.

THE COMPREHENSIVE HIGH SCHOOL
18,000 comprehensive public senior high schools enroll roughly 85 percent of the American youth; the balance are enrolled in independent and parochial high schools. In a comprehensive high school, students are drawn from an entire community and thereby reflect diverse and heterogeneous abilities, backgrounds, and interests; its education programs are sufficiently diverse to serve the needs of the heterogeneous student body. The typical American public high school sets out to accomplish three specific goals:

1   To provide a sound general education for all future citizens regardless of status or vocation

2   To provide vocational programs leading to skills marketable at the time of graduation from grade 12

3   To provide advanced academic electives for those students continuing their education at colleges and universities

BIG-CITY SCHOOLS

Some urban school systems are threatened by the necessity to shut down for lack of funds. Teachers unions do, in fact, close urban schools from time to time. Racial strife over integration makes a mockery of education in citizenship. Violence and drug abuse in inner-city schools reflects the despair of poverty outside the schools.

If the schools of the large cities do nothing more, they must develop the basic skills in their students. Large numbers of students receive high school diplomas who can barely read and write; equally large numbers drop out of school before graduation.

The second most noticeable failure within urban schools is the lack of adequate vocational training. In some large cities vocational training is conducted solely in separate vocational high schools. In too many instances, students without sufficient motivation and ability to carry rigorous programs in academic high schools are forced into watered-down general academic programs with little value.

WEALTHY SUBURBAN SCHOOLS

In wealthy suburban high schools many affluent students are turned off by school. The drug culture, a decline in interest in extracurricular activities and "school spirit," anti-intellectualism among many of the brightest students, general ennui and apathy, a turning inward with seeming reluctance or inability to communicate—these are disturbing symptoms of a deep malaise found in some of the affluent suburban high schools.

The Commission recommends pluralistic approaches to common ends:

Local school boards, with community and professional assistance, should identify the overall ends and objectives of the public schools, deliberately encourage experimentation with a diversity of means to those objectives, and insist upon accountability from teachers and administrators (p. 64).

Improvement of the nation's schools is the first educational priority in the nation; and within the schools, improvement in the basic skills, especially in large city schools, is the first priority. Colleges and universities should recognize this fact and help to provide the resources, incentives, and rewards for faculty members who commit themselves to this task (p. 67).

Each state should undertake a review and analysis of the general education requirements for graduation from high school. Objectives should be clearly established and new means to these objectives should be explored, including the possibility that students can "test out" of graduation requirements. In addition, the relationship of general education at the high school to that at the college level, especially in grades 13 and 14, should be explored with a view toward ways that the general education requirements at both levels might be linked together to provide continuity and to prevent wasteful overlap and duplication. School and college faculty members should work together on this set of problems under the sponsorship of local, state, and national organizations such as the College Board and professional associations. More of the responsibility for general education should be assumed by the high schools (pp. 69–70).

Each state through its coordinating mechanisms should study carefully and define the roles of public high schools, area vocational schools, community colleges, and proprietary schools with respect to vocational and technical programs (p. 71).

Curriculum development in the humanities and social studies has lagged behind mathematics and science. Schools and colleges, together with funding agencies, should foster new programs and approaches (p. 73).

The Carnegie Commission recommends a major national study of the entire set of relationships that exist between school systems, state bureaucracies, school and college teachers, and the educational materials industry in the production and selection of materials. The purpose of the study would be to seek ways to improve the system by which curricular materials are chosen, created, and marketed. Such a study should shed light as well upon the difficulties and problems associated with the widespread adoption of educational technology (p. 74).

Schools and colleges alike should remember that experimentation carries with it the price of accountability. No new programs at either level should be initiated without clear criteria for evaluation (p. 77).

NEW STRUCTURAL PATTERNS

Experimentation with the structure of education, especially at the interface of school and college, might well reduce much of the present harmful discontinuity that exists. The intent of structural change is not to substitute one lockstep for another; it is to provide options, to enable the student to find the right program at the right time. Such experimentation should include:

■ Establishing middle colleges providing the last two years of high school and the first two years of college

■ Commencing school at age four

■ Reducing the current 13-year K through 12 sequence to 12 years while maintaining quality

■ Maintaining the present K through 12 sequence but aiming, by high school graduation, at providing most students a curriculum that a good college would consider the equivalent of its lower-division general education program

■ Enabling high school students to test out of graduation requirements in order to go to college early or to stop out for a year of work or service

■ Designing three-year bachelor's degree programs

■ Allowing bright students to take either an overload of courses throughout the normal academic year or to accelerate by taking summer school courses

- Granting college credit for the senior year at high school

- Increasing the numbers of schools and colleges that admit high school students at the end of grade 10 or grade 11

The Commission recommends:

Schools and colleges should experiment with different structural models designed to provide a student with options that will enable him to find the right program at the right time. Such experimentation challenges the current structure and its traditional break between school and college at the end of grade 12. Liberal arts colleges should consider enrolling students at grade 11 and awarding the bachelor's degree after grade 14 or 15; there should be experimentation with public education at age 4; some school systems should eliminate a year from the K through 12 sequence; other school systems should stress general education equivalent to that found at good colleges; students should be able to "test out" of high school graduation requirements; there should be expanded programs of college credit for the senior year of high school, concurrent enrollment of students in school and college, and early admission to college; options other than college attendance should be made available for high school graduates (p. 83).

THE EDUCATION OF SCHOOL TEACHERS AND ADMINISTRATORS

Teacher education is the largest single enterprise within American higher education. More than 80 percent of all four-year colleges and universities prepare teachers, and more than one-third of all bachelor's degrees each year go to men and women prepared as either elementary or secondary school teachers. The education of teachers must be recognized as a responsibility of the whole university in order to take their needs into account in the design of arts and science courses.

In the last 10 years, far more attention has been paid in education literature to the training of school teachers than to that of school administrators. In the long run, our ability to select effective and sensitive school administrators will be enhanced by the availability of performance criteria and by further research on administrator effectiveness.

The Commission recommends:

At present too many white, middle-class teachers are prepared in essentially nonspecific ways for general purpose assignments. The problems of the large urban schools, small rural schools, bilingual-bicultural schools, and wealthy suburban school districts require teachers trained for these separate constituencies. University faculties of arts and sciences and education should concentrate more upon training teachers for different kinds of schools. Because of the variety of tasks there can be no single model of a teacher-training program, and the National Council for the Accreditation of Teacher Education and state accrediting associations should encourage diversity. A common element in all preservice programs should be an emphasis upon bringing theory and practice together in clinical settings (p. 96).

Greater emphasis should be placed on inservice education of a different kind from that traditionally available. Local teacher centers that focus on teachers' problems and that utilize the resources of the university should be encouraged and their effects carefully evaluated (p. 96).

Special efforts should be made to recruit able administrators from outside the field as well as members of minority groups and women into the profession of school administration (pp. 99–100).

Given the diversity of school districts, there can be no single model of an administrator training program. Common elements in all programs should be the use of the resources of the whole university and experimentation with different ways of combining theory and practice in clinical settings (p. 100).

Greater emphasis should be placed on inservice training as a way of keeping administrators up-to-date and as a vehicle for school improvement (p. 100).

Universities, in conjunction with state school boards associations, should experiment with various means of providing school board members with information on crucial issues (p. 100).

CONCLUSION

The two worlds of school and college tend to be quite different. Even today, school teachers distrust the academic elitism of the colleges, and college teachers are often disdainful of anti-intellectualism in the schools. School teachers and administrators are activists and practical problem-solvers on a day-to-day basis; university faculty members like to study problems over time.

Colleges and universities should encourage school-college collaboration on substantive matters through promotion and reward policies that recognize the importance of such activities (p. 103).

Though often different in temperament, training, and style, school and college teachers and administrators must work together to reduce many of the present undesirable discontinuities in the relationships between school and college (p. 108).

There are at least five common interests that call for closer school-college ties in the era ahead. First is the need to make equality of educational opportunity a reality. Second is the challenge to traditional curricula and structure at both levels. Third is the necessity for a response to fairly widespread public disenchantment with education at both levels. This disenchantment is tied to the fourth common interest, namely, the need to maximize the use of limited financial resources. And, fifth, the unity of educational welfare must be recognized.

Activities having to do with the substantive matters discussed in this report should be initiated by five different agencies: state education offices, educational institutions, testing agencies, and the federal government (p. 108).

OPPORTUNI-TIES FOR WOMEN IN HIGHER EDUCATION

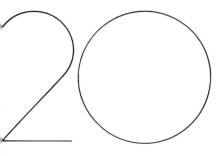

THEIR CURRENT PARTICIPATION, PROSPECTS FOR THE FUTURE, AND RECOMMENDATIONS FOR ACTION (SEPTEMBER 1973)

This report is concerned with only one aspect of the women's movement: equality of opportunity for participation of women in higher education. But this is an extremely important aspect of the movement because women want an equal opportunity to benefit from the intellectual and cultural experience of higher education, whatever their future roles in life.

Relatively few women are in the higher ranks of university and college faculties. This suggests a lack of equal opportunity for women scholars and a loss of talent to society.

THE MANY ROLES OF COLLEGE-EDUCATED WOMEN

Some recent studies are beginning to shed light on relationships between women's education and their roles as wives, mothers, and participants in community activities.

LABOR FORCE PARTICIPATION

In the past, it has sometimes been argued that college education, and particularly graduate and professional education, for women is a poor social investment, because women who marry are relatively unlikely to participate in the labor force. The argument has been used especially frequently in relation to medical education and to graduate education in the natural sciences, which are costly and heavily subsidized. But the social benefits of college education for women are by no means confined to their productivity in the labor force and, in any case, graduates of women's colleges and women with advanced degrees tend to have relatively high rates of labor force participation.

MALE AND FEMALE PROFESSIONS

In the United States, college-educated women and men are distributed very differently among the professions. Women are overwhelmingly predominant in nursing. They also comprise a substantial majority of elementary and secondary school teachers—more so at the elementary than at the secondary level. On the other hand, as is well known, there have tended to be relatively few women in medicine, dentistry, law, the ministry, engineering, the natural sciences, business administration, and economics. Detailed occupational data from the 1970 census, however, show pronounced increases in the number of women in traditionally male professions.

WOMEN ENTERING HIGHER EDUCATION

Throughout the present century, women have been more likely to graduate from high school and less likely to enter college than men in the same age group. Some of the reasons for lower college enrollment among women are:

■ Low socioeconomic status has tended to be more of a barrier to enroll-ment in college for women than for men.

■ Almost from the moment of birth, boys and girls are subject to a wide variety of cultural influences that tend to prepare them for differentiated roles in life.

■ Beginning at about the ninth grade, students are given vocational aptitude tests, but in some cases these test differ for the two sexes.

DISCRIMINATION IN ADMISSIONS?

The proportion of students entering higher education who are women is now nearly 50 percent, but the proportion of undergraduates who are women varies widely in different types of institutions.

Under Title IX of the Education Amendments of 1972, sex discrimina-tion is prohibited in the admission of students to institutions of higher education receiving federal financial assistance, but the provision does not apply to undergraduate education in private institutions. There is also an exception for undergraduate education in public institutions that have, from their establishment, admitted students of only one sex.

The Commission believes that, in general, colleges and universities should use the same standards in admitting men and women. In fact, there is a case for using a lower cutoff point for women on high school grades and test scores than for men.

The Commission recommends:

The first priority in the nation's commitment to equal educational opportunity for women should be placed on changing policies in preelementary, elementary, and secondary school programs that tend to deter women from aspiring to equality with men in their career goals. This will require vigorous pursuit of appropriate policies by state and local boards of education and implementation by school ad-ministrators, teachers, and counselors (p. 56).

There should be no discrimination on the basis of sex in the use of either high school grades or test scores as admissions criteria (p. 57).

Efforts to eliminate sex bias from vocational interest questionnaires should be encouraged, as should research designed to achieve a more adequate under-standing of similarities and differences in patterns of vocational choices among men and women (p. 57).

Policies that prevent part-time study or that discriminate against admission of adults desirous of continuing their education should be liberalized to permit en-rollment of qualified mature men and women whose education has been inter-rupted because of family responsibilities or for other reasons. High school or college records should not be ruled inapplicable as evidence of eligibility for ad-mission simply because the records were acquired some years earlier (p. 57).

WOMEN AS UNDERGRADUATES

Women have slightly higher dropout rates than men, but those who stay in college receive their bachelor's degrees more quickly. In view of the role played by marriage and childbearing in interrupting the progress of women in higher education, policy changes that make it possible for a student to earn a bachelor's degree in less than four years seem particularly desirable for women.

CHOICES OF FIELDS

The fields women have traditionally chosen as majors in college are closely related to the types of professional jobs in which women have been represented in large proportions. To some degree, their choices, especially their preferences for the humanities and the arts, have also reflected the cultural interests of women who have expected to devote themselves to being wives and mothers after college. They have been represented in larger proportions in such fields as education, home economics, library science, social work, and nursing.

Especially important in colleges and universities are policies that encourage women to enter fields that have been regarded as traditionally male. Such changes are especially needed in leading research universities. Women should also be encouraged to study languages like Russian and Japanese, and not only English or French. In addition, there is a current demand for bilingual teachers who know Spanish and English. Colleges and universities should adjust their resources to changing student choices of fields in the next few years while enrollment continues to grow, for it will be much more difficult to achieve flexibility in this respect as enrollment levels off in the late 1970s and early 1980s.

We believe that women should have the opportunity to develop their mental capacities and utilize their abilities in whatever field of study is of greatest interest to them.

WOMEN'S COLLEGES

Women's colleges have played a unique role in the development of higher education for women. Many of them were established when many private colleges and universities, and some public institutions, were exclusively male. Over the decades, however, coeducational institutions came to be overwhelmingly predominant in higher education.

An emerging problem for women's colleges is the absence from their curricula of such subjects as business administration and engineering. Whether students should be encouraged to major in business administration at the undergraduate stage is questionable, but courses like accounting may usefully be taken by undergraduate economics majors. Women's colleges would be well advised to enter into arrangements, whenever possible, with neighboring male or coeducational institutions to enable their students to enroll in accounting courses or to undertake an engineering program rather than attempting to develop their own programs in these fields.

WOMEN'S STUDIES

One of the most decisive effects of the women's movement in higher education has been the growth of women's studies. But only a small minority of women's courses appear to be concerned with the women's movement as such. Most of them are oriented to a particular discipline: for example, women in history, women in literature, the psychology of women, women in the economy, and women's legal rights.

For the present, women's courses and women's study programs serve an important purpose. However, in the longer run women's courses should be presented within relevant existing departments, and women's undergraduate study programs should take the form of interdisciplinary group majors or elective group course selections under the auspices of existing departments. The same general principles should apply in relation to graduate courses.

Not only should colleges and universities take immediate steps to strengthen occupational counseling programs generally in this era of a changing job market for college graduates, but they should also take special steps to strengthen career counseling programs for women. Counselors should be trained to discard outmoded concepts of male and female careers and to encourage women in their abilities and aspirations (p. 79).

Colleges and universities have a responsibility to develop policies specifically designed to bring about changes in the attitude of administrators and faculty members, where these have been antagonistic to enrollment of women in traditionally male fields (p. 79).

Because of the evidence that many women enter college with inadequate mathematical training, special provision should be made to ensure that women desiring to major in fields calling for extensive use of mathematics are encouraged to make up this deficiency in order to enter the fields of their choice (p. 79).

Opportunities for women to participate in competitive sports should be strongly encouraged (p. 79).

The movement to introduce courses on women and interdisciplinary women's study programs should be encouraged by institutions of higher education, at least on a transitional basis, but these courses and programs should be organized within existing disciplines and not under separate departments of women's studies (pp. 79–80).

WOMEN IN GRADUATE AND PROFESSIONAL SCHOOLS

Women form a somewhat smaller proportion of graduate than of undergraduate students, although enrollment rates of women in graduate programs have been rising rapidly. A major factor explaining the lower proportion of women in graduate than in undergraduate education is that, as women reach the age group in which students tend to enter graduate school, 22 to 24, the proportion who are married increases, as does the proportion who have children.

MARITAL STATUS AND AGE

Women in graduate school are more likely to be single (41 percent) than men (31 percent), reflecting the problems married women encounter in attending graduate school, especially if they have children. Although the median age of both male and female graduate students was between 26 and 27, they differed markedly in age distribution. The most striking and significant difference was that relatively large proportions of both the married and divorced women were aged 35 and older.

CHOICE OF FIELDS

A very large proportion of women in graduate school are enrolled in such fields as education, library science, and social welfare, in which relatively few students go on for a doctor's degree. In 1970, 53 percent of the master's degrees were awarded to women in the field of education. Another 13 percent were in "other social sciences" (chiefly social welfare) and in library science. The sizable proportion (about 17 percent) in arts and humanities probably included many women who were planning to go into secondary education and did not expect to go on for doctor's degrees.

RETENTION RATES AND RELATIVE ABILITY

Women are more likely to drop out of graduate school than are men. Even among the students who were rated "excellent" by their professors, and who presumably would have qualified for second year support, dropout rates were considerably higher for women than for men. One suspects that many of these women dropped out because of marriage and childbearing, but the relevant data on this point are not available.

Most of the available evidence suggests that women who enter graduate school are able and that women who receive the doctorate are more able, on the average, than men who receive the doctorate. We have noted that women receive higher grades in college than men. Among the graduate students questioned in the Carnegie Commission Survey of Faculty and Student Opinion, 1969, about 24 percent of the women, as compared with 17 percent of the men, reported an undergraduate grade point average of A. Only 11 percent of the women, as contrasted with 22 percent of the men, reported undergraduate averages of C or less.

IS THERE DISCRIMINATION?

Discrimination may be a more serious problem at the graduate than at the undergraduate level, but it is difficult to document.

Probably the most important factors tending to discriminate against women in admission to graduate study are a variety of rules and informal policies discouraging admission of students who wish to study on a part-time basis. Faced with a choice between a married woman planning to study part-time and a student who plans full-time graduate work, a department is highly likely to favor the full-time student.

There should be no discrimination on the basis of sex or marital status in admitting students to graduate and professional schools (p. 106).

Departments and schools should be required to maintain complete records on all applicants for admission to graduate and professional education and to make these records available to administrative officers on request. They should also be required to maintain records indicating that, in any programs designed to recruit able graduate students, equal efforts have been made to recruit women as well as men, for example, through letters or circulars addressed to departments in women's colleges as well as to those in male and coeducational institutions (p. 106).

Rules and policies that discriminate against the part-time graduate or professional student should allow for exceptions to accommodate men or women whose family circumstances require them to study on a part-time basis. Any limitation on the total number of graduate or professional students admitted by departments or schools and by the institution as a whole should be applied on a full-time equivalent rather than on a head-count basis (p. 106).

Policies requiring students to obtain advanced degrees within a certain number of years should allow for a limited extension of the period for those graduate students whose family circumstances require them to study on a part-time basis (p. 106).

There should be no discrimination on the basis of sex or marital status in appointing teaching or research assistants or in awarding fellowships. Furthermore, part-time graduate and professional students should not be barred from eligibility for fellowships. In addition, there should be no antinepotism rules in connection with these appointments or awards (p. 106).

A woman desiring to enter graduate or professional school after some years away from higher education, and generally meeting departmental standards for admission (e.g., in her undergraduate grade-point average), should be given an opportunity to make up for her inability to meet any special requirements, such as specific mathematical requirements. Under no circumstances should she be denied admission because her undergraduate education occurred some years earlier (p. 107).

Positive attitudes on the part of faculty members toward the serious pursuit of graduate study and research by women are greatly needed. College and university administrations should assume responsibility for adoption of policies that will encourage positive, rather than negative, attitudes of faculty members in all fields (p. 107).

WOMEN AS FACULTY MEMBERS AND ACADEMIC ADMINISTRATORS
Women represented only 27 percent of college faculty members in 1971–72. However, there is a tendency for ratios of women to men to be much smaller in universities, and especially in highly research-oriented universities, than in other types of institutions. And, during the decade of the most explosive growth in the history of higher education—the 1960s —women lost ground as a percentage of members of regular faculty ranks

in four-year institutions, especially at the associate professor level, and gained ground only at the instructor level.

THEIR RELATIVE SALARIES

The pattern of lower salaries of women faculty members requires complex analysis to determine whether the salary differences suggest discrimination against women or are explained by relatively objective factors, such as the smaller percentage of women faculty who have Ph.D.'s.

IS THERE DISCRIMINATION?

In virtually all public institutions and in many private institutions that have formal salary structures, discrimination does not take the form of paying a woman a lower salary than a man when she is in the same step of the same rank, but it does take the form of not moving her up through the steps and ranks as quickly.

It is doubtful that this discrimination results from deliberate decisions of college and university administrators. Instead it stems from myriads of individual decisions within departments and schools that do the actual recruiting and selecting of faculty members (subject to subsequent administration approval) and that initiate recommendations for merit increases and promotions.

But college and university administrations have been guilty of indifference to the problem. Now, under pressure from the federal government and from women's committees, institutions are developing affirmative action policies that embody intensive scrutiny of departmental procedures.

WOMEN IN ADMINISTRATION

Women are practically nonexistent in top academic administrative positions, although the Catholic women's colleges are an exception. In the latter part of 1971, virtually no four-year coeducational institution was headed by a women. Among the nonsectarian women's colleges there were only eight female presidents.

THE PROSPECTS

As the rate of increase of enrollments in higher education declines in the 1970s, it will become increasingly difficult to correct sexual and social imbalances on college and university faculties.

But it is exceedingly important for universities and colleges to take vigorous steps to correct imbalances in the immediate future, while enrollment increases continue to stimulate modest increases in the demand for faculty members. The most rapid increases in enrollment are now occurring in two-year colleges, where sexual imbalances on faculties are least serious. It would have been far easier to provide increased opportunities for women on faculties a decade ago, when enrollments were rising rapidly.

AFFIRMATIVE ACTION
Beginning in about 1968, pressure began to be applied to colleges and universities to develop affirmative action policies that would improve employment opportunities for women.

Federal government intervention in this matter is justified because of previous institutional neglect of this significant aspect of civil rights, but it is imposing a heavy price in terms of potential interference with the autonomy of institutions and in terms of the detailed record-keeping and reporting and the time-consuming negotiations that are required.

However, we strongly believe that colleges and universities should take the initiative, without waiting for federal pressure, to develop affirmative action policies and to see that they are carried out. Probably the most serious handicap facing married women desirous of a teaching career in higher education, especially in research-oriented universities, is that in the very age range in which men are beginning to achieve a reputation through research and publication, 25 to 35, married women are likely to be bearing and rearing children. In some fields, in which the advancement of knowledge proceeds very rapidly, particularly the natural sciences and some of the social sciences, it may be very difficult for a woman to recover the ground lost by withdrawing from professional activity during this period.

All colleges and universities covered by federal affirmative action requirements relating to employment should proceed to develop adequate written statements of affirmative action policy and should take active steps to see that the goals of the affirmative action policy are achieved within a reasonable period of time. To expedite achieving such goals, every large college or university should appoint one or more affirmative action officers, whose policies should be guided by an appropriately constituted advisory committee or council. Small colleges may find it preferable to assign affirmative action responsibilities to an existing administrator or faculty member.

Every affirmative action policy, as it concerns the employment of faculty members, should include at least the following provisions relating to sex discrimination:

1   Departments and schools should actively recruit women and maintain records that indicate the steps they have taken in this recruitment program. Efforts should be made to recruit women who are members of minority groups through recruitment plans especially designed to seek them out. Serious consideration should be given to appointing qualified women lecturers to regular faculty positions.

2   Every department and school in an academic institution should establish, in consultation with the administration of the college or university, a goal relating to the relative representation of women on its regular faculty (assistant professor to full professor). In determining these goals, every appropriate source of information

on the relative size of available pools of qualified women and men should be consulted—not just those indicated in the federal guidelines. A reasonable timetable for achieving the goals should be developed, but allowance should be made for special difficulties that may be encountered in adhering to the timetable, especially in fields in which there are currently relatively few women with doctor's degrees and in which competition among institutions for this limited pool of talent is likely to be intense. Special consideration should be given to women who meet the institution's standards of competence in terms of both realized and potential ability, even though they may have had a less substantial record of achievement in terms of research and publication than men who are being considered for the same positions. Standards of competence vary by type of institution. In practice, however, they are often only vaguely defined. Where this is a problem, they should be made more explicit.

3   Part-time appointments should not be discouraged for men and women whose family circumstances make such appointments desirable. Institutions may find it advantageous to distinguish, as some have done, between (1) part-time appointments and (2) appointments to the faculty of persons whose principal employment is elsewhere and who come to the campus to give one or two specialized courses. For example, fringe benefits, prorated on the basis of the proportion of a full-time appointment, are more appropriate for the first type of part-time employee.

4   Policies requiring decisions on the granting of tenure to be made within a given period of years should permit a limited extension of the time period for persons holding part-time appointments. Men and women holding part-time appointments for family reasons should be permitted to achieve tenure on a part-time basis. In such cases, tenure on a full-time basis at some future time would not be ensured, but the institution should attempt to shift the individual's status to a full-time tenured position when desired if budgetarily possible and academically appropriate.

5   Faculty members holding part-time appointments for family reasons should not be barred from service on departmental or campus committees and should, if holding an appropriate faculty rank, be eligible for membership in the academic senate.

6   There should be no antinepotism rules applying to employment within the institution or campus as a whole, or within individual units, such as departments, schools, and institutes. However, a husband or wife should not be involved in a decision relating to his or her spouse.

7   There should be equal treatment of men and women in all matters relating to salary, fringe benefits, and terms and conditions of employment.

8   Women should be entitled to maternity leave for a reasonable length of time, and affirmative action plans should include specific provisions relating to the definition of a reasonable length of time, rights to accumulated leave, and other relevant considerations (pp. 146–150).

The affirmative action program should also provide for an effective internal grievance procedure, if the institution does not already have one. An effective grievance procedure should result in minimizing litigation (p. 150).

We support the objectives of federal policies aimed at ensuring that institutions of higher education having contracts with the federal government pursue effective affirmative action programs, but we believe that these federal policies should be carried out in relation to each institution with due regard for the sensitive characteristics of academic employment, and for the difficulties that may be encountered in meeting affirmative action goals and timetables (p. 150).

The power to delay or cancel contracts should not be used in connection with complaints by individuals, which are best handled, as is now required, by the Equal Employment Opportunity Commission under Title VII of the Civil Rights Act of 1964. Institutions should be given adequate warning before contracts are delayed and should be entitled to a hearing, as is now required, before any existing contract is canceled. Moreover, we do not believe that any existing contracts should be canceled unless a pattern of discrimination has persisted for a considerable period of time and the institution has failed to take steps to correct it. The ultimate sanction of debarring an institution from eligibility for future contracts should be reserved only for the most extreme cases in which a pattern of discrimination is deliberate and has persisted for a lengthy period of time. Final decisions on withholding contract funds should be made only by the Secretary of Labor, on the recommendation of the Secretary of Health, Education and Welfare (p. 150).

The lengthy delays that have sometimes characterized HEW procedures, on the one hand, and the prolonged delays that have been involved in the development or implementation of adequate affirmative action plans by institutions, on the other, are equally unwise and should be avoided in the future (pp. 150–151).

We define a pattern of discrimination as involving one or more of the following situations:

(a) Failure to develop an adequate affirmative action plan within a reasonable period of time;

(b) Lack of evidence that the institution is making an effort to achieve its affirmative action goals; or evidence of widespread faculty or administrative attitudes that are antagonistic to the achievement of the affirmative action goals;

(c) Lack of progress in achieving its affirmative action goals within a reasonable period of time (p. 150).

Colleges and universities should take especially vigorous steps to overcome a pervasive problem of absence of women in top administrative positions. Women should be given opportunities by their departments to serve as department chairmen, because academic administrators are usually selected from among persons who have served ably as department chairmen. Most important, in addition, is an administrative stance that is highly positive toward providing opportunities for women to rise in the administrative hierarchy. Also very important is the provision of management training opportunities for both men and women who have potential administrative ability but do not hold administrative positions (p. 151).

NEEDED CAMPUS FACILITIES

Throughout this report, we have referred in a variety of contexts to the need for broader options and greater freedom of choice for women to make maximum use of their abilities. We add here two further considerations.

CONTINUING EDUCATION FOR WOMEN

One of the most important recent developments in higher education has been the movement to provide increased opportunities for nontraditional study for adults. Women are major beneficiaries of this movement. It is sometimes argued that centers for continuing education should be established for women alone.

The Commission recommends:

Large campuses should have an administrative officer specifically concerned with ensuring that qualified adults are given opportunities to pursue undergraduate or graduate study on a full-time or part-time basis. Whether there should be a separate center for continuing education of women should be decided in the light of the circumstances prevailing on any given campus. We believe that there is often a case for a center primarily concerned with the education problems of mature women, but that the need for such a center may be transitional and that in the future the concept of continuing educational opportunities for mature women is likely to be so thoroughly accepted that a center especially oriented toward women's problems may no longer be desirable or necessary (p. 158).

The existence of separate institutions for nontraditional study should not be used as an excuse for denying qualified adults of either sex the opportunity to study on traditional campuses on a full-time or part-time basis (p. 158).

The Commission reiterates its support of the development of external degree and other nontraditional study programs, emphasizing the need, that has not in all cases been observed, for high quality in such programs. They are especially important in relation to the special needs of mature married women for continuing education (pp. 157–158).

THE PROBLEM OF CHILD CARE

In recent years many colleges and universities have been confronted with demands to establish child-care centers, and many have responded. Although women students and faculty members share needs for child-care services with working mothers generally, the needs of women on campuses are often for part-time care only.

Colleges and universities should be responsive to campus groups seeking to develop child-care services. An essential step is to appoint a carefully selected committee to study various possible types of child-care services, including those already available in the community, and to recommend a plan for making such services available to students and employees of the institution. The committee should include faculty members drawn from appropriate departments, parents, and persons knowledgeable about community resources.

We believe that in most situations, especially for smaller campuses, it will be preferable for the academic institution to cooperate with other community groups in ensuring the availability of adequate child-care services in the community. If campus facilities are desired on or near large campuses, we believe, consistent with our general view that an academic institution should not assume functions that are not central to its main purposes, that it will usually be preferable to seek an arrangement under which the child-care services will be provided under the auspices of a separate board of directors and not as a direct function of the academic institution. The board of directors would be expected to ensure adequate financing and adequate standards for the child-care services.

We believe that student-parents should be expected to pay for child-care services on the basis of sliding scale fees according to their incomes and that parents who are employees of the institutions would normally be expected to pay for the full cost of services. Subsidies to meet the needs of low-income student-parents should be sought from extramural public and private sources and should not normally be sought from the academic institution's regular budget (pp. 162–163).

CONCLUSION

Attitudes of people toward sex roles are changing rapidly, but no one can envisage exactly how sex roles and family structure will evolve in the future. There might even be a swing of the pendulum away from the liberalized attitudes displayed by many people today as there was a backward swing of the pendulum following the granting of women's suffrage. We hope and expect, instead, a steady trend toward full equality of opportunity for women in academic life.

TOWARD A LEARNING SOCIETY

ALTERNATIVE CHANNELS TO LIFE, WORK, AND SERVICE (OCTOBER 1973)

Education is too often perceived as an activity that occurs only at certain times in people's lives, in certain institutional settings, at certain times of the day, and in a certain few accepted formats. At the postsecondary level, education is most immediately thought of in terms of colleges and universities.

THE TOTALITY OF POSTSECONDARY EDUCATION
In 1900, only 6 of each 100 persons 17 years old graduated from high school; by 1970, 75 of each 100 17-year-olds graduated from high school and more than 50 percent of the high school graduates went on to college. As the proportion of high school graduates attending college increased, those who did not go to college began to feel more sharply the economic and social handicaps of not having a college degree. This situation gave impetus to a national push for equality of educational opportunity and its implementation through universal access to college. But, for many people, college is neither the only effective post–high school education option nor the best one.

POSTSECONDARY EDUCATION AND HIGHER EDUCATION
Efforts to contrast higher education and the remainder of postsecondary education are complicated by the use of certain terms that suggest that postsecondary education that does not occur in colleges and universities is somehow less important, more remote, or of secondary status. In the United States, since the mid-nineteenth century, the meaning of the term *higher education* and the content of degree programs has been gradually expanded to incorporate much that would be considered *further education* or *vocational training* in other nations.

Today the distinctions between higher education programs and other postsecondary education seems to turn more on whether degree credit is awarded than on the intrinsic nature of the activity leading to credit. Even this distinction becomes somewhat artificial as some colleges begin to award college credit on a post hoc basis, as the right to grant degrees is extended, at least under some circumstances, to private specialty schools and to rapidly developing new branches of existing institutions.

LIFELONG LEARNING
Education generally calls to mind the passage of youth through the schools into adulthood, a stage presumably reached somewhere around age 18 or 21. The age of students is, itself, therefore regarded as a distinguishing feature of certain types of institutions of postsecondary education. Statistically, about 42 percent of all students on college and university campuses are adults.

The presence of such large proportions of adults in the student bodies of colleges and universities calls into question the view that learning

TABLE 5   Estimated number of program enrollments and FTE enrollments beyond regular elementary and secondary education, by source, 1970

SOURCE	PROGRAM ENROLLMENTS		FTE ENROLLMENTS	
	NUMBER* (THOUSANDS)	PERCENT¶	NUMBER‡ (THOUSANDS)	PERCENT¶
Total, higher education and other postsecondary education	73,800†	100.0	17,600	100.0
Higher education				
1 Colleges and universities (full-time degree credit)	8,900	12.1	8,900	50.6
2 Colleges and universities (part-time degree credit and non-degree credit)	6,300	8.5	1,950	11.1
Other postsecondary education				
1 Elementary and secondary schools	3,900	5.3	300	1.7
2 Other public postsecondary programs	1,000	1.4	350	2.0
3 Specialty schools:				
Proprietary (except correspondence)	3,800	5.1	1,350	7.7
Correspondence schools	2,000	2.7	50	0.3
4 Employers and associations (except armed forces):				
Apprenticeship (registered)	400	0.5	100	0.6
Apprenticeship (nonregistered)	200	0.3	50	0.3
Safety instruction	15,700	21.3	300	1.7
Job orientation	7,400	10.0	550	3.1
Other organized instruction	8,100	11.0	1,650	9.4
5 Armed forces:				
Initial training	650	0.9	550	3.1
Correspondence	1,300	1.8	50	0.3
Other organized instruction	1,100	1.5	850	4.8
6 Prison	200	0.3	§	0.1
7 Other government programs:				
Work Incentive Program, Job Corps, Neighborhood Youth Corps (out-of-school)	250	0.3	50	0.3
Agricultural extension and other	500	0.7	50	0.3
8 Unions	100	0.1	§	§
9 Other organized programs (e.g., TV, churches and synagogues, community organizations, libraries and museums, etc.)	10,000	13.6	400	2.3
10 Tutors	2,000	2.7	100	0.6

* Estimated number of persons who participated at some time during the year; excludes informal learning at home, on the job, or elsewhere, and exclusively self-study.

† May overstate the number of separate persons by a factor of approximately 1.3 because of multiple program enrollments during the year.

‡ FTE is defined as 391 classroom hours, the estimated number of hours spent face-to-face in instructional setting by full-time degree-credit college students.

§ Less than 12,500, or less than 0.1 percent.

¶ Detail may not add to total because of rounding.

Source: Carnegie Commission staff, 1973.

beyond the high school is solely a preparation for life. It is, instead, a part of life itself—and as much so at a college or university as it is at other postsecondary institutions of education.

TRENDS IN ADULT LEARNING

As part of the Current Population Survey (CPS) in May 1969, all persons 35 years old and over, and those 17 to 34 years of age who were not enrolled in regular school full time, were asked if they had participated in education and training activities during the previous year. An estimated 13.2 million Americans or 11.0 percent of the 119.7 million "eligible" adults said that they had participated.

Preliminary unpublished tabulations from the third CPS survey taken in 1972 indicate that some 15.7 million persons, or approximately 12 percent of the "eligible" adult population, participated in adult education activities during the year immediately preceding.

The increases observed in the Current Population Survey reinforce the findings of other surveys carried out under private auspices.

EDUCATION AND TRAINING FOR WORK

Although we have repeatedly emphasized that training people for occupational performance is but one of many important functions of postsecondary education, many of the issues surrounding educational policy legitimately concern how best to serve new labor force entrants, as well as other workers who have continuing or recurrent education and training needs.

Among youth who complete high school but do not go on to college, the first channels through which they emerge into the work force are the various curricula at the secondary school level. The unemployment rate of young school drop-outs tends to be about twice the rate of those who complete the 12th grade.

PATTERNS OF POSTSECONDARY EDUCATION AND TRAINING TO 1980

Many factors influence the future course of postsecondary education. Among them are (1) characteristics of the environment (for example, work and home life), that encourage learning activity; (2) opportunities (for example, time) for learning; (3) the presence or absence of attractive competing uses of time; (4) the expected "pay off" (both monetary and nonmonetary) to learning activity; (5) how adept a person is at learning; (6) the effectiveness and efficiency with which potential sources of learning respond to learning needs; and (7) methods of financing postsecondary learning.

We have estimated that there were 73.8 million program enrollments in all postsecondary educations and training activities in 1970. Because some people enroll in more than one program during the year, however, the total number of persons enrolled is estimated at 56 million. If the degree-credit enrollment (8.9 million) is excluded, then 47 million persons—mainly adults—were engaged in postsecondary education and training activities.

Judging the magnitude of postsecondary education by "head-count" enrollments alone can be misleading, however. Some of the learners thus counted are instructed for an hour or less a week while others pursue more time-consuming studies. Some take instruction of only a few weeks duration, while others may take it for a year or more. The demands of individual learners on institutional resources, therefore, vary significantly.

Adult learning activity will increase generally in the years to come. The educational attainment of our population is increasing generally, and a strong positive relationship has been found between participation in adult education and the highest year of school completed.

NEW FUNDING FOR POSTSECONDARY EDUCATION

In contemplating the financing of educational opportunities beyond the high school, one could argue that an ideal system should make it possible for one to undertake further education and training at the time(s) in one's life when it can most effectively contribute to his or her career and development. For many persons the period immediately after high school may not be the most effective time—because of career indecision, immaturity, motivation, alternative interests, or family responsibilities.

Tuition costs are a recognizable barrier to attendance at college, and higher educational institutions, as well as federal and state student-aid programs, have attempted to alleviate this problem for the student from a low-income family.

Adult students who no longer receive parental aid frequently find the tuition barrier more imposing, and scholarship programs less well adapted to their needs, than younger students. In addition, tuition policies in public institutions often penalize the adult student.

As one analyzes the economic and technological history of modern society, the movement toward recurrent lifetime education with adequate provision to offset personal income loss appears to be a logical step for the last quarter of the twentieth century. Particularly in the United States, where universal access to collegiate education is now nearly assured to all youth, the next step in the evolution of our educational system would seem to be the assurance that lifetime educational opportunities be within reach of all motivated adults.

There seems to be little doubt, given the nature of today's society, that recurrent education is an increasingly important need; whether this need is converted into a "demand"—in the economist's sense of the word —hinges largely upon when and how society tackles the problem of financing. Adults are unlikely to be served well by merely adding on to the present arrangements for financing postsecondary education; rather, it seems evident that a bold new program of universal lifetime financing will be required.

GENERAL OBJECTIVES

We set forth the following objectives to alleviate problems arising in the funding of postsecondary education, the provision of adequate educational opportunities, the coordination of postsecondary education, the accreditation of systems of higher education, and the recognition of student achievement in postsecondary education, and the development of counseling and information centers for nontraditional students:

Every person will have available to him, throughout his life, financial assistance for at least two years of postsecondary education. For at least part of the entitlement, there will be no restrictions as to the type of educational institution the recipient might elect to attend (p. 69).

The states will make adequate provision, within the full spectrum of their postsecondary education resources, for educational opportunities adequate to the divergent needs of all their citizens (p. 69).

State coordinating agencies will become increasingly aware of the resources of all postsecondary institutions in their states and, in partnership with those affected, will utilize their influence to assure adequate financial support for their institutions and to minimize unnecessary duplication of specialized programs in colleges and universities and other institutions offering postsecondary education (p. 70).

Collection and dissemination of information on all forms of postsecondary education will be given high priority by federal and state educational statistical agencies (p. 71).

Educational Opportunity Counseling Centers, such as those we recommended in our report *The Campus and the City* and other appropriate local agencies will have as one of their responsibilities the development and distribution of information about postsecondary educational resources including, but also in addition to, colleges and universities (p. 71).

The current system of accreditation by institutional associations will be supplemented by a second system instituted by state and federal governments for the purpose of validating fiscal stability, legitimacy of advertising claims, and general quality of instruction. Those responsible for administering such validation will be restrained, by all means feasible, from regulation of postsecondary education, and will seek to establish minimum rather than optimum standards for the accreditation they are empowered to bestow (p. 75).

Colleges and universities will successfully resist pressures to grant degree credit for those activities and experiences that are not clearly planned as part of an academic learning program designed to meet the educational goals recognized by the degrees offered (p. 77).

Institutions of postsecondary education will grant degrees, certificates, and honors at more frequent intervals than they now do (p. 77).

Undergraduate and professional degrees will increasingly become only a part of the cumulative record of an individual's educational accomplishments. Ultimately, the degrees will become less important than the total record as evidence of such accomplishments (p. 77).

SPECIFIC OBJECTIVES

In this section we narrow the discussion to suggest specific objectives that might be sought in our endeavors to move more surely toward a learning society. Some of the objectives concern particular types of education and specific alternatives to colleges and universities as sources of learning. Others involve fairly specific issues that arise from an expanded view of postsecondary education. Whereas most of the general objectives discussed above are long-range, the specific objectives discussed in this section tend to be short-range. Many of them could be achieved by immediate action:

The provision of part-time learning opportunities will be considered a legitimate function of all colleges or universities, regardless of their level of instruction or type of control. After deliberation, some institutions will elect not to perform this function, but their decisions will be based on particular objectives they have set for themselves because of policy options, limitations of space, finances, or facilities, and not on a belief that such instruction is inherently inappropriate to colleges and universities (p. 85).

Once admitted to a college or university for academic studies, qualified part-time students will be eligible to take courses in the regular departments of the institution and will be accorded the same campus privileges that are accorded to full-time students (p. 85).

Wherever academic programs are offered for students who are adults of all ages, the rules for student conduct, campus traditions, and the learning environment will be hospitable to them, and will not discriminate against older students (p. 85).

Institutions of higher education will not offer part-time students courses that exceed levels of instruction maintained in courses offered to full-time students. Two-year institutions will not offer upper-division or professional instruction to part-time students. Vocational schools that do not offer general education to full-time students will not offer it to part-time students (p. 86).

States will periodically review their statutes to make certain that they adequately protect students against fraudulent claims and unfair business practices that may characterize operations of some private specialty schools (p. 88).

Elementary and secondary schools will continue to play a significant role in the provision of educational opportunities appropriate to their resources to persons of all ages in the communities where they are located (p. 89).

College- and school-based vocational education will emphasize general knowledge common to broad groups of occupations in addition to providing training for specific skills. Industry will continue to accept responsibility for training persons to perform skills required by specific tasks on the job (p. 91).

When they do not have skill-training expertise in their own companies, businesses will seek agreements with educational institutions to provide technical aid for the development of industry-based skill-training programs and for the evaluation of such programs (p. 91).

Research and development funds will be made available by the Office of Education and the Department of Labor to facilitate the development of the theoretical knowledge and technical expertise needed to service agreements between post-secondary educational institutions and industry for the development of skill-training programs (p. 91).

Educational institutions that have well-developed instructional technology will avail businesses and industry of opportunities to tie plant-site classrooms to tele-vised instruction originating on the campus, and will make available audio-video-tape instruction or computer-assisted instruction on subjects relevant to business and industry training programs (p. 91).

Apprenticeship, internship, and in-service training will be used more widely than they are today to prepare persons for their life work in many professions, para-professions, and occupations (p. 93).

Educational activity provided by the armed forces to officers and enlisted men at postsecondary levels will yield credit that is widely accepted as servicemen are transferred from military base to military base. Some of this instruction will be of a quality that is widely accepted for course-credit in civilian educational institutions after the serviceman student is discharged (pp. 94–95).

The efforts of community colleges and four-year colleges to provide degree-credit instruction for military personnel and civilians living within commuting distance of such installations will be encouraged and increased (p. 95).

Enlisted men, as well as officers, will have increasing opportunities to participate in postsecondary education at civilian centers of postsecondary learning through education leave programs subsidized by the armed services (p. 95).

Local, state, and national governments will provide more opportunities for persons to render public service through well-organized programs, and those who engage in national service will be able to earn financial benefits toward education in addition to their regular in-service compensation (p. 96).

Learning Pavilions designed and operated to encourage and facilitate independent adult learning will be developed in urban centers and in areas that are remote from institutions of postsecondary education. Funding responsibility for construction and operation of such facilities will reside with metropolitan or county governments (p. 97).

Public libraries and museums will increasingly recognize their potentials as sources for guidance and independent study that can be utilized to meet the standards and objectives of postsecondary-level instruction (p. 98).

Educational institutions located within accessible range of prisons and having at their disposal well-developed instructional technology will make remote-access instruction and independent learning materials available to prison education programs at minimum costs (p. 99).

Before taking on a new educational function, institutions will determine the relationship of that function to their educational mission and will ascertain whether there are existing alternative educational resources to meet the particular educational need to be served. If such alternative resources exist, the possibility of contractual agreements with other institutions to secure the services, or the possibility of joint enrollment of the learner, will be explored before a new program is developed (pp. 99–100).

CONCLUSION

A distinguishing feature of the new era of postsecondary education in the United States is that there will be more students of all ages. Many of the new learners will be older than those customarily regarded as of college age. But some of them will be younger persons who prefer more flexible forms of education than are now generally available at colleges and universities.

Fortunately, the learning society is emerging at a time when our colleges and universities and other institutions of postsecondary education are best able to deal with it. The rapid, almost frantic growth of the 1950s and 1960s is over. Many states have created coordinating agencies that can be used for planning and developing the diversity of channels and opportunities that are needed to serve new students in the new age of learning. The opportunity to proceed with such plans and developments should not be allowed to pass unheeded.

WHO
SHOULD
DO
WHAT?

In this section, all the Commission's recommendations are arranged according to the persons, agencies, and institutions most directly affected by them and most likely to be able to take the necessary steps to implement them. It should be remembered, however, that action on many of the recommendations require the concerted efforts of many different people.

THE FEDERAL GOVERNMENT

GENERAL POLICIES

The balance of public support for higher education must shift over the coming decade if the goal of universal access is to be achieved, and federal funds should partially relieve the states of added financial burdens resulting from the expected expansion in higher education. We recommend that federal support of higher education should gradually expand to about one-half of the total governmental contributions by the early 1980s *(Higher Education: Who Pays? Who Benefits? Who Should Pay?).*

Institutions of higher education and governments at all levels should not restrict undergraduate opportunities to enroll in college or to receive student aid because of less favorable trends in the job market for college graduates than have prevailed in the recent past *(College Graduates and Jobs).*

The federal and state governments should develop and implement policies to preserve and strengthen private institutions of higher education *(New Students and New Places).*

The federal government should not only stabilize its support of graduate training and research, but should attempt to stabilize the scope of activities, like the space program, that have in the past involved sudden and sharp shifts in the demand for scientists and engineers *(College Graduates and Jobs).*

A separate federal law and separate state laws should be enacted governing collective bargaining by faculty members in both private and public institutions and should be responsive to the special circumstances that surround their employment. If this is not possible, then separate provisions should be made in more general laws, or leeway should be provided for special administrative interpretations *(Governance of Higher Education).*

We support the objectives of federal policies aimed at ensuring that institutions of higher education having contracts with the federal government pursue effective affirmative action programs, but we believe that these federal policies should be carried out in relation to each institution with due regard for the sensitive characteristics of academic employment and for the difficulties that may be encountered by individual departments and schools in meeting affirmative action goals and timetables *(Opportunities for Women in Higher Education).*

The power to delay or cancel contracts should not be used in connection with complaints by individuals, which are best handled, as is now required, by the Equal Employment Opportunity Commission under Title VII of the Civil Rights Act of 1964 *(Opportunities for Women in Higher Education).*

Institutions should be given adequate warning before contracts are delayed and should be entitled to a hearing, as is now required, before any existing contract is canceled. Moreover, we do not believe that any existing contracts should be canceled unless a pattern of discrimination has persisted for a considerable period of time and the institution has failed to take steps to correct it. The ultimate sanction of debarring an institution from eligibility for future contracts should be reserved only for the most extreme cases in which a pattern of discrimination is deliberate and has persisted for a lengthy period of time. Final decisions on withholding contract funds should be made only by the Secretary of Labor, on the recommendation of the Secretary of Health, Education and Welfare *(Opportunities for Women in Higher Education)*.

The lengthy delays that have sometimes characterized HEW procedures, on the one hand, and the prolonged delays that have been involved in the development or implementation of adequate affirmative action plans by institutions, on the other, are equally unwise and should be avoided in the future *(Opportunities for Women in Higher Education)*.

We define a pattern of discrimination as involving one or more of the following situations: *(a)* Failure to develop an adequate affirmative action plan within a reasonable period of time; *(b)* Lack of evidence that the institution is making an effort to achieve its affirmative action goals or evidence of widespread faculty or administrative attitudes that are antagonistic to the achievement of the affirmative action goals; *(c)* Lack of progress in achieving its affirmative action goals within a reasonable period of time *(Opportunities for Women in Higher Education)*.

It should be unlawful to interfere in any way with any person's exercise of his constitutional rights. Aggrieved persons should be able to bring civil action for appropriate relief, and United States district courts should be given original jurisdiction to grant permanent or temporary injunctions, temporary restraining orders, or any other orders, and to award damages *(Dissent and Disruption)*.

A National Foundation for the Development of Higher Education should be established whose functions would be to encourage, advise, review, and provide financial support for institutional programs designed to give new directions in curricula, to strengthen essential areas that have fallen behind or never been adequately developed because of inadequate funding, and to develop programs for improvement of educational processes and techniques *(Quality and Equality)*.

The Foundation should be granted $50 million, to be allocated to states and regions which would, working with the advice and assistance of the Foundation, make further plans for the effective growth of the states' postsecondary educational system. In the development of these plans the Foundation and the states should give particular attention to creation of an adequate system of community colleges and to stimulation and coordination of the states' occupational and technical educational resources *(Quality and Equality)*.

AID TO STUDENTS
The present program of educational opportunity should be strengthened and expanded by providing:
1   That the level of funding be increased so that all college students with demonstrated need will be assured of some financial aid to meet expenses at institutions which they select.
2   That grants based on need be available for a period not to exceed four years of undergraduate study and two years of study toward a graduate degree *(Quality and Equality)*.

The work-study program should be continued and expanded with federal funding sufficient to enable those undergraduate students who meet, in general terms, the federal need criteria to earn up to $1,000 during the academic year, working not more than the equivalent of two days per week. Off-campus assignments of educational importance, such as tutorial work, should be encouraged *(Quality and Equality)*.

The Veterans' Educational Benefit Programs should be continued and the benefits under such programs should be revised automatically to keep pace with rising living and educational costs *(Quality and Equality)*.

A doctoral fellowship program should be established with selection based upon demonstrated academic ability without reference to need, with fellowships in the amount of $3,000 annually for a maximum of two years to graduate students advanced to candidacy for a Ph.D or equivalent research doctorate. The total number of such first-year fellowships awarded should equal one-half of the average of the national total of doctorates earned in the fourth, third, and second year preceding the year in which the fellowships are awarded. In each year an additional number of fellowships equal to 10 percent of the total just described would be allocated for expansion into neglected or developing fields *(Quality and Equality)*.

A federal program should be established with grants in amounts up to $4,000 a year for medical and dental students from low-income families and for students from low-income families enrolled in associate and assistant programs in medical and dental schools *(Higher Education and the Nation's Health)*.

All persons, after high school graduation, should have two years of post-secondary education placed "in the bank" for them to be withdrawn at any time in their lives when it best suits them *(Less Time, More Options)*.

The federal government should charter a National Student Loan Bank as a nonprofit corporation financed by the sale of governmentally guaranteed securities, which would serve all eligible students regardless of need. The fund should be self-sustaining, except for catastrophic risks, and should permit borrowing up to a reasonable limit that would reflect both tuition charges and subsistence costs. Loan repayments should be based upon income currently earned, and up to 40 years should be permitted for repayment. Provision should be made for public subsidy of catastrophic risks *(Higher Education: Who Pays? Who Benefits? Who Should Pay?).*

The Basic Opportunity Grants program should be fully funded. This legislation, already on the books, is a major step in providing critically needed assistance to both students and institutions of higher education *(Higher Education: Who Pays? Who Benefits? Who Should Pay?).*

The 50 percent of cost limitation for Basic Opportunity Grants for lower-division students should be raised, perhaps in steps, to 75 percent over the next few years *(Higher Education: Who Pays? Who Benefits? Who Should Pay?).*

In the future the $1,400 ceiling on Basic Opportunity Grants should be raised gradually in line with increases in educational and subsistence costs *(Higher Education: Who Pays? Who Benefits? Who Should Pay?).*

The federal government should appropriate full funding for state student incentive matching grants. We also recommend that the federal program be modified in the next several years to provide one-fourth of all state awards that meet the criterion of making up, for students with full need, the difference between federal Basic Opportunity Grants, and the full cost of attending college in the first two years at public institutions, and a significant fraction of the difference in upper-division years. The awards would be reduced by appropriate amounts for students with less than full need *(Higher Education: Who Pays? Who Benefits? Who Should Pay?).*

An undergraduate student holding an educational opportunity grant and receiving added grants from nonfederal sources should be given a supplementary federal grant in an amount matching the nonfederal grants but not exceeding one-quarter of the student's original educational opportunity grant *(Quality and Equality).*

Each college and university should be given a scholarship fund for needy students equal to 10 percent of the total sum of educational opportunity grants (not including supplementary matching grants) held by students at that institution, such funds to be allocated by the institution to students as determined by the institution's own definition of student need *(Quality and Equality).*

Existing legislation should be revised to enable all postsecondary vocational and technical students to apply for grants on the basis of need regardless of whether such students are enrolled in community colleges, area vocational schools, or public adult schools. Work-study programs should also be available to vocational and technical students in all these institutions, and, in addition, to students in proprietary schools. To participate in either of these programs, each institution should be officially recognized as providing a particular program in which the student is enrolled at an acceptable standard of instruction *(Quality and Equality).*

A national service educational benefit program should be established making educational grants available for service in various programs such as the Peace Corps or Vista, with the amount of the benefits set at some percentage of veterans' educational benefits *(Quality and Equality).*

AID TO INSTITUTIONS
The federal government should establish a program of cost-of-education supplements to colleges and universities based on the numbers of students enrolled in the institutions who hold grants awarded on the basis of financial need. Under this program, it is recommended that any college or university officially recognized as being eligible for participation in this program by the Office of Education be paid $500 for each undergraduate student at the institution that is a recipient of a grant from the federal government which was made to the student because of his financial need. Proportionate cost-of-education supplements would be paid to institutions for any part-time students who are enrolled at that institution and who hold such grants *(Institutional Aid).*

Institutions should be paid a cost-of-education supplement amounting to $5,000 for each federal doctoral fellow enrolled at that institution *(Institutional Aid).*

The cost-of-education supplements accompanying the doctoral fellowships recommended in the Commission's first Special Report should be available only to those institutions that charge the doctoral recipient a fee that is not affected by his residency status *(The Capitol and the Campus).*

The Commission recommends increased funding for the following three programs: aid to developing institutions ($100 million in 1970–71), library support ($100 million in 1970–71), and international studies ($25 million in 1970–71). In addition, to stimulate cooperative programs among community colleges and universities for the preparation and re-education of community college teachers and counselors, the Commission recommends $25 million in 1970–71 for an expanded special program of federal training grants *(Quality and Equality).*

Funds should be made available to colleges and universities for specific programs to meet the present needs of inner-city schools and of desegregated schools with heterogeneous classroom enrollments *(A Chance to Learn)*.

The Commission also recommends a similar allocation of funds for meeting the present needs of rural schools in disadvantaged areas *(A Chance to Learn)*.

The present federal aid program of guidance, counseling, and testing for identification and encouragement of able students should be expanded, and funding for the program should be increased to $30 million in 1970–71, rising to $40 million in 1976–77 *(Quality and Equality)*.

Certain universities should be selected on the basis of program proposals submitted to national panels to undertake specific graduate talent search and development programs, and federal funding should be made available for such programs in the amount of $25 million in 1970–71, rising to $100 million in 1976–77 *(Quality and Equality)*.

Construction grants should be made available to provide one-third of total costs for construction and needed renovation of academic facilities.
    Funding levels for the academic facilities construction program should be increased to provide sufficient loan funds for an additional one-third of needed new construction costs *(Quality and Equality)*.

In recognition of the special urgency and problems involved in the planning and development tasks that face colleges founded for Negroes, the Commission recommends that a special subdivision for the development of black colleges and universities be created within the National Foundation for Development of Higher Education previously proposed in our report, *Quality and Equality*. The purpose of this division, in which Negroes should have a vital role in advisory and management capacities, would be to aid colleges and universities founded for Negroes to develop and implement new programs and activities that respond to the challenges that confront them as institutions in transition. To fund this division, the Commission recommends that an average of $40 million annually in the 1970s from the proposed funding to The Developing Institutions Program be channeled through the division for allocation to those black colleges working with the division toward the development and implementation of specific proposals for modification and expansion of the range of curricular offerings at the institution, or for the development of consortia to facilitate such changes, or to effect mergers among institutions to enable the desirable transition *(From Isolation to Mainstream)*.

The National Foundation on the Arts and Humanities should provide grants for university-based cultural activities available to both the campus and its neighbors and for cooperative endeavors involving higher education and city museums and performing arts centers *(The Campus and the City).*

To meet many of the basic financial problems of black colleges we recommend that the federal government adopt the full program of recommendations in *Quality and Equality* as revised June 1970, and we also recommend adoption of the federal funding proposals in the Commission's report, *Higher Education and the Nation's Health.*

We recommend that $1 million annually be earmarked from planning funds assigned to the National Foundation for the Development of Higher Education to aid states and black colleges to plan for their growth and transition. If the Foundation is not established at an early date, thus delaying the creation of the subdivision within the Foundation, the Commission recommends that the above-described responsibilities be assigned to a special commission appointed by the President of the United States in consultation with representatives of institutions founded for Negroes and that the funds which would have been channeled through the subdivision be assigned to this special commission *(From Isolation to Mainstream).*

The federal government should assist community colleges by providing (1) funds for state planning: (2) start-up grants for new campuses; (3) construction funds; (4) cost-of-education allowance for low-income students attending the colleges; (5) grants, work-study opportunities, and loans for students; and (6) an expanded program of federal training grants to stimulate expansion and improvement of graduate education programs for community college teachers, counselors, and administrators *(The Open-Door Colleges).*

The federal government should grant cost-of-education supplements to colleges and universities based on the numbers and levels of students holding federal grants enrolled in the institutions *(Quality and Equality).*

A grant amounting to 10 percent of the total research grants received annually by an institution should be made to that institution to be used at its discretion *(Quality and Equality).*

Colleges and universities officially recognized as eligible for participation in this program (cost-of-education supplements) by the Office of Education should receive a grant of $200 for each student who receives a subsidized loan, provided, however, that no such payment shall be made for students who hold federal grants or for students who borrow less than $200 during the fiscal year *(Institutional Aid).*

The proposed National Foundation for Postsecondary Education and the proposed National Institute for Education should be established, and the proposed National Foundation for Postsecondary Education should be assigned responsibility for the utilization of instructional technology. Grants to support research and development activities in the field of instructional technology for higher education should be made by the proposed National Institute of Education *(The Fourth Revolution)*.

RESEARCH PROGRAMS

Federal research funds expended within higher education should be maintained steadily at a level of about 0.3 percent of the gross national product *(The Purposes and the Performance of Higher Education in the United States)*.

Federal grants for university-based research (not including federal contract research centers), regardless of changing priorities for defense and space research, should be increased annually (using grants in 1967–68 as a base) at a rate equal to the five-year moving average annual rate of growth in the gross national product *(Quality and Equality)*.

Federal research funds should be substantially increased for the social sciences, humanities, and creative arts from their current level of about 7 percent of the amount for science *(The Purposes of the Performance of Higher Education in the United States)*.

The Commission endorses an intensive research and experimental undertaking in the area of education similar to that made possible in medical practice through the National Institutes of Health *(A Chance to Learn)*.

Funds for basic research should be concentrated on highly productive centers and individuals, and money for applied research should be subject to periodic reassignment to reflect the decline of old and the rise of new potentialities *(The Purposes and the Performance of Higher Education in the United States)*.

Federal financial support of research in university health science centers should be maintained at its present percentage of the gross national product; funds should be made available to support research on methods of achieving greater efficiency in health manpower education and in the delivery of health care as well as for biomedical research; federal allocations should cover the total cost of research projects and not less than 10 percent and not more than 25 percent of the research grants to any university health science center should take the form of institutional grants rather than grants for specific research projects *(Higher Education and the Nation's Health)*.

Health manpower research programs in the Department of Health, Education and Welfare should be expanded and strengthened in cooperation with the Department of Labor to encompass broad continuous studies of health manpower supply and demand. Research funds should be made available for specialized studies of these problems in university health science centers and appropriate university research institutes *(Higher Education and the Nation's Health)*.

MEDICAL EDUCATION

The Commission recommends establishment of a substantial program of federal aid for medical education and health services for the purposes of:

■ Stimulating expansion of capacity at existing medical schools
■ Planning additional medical schools distributed on a geographical basis to provide needed service to areas not now served
■ Expanding educational facilities and developing new programs for the training of medical care support personnel
■ Increasing availability of health services in the community of the medical schools and the quality of health care delivery *(Quality and Equality)*.

The number of medical school entrants should be increased to 15,300 by 1976 and to 16,400 by 1978. Toward the end of the 1970s, the question of whether the number of entrant places should continue to be increased will need to be reappraised. The expansion in the number of medical school entrants should be accomplished through an average expansion of about 30 to 44 percent in existing and developing schools by 1978, with nine new schools accounting for about 900 to 1,350 entrant places, adding another 8 to 13 percent. The number of dental school entrants should be increased at least to 5,000 by 1976 and to 5,400 by 1980 *(Higher Education and the Nation's Health)*.

An Educational Opportunity Bank for medical and dental students, including house officers, should be established, with repayment excused during periods of house officer training and during two years of military service *(Higher Education and the Nation's Health)*.

A voluntary national health service corps should be developed. As an incentive for participation in the corps, an M.D. or D.D.S. would be excused from loan repayments during periods of service, and 25 percent of the maximum indebtedness he is eligible to incur would be forgiven *(Higher Education and the Nation's Health)*.

The Commission recommends (1) cost-of-instruction supplements to university health science centers for each medical and dental student enrolled; (2) bonuses for expansion of enrollment; (3) cost-of-instruction supplements to university health science centers and their affiliated hospitals for each house officer; and (4) bonuses for curriculum reform. The supplements and bonuses would also be available for each student enrolled in physician's and dentist's associate and assistant programs

as well as for students in the last year of premedical or predental education if curriculum reform is designed to achieve a reduction in the total
duration of preprofessional and professional education *(Higher Education and the Nation's Health).*

The Commission recommends (1) construction grants for university
health science centers and area health education centers in amounts up
to 75 percent of total construction costs, with the remaining 25 percent
available in the form of loans; and (2) start-up grants for new university
health science centers in amounts not exceeding $10 million per center
(Higher Education and the Nation's Health).

A National Health Manpower Commission should be appointed to make a
thorough study of changing patterns of education and utilization of health
manpower, with particular reference to new types of allied health workers, of changing patterns of health care delivery, and of the feasibility
of national licensing requirements for all health manpower *(Higher Education and the Nation's Health).*

Federal payments to medical and dental institutions should be adjusted
for schools with three-year programs to enable those schools to receive
the same amount of institutional aid as they would if they were four-year
schools. This adjustment should be made until about 1970 but then
should be reviewed *(Higher Education and the Nation's Health).*

The Commission recommends the strengthening of existing federal legislation for regional, state, and local health planning to encompass regional
planning of all health manpower education and health care facilities. The
university health science centers, along with their affiliated area health
education centers, should have central responsibility for the planning of
health manpower education, while the central responsibility for planning
changes in the delivery of health care should be in the hands of regional
agencies, in cooperation with state and local agencies, as well as appropriate private institutions. Continuing education of health manpower
should be a major concern of the university health science centers and
area health education centers with federal funds providing 50 percent of
the financial support of such programs *(Higher Education and the Nation's Health).*

URBAN PROGRAMS
An Urban-Grant program should be established which would provide 10
grants to carefully selected institutions for the purpose of undertaking a
comprehensive urban commitment for each institution. These grants
should not exceed $10 million each for a 10-year period with reviews
every two years *(The Campus and the City).*

Within the level of research funding which we recommended in *Quality and Equality,* high priority should be given to both basic and applied social science research *(The Campus and the City).*

The network of urban observatories should be continued and each observatory should be funded at approximately $100,000 per year *(The Campus and the City).*

The new National Institute of Education should make grants available to those institutions that are conducting systematic experiments with remedial education *(The Campus and the City).*

From funds allocated to the Secretary of Health, Education and Welfare for innovation and reform in higher education, grants should be made available for development and testing of new techniques for assessing individual competencies *(The Campus and the City).*

THE NEW TECHNOLOGY

The federal government should continue to provide a major share of expenditures required for research and development in instructional technology and for introduction of new technologies more extensively into higher education at least until the end of the century. The total level of federal government support for these purposes should be at least $100 million in 1973 and should rise to 1 percent of the total expenditures of the nation on higher education by 1980 *(The Fourth Revolution).*

The federal government should assume full financial responsibility for the capital expenditures required initially to establish one cooperative learning-technology center every three years between 1973 and 1992 *(The Fourth Revolution).*

The federal government should provide at least one-third of the funds required for the operation of cooperative learning-technology centers for the first 10 years of their operation *(The Fourth Revolution).*

DISSEMINATION OF DATA

The Commissioner of Education should designate a unit within the Office of Education, with an appropriate advisory committee, reporting to the Commissioner, to develop standard definitions and methods of reporting to ensure the coordination, evaluation, and dissemination of available data *(A Chance to Learn).*

The U.S. Office of Education should develop a more accurate definition of enrollment in occupational programs and expand its statistics to include changes in enrollment by field of study *(The Open-Door Colleges).*

The U.S. Bureau of Labor Statistics and the U.S. Office of Education should develop revised estimates of the future demand for teachers that take into account, as existing projections do not, the growing demand for teachers in preelementary education and in such other settings as adult education programs. There is also a need for revised estimates of supply that take account of the declining enrollment in undergraduate education programs and a possible future decline in enrollment in master's degree in education programs *(College Graduates and Jobs)*.

Federal government agencies involved in studies of health manpower should continuously review projections of supply and demand during the 1970s *(College Graduates and Jobs)*.

The federal government should give high priority to the development of more adequate, sophisticated, and coordinated programs of data gathering and analysis relating to highly educated manpower. Because professional associations can be particularly helpful in these efforts, we also believe that federal government agencies should develop programs designed to elicit and support the efforts of these associations *(College Graduates and Jobs)*.

Federal and state government agencies and other appropriate bodies should undertake studies of the implications of the changing job market for holders of master's degrees and for enrollment in master's programs *(College Graduates and Jobs)*.

The international migration of students and professional personnel should be explicitly incorporated into analyses of changes in demand and supply, and opportunities for student places and student aid for foreign students in the United States should not be curtailed *(College Graduates and Jobs)*.

Federal government agencies should take steps to improve the flow of current occupational information and to make it available more promptly *(College Graduates and Jobs)*.

The Carnegie Commission recommends a major national study of the entire set of relationships that exist between school systems, state bureaucracies, school and college teachers, and the educational materials industry in the production and selection of materials. The purpose of the study would be to seek ways to improve the system by which curricular materials are chosen, created, and marketed. Such a study should shed light as well upon the difficulties and problems associated with the widespread adoption of educational technology *(Continuity and Discontinuity)*.

OBJECTIVES FOR THE FUTURE

Every person will have available to him, throughout his life, adequate funding for at least two years of postsecondary education. For at least part of the entitlement, there will be no restrictions as to the type of educational institution the recipient might elect to attend *(Toward a Learning Society)*.

Collection and dissemination of information on all forms of postsecondary education will be given high priority by federal and state educational statistical agencies *(Toward a Learning Society)*.

Research and development funds will be made available by the Office of Education and the Department of Labor to facilitate the development of the theoretical knowledge and technical expertise needed to service agreements between postsecondary educational institutions and industry for the development of skill-training programs *(Toward a Learning Society)*.

Educational activity provided by the armed forces for enlisted men at postsecondary levels will yield credit that is widely accepted as servicemen are transferred from military base to military base. Some of this instruction will be of a quality that is widely accepted for course credit in civilian educational institutions after the serviceman student is discharged *(Toward a Learning Society)*.

Enlisted men, as well as officers, will have increasing opportunities to participate in postsecondary education at civilian centers of postsecondary learning through education leave programs subsidized by the armed services *(Toward a Learning Society)*.

STATE AND LOCAL GOVERN- MENTS

GENERAL POLICY

State governments should continue to exercise major responsibility, in cooperation with the local governments and private institutions, for maintaining, improving, and expanding systems of postsecondary education adequate to meet the needs of the American people *(The Capitol and the Campus)*.

State governments should develop and implement policies to preserve and strengthen private institutions of higher education *(New Students and New Places)*.

State laws, where they do not now permit it, should provide faculty members in public institutions the opportunity of obtaining collective bargaining rights. One alternative under such laws should be choice of no bargaining unit *(Governance of Higher Education)*.

State financing authorities and local agencies should review their policies for funding community colleges to determine whether adequate funds are being made available for this segment of higher education with its difficult and important tasks *(The Campus and the City)*.

COORDINATION AND PLANNING

A state's initial development of a broad postsecondary educational plan should be undertaken by a commission appointed for that purpose with a small staff augmented by special task forces as needed, selected so as to assure participation by both public representatives and leaders of educational constituencies *(The Capitol and the Campus)*.

The Commission recommends:

■ That states review the funding levels of their coordinating agencies to determine if the levels permit attention to the broader functions of coordination or only to those minimal duties legally required of the agencies.

■ That states take steps to attract staff members of the ability, stature, and sensitivity required to carry out the complex tasks of the agencies (e.g., salary level increases, opportunities for educational and research leaves, and adoption of certain other fringe benefits usually available to members of the academic community).

■ That states with heavy institutional representation in the composition of their boards take steps to increase the proportion of lay members and to introduce appropriate nominating techniques for appointment of outstanding noninstitutional members regardless of who has the final appointing authority.

■ That boards seek to increase acceptance by the institutions through:

1 more effective consultation with the entire range of postsecondary institutions
2 experimentation with a program of limited term exchanges of personnel between agency and institutional staffs

3   establishment of joint board staff and institutional staff seminars or workshops focused on state educational concerns

■ That institutions examine their own levels of cooperativeness to determine whether failures to respond to advisory agencies might lead more surely and quickly to establishment of regulatory agencies *(The Capitol and the Campus).*

As minimum elements in any state planning effort, attention should be given to:

■ Present and future access to postsecondary education, including need for student spaces, student financial aid programs, geographic availability of institutions, and admission standards for types of institutions
■ Appropriate functions for the various types of institutions within postsecondary education, including degrees to be granted, research activities, and public service functions
■ Orderly growth of postsecondary education—including location of new campuses, development of new schools, and optimum size of institutions
■ Articulation among the various elements of postsecondary education and within secondary education

In setting the parameters for these planning functions, state agencies should:

■ Take into account the present and potential contributions to state needs of all types of postsecondary institutions, including universities, colleges, private trade and technical schools, area vocational schools, industry and unions and other agencies providing various forms of postsecondary education
■ Encompass the entire timespan of a person's postsecondary education needs from immediately after high school throughout life

The Commission further recommends that states, in developing both their short- and longer-range plans, give greater attention to institutional diversity, and to building sufficient flexibility into both institutional and system-wide plans to permit adaptation as educational processes and needs change *(The Capitol and the Campus).*

Coordinating agencies should be granted the following authorities to be exercised within the context of the long-range plans or guidelines established for the state:

1   To approve or disapprove new institutions, branches, or centers, and where appropriate, to take active steps toward establishment of new institutions.
2   To approve all new degree programs at the doctoral level, and new master's and baccalaureate programs in general fields not previously offered, and in high-cost fields.
3   To allocate funds under state-administered federal programs *(The Capitol and the Campus).*

While recognizing the need for more effective coordination of postsecondary education at the state level, states should strongly resist:

1 Investing coordinating agencies with administrative authority, particularly over budget matters, or

2 Establishing single governing boards except in those states in which a special combination of historical factors and present circumstances make such agencies more feasible than other types of coordinating agencies *(The Capitol and the Campus)*.

State planning agencies should give very high priority in the next few years to careful adaptation of teacher education to the changing needs of a period of shrinking job opportunities for elementary and secondary school teachers. We believe that consolidation of teacher education into a more limited number of institutions that can offer high-quality training would be generally preferable to a cutting back of teacher education on an across-the-board basis. States should encourage the participation of private as well as public colleges and universities in such planning. We also recognize that many state colleges that have largely concentrated on teacher education will need to develop more comprehensive programs if they are to serve students effectively, and that in sparsely populated states this will require division of labor among such state colleges in adding new fields or in some cases a merger of two or more such state colleges into a single location.

State coordinating councils and similar agencies should develop strong policies (where these do not now exist) for preventing the spread of Ph.D. programs to institutions that do not now have them. In addition, every effort should be made to prevent the establishment of new Ph.D. programs in particular fields of study in institutions that now have Ph.D. programs unless an exceptionally strong case can be made for them. We also strongly recommend the continuous review of existing degree programs with a view to eliminating those that are very costly or of low quality and the concentration of highly specialized degree programs on only one or two campuses of multicampus institutions *(College Graduates and Jobs)*.

All state plans for the development of two-year institutions of higher education should provide for comprehensive community colleges which will offer meaningful options for college-age students and adults among a variety of educational programs, including transfer education, general education, remedial courses, occupational programs, continuing education for adults, and cultural programs designed to enrich the community environment. Within this general framework there should be opportunities for varying patterns of development and for the provision of particularly strong specialties in selected colleges *(The Open-Door Colleges)*.

For the sake of quality of programs, economy of operation, and easy availability, state plans should provide for community colleges generally ranging in size from about 2,000 to 5,000 daytime students, except in sparsely populated areas where institutions may have to be somewhat smaller, and in very large cities, where they may have to be somewhat larger *(The Open-Door Colleges)*.

States with community college systems should undertake continuing evaluation studies of the experiences of these colleges, with particular reference to student achievement during the two-year educational period and their subsequent education and employment *(The Open-Door Colleges)*.

A basic reassessment of a state's postsecondary educational plan should be undertaken by the advisory coordinating board, if such exists, or by a commission appointed for that purpose every five or ten years or whenever it becomes apparent that such a reassessment is essential to reflect adequately the totality and interaction of changing conditions and educational needs *(The Capitol and the Campus)*.

State plans and multicampus system plans should provide for specialization by field and for differentiation of general functions among campuses and groups of campuses *(Reform on Campus)*.

Consideration should be given to establishing campus by campus a series of coherent options for a broad learning experience among which students may choose *(Reform on Campus)*.

Individual institutions of higher education and state planning agencies should place high priority in the 1970s and 1980s on adjusting their programs to changing student choices of fields that will occur in response both to pronounced occupational shifts in the labor market and to changing student interests and concerns. High priority should also be placed on continued flexibility in the use of resources to facilitate such adjustments *(College Graduates and Jobs)*.

Each state should undertake a review and analysis of the general education requirements for graduation from high school. Objectives should be clearly established and new means to these objectives should be explored, including the possibility that students can "test out" of graduation requirements. In addition, the relationship of general education at the high school to that at the college level, especially in grades 13 and 14, should be explored with a view toward ways that the general education requirements at both levels might be linked together to provide continuity and to prevent wasteful overlap and duplication. School and college faculty members should work together on this set of problems under the sponsorship of local, state, and national organizations such as the College Board and professional associations. More of the responsibility for general education should be assumed by the high schools *(Continuity and Discontinuity)*.

Each state through its coordinating mechanisms should study carefully and define the roles of public high schools, area vocational schools, community colleges, and proprietary schools with respect to vocational and technical programs *(Continuity and Discontinuity)*.

Universities, in conjunction with state school boards associations, should experiment with various means of providing school board members with information on crucial issues *(Continuity and Discontinuity)*.

States should consider carefully the adverse affects of enrollment limits at the graduate level for out-of-state students *(The Capitol and the Campus)*.

BROADENING THE SCOPE

The comprehensive public community college has a unique and important role to play in higher education, and public two-year colleges should be actively discouraged by state planning and financing policies from converting to four-year institutions *(The Open-Door Colleges)*.

Coordinated efforts should be made at the federal, state, and local levels to stimulate the expansion of occupational education in community colleges and to make it responsive to changing manpower requirements. Continuing education for adults, as well as occupational education for college-age students, should be provided *(The Open-Door Colleges)*.

Service and other employment opportunities should be created for students between high school and college and at stop-out points in college through national, state, and municipal youth programs, through short-term jobs with private and public employers, and through apprenticeship programs in the student's field of interest; and students should be actively encourage to participate *(Less Time, More Options)*.

State plans for two-year institutions should not provide for new, two-year, strictly academic branches of universities or new specialized two-year technical institutions, although there may be a case for exceptions under special circumstances prevailing in some of the states. Where such institutions now exist, they should be urged to broaden their programs as rapidly as possible so that they may fulfill the general purposes of comprehensive community colleges. The continuing existence of specialized two-year institutions, if the decision is to continue them in their narrow specialization, should not stand in the way of the establishment of comprehensive community colleges in the same areas. We also recommend that state plans should place major emphasis on the allocation of vocational education funds to comprehensive community colleges rather than to post-high school area vocational schools or other noncollegiate institutions *(The Open-Door Colleges)*.

Coordinating councils, consortia, and multicampus systems should adopt policies of clear differentiation of functions among campuses and of assigned specializations among fields. Such differentiation of functions should follow the logic of complementarity of interests *(The Purposes and the Performance of Higher Education in the United States)*.

State and federal government agencies, as well as private foundations, should expand programs of support for the development of external degree systems and open universities along the lines of programs initiated within the last year or so. It will also be important for governmental bodies and foundations to provide funds for evaluation of these innovative programs as they develop *(New Students and New Places)*.

Public policy should be directed to improvement of existing channels into adult life and to the creation of new channels—college being only one of several preferred channels *(The Purposes and the Performance of Higher Education in the United States)*.

Nine new university health science centers should be developed *(Higher Education and the Nation's Health)*.

Area health education centers should be developed in areas at some distance from university health science centers which do not have sufficiently large populations to support university health science centers of their own, and in a few metropolitan areas needing additional training facilities but not full health science centers. These area centers would be affiliated with the nearest appropriate university health science center and would perform somewhat the same functions recommended for university health science centers, except that the education of M.D. and D.D.S. candidates would be restricted to a limited amount of clinical education on a rotational basis, and research programs would be largely restricted to the evaluation of local experiments in health care delivery systems *(Higher Education and the Nation's Health)*.

Open-access opportunities should be provided into most and perhaps all of these channels, and such access should be subject to public financial support where and as appropriate and not restricted to college attendance alone *(The Purposes and the Performance of Higher Education in the United States)*.

Community colleges or equivalent facilities should be established within commuting range of potential students in all populous areas *(A Chance to Learn)*.

The expansion of postsecondary educational opportunities should be encouraged outside the formal college in apprenticeship programs, proprietary schools, in-service training in industry, and in military programs; appropriate educational credit should be given for the training received; and participants should be eligible where appropriate for federal and state assistance available to students in formal colleges *(Less Time, More Options).*

To take advantage of the opportunities afforded by interstate mobility of students, states should enter into reciprocity agreements for the exchange of both undergraduates and graduate students in those situations where the educational systems in each of the states will be enhanced by such an exchange agreement *(The Capitol and the Campus).*

States should give careful consideration to adoption of policies encouraging a lower age of entrance into the public schools, specifically at the age of four *(College Graduates and Jobs).*

PROVIDING FOR ACCESS
Each state should plan universal access to its total system, but not necessarily to each of its institutions, since they vary greatly in their nature and purpose *(A Chance to Learn).*

The Commission recommends that:
1   All states, but particularly those with ratios below 70 percent, take steps to increase the percentage of high school students who remain in high school and successfully complete the high school program.
2   States that rank low in terms of the proportion of students going on to higher education substantially increase their financial commitment to higher education.
3   State and local communities implement the Commission's recommendations for establishing 230–280 additional open-door community colleges as set forth in the Commission's report *The Open-Door Colleges.*
4   States showing a low proportion of their students within commuting distance of free-access colleges immediately undertake an evaluation of their higher education system to determine if, in fact, it lacks open access as a system and, if so, what steps need be taken to achieve reasonable open access *(The Capitol and the Campus).*

All states should enact legislation providing admission to public community colleges of all applicants who are high school graduates or are persons over 18 years of age who are capable of benefiting from continuing education *(The Open-Door Colleges).*

States having a ratio of less than 30 places in both public and private higher education in the state for every 100 18- to 21-year-olds in the state should take emergency measures to increase the availability of higher education in the state *(The Capitol and the Campus).*

Appropriate state and local agencies should take steps to improve availability of student places in colleges and universities in those areas which now have less than 2.5 places available per 100 population *(The Campus and the City).*

Through the coordinated efforts of federal, state, and local governments, the goal of providing a community college within commuting distance of every potential student should be attained by 1980. In sparsely populated areas, where it is not feasible to provide institutions within commuting distance of every student, residential community colleges are needed. State plans should also designate selected urban community colleges to provide housing arrangements for students from smaller communities and rural areas in order to encourage maximum access to specialized occupational programs. The Commission estimates that, to achieve this goal, about 230 to 280 new, carefully planned community colleges will be needed by 1980 *(The Open-Door Colleges).*[1]

Policies should be developed in all states to facilitate the transfer of students from community colleges to public four-year institutions. Whenever public four-year institutions are forced, because of inadequacies of budgets, to reject students who meet their admission requirements, top priority should be given to qualified students from community colleges within the state. Private colleges and universities should also develop policies encouraging admission of community college graduates. In addition, there should be no discrimination against students transferring from community colleges in the allocation of student aid *(The Open-Door Colleges).*

Careful studies should be made in certain areas to determine whether present patterns of nonresident enrollment correspond closely with those of 1968 and, if so, to take whatever steps are necessary to expand facilities for higher education *(The Campus and the City).*

Appropriate state and local agencies should undertake an evaluation of the adequacy of the number of higher education student places in many areas of the country *(The Campus and the City).*

State plans for the growth and development of public institutions of higher education, in general, should incorporate minimum full-time-equivalent enrollment objectives of (1) 5,000 for doctoral; (2) 5,000 for comprehensive; (3) 1,000 for liberal arts; and (4) 2,000 for two-year. Maximum full-time-equivalent should be 20,000; 10,000; 2,500; and 5,000, respectively *(New Students and New Places).*

State and local planning bodies should develop plans for the establishment by 1980 of about 60 to 70 new comprehensive colleges and 80 to 125 new community colleges in large metropolitan areas with populations

---

[1] Because of the establishment of many new colleges and the availability of new information, the Commission revised its estimate of new community colleges needed by 1980. In *New Students and New Places* (October 1971) it estimated a need for 175 to 235 new community colleges.

of 500,000 or more. In determining the location of these new institutions within metropolitan areas, particular emphasis should be placed on the provision of adequate open access places for students in inner-city areas *(New Students and New Places)*.

State and local planning agencies should develop plans for about 80 to 105 new comprehensive colleges including those already recommended for large metropolitan areas *(New Students and New Places)*.

State and local planning agencies should develop plans for the establishments of about 175 to 235 new community colleges in all, including those already recommended for large metropolitan areas, by 1980 *(New Students and New Places)*.

FINANCING HIGHER EDUCATION

States with a present expenditure of less than 0.6 percent of per capita personal income spent through state and local taxes for higher education should take immediate steps to increase their financial support of higher education *(The Capitol and the Campus)*.

States should expand their contributions to the financing of community colleges so that the state's share amounts, in general, to one-half or two-thirds of the total state and local financial burden, including operational and capital outlay costs. The Commission opposes the elimination of any local share on the ground that, if local policy-making responsibility is to be meaningful, it should be accompanied by some substantial degree of financial responsibility. In addition, the Commission believes that, in providing its share, the state should ensure that total appropriations for operating expenses are large enough to permit the institution to follow a policy of either no tuition or very low tuition *(The Open-Door Colleges)*.

States with regressive tax structures should develop more progressive tax systems in the interest of greater equity and adequacy in the financing of education and other public services *(Higher Education: Who Pays? Who Benefits? Who Should Pay?)*.

States which do not presently have a strong private sector should consider the desirability of making the equivalent of land grants to responsible groups who can demonstrate financial ability to operate new private institutions. Such grants should encourage groups to start new institutions or to open branches of existing well-established institutions in the granting state *(The Capitol and the Campus)*.

States should enter into agreements, or make grants, for the purpose of continuing certain educational programs at private institutions (for example, Florida and Wisconsin grants to private medical schools). These should be selected after consideration of special manpower needs, evaluation of existing student places for these programs in public institutions and the relative cost of expanding public capacity or supporting and expanding private programs *(The Capitol and the Campus)*.

Those states that do not already have programs enabling private institutions to borrow construction funds through a state-created bond-issuing corporation should take steps to develop such agencies if the private institutions can demonstrate the need for them *(The Capitol and the Campus)*.

In developing their policies for state aid to private institutions, states should study and adopt policies providing financial incentive for expansion in those cases in which private institutions are clearly much too small for efficient operation, but state policies should not be designed to force growth on private institutions of demonstrably high quality which are desirous of retaining unique characteristics associated with their comparatively small size. In some states it may be desirable, also, to study and adopt policies providing financial assistance for merger of very small private institutions in appropriate cases *(New Students and New Places)*.

States should recognize the public-service demands made on public institutions and provide funds for such services *(The Campus and the City)*.

For those few states in which the above recommendations prove inadequate, and this might be the situation in states which rely heavily on private universities and colleges, the Commission recommends that each resident student be given cost-of-education vouchers which would entitle any private institution selected by the student to receive a state payment increasing gradually each year up to an amount equal to one-third of the subsidy granted by the state for students at the same levels attending comparable public institutions *(The Capitol and the Campus)*.

TUITION POLICIES
State governments should take positive steps toward a gradual narrowing of the tuition differential between public and private institutions in their jurisdictions. This can be accomplished through adjustments in tuition levels at public institutions with an accompanying statewide program of student aid that will minimize the cost to the low-income student, by a program of direct or indirect support to private institutions to enable them to keep tuition charges from rising unduly rapidly, or by a combination of both *(Higher Education: Who Pays? Who Benefits? Who Should Pay?)*.

States should revise their legislation, wherever necessary, to provide for uniform low tuition or no tuition charges at public two-year colleges *(The Open-Door Colleges)*.

States and public institutions that find it necessary to increase tuition and other required instructional fees should not increase such fees at a rate higher than the rate at which per capita personal disposal income rises, except that institutions which have kept their fees unusually low for many years may find it necessary to exceed this rate in initial increases *(The Capitol and the Campus).*

States should establish a program of tuition grants for both public and private institutions to be awarded to students on the basis of financial need. Only after establishment of a tuition grants program should states consider raising tuition levels at public institutions. To avoid upward pressures on private tuition from such grants, states would need to set a maximum tuition grant *(The Capitol and the Campus).*

To alleviate some of the problems resulting from nonresident policies, the Commission recommends that:

1   States, possibly working through the Education Commission of the States, carefully review their residence requirements and modify them if necessary for the purpose of granting immediate residence status to students whose families came to the state for other than educational reasons.

2   States, possibly working through the Education Commission of the States, cooperate for the purpose of developing relatively standard residence criteria and that each state review the implementation of requirements of its own institutions to ensure similar application of the criteria among public institutions *(The Capitol and the Campus).*

MEDICAL EDUCATION

States should continue to provide substantial financial support for medical and dental education, and states that have lagged in the past should plan for significant increases in expenditures for this purpose. Also, states should provide financial support for medical and dental education in private institutions. In addition, the states should provide major financial support for house officer training and for the education of allied health personnel. The states, in cooperation with universities and with regional and local planning bodies, should also play a major role in the development of plans for the location of university health science centers, area health education centers, and comprehensive colleges and community colleges providing training for allied health personnel *(Higher Education and the Nation's Health).*

The Commission recommends the development of 126 new area health education centers, to be located on the basis of careful regional planning *(Higher Education and the Nation's Health).*

Vigorous efforts should be made at the state level to develop training programs in nursing and allied health professions in state colleges and community colleges in those states that have lagged in the past *(College Graduates and Jobs).*

METROPOLITAN AREAS

Mayors of major cities should assign someone on their staff primary responsibility for liaison with higher education in the city *(The Campus and the City)*.

In each metropolitan area with population in excess of 1 million, we recommend establishment of: (1) a Metropolitan Higher Education Council, and (2) a Metropolitan Educational Opportunity Center *(The Campus and the City)*.

We recommend that the (Metropolitan Educational Opportunity) centers be funded one-half from local sources and one-half from state and federal sources. We also recommend that funding for administrative expenses of the metropolitan councils be similarly shared, with one-half from local sources and one-half from state and federal sources *(The Campus and the City)*.

COLLEGES FOUNDED FOR NEGROES

The examples of special effort made by North Carolina and certain other states to overcome the historical disadvantages of their colleges founded for Negroes should be followed by other states in which such institutions are located *(From Isolation to Mainstream)*.

Coordinating agencies and boards of higher education in the several states where there are black colleges should make studies of compensation paid to faculty members in comparable ranks at all state-supported institutions and advise legislative bodies of inadequacies where they exist. The Commission also recommends that states give careful consideration to providing aid for private institutions of higher education *(From Isolation to Mainstream)*.

INSTITUTIONAL INDEPENDENCE

Academic policies set by state agencies should be of a broad nature and should not interfere with the more specific professional academic judgments about faculty appointments, courses of study, admission of individual students, grades and degrees for individual students, specific research projects, appointment of academic and administrative staff and leadership, and protection of academic freedom *(Governance of Higher Education)*.

The Commission recommends that:

1 Public and private institutions seek to establish guidelines clearly defining the limitations on state concern and state regulation or control.

2 A special commission on institutional independence be established within the American Council on Education; this commission, which should

consist of both ACE members and public members, would be assigned responsibility for reviewing external interference with institutional independence and issuing findings after such reviews.

3   Elected officials (unless elected for that specific purpose) not serve as members of governing boards of public institutions or coordinating agencies.

4   A system be developed to assure adequate screening and consultation prior to appointments to governing boards, regardless of who has the final authority to appoint *(The Capitol and the Campus)*.

State grants to institutions for general support should be based on broad formulas and not line-item control *(Governance of Higher Education)*.

Coordinating agencies at the state level should seek to establish, in cooperation with public and private institutions of higher education, guidelines defining areas of state concern and areas of institutional independence that avoid detailed control *(Governance of Higher Education)*.

The Commission recommends: (1) that governors not serve as chairmen or voting members of state coordinating agencies or governing boards of colleges and universities; and (2) that appointments by the governor to governing boards of state colleges and universities, and to state coordinating and/or planning agencies, be made with the advice and consent of the Senate *(The Capitol and the Campus)*.

We conclude that actions by society in response to coercion and violence be undertaken only with reference to those specific individuals and groups who engage in it. A campus as a whole, or a system as a whole, or higher education as a whole, should not be penalized *(Dissent and Disruption)*.

Innovations in programs and in policies should be encouraged by public authorities by influence and not by control *(Governance of Higher Education)*.

The Commission recommends that:

1   If an existing state agency such as the budget office or finance office undertakes budget review for higher education, the coordinating agency should not be given the responsibility for an independent budget review, but should instead be involved in the budget review process of the other state agency. This involvement should include, at the very minimum, the availability of the budget analyst's data, including the institution's presentations and the budget department's analysis; and representatives of the coordinating agencies should attend and participate in all hearings on the appropriation request. In some instances, it may also be possible for members of the coordinating agency staff to work with the budget analyst's staff in a consultative capacity in making the budget review.

2   If there is no existing state agency which does or can undertake budget review for higher education, budget review, as opposed to budget control, could be assigned to the coordinating agency.

3   Although the Commission recommends against investing coordinating agencies with authority to control institutional budgets, it does recommend that states grant to coordinating agencies some funds which the agency itself can grant to institutions to encourage quality improvement and experimentation and innovation consistent with the state's long-range educational goals. Agencies allocating funds for these purposes should regularly evaluate the programs developed with such funds.

4   Coordinating agencies should be assigned certain program review responsibilities and authority consistent with their educational planning functions

5   Coordinating agencies should act in an advisory capacity on matters such as:

Effective use of resources
Educational quality
Access to postsecondary education
Appropriate functions for the various types of institutions
Articulation among the various elements within postsecondary education

6   Coordinating agencies should serve as a buffer and communicator.

Explaining the above matters to agencies of the state government and to the public
Developing mutual understanding of common goals among the elements of postsecondary education
Protecting the institutions, when necessary, from legislative, executive, or public interference in carrying out their educational functions *(The Capitol and the Campus)*.

Universities, colleges, and state planning agencies should carefully study and adopt plans for the development of cluster colleges. The federal government, the states, and private foundations should make funds available for research evaluating the comparative experience of these colleges *(New Students and New Places)*.

Major funding sources, including states, the federal government, and foundations, should recognize not only the potential of new and developing extramural systems for expanding learning opportunities, but also the crucial roles such systems should play in the ultimate development of instructional technologies. Requests by these systems for funds with which to introduce and use new instructional programs, materials, and media should be given favorable consideration *(The Fourth Revolution)*.

OBJECTIVES FOR THE FUTURE
The states will make adequate provision, within the full spectrum of their postsecondary educational resources, for educational opportunities

adequate to the divergent needs of all of their citizens *(Toward a Learning Society).*

State coordinating agencies will become increasingly aware of the resources of all postsecondary institutions in their states and will utilize their influence to assure its adequate financial support and to minimize unnecessary duplication of specialized programs in colleges and universities and other institutions offering postsecondary education *(Toward a Learning Society).*

Educational Opportunity Counseling Centers, such as those we recommended in our report, *'The Campus and the City',* and other appropriate local agencies will have as one of their responsibilities the development and distribution of information about postsecondary educational resources other than colleges and universities *(Toward a Learning Society).*

States will periodically review their statutes to make certain that they adequately protect students against fraudulent claims and unfair business practices that may characterize operations of some private specialty schools *(Toward a Learning Society).*

Local, state, and national governments will provide more opportunities for persons to render public service through well-organized programs, and those who engage in national service will be able to earn educational benefits in addition to their regular in-service compensation *(Toward a Learning Society).*

Public libraries and museums will increasingly recognize their potentials as sources for guidance and independent study that can be utilized to meet the standards and objectives of postsecondary-level instruction *(Toward a Learning Society).*

PARENTS AND STUDENTS

EDUCATIONAL OPTIONS

The total postsecondary age group should become more the subject of concern, and attention should be comparatively less concentrated on those who attend college *(The Purposes and the Performance of Higher Education in the United States)*.

Reasonable efforts should be made to reduce the ranks of the reluctant attenders *(Reform on Campus)*.

More work and service opportunities should be created for students by government and industry and nonprofit agencies, and students should be encouraged to pursue these opportunities, including, occasionally, through "stop-outs" *(The Purposes and the Performance of Higher Education in the United States)*.

FINANCES

Over the next few years, the taxpayer's share of monetary outlays in higher education should be increased modestly, as student-aid funds expand to assist students from low-income families *(Higher Education: Who Pays? Who Benefits? Who Should Pay?)*.

RIGHTS AND RESPONSIBILITIES

Conduct codes should be prepared with student involvement in the process of their preparation, ombudsmen or their equivalent should be appointed, and formal grievance machinery should be available and should end in impartial judicial tribunals *(Governance of Higher Education)*.

Representatives of the administration, the faculty, and the students should participate in establishing guidelines and procedures for relations between a campus and law enforcement authorities. These guidelines should be made public *(Dissent and Disruption)*.

The view that a campus is a sanctuary from the processes of the law and law enforcement should be totally rejected *(Dissent and Disruption)*.

We conclude that students and faculty members are divided, as is American society, about means and ends; but they stand predominantly, as does American society, against disruption and violence and for ordered change *(Dissent and Disruption)*.

GOVERNANCE

Students should serve on joint faculty-student (or trustee-student or administrative-student) committees with the right to vote or should have their own parallel student committees with the right to meet with faculty, trustee, and administrative committees in areas of special interest and competence such as educational policy and student affairs. Students serving on such committees should be given staff assistance *(Governance of Higher Education)*.

Students should be given the opportunity to evaluate the teaching performance of faculty members, and students should be involved in periodic reviews of the performance of departments *(Governance of Higher Education)*.

Students should be associated with the evaluation of teaching performance *(Reform on Campus)*.

Students should be added more generally as voting members to curriculum committees in departments, group majors, and professional schools where there are majors, and on committees concerned with broad learning experiences. If they are not added as members, they should be given some other forum for the expression of their opinions *(Reform on Campus)*.

On campuses where organized protest does occur, faculty and student marshals might be available to monitor these events and to report on violations of campus rules and excessive actions by law enforcement officers. The marshals should be organized so that they are available on a regular, ongoing basis *(Dissent and Disruption)*.

OBJECTIVE FOR THE FUTURE
Apprenticeship, internship, and in-service training will be used more widely than they are today to prepare persons for their life work in many professions, paraprofessions, and occupations *(Toward a Learning Society)*.

FACULTY

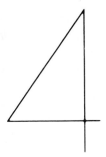

CURRICULUM

The curriculum as a whole should be reviewed, campus by campus, in consultation with high school leaders, to assess its broad relevance not only to appropriate student interests but also to prior and subsequent learning experiences *(Reform on Campus).*

More faculty attention and more funds, on a comparative basis, should be devoted to lower-division students *(Reform on Campus).*

Greater attention in the curriculum should be given to (*a*) the creative arts and (*b*) world cultures *(Reform on Campus).*

Because expanding technology will extend higher learning to large numbers of people who have been unable to take advantage of it in the past, because it will provide instruction in forms that will be more effective than conventional instruction for some learners in some subjects, because it will be more effective for all learners and many teachers under many circumstances, and because it will significantly reduce costs of higher education in the long run, its early advancement should be encouraged by the adequate commitment of colleges and universities to its utilization and development and by adequate support from governmental and other agencies concerned with the advancement of higher learning *(The Fourth Revolution).*

Since a grossly inadequate supply of good quality instructional materials now exists, a major thrust of financial support and effort on behalf of instructional technology for the next decade should be toward the development and utilization of outstanding instructional programs and materials. The academic disciplines should follow the examples of physics and mathematics in playing a significant role in such efforts *(The Fourth Revolution).*

More opportunities should be created for students to gain community service and work experience *(Reform on Campus).*

Colleges and universities that are responsible for the training of prospective university, college, and high school teachers should begin now to incorporate in their curricula instruction on the development of teaching-learning segments that appropriately utilize the expanding technologies of instruction *(The Fourth Revolution).*

Existing graduate education warrants a thorough review *(Reform on Campus).*

Any further general expansion of graduate education should proceed only after the most careful consideration *(Reform on Campus).*

High priority should be given to adaptation of teacher-training programs to changing needs. There should be increased emphasis on specialized training to prepare teachers for service in ghetto schools, in programs for mentally retarded or physically handicapped children, in early child development programs and day-care centers, and in vocational education programs *(College Graduates and Jobs)*.

At present too many white, middle-class teachers are prepared in essentially nonspecific ways for general purpose assignments. The problems of the large urban schools, small rural schools, bilingual-bicultural schools, and wealthy suburban school districts require teachers trained for these separate constituencies. University faculties of arts and sciences and education should concentrate more upon training teachers for different kinds of schools. Because of the variety of tasks there can be no single model of a teacher training program, and the National Council for the Accreditation of Teacher Education and state accrediting associations should encourage diversity. A common element in all preservice programs should be an emphasis upon bringing theory and practice together in clinical settings *(Continuity and Discontinuity)*.

The initiation of programs for an individualized "foundation year" should be available on an optional basis to all interested students *(A Chance to Learn)*.

University health science centers should give serious consideration to curriculum reforms. Their admission policies should be made more flexible and their programs more responsive to the expressed needs of students. Greater emphasis should be placed on comprehensive medicine in both the M.D.-candidate program and in graduate medical education. In all phases of medical and dental education, including residency programs, there should be more careful integration of abstract theory and clinical experience. Residency programs should be planned and reviewed by the entire faculty, and residency training should include experience in community hospitals, neighborhood clinics, and other facilities, as well as in teaching hospitals *(Higher Education and the Nation's Health)*.

All university health science centers should consider the development of programs for the training of physician's and dentist's associates and assistants, where they do not exist, and, wherever feasible, such programs should be initiated forthwith *(Higher Education and the Nation's Health)*.

Comprehensive colleges and community colleges should develop and expand their curricula in the allied health professions where this has not been done, and they should also seek and accept guidance from university health science centers and area health education centers in the planning and evaluation of these educational programs *(Higher Education and the Nation's Health)*.

There should be an increased emphasis on basic programs of education in the health sciences—in curricula leading to associate's, bachelor's, and master's degrees—to provide a uniform core of training for nurses, allied health workers, physicians, dentists, and persons preparing themselves for administrative, educational, and research careers in the health field *(College Graduates and Jobs).*

The training of health care personnel should be substantially expanded for the immediate future to eliminate the one remaining major deficit in highly trained manpower *(The Purposes and the Performance of Higher Education in the United States).*

Though often different in temperament, training, and style, school and college teachers and administrators must work together to reduce many of the present undesirable discontinuities in the relationships between school and college *(Continuity and Discontinuity).*

The movement to introduce courses on women and interdisciplinary women's study programs should be encouraged by institutions of higher education, at least on a transitional basis, but these courses and programs should be organized within existing disciplines and not under separate departments of women's studies *(Opportunities for Women in Higher Education).*

Curriculum development in the humanities and social studies has lagged behind mathematics and science. Schools and colleges, together with funding agencies, should foster new programs and approaches *(Continuity and Discontinuity).*

Curricula should be examined to be certain they reflect the history, culture, and current roles of minority groups *(The Purposes and the Performance of Higher Education in the United States).*

DEGREE STRUCTURES

Colleges and universities should use great caution in adopting new degree programs, and they should conduct periodic reviews of existing degree programs, with a view to eliminating those in which very few degrees are awarded, whether or not they are required to do so by state coordinating bodies. Coordinating bodies may also need to conduct such reviews if the institutions fail in their responsibilities. In multicampus institutions, there is a strong case for confining highly specialized degree programs to only one or two campuses within the system *(The More Effective Use of Resources).*

A degree (or other form of credit) should be made available to students at least every two years in their careers (and in some cases every year) *(Less Time, More Options).*

The time to get a degree should be shortened by one year to the B.A. and by one or two more years to the Ph.D. and to M.D. practice *(Less Time More Options)*.

Certain new degrees should be widely accepted: master of philosophy and doctor of arts *(Less Time, More Options)*.

Professional schools and academic departments should cooperate in the development of joint degree programs in response to emerging societal problems and in response to the advancement of knowledge or technological change *(Less Time, More Options)*.

All two-year colleges should award an associate of arts or associate of applied science degree to all students who satisfactorily complete a two-year prescribed curriculum, and students who enter with adequate advanced standing should have the option of earning the associate degree in less than two years. Non-degree-credit courses should be confined to short-term courses and to training of the skilled craftsman type, for which certificates should be provided, and to remedial work *(The Open-Door Colleges)*.

Leading research universities should refrain from cutbacks in graduate programs except on a carefully considered, selective basis. We also recommend that institutions with less emphasis on research consider curtailment or elimination, on a selective basis, of Ph.D. programs that are not of high quality or that are too small to be operated economically. We urge great caution in the development of new Ph.D. programs in particular fields at existing doctoral-granting institutions and do not believe that there is a need for any new Ph.D.-granting institutions, although some or even many institutions will be introducing the B.A. degree *(The More Effective Use of Resources)*.

Policies requiring students to obtain advanced degrees within a certain number of years should allow for a limited extension of the period for those graduate students whose family circumstances require them to study on a part-time basis *(Opportunities for Women in Higher Education)*.

The Commission reiterates its support of the development of external degree and other nontraditional study programs, emphasizing the need, that has not in all cases been observed, for high quality in such programs. They are especially important in relation to the special needs of mature married women for continuing education *(Opportunities for Women in Higher Education)*.

The continued development of doctor of arts programs should be encouraged. We consider the doctor of arts a more suitable degree than the Ph.D. for many types of employment *(College Graduates and Jobs)*.

EXPANDING OPTIONS FOR STUDENTS

More broad learning experiences should be made available to students, and more opportunities for creative activity should be provided as through independent study and the creative arts (*The Purposes and the Performance of Higher Education in the United States*).

Urban campuses, in appropriate instances, should offer certain portions of their programs in off-campus facilities—at industrial plants, in business and government offices, and at public libraries and schoolrooms in residential areas (*The Campus and the City*).

Cluster and theme colleges within large institutions should provide particularly good opportunities for diversity (*Reform on Campus*).

Most professional schools and academic departments should be actively involved, along with their institutions, in developing policies that encourage students to stop out between high school and college, or after several years of undergraduate education, or between undergraduate and graduate work, and should assist those students to gain relevant work experience during periods away from school. Of equal importance are policies that facilitate part-time study for the working student (*College Graduates and Jobs*).

Community colleges should provide adequate resources for effective guidance, including not only provision for an adequate professional counseling staff but also provision for involvement of the entire faculty in guidance of students enrolled in their courses. The Commission also recommends that all community college districts provide for effective coordination of their guidance services with both counseling and placement services with those of the public employment offices and other appropriate offices (*The Open-Door Colleges*).

ENROLLMENT

Colleges and universities have a responsibility to develop policies specifically designed to bring about changes in the attitudes of administrators and faculty members where these have been antagonistic to enrollment of women in traditionally male fields (*Opportunities for Women in Higher Education*).

In developing their plans for expansion, university health science centers should adopt programs designed to recruit more women and members of minority groups as medical and dental students (*Higher Education and the Nation's Health*).

Because of the evidence that many women enter college with inadequate mathematical training, special provision should be made to ensure that women desiring to major in fields calling for extensive use of mathematics are encouraged to make up this deficiency in order to enter the fields of their choice *(Opportunities for Women in Higher Education)*.

Rules and policies that discriminate against the part-time graduate or professional student should allow for exceptions to accommodate men or women whose family circumstances require them to study on a part-time basis. Any limitation on the total number of graduate or professional students admitted by departments or schools and by the institution as a whole should be applied on a full-time-equivalent rather than on a head-count basis *(Opportunities for Women in Higher Education)*.

INNOVATION, SERVICE, AND RESEARCH

The process of change in each institution should be examined to assure (a) that innovations can be initiated without unnecessary impediments, (b) that all innovations of significance are subject to subsequent evaluation and review, and (c) that all experimental programs include a specific time plan for their termination or for their incorporation into the mainstream of the academic program *(Reform on Campus)*.

Service should be extended on a more even-handed basis to groups and persons in connection with problems where it may be helpful, subject to the major limitation that any service should be appropriate to the educational functions of higher education. *(The Purposes and the Performance of Higher Education in the United States)*.

Colleges should develop programs to serve new constituencies, especially adults and transfers from two-year colleges *(The Purposes and the Performance of Higher Education in the United States)*.

In communities where effective desegregation of local school systems has not been achieved, institutions of higher education should offer their resources of research and consultation to local school administrators and other community leaders *(A Chance to Learn)*.

Experimental programs for the early development of verbal skills should be sponsored and administered by institutions of higher education with active participation from members of the community *(A Chance to Learn)*.

Colleges founded for Negroes should utilize the present period of transition for curriculum innovation and enrichment, and most of them should concentrate on developing, in addition to general liberal arts courses, strong comprehensive undergraduate programs in preprofessional subjects and in subjects that prepare students for advanced education and high-demand occupations *(From Isolation to Mainstream)*.

Those Negro colleges with strong resources and successful operating programs of Afro-American instruction and research should be encouraged to seek special financial support for the further development of such endeavors, and foundations and governments should favorably consider requests for such support *(From Isolation to Mainstream)*.

There should be increased emphasis in educational programs on providing experience in working with other health care personnel as a team *(College Graduates and Jobs)*.

There should be increased emphasis on encouraging research on alternative ways of utilizing health manpower. There is a need for studies evaluating innovations in health care delivery, and there is also a need for comparative studies on differing patterns of utilization of health manpower in selected countries, especially with a view to determining how a number of other industrial countries have achieved lower infant mortality rates and higher life expectancy rates than the United States, despite lower physician-population ratios. *(College Graduates and Jobs)*.

Professional schools in universities and colleges should undertake the responsibility for providing guidance and advice in connection with programs of continuing education for members of their professions, whether these are provided under the auspices of extension divisions, evening school programs of the professional schools, or in other ways *(College Graduates and Jobs)*.

All programs of professional education involving human services should seek to incorporate clinical or operational experience in the student's training, but we would also warn that successful clinical training requires careful planning, evaluation, and adaptation to changing needs *(College Graduates and Jobs)*.

Agencies and individuals that have been conducting studies of future supply and demand for Ph.D.'s should continue to review and update their work. We are impressed by the differences in outlook among fields and believe that the time has come for increased emphasis on projections relating to individual fields or groups of fields and less reliance on broad aggregative studies *(College Graduates and Jobs)*.

To help maintain differentiation of function and to reduce excessive tension within state systems, two steps should be taken: (1) There should be experimentation on a large scale with doctor of arts degrees as a teaching alternative to the research Ph.D; and (2) there should be a redefinition of institutional quality to focus upon the value added by the college experience itself *(Continuity and Discontinuity)*.

Schools and colleges alike should remember that experimentation carries with it the price of accountability. No new programs at either level should be initiated without clear criteria for evaluation *(Continuity and Discontinuity)*.

PROFESSIONAL OBLIGATIONS

The Commission recommends:

Carefully studying and adopting a varied mixture of class size at the different levels of instruction and establishing appropriate average class sizes that different departments may be expected to meet

Seeking to prevent undue proliferation of courses by periodic review of the totality of course offerings in a department

Involving the faculty in developing policies directed toward achieving appropriate and equitable teaching loads

Establishing standards relating to a reasonable maximum amount of time to be spent in consulting activities

Maintaining reasonable and equitable policies relating to sabbatical leave for all career members of the faculty, including assistant professors

Analyzing costs of support personnel, in comparison with those of other similar institutions with a view to identifying possible excessive costs in some aspects of support functions, but also of making certain that these functions are being conducted efficiently and that highly paid faculty members are not performing functions that could be delegated to lower paid support personnel *(The More Effective Use of Resources).*

Faculties in each institution should undertake the most careful analysis of the implications of collective bargaining and, more broadly, of which of the alternative forms of governance they prefer *(Governance of Higher Education).*

Faculties should be granted, where they do not already have it, the general level of authority as recommended by the American Association of University Professors *(Governance of Higher Education).*

Representation and bargaining units should be composed of faculty members, including department chairmen *(Governance of Higher Education).*

The approach to contract coverage should be one of restraint, with the contract covering economic benefits and with academic affairs left (or put) in the hands of the faculty senate or equivalent council *(Governance of Higher Education).*

Tenure systems should be so administered in practice (1) that advancements to tenure and after tenure are based on merit, (2) that the criteria to be used in tenure decisions are made clear at the time of employment, (3) that codes of conduct specify the obligations of tenured faculty members, (4) that adjustments in the size and in the assignments of staff in accord with institutional welfare be possible when there is a fully justifiable case for them, (5) that fair internal procedures be available to hear any cases that may arise, and (6) that the percentage of faculty members with tenure does not become excessive *(Governance of Higher Education).*

Persons on a 50 percent time basis or more should be eligible for tenure, but the time elapsed before a decision on tenure must be made should be counted on a full-time-equivalent basis *(Governance of Higher Education).*

Teaching performance should be the basic criterion for rewards to faculty members, except in research universities where research, of necessity, is of equal or greater importance *(Reform on Campus).*

Colleges and universities should examine their utilization of faculty time and in particular they should do so if their student-faculty ratios fall below the following median levels for their categories.

	PUBLIC	PRIVATE
Research universities	22.0 (weighted)	16.0 (weighted)
Other doctoral-granting universities	21.6 (weighted)	22.0 (weighted)
Comprehensive universities and colleges I	19.7 (weighted)	18.6 (weighted)
Comprehensive universities and colleges II	17.9 (weighted)	16.5 (weighted)
Liberal arts colleges I	*	12.2 (unweighted)
Liberal arts colleges II	*	14.3 (unweighted)
Two-year colleges	19.2 (unweighted)	15.4 (unweighted)

* There are no public liberal arts colleges I, and data have not been included on public liberal arts colleges II, because the number of these colleges reporting the necessary information was very small.

NOTE: The weight for graduate as against undergraduate students is 3 to 1 in universities and 2 to 1 in comprehensive colleges.

SOURCE: *The More Effective Use of Resources.*

Special efforts should be made to find qualified members of minority groups and women for inclusion in the "pool" of candidates for consideration when faculty appointments are being made; and such persons should be given special consideration in employment for faculty positions where their employment will lead to the creation of a more effective total academic environment for the entire student group that will be affected *(The Purposes and the Performance of Higher Education in the United States).*

Colleges and universities should encourage school-college collaboration on substantive matters through promotion and reward policies that recognize the importance of such activities *(Continuity and Discontinuity).*

There should be no discrimination on the basis of sex or marital status in appointing teaching or research assistants or in awarding fellowships. Furthermore, part-time graduate and professional students should not be barred from eligibility for fellowships. In addition, there should be no antinepotism rules in connection with these appointments or awards *(Opportunities for Women in Higher Education)*.

Enhanced emphasis should be placed on advising as an increasingly important aspect of higher education *(Reform on Campus)*.

OBJECTIVES FOR THE FUTURE

Colleges and universities will successfully resist pressures to grant degree credit for those activities and experiences that are not clearly planned as part of an academic learning program designed to meet the educational goals recognized by the degrees offered *(Toward a Learning Society)*.

Institutions of postsecondary education will grant degrees, certificates, and honors more frequently than they now do. They will also devise frequent recognition for specific outstanding academic achievements and for service to the institution and its members *(Toward a Learning Society)*.

Undergraduate and professional degrees will increasingly become only a part of the cumulative record of an individual's educational accomplishments. Ultimately, the degree will become less important than the total record as evidence of such accomplishments *(Toward a Learning Society)*.

Wherever academic programs are offered for students who are adults of all ages, the rules for student conduct, campus traditions, and the learning environment will be hospitable to them and will not discriminate against older students *(Toward a Learning Society)*.

The provision of part-time learning opportunities will be considered a legitimate function of all colleges and universities, regardless of their level of instruction or type of control. After deliberation, some institutions will elect not to perform this function, but their decisions will be based on particular objectives they have set for themselves because of policy options, limitations of space, finances, or facilities, and not on a belief that, such instruction is inherently inappropriate to colleges and universities *(Toward a Learning Society)*.

College- and school-based vocational education will emphasize general knowledge common to broad groups of occupations rather than provide training for specific skills. Industry, on the other hand, will accept responsibility for training persons to perform skills required by specific tasks on the job *(Toward a Learning Society)*.

ADMINIS-TRATORS

5

EXPANDING OPTIONS

Alternative avenues by which students can earn degrees or complete a major portion of their work for a degree should be expanded to increase accessibility of higher education for those to whom it is now unavailable because of work schedules, geographic location, or responsibilities in the home *(Less Time, More Options)*.

Opportunities should be expanded for students to alternate employment and study, as in the "sandwich" programs in Great Britain and in programs at some American colleges *(Less Time, More Options)*.

Opportunities should be created for persons to re-enter higher education throughout their active careers in regular daytime classes, nighttime classes, summer courses, and special short-term programs, with degrees and certificates available as appropriate *(Less Time, More Options)*.

We recommend consideration of the establishment of learning pavilions at community colleges and comprehensive colleges located in central cities *(The Campus and the City)*.

Institutions of higher education should contribute to the advancement of instructional technology not only by giving favorable consideration to expanding its use, whenever such use is appropriate, but also by placing responsibility for its introduction and utilization at the highest possible level of academic administration *(The Fourth Revolution)*.

Colleges and universities should supplement their instructional staffs with qualified technologists and specialists to assist instructors in the design, planning, and evaluation of teaching-learning units that can be used with the expanding instructional technologies. Institutions of higher education at all levels should develop their potentials for training specialists and professionals needed to perform the new functions that are associated with the increasing utilization of instructional technology on the nation's college and university campuses *(The Fourth Revolution)*.

Colleges and universities should provide incentives to faculty members who contribute to the advancement of instructional technology. Released time for the development of instructional materials and promotions and salary improvement for successful achievement in such endeavors should be part of that encouragement *(The Fourth Revolution)*.

Colleges enrolling large numbers of disadvantaged or minority students should review their institutional programs to determine if they are designed to meet the educational needs of the students involved *(The Campus and the City)*.

University health science centers and area health education centers should provide leadership in encouraging the development and expansion of continuing education programs for nurses and allied health workers in appropriate educational institutions *(College Graduates and Jobs)*.

Cultural and "life-long learning" facilities and opportunities should be made available to the general public on an expanded basis *(The Purposes and the Performance of Higher Education in the United States)*.

ADMISSIONS POLICIES

College admissions officers should be appointed with great care because their work is intimately tied to the primary mission of the institution. If possible, they should have both faculty status and a prominent place in the administrative hierarchy *(Continuity and Discontinuity)*.

Admissions policies should be examined to assure that they serve both the cause of diversity within higher education and also the possibilities for diversity at the high school level *(Reform on Campus)*.

Colleges and universities should give careful attention to recruitment policies designed not only to maintain adequate enrollments but also to achieve such objectives as equality of opportunity, broad geographical distribution wherever feasible, and diversity in the student body. As we approach a period of stationary enrollment, many public institutions of higher education will need to place greater emphasis than they have in the past on recruitment programs aimed at maintaining adequate enrollments *(The More Effective Use of Resources)*.

Graduate and professional schools should give special consideration to the graduates of Negro colleges who are candidates for admission, and we reaffirm our recommendations that federal grants and loans be provided to assist students from low-income families who enroll in graduate and professional schools *(From Isolation to Mainstream)*.

Graduate and professional departments should coordinate recruiting of disadvantaged students *(A Chance to Learn)*.

Four-year colleges generally should be prepared to accept qualified transfer students and give them appropriate credit for the work they have already completed *(A Chance to Learn)*.

Every student accepted into a program requiring compensatory education should receive the necessary commitment of resources to allow his engagement in an appropriate level of course work by the end of no more than two years *(A Chance to Learn)*.

Colleges and universities should make a special effort to identify and support, at all levels of their college and graduate preparation, young Negro men and women who show promise of becoming college teachers. Colleges founded for Negroes should seek assistance from state governments and foundations for programs that will pay the salaries of their faculty members while they complete work for their doctorates at other institutions *(From Isolation to Mainstream)*.

Institutions of higher education should seek to increase their retention rates through improved counseling programs, where these are deficient, and through establishing the practice of conducting an "exit interview" with every student who plans to withdraw *(The More Effective Use of Resources)*.

Private colleges should reexamine their admissions policies to determine whether expansion of open-admission or flexible-admission student places in their institutions would be compatible with their particular educational missions *(The Campus and the City)*.

Admission standards should be relaxed for members of disadvantaged groups, provided that the chances are good that such students can meet graduation requirements in full *(The Purposes and the Performance of Higher Education in the United States)*.

Experimentation with college admissions practices should be encouraged. In particular, more experimentation is needed to determine the quality of testing as a basis for admission and placement, the importance of student motivation and life experience as indicators of promise, and the feasibility of deferred admissions as a means of providing educational flexibility for students *(Continuity and Discontinuity)*.

Colleges should review their admissions requirements and, except for competence in the basic skills of reading, writing, and arithmetic, should not require or suggest particular courses of study at the secondary level unless such requirements or suggestions are tied explicitly to the colleges' own degree requirements or to those of the system of which they are a part *(Continuity and Discontinuity)*.

Both public and private institutions should give careful attention to admissions policies suitable to an era characterized by universal access to the total system of higher education and by a no-growth enrollment trend. Public agencies, including coordinating councils and state planning commissions, should determine general policies on student admissions within state systems, including policies with respect to number of places, equality of access by race, age, and sex, and the level of academic admissibility among types of institutions. Decisions on individual students should be left to each campus *(Continuity and Discontinuity)*.

There should be no discrimination on the basis of sex in the use of either high school grades or test scores as admissions criteria *(Opportunities for Women in Higher Education)*.

Policies that prevent part-time study or that discriminate against admission of adults desirous of continuing their education should be liberalized to permit enrollment of qualified mature men and women whose education has been interrupted because of family responsibilities or for other reasons. High school or college records should not be ruled inapplicable as evidence of eligibility for admission simply because the records were acquired some years earlier *(Opportunities for Women in Higher Education).*

There should be no discrimination on the basis of sex or marital status in admitting students to graduate and professional schools *(Opportunities for Women in Higher Education).*

A women desiring to enter graduate or professional school after some years away from higher education and generally meeting departmental standards for admission (e.g., in her undergraduate grade-point average) should be given an opportunity to make up for her inability to meet any special requirements, such as specific mathematical requirements. Under no circumstances should she be denied admission because her undergraduate education occurred some years earlier *(Opportunities for Women in Higher Education).*

The existence of separate institutions for nontraditional study should not be used as an excuse for denying qualified adults of either sex the opportunity to study on traditional campuses on a full-time or part-time basis *(Opportunities for Women in Higher Education).*

Large campuses should have an administrative officer specifically concerned with ensuring that qualified adults are given opportunities to pursue undergraduate or graduate study on a full-time or part-time basis. Whether there should be a separate center for continuing education of women should be decided in the light of the circumstances prevailing on any given campus. We believe that there is often a case for a center primarily concerned with the educational problems of mature women, but that the need for such a center may be transitional and that in the future the concept of continuing educational opportunities for mature women is likely to be so thoroughly accepted that a center especially oriented toward women's problems may no longer be desirable or necessary *(Opportunities for Women in Higher Education).*

ENROLLMENT AND TUITION
There should be a greater mixing of age groups on campus through providing more opportunities for older persons to take classes and to obtain needed financial support *(The Purposes and the Performance of Higher Education in the United States).*

No tuition or very low tuition should be charged for the first two years in public institutions including community colleges, state colleges, and universities *(The Capitol and the Campus)*.

Public institutions—and especially the community colleges—should maintain a relatively low tuition policy for the first two years of higher education. Such tuition should be sufficiently low that no student, after receipt of whatever federal and state support he or she may be eligible for, is barred from access to some public institution by virtue of inadequate finances *(Higher Education: Who Pays? Who Benefits? Who Should Pay?)*.

Public colleges and universities should carefully study their educational costs per student and consider restructuring their tuition charge at upper-division and graduate levels to more nearly reflect the real differences in the cost of education per student, eventually reaching a general level equal to about one-third of educational costs *(Higher Education: Who Pays? Who Benefits? Who Should Pay?)*.

Private colleges and universities should increase their tuition charges at a rate that is no more rapid than the increase in per capita disposable income. The rate of increase in tuition should be less pronounced than this, if at all possible *(Higher Education: Who Pays? Who Benefits? Who Should Pay?)*.

Private colleges and universities also should carefully study their educational costs per student and consider restructuring their tuition charges, so that tuition is relatively low for lower-division students, somewhat higher for upper-division students, and considerably higher for graduate and professional students *(Higher Education: Who Pays? Who Benefits? Who Should Pay?)*.

The Commission recommends a relatively low uniform national tuition policy for institutions providing medical and dental education *(Higher Education and the Nation's Health)*.

The governing boards, administrations, and faculties of most colleges founded for Negroes should plan to accommodate enrollments which may double on the average, certainly by the year 2000 and possibly by 1980 *(From Isolation to Mainstream)*.

By the year 2000, colleges founded for Negroes should have enrollments in keeping with the guidelines suggested for all institutions of higher education of comparable types. Comprehensive colleges should have 5,000 students. Liberal arts colleges should have at least 1,000 students. Public community colleges should have at least 2,000 students. Colleges with very low enrollments and with little prospect of meeting these goals should consider relocation or merging with other institutions which have complementing programs and facilities *(From Isolation to Mainstream)*.

AFFIRMATIVE ACTION

Colleges should closely examine their admissions policies with respect to sex, race, and age. They should then be certain that their admissions practices implement those policies that relate to social justice in higher education. Separate prediction equations for men and women, minority students, and adults should be developed and, where feasible, differential prediction by general field of study should be used *(Continuity and Discontinuity)*.

Community colleges should provide remedial education that is flexible and responsive to the individual student's needs; such programs should be subject to continual study and evaluation, and community colleges should seek the cooperation of other educational institutions in providing for remedial education. In addition, the Commission reaffirms its recommendation that an individualized "foundation year" be made available on an optional basis to all interested students *(The Open-Door Colleges)*.

All institutions should accept responsibility to serve the disadvantaged minorities at each of the levels at which they provide training, and universities should accept a special responsibility to serve a substantially greater representation of currently disadvantaged minorities in their graduate programs *(A Chance to Learn)*.

Historically white colleges in the North and in the South should consider appointing blacks to some of the administrative positions open at their institutions. Organization of advanced management seminars and short courses for administrators at colleges founded for Negroes, supported at least partially by foundations and business firms, is also recommended.

We also suggest that colleges and universities develop programs and prepare proposals to the government and foundations for support of administrative intern programs for black students *(From Isolation to Mainstream)*.

Each institution should issue an annual report on its present and potential contributions to equality of opportunity *(A Chance to Learn)*.

Departments and schools should be required to maintain complete records on all applicants for admission to graduate and professional education and to make these records available to administrative officers on request. They should also be required to maintain records indicating that, in any programs designed to recruit able graduate students, equal efforts have been made to recruit women as well as men. For example, through letters or circulars addressed to departments in women's colleges as well as to those in male and coeducational institutions *(Opportunities for Women in Higher Education).*

Positive attitudes on the part of faculty members toward the serious pursuit of graduate study and research by women are greatly needed. College and university administrations should assume responsibility for adoption of policies that will encourage positive, rather than negative, attitudes of faculty members in all fields *(Opportunities for Women in Higher Education).*

Colleges and universities should take especially vigorous steps to overcome a pervasive problem of absence of women in top administrative positions. Women should be given opportunities by their departments to serve as department chairmen, because academic administrators are usually selected from among persons who have served ably as department chairmen. Most important is an administrative stance that is highly positive toward providing opportunities for women to rise in the administrative hierarchy. Also very important is the provision of management training opportunities for both men and women who have potential administrative ability but do not hold administrative positions *(Opportunities for Women in Higher Education).*

INSTITUTIONAL POLICY

Campuses should not add and, where feasible, should eliminate operational, custodial, and service functions which are not directly tied to academic and educational activities and which can be performed as well or better by other agencies *(The Purposes and the Performance of Higher Education in the United States).*

All relatively large institutions of higher education should maintain an office of institutional research or its equivalent and relatively small institutions should seek to enter into arrangements with nearby similar institutions to conduct jointly sponsored programs of institutional research *(The More Effective Use of Resources).*

Institutions of higher education engaged with faculty unionism should employ staff members or consultants who are experienced in collective bargaining negotiations and consider the possibility of agreements that will induce increases in the productivity of faculty members and other academic employees without impairing educational effectiveness *(The More Effective Use of Resources).*

Significant actions which could be construed as violations of the general law should be handled by the outside courts. A corollary is that campus authorities have an obligation to report significant violations of the general law that come to their attention *(Dissent and Disruption).*

Careful consideration should be given to use of *(a)* ombudsmen, *(b)* hearing officers, and *(c)* campus attorneys *(Dissent and Disruption)*.

Universities with university health science centers should seek to ensure that management of these centers is organized in such a way as to enable the centers to meet the greatly increased responsibilities they are now being asked to fulfill. Among the policies that are likely to contribute to effective management are (1) separate but coordinated administration of health science centers and teaching hospitals and, where feasible, reliance on agreements with affiliated hospitals rather than ownership of a teaching hospital, and (2) development of an able core of middle managers to assume responsibility for the more routine administrative functions *(The More Effective Use of Resources)*.

BUDGETARY MATTERS
Institutions of higher education, especially those with relatively high administrative costs, should conduct analyses of these costs with a view to identifying functions or parts of the institution in which these costs may be excessive or in which there is evidence of administrative inefficiency *(The More Effective Use of Resources)*.

We recommend that campuses consider the following special policies for increasing their flexibility to adjust to a period of a declining rate of growth:
- Recapturing certain vacated positions for central reassignment, as recommended earlier
- Hiring temporary and part-time faculty members
- Providing that tenure does not necessarily apply only to the specific original assignment of specialized field and location
- Employing persons with subject-matter flexibility, as made easier in the training for the doctor of arts degree, and by encouraging persons to shift fields where this is desirable and possible
- Providing opportunities for early retirements on a full-time or part-time basis *(The More Effective Use of Resources)*.

The Commission recommends (1) that long-range plans for capital expansion be continually revised to meet changing circumstances, (2) that adequate allowance be made for meeting increased debt service and maintenance costs on the basis of several alternative and relatively conservative estimates of the behavior of future income, and (3) that capital and operating budgets be consolidated (with the capital budget converted to a rental costs basis), so that shifts can be made from one allocation to the other at the discretion of the board of trustees *(The More Effective Use of Resources)*.

Capital investment plants should give full advance consideration to the possible impact of accelerated degree programs *(The More Effective Use of Resources).*

Colleges and universities should develop a "self-renewal" fund of 1 to 3 percent each year taken from existing allocations *(The More Effective Use of Resources).*

All institutions of higher education should place emphasis on policies that will ensure budgetary flexibility. Combinations of policies that will achieve this goal will vary from institution to institution but may well include elements of (1) selective cutbacks, (2) across-the-board budgetary cuts, (3) consolidation of existing programs, (4) readaptation of existing programs, (5) "every tub on its own bottom," and (6) central reassignment of positions vacated due to resignation, retirement, or death. *(The More Effective Use of Resources).*

Institutions of higher education should develop plans for gradually shifting to a practice of requiring budgets of departments and other units to include a rental charge for the space they occupy and the equipment they use *(The More Effective Use of Resources).*

Institutions of higher education should seek economies in computer expenditures by (1) contracting for computer services where this is found to be advantageous, (2) charging the full costs of computer services used in instruction and departmental research against departmental budgets, (3) charging the full costs of computer services used in extramurally financed research against the relevant research budgets, and (4) sharing computer facilities with nearby institutions of higher education where this appears to be a more advantageous solution than contracting out *(The More Effective Use of Resources).*

Colleges and universities should minimize cash balances held in checking accounts and make certain, especially in large institutions, that purchasing functions and inventory management are handled by persons with adequate special training *(The More Effective Use of Resources).*

Institutions of higher education should seek to alter their budgetary procedures in such a way as to induce cost-saving changes, giving special attention to the possibilities of permitting departments and schools to carry over from year to year significant proportions of unspent balances in their budgets and of permitting them to retain a portion of the budgetary savings resulting from innovation or investment in more efficient equipment. Ways and means of providing monetary compensation, probably principally in the form of special awards, for employees who make constructive suggestions for innovations that result in economies should be developed.

Because changes in budgetary procedures in public institutions of higher education will often require changes in state legislation or administrative regulations, it may be necessary for institutions to seek permission to carry out pilot projects designed to demonstrate that changes in procedures will yield economies. The Commission recommends that state coordinating councils and boards seek to encourage such projects *(The More Effective Use of Resources)*.

Institutions of higher education should consider the establishment of committees including faculty, students, and administrators to serve in an advisory capacity in relation to the preparation of the budget when severe cuts must be made. Where it is not considered feasible or desirable to establish such committees, the more traditional practice of holding hearings on major budgetary decisons can provide faculty and students with opportunities to express their views *(The More Effective Use of Resources)*.

FACILITATION

The Commission recommends careful study of space utilization standards and their reasonable application *(The More Effective Use of Resources)*.

Institutions of higher education should carefully consider programs of year-round operation, but also recognize that the conditions that determine whether net savings will be achieved through year-round operation are complex and require careful study and planning *(The More Effective Use of Resources)*.

Increased emphasis should be placed on the development and training of a staff of middle managers who could assume many of the day-to-day functions of department chairmen, deans, and top administrators, thereby (1) reducing the amount of released faculty time required for administration; (2) providing more efficient and consistent administrative policies and practices; and (3) providing experienced and informed professional assistance to faculty members assuming new administrative responsibilities. There should likewise be emphasis on providing specialized training for nonacademic administrators. The Commission also recommends that the president of the institution be given adequate assistance from a highly capable staff *(The More Effective Use of Resources)*.

Institutions of higher education should devote a portion of their summer schedule and facilities for camps for educationally disadvantaged children *(A Chance to Learn)*.

Universities with health science centers should develop plans for accelerating premedical and medical education. The Commission also recommends that plans be developed for shortening the total duration of predental and dental education where it is unnecessarily prolonged.

We particularly favor a program calling for three years (instead of four) after the B.A. to obtain the M.D. or D.D.S. and a three-year residency (instead of the typical four years for internship and residency) *(Higher Education and the Nation's Health).*

Universities with health science centers, and especially those developing new centers, should consider plans for (1) greater integration of preprofessional and professional curricula, (2) increasing the student's options so that basic training in health-related sciences can lead to training for a variety of health-related professions as well as medicine and dentistry, (3) awarding a master's degree at the end of this basic training period, and (4) integrating instruction in the basic sciences on main university campuses if this can be accomplished without major costs associated with the shift, without interfering with integration of basic science and clinical science instruction, and without delaying the opportunities for students to have early contact with patients.

In addition, the Commission recommends that existing two-year medical schools that do not lead to M.S.-candidate education within the same university system convert to provide full M.D.-candidate education as soon as possible and that no new two-year schools of this type be established.

The Commission also recommends that new public health schools be made parts of university health science centers and that existing public health schools become parts of such centers as soon as possible.

The Commission recommends that new university health science centers consider providing clinical instruction in selected hospitals on the British model *(Higher Education and the Nation's Health).*

University health science centers should be responsible, in their respective geographic areas, for coordinating the education of health care personnel and for cooperation with other community agencies in improving the organization of health care delivery. Their educational and research programs should become more concerned with problems of health care delivery and the social and economic environment of health care. All new medical and dental schools should be parts of university health science centers, and, wherever feasible, existing separate medical and dental schools should likewise become parts of university health science centers *(Higher Education and the Nation's Health).*

University administrations should appoint appropriate officers to develop plans for the expansion of university health science centers and for their transformation to perform the broad educational, research, and community service functions recommended in this report. University administrations should also be actively involved in the planning of area health education centers. To accomplish these objectives will often require administrative changes in the university and in the health science centers as well. Careful integration of instruction in the biomedical sciences and social sciences between university health science centers and departments on major university campuses should be achieved *(Higher Education and the Nation's Health).*

Colleges founded for Negroes should initiate proposals to state coordinating councils, boards of education, and other educational agencies for the support and development of seminars, special training institutes, and classes to improve the skills of elementary and secondary school teachers *(From Isolation to Mainstream).*

The library should become a more active participant in the instructional process with an added proportion of funds, perhaps as much as a doubling *(Reform on Campus).*

The introduction of new technologies to help libraries continue to improve their services to increasing numbers of users should be given first priority in the efforts of colleges and universities, government agencies, and other agencies seeking to achieve more rapid progress in the development of instructional technology *(The Fourth Revolution).*

Colleges and universities should be responsive to campus groups seeking to develop child care services. An essential step is to appoint a carefully selected committee to study various possible types of child care services, including those already available in the community, and to recommend a plan for making such services available to students and employees of the institution. The committee should include faculty members drawn from appropriate departments, parents, and persons knowledgeable about community resources.

We believe that in most situations, especially for smaller campuses, it will be preferable for the academic institution to cooperate with other community groups in ensuring the availability of adequate child care services in the community. If campus facilities are desired on or near large campuses, we believe, consistent with our general view, that an academic institution should not assume functions that are not central to its main purposes, that it will usually be preferable to seek an arrangement under which the child care services will be provided under the auspices of a separate board of directors and not as a direct function of the academic institution. The board of directors would be expected to ensure adequate financing and adequate standards for the child care services.

We believe that student-parents should be expected to pay for child care services on the basis of sliding scale fees according to their incomes and that parents who are employees of the institution would normally be expected to pay for the full cost of services. Subsidies to meet the needs of low-income student-parents should be sought from extramural public and private sources and should not normally be sought from the academic institution's regular budget *(Opportunities for Women in Higher Education).*

STUDENT SERVICES

Colleges and universities should seek maximum economies in the operation of auxiliary services. These may be achieved through (1) contracting out, especially in small colleges and universities, (2) the development of student cooperative housing, and (3) employing students in food and room service activities. Students should be charged for services on a full-cost basis, and those who cannot afford these charges should be assisted through student aid or jobs *(The More Effective Use of Resources).*

Colleges and universities should inaugurate programs designed to discourage poorly motivated students from entering and from continuing once they have entered. These programs should be designed to include appropriate counseling of applicants, generally through the admissions office, as well as counseling of all undergraduate students, perhaps through the medium of a regular annual review *(The More Effective Use of Resources).*

More attention should be paid to the occupational training interests of students and to occupational counseling and guidance as students and adults seek to adjust to changing labor market conditions *(The Purposes and the Performance of Higher Education in the United States).*

Colleges and universities should seek maximum effectiveness in the allocation of student-aid funds through limiting aid given exclusively in the form of grants to the neediest and most disadvantaged students, while providing combinations of grants, loans, and work opportunities to less needy students *(The More Effective Use of Resources).*

Colleges and universities should review their student services, with particular reference to reducing the extent of subsidization of these services where it seems justified. However, in view of the critical need for counseling services for disadvantaged students, the changes that are occurring in patterns of participation in higher education, and the complex shifts that are taking place in the labor market for college graduates, we believe that counseling services need to be expanded rather than contracted in many colleges and universities *(The More Effective Use of Resources).*

Commuter institutions should make available lockers, study and lounge areas, and other physical facilities designed to meet the special need of commuters, and scheduling of educational programs and activities should be undertaken with the commuter in mind *(The Campus and the City).*

Colleges and universities should take immediate steps to strengthen occupational counseling programs available to their students. We also recommend that college placement services be strengthened where they have not been well developed. Professional schools should maintain their own placement programs for those receiving master's, first-professional, and doctor's degrees, while arts and science departments should have their own placement programs for students at the doctoral level *(College Graduates and Jobs).*

Opportunities for women to participate in competitive sports should be strongly encouraged *(Opportunities for Women in Higher Education).*

Not only should colleges and universities take immediate steps to strengthen occupational counseling programs generally in this era of a changing job market for college graduates, but they should also take special steps to strengthen career counseling programs for women. Counselors should be trained to discard outmoded concepts of male and female careers and to encourage women in their abilities and aspirations *(Opportunities for Women in Higher Education).*

COOPERATION
Colleges and universities should continue to seek ways of sharing facilities, courses, and specialized programs through cooperative arrangements; existing consortia should make continuous efforts toward increasing the effectiveness of their cooperative programs; and institutions—especially small colleges—that are not now members of consortia should carefully consider possibilities for forming consortia with neighboring institutions *(New Students and New Places).*

Until qualified scholars and teachers become more plentiful, exchanges of visiting professors, joint appointments, and other arrangements which enable talented people to serve more than one institution should be attempted as a means of expanding the pool of teaching talent available to colleges founded for Negroes *(From Isolation to Mainstream).*

Recruiting and counseling pools should be established among neighboring colleges and universities to coordinate resources and staff efforts for admitting educationally disadvantaged candidates *(A Chance to Learn).*

Institutions of higher education, either alone or in conjunction with local schools, should establish educational opportunity centers to serve areas with major concentrations of low-income populations *(A Chance to Learn).*

URBAN RELATIONS
Universities and colleges should develop long-range plans which give adequate attention to the interaction between the campus and the neighborhood in which it is located *(The Campus and the City).*

Where appropriate, colleges and universities should participate actively in urban-renewal activities, but only in unusual circumstances should this participation extend to investment of scarce institutional resources in housing development for the general community *(The Campus and the City).*

Institutions should limit their need for expansion into scarce urban space by better use of existing space *(The Campus and the City).*

An Urban Affairs Advisory Council including faculty, administration, and student representatives should be appointed to consult with the vice-chancellor of urban affairs *(The Campus and the City).*

Colleges and universities should develop overall policies concerning appropriate urban activities for their institutions to avoid response to new proposals on an ad-hoc basis without reference to consistency with the educational mission of the institution *(The Campus and the City).*

Institutions of higher education should undertake those community service activities which:

Revitalize its educational functions and constitute an integral part of its educational program

Are within the institutional capacity both in terms of personnel and resources

Are not duplicative of the services of other urban institutions

We further recommend that quasi-university agencies be established through which faculty members and/or students could provide services, even on controversial matters, without directly involving the university or college in its corporate capacity *(The Campus and the City).*

Urban community colleges, in order to serve more fully their urban clientele, should give careful consideration to the following:

1 Establishment of multiple campuses in a metropolitan area rather than concentration of all students on one campus, and the development of some specialization of educational missions among the various campuses

2 Systematic experimentation and evaluation of remedial and developmental programs

3 Possible early admission of urban high school students requiring remedial work or seeking immediate entry into vocational training programs *(The Campus and the City).*

Both planning agencies and urban-located institutions should review and analyze the educational resources in their areas and the educational needs of urban students to determine whether use of such experimental approaches as those described above, or others that may be developed, are desirable to expand effective options for postsecondary educational opportunities in the metropolitan areas *(The Campus and the City).*

Colleges and universities should seek to assist the surrounding areas through the operation of their employment and purchasing policies *(The Campus and the City).*

Regardless of rights given them by charter, colleges and universities should pay the usual taxes on any property held by them for noneducational purposes, and when expanding their campuses, should make every effort to develop the property in such as way as to permit its continuation on the tax rolls *(The Campus and the City)*.

Large universities located in urban areas should appoint a vice-president or vice-chancellor for urban affairs who would be concerned with the university-urban interface in terms of the urban impact of the university's educational, service, research, and corporate functions *(The Campus and the City)*.

OBJECTIVES FOR THE FUTURE

Once admitted to a college or university for academic studies, qualified part-time students will be eligible to take courses in the regular departments of the institution and will be accorded the same campus privileges that are accorded to full-time students *(Toward a Learning Society)*.

Educational institutions that have well-developed instructional technology will avail business and industry of opportunities to tie plant-sized classrooms to televised instruction originating on the campus, and will make available audio-videotape instruction or computer-assisted instruction on subjects relevant to business and industry training programs *(Toward a Learning Society)*.

The efforts of community colleges and four-year colleges to provide degree-credit instruction for military personnel and civilians living within commuting distance of such installations will be encouraged and increased *(Toward a Learning Society)*.

Learning pavillions designed and operated to encourage and facilitate independent adult learning will be developed in urban centers and in areas that are remote from institutions of postsecondary education. Funding responsibility for construction and operation of such facilities will reside with metropolitan or county governments *(Toward a Learning Society)*.

Educational institutions located within accessible range of prisons and having at their disposal well-developed instructional technology will make remote-access instruction and independent learning materials available to prison education programs at minimum costs *(Toward a Learning Society)*.

TRUSTEES

BOARD MEMBERSHIP

Board membership should reflect the different age, sex, and racial groups that are involved in the concerns of the institution. Faculty members from other institutions and young alumni should be considered for board memberships *(Governance of Higher Education)*.

Elected officials with the power of budgetary review should not serve as members of governing boards of public institutions over which they exercise such review because of the conflict of interest and the resulting double access to control, and because of the partisan nature of their positions *(Governance of Higher Education)*.

Members of governing boards of public institutions (where the governor makes the appointments) should be subject to appropriate mechanisms for nominating and screening individuals before appointment by the governor to assure consideration of properly qualified individuals, or to subsequent legislative confirmation to reduce the likelihood of purely politically partisan appointments, or to both *(Governance of Higher Education)*.

Faculty members, students, and alumni should be associated with the process of nominating at least some board members in private and public institutions, but faculty members and students should not serve on the boards of institutions where they are enrolled or employed *(Governance of Higher Education)*.

INSTITUTIONAL FUNCTIONS

All secret research should be eliminated from all campuses as a matter of national policy, except under quite unusual circumstances *(The Purposes and the Performance of Higher Education in the United States)*.

Institutions of higher education should seek to avoid and to eliminate noncomplementary functions *(The Purposes and the Performance of Higher Education in the United States)*.

Schools of osteopathy should be converted to schools of medicine wherever feasible *(Higher Education and the Nation's Health)*.

Each institution of higher education should survey periodically the totality of the functions it performs to be sure that none of them contradict the ethos of academic life, and that none of the nonacademic functions could be as well or better performed by some quasi-university or external agency *(The Purposes and the Performance of Higher Education in the United States)*.

Diversity among institutions and within them should be a major goal of higher education, and one test of institutions and of their major segments should be how successful they have been in defining their special characteristics and how successful they are in achieving them *(Reform on Campus).*

As debates inevitably proceed in the coming years over the reordering of national goals, the goal of fulfilling the aspirations of many young people for more useful roles in our society should be given high priority, along with the more widely recognized goal of overcoming critical human, urban, and environmental problems *(College Graduates and Jobs).*

PROVIDING FOR GOVERNANCE

Boards should consider faculty and student membership on appropriate board committees, or the establishment of parallel committees with arrangements for joint consultation *(Governance of Higher Education).*

Boards periodically should review the arrangements for governance—perhaps every four or five years—to be certain that they fit the current needs of the institution and are appropriate to the various functions being performed *(Governance of Higher Education).*

Boards should seek active presidents and give them the authority and the staff they need to provide leadership in a period of change and conflict *(Governance of Higher Education).*

Boards may wish to consider the establishment of stated review periods for presidents so that withdrawal by the president or reaffirmation of the president may be managed in a more effective manner than is often now the actual situation. Faculty members and students should be associated in an advisory capacity with the process of review as they are in the initial appointment *(Governance of Higher Education).*

Campus rules should be formulated which regulate the time, place, and manner of peaceful assemblies *(Dissent and Disruption).*

Governance arrangements should provide: (1) adequate academic options from among which students may choose, and (2) the right to be heard on important campus issues *(Governance of Higher Education).*

In every local community college district there should be an elected or appointed board of directors with substantial powers relating to the development and administration of community colleges within the district. The Commission also recommends that local boards delegate substantial responsibility to the administration and faculty and provide for student participation in decisions relating to educational policy and student affairs. When community colleges are part of the state university system, there should be a local advisory board with substantial influence *(The Open-Door Colleges).*

Higher education should take responsibility and undertake needed reforms internally rather than wait for them to be imposed externally as they are in so many other nations *(Reform on Campus).*

FISCAL POLICY

Colleges and universities should (1) aim to maximize long-term total return in the investment of endowment funds, (2) delegate responsibility for portfolio management to an able professional, and (3) generally follow modern principles of endowment management *(The More Effective Use of Resources).*

Public institutions of higher education, as well as private institutions, should pursue systematic and vigorous policies aimed at attracting additions to their endowment funds *(The More Effective Use of Resources).*

One to three percent of all funds should be taken each year from existing programs, set aside as self-renewal funds, and directed to new or expanded programs *(Reform on Campus).*

Higher education should undertake internally the constructive actions necessary to get more effective use of resources and not wait for less constructive—and sometimes destructive—actions to be required because of external initiative *(The More Effective Use of Resources).*

PROTECTING DISSENT

The principles of academic freedom for faculty members should be preserved where they are now effective and extended into areas where they do not now prevail, and the essential institutional independence of the campus should be fully protected by society to assure the continuance of the possibilities of critical evaluation of society by individual faculty members and students *(The Purposes and the Performance of Higher Education in the United States).*

Each institution of higher education should establish a policy of self-restraint against disruptive activities, against improper use of campus facilities, against improper political indoctrination of students, against selection and promotion of faculty members in accordance with their political beliefs, and against commitment of the institution as such to the pursuit of specific external political and social changes; each institution should be prepared to defend its own integrity *(The Purposes and the Performance of Higher Education in the United States).*

Regular procedures and channels for hearing grievances and suggestions directed to the campus should be established and be well publicized; decisions should be based on wide consultation with those segments of the campus affected by them; and decisions and the rationale behind them should be made widely known *(Dissent and Disruption).*

Evaluation of and response to events on a campus should be based upon the distinction between dissent and disruption. Dissent should be protected as a democratic right and a major means of renewal for society; and repression should be rejected. Disruption should be met by the full efforts of the campus to end it and, where necessary, by the general law, while guarding against excessive force by law enforcement personnel *(Dissent and Disruption)*.

Presidents should be given the authority to deal with emergency situations, and they should seek advice from preexisting consultative groups drawn from the campus community. The administration should keep the campus and its trustees informed of the decisions and the rationale behind them *(Dissent and Disruption)*.

In cases of nonviolent disruption, to the extent possible, procedures internal to a campus should be used initially and nonviolent actions should be met by responses which do not use force. Violent actions, involving injury to persons or more than incidental damage to property, should be met immediately by enforcement of the law, using internal and external personnel to the full extent necessary *(Dissent and Disruption)*.

Members of a campus should be tried or punished only for alleged violations of existing codes or regulations; therefore, these should be regularly reexamined. Such regulations should be consistent with the bill of rights and responsibilities adopted by a campus *(Dissent and Disruption)*.

In serious cases involving "rights and responsibilities" of members of the campus community and possible campus penalties beyond those for violation of the external law, campus judicial tribunals should be composed partially or wholly of external persons, defined as persons drawn from outside the particular school or college or campus whose members are involved in the dispute *(Dissent and Disruption)*.

We conclude that dissatisfactions on campuses and their public expression should be viewed as the reflection of many problems and conditions both in society and on the campuses. Both campus and society share responsibility. Dissenters are also responsible for their tactics in advancing their goals—for some of their tactics are the source of the dissatisfactions and negative reactions of the public at large *(Dissent and Disruption)*.

PERSONNEL POLICY

The principle of tenure should be retained and extended to campuses where it does not now apply *(Governance of Higher Education)*.

The affirmative action program should also provide for an effective internal grievance procedure, if the institution does not already have one. An effective grievance procedure should result in minimizing litigation *(Opportunities for Women in Higher Education)*.

All colleges and universities covered by federal affirmative action requirements relating to employment should proceed to develop adequate written statements of affirmative action policy and should take active steps to see that the goals of the affirmative action policy are achieved within a reasonable period of time. To expedite achieving such goals, every large college or university should appoint one or more affirmative action officers, whose policies should be guided by an appropriately constituted advisory committee or council. Small colleges may find it preferable to assign affirmative action responsibilities to an existing administrator or faculty member.

Every affirmative action policy, as it concerns the employment of faculty members, should include at least the following provisions relating to sex discrimination:

1   A requirement that departments and schools should actively recruit women and maintain records that indicate the steps they have taken in this recruitment program. Special efforts should be made to recruit women who are members of miniority groups through recruitment plans especially designed to seek them out. Serious consideration should be given to appointing qualified women lecturers to regular faculty positions.

2   A requirement that every department and school in an academic institution should establish, in consultation with the administration of the college or university, a goal relating to the relative representation of women on its regular faculty (assistant professor to full professor). In determining these goals, every appropriate source of information on the relative size of available pools of qualified women and men should be consulted—not just those indicated in the federal guidelines. A reasonable timetable for achieving the goals should be developed, but allowance should be made for special difficulties that may be encountered in adhering to the timetable, especially in fields in which there are currently relatively few women with doctor's degrees and in which competition among institutions for this limited pool of talent is likely to be intense. Special consideration should be given to women who meet the institution's standards of competence in terms of both realized and potential ability, even though they may have had a less substantial record of achievement in the terms of research and publication than men who are being considered for the same positions. Standards of competence vary by type of institution. In practice, however, they are often only vaguely defined. Where this is a problem, they should be made more explicit.

3   Part-time appointments should not be discouraged for men and women whose family circumstances make such appointments desirable. Institutions may find it advantageous to distinguish, as some have done, between (1) such part-time appointments and (2) appointments to the faculty of persons whose principal employment is elsewhere and who come to the campus to give one or two specialized courses. For example, fringe benefits, prorated on the basis of the proportion of a full-time

appointment, are more appropriate for the first type of part-time employee.

4   Policies requiring decisions on the granting of tenure to be made within a given period of years should permit a limited extension of the time period for persons holding part-time appointments. Men and women holding part-time appointments for family reasons should be permitted to achieve tenure on a part-time basis. In such cases, tenure on a full-time basis at some future time would not be ensured, but the institution should attempt to shift the individual's status to a full-time tenured position when desired if budgetarily possible and academically appropriate.

5   Faculty members holding part-time appointments for family reasons should not be barred from service on departmental or campus committees and should, if holding an appropriate faculty rank, be eligible for membership in the academic senate.

6   There should be no antinepotism rules applying to employment within the institution or campus as a whole, or within individual units, such as departments, schools, and institutes. However, a husband or wife should not be involved in a decision relating to his or her spouse.

7   There should be equal treatment of men and women in all matters relating to salary, fringe benefits, and terms and conditions of employment.

8   Women should be entitled to maternity leave for a reasonable length of time, and affirmative action plans should include specific provisions relating to the definition of a reasonable length of time, rights to accumulated leave, and other relevant considerations *(Opportunities for Women in Higher Education).*

OBJECTIVES FOR THE FUTURE
Institutions of postsecondary education will not offer part-time students courses that exceed levels of instruction maintained in courses offered to full-time students. Two-year institutions will not offer upper-division or professional instruction to part-time students. Vocational schools that do not offer general education to full-time students will not offer it to part-time students *(Toward a Learning Society).*

Before taking on a new educational function, institutions will determine the relationship of that function to their educational mission and ascertain whether there are existing alternative educational resources to meet the particular educational need to be served. If such alternative resources exist, the possibility of contractual agreements with other institutions to secure the services, or the possibility of joint enrollment of the learner, will be explored before a new program is developed *(Toward a Learning Society).*

RELATED CENTERS OF ACTION

ACCREDITING AND TESTING AGENCIES

The Commission recommends a single program of institutional accreditation for two-year colleges and the elimination of accreditation of specialties. The contribution of professional associations in the evaluation of specialized programs should be made through cooperation with the regional accrediting bodies *(The Open-Door Colleges)*.

Testing agencies should initiate the development of a family of admissions and placement tests, with special versions prepared for individuals with particular educational and career aspirations *(Continuity and Discontinuity)*.

Testing agencies, through new testing techniques, should aid colleges in developing appropriate criteria and measures of value added to reflect a diversity of institutional objectives and outcomes *(Continuity and Discontinuity)*.

Efforts to eliminate sex bias from vocational interest questionnaires should be encouraged, as should research designed to achieve a more adequate understanding of similarities and differences in patterns of vocational choices among men and women *(Opportunities for Women in Higher Education)*.

Schools, colleges, and testing agencies should work together in developing a complete and coherent information system that enables sound decision-making by both students and colleges. Colleges should prepare frank, accurate, and complete descriptive materials, so that students will know as much about colleges as the colleges know about students *(Continuity and Discontinuity)*.

REGIONAL ASSOCIATIONS AND CONSORTIA

Regional plans for the development of Ph.D. programs along the lines of those of the New England Board of Higher Education and the Southern Regional Education Board should be strengthened and extended to regions that do not now have them. We also recommend far more extensive use of consortium arrangements that involve planning for concentration of development of Ph.D. programs in particular fields in individual members of the consortium as well as the rights of students to cross-register for individual courses or fields of concentration. Such plans should call for developing the strength of an individual institution in a group of related fields, such as the physical sciences or the social sciences *(College Graduates and Jobs)*.

All appropriate agencies such as U.S. Office of Education, the Southern Regional Education Board, and Western Interstate Commission for Higher Education should give high priority to the development of more adequate data on the behavior of costs, income, and output in higher education *(The More Effective Use of Resources).*

Two or more regional centers for research on the academically disadvantaged and for training teachers for work with students thus defined should be established. Such centers should be developed, wherever possible, with the cooperation of both predominantly black and predominantly white schools of education *(From Isolation to Mainstream).*

By 1922, at least seven cooperative learning-technology centers, voluntarily organized on a regional basis by participating higher educational institutions and systems, should be established for the purpose of sharing costs and facilities for the accelerated development and utilization of instructional technology in higher education *(The Fourth Revolution).*

The Commission recommends the development and strengthening of consortia in higher education. It also welcomes developments that are occurring in several states in the direction of increased cooperation and sharing of facilities by public and private institutions of higher education, and urges that such collaboration be considered in all states *(The More Effective Use of Resources).*

Professional schools in universities and colleges should undertake the responsibility for cooperating with and providing guidance for comprehensive colleges and community colleges in the development of paraprofessional training programs, as we have earlier recommended in the case of university health science centers *(College Graduates and Jobs).*

In those areas where multiple college applications are a problem, clearinghouse operations utilizing single application forms, transcripts, and school report forms should be developed. Concern for the small amount of college autonomy involved should be less important than better service to students *(Continuity and Discontinuity).*

PROFESSIONAL ASSOCIATIONS

In virtually all professional fields, increased attention should be devoted to providing students with opportunities to proceed along carefully planned and at the same time flexible career training ladders *(College Graduates and Jobs).*

In all professional fields, careful and sustained attention needs to be given to adaptation of educational programs to the advancement of knowledge and technological change and to society's changing problems and needs *(College Graduates and Jobs).*

Professions, wherever possible, should create alternate routes of entry other than full-time college attendance and reduce the number of narrow, one-level professions which do not afford opportunities for advancement *(Less Time, More Options).*

The Commission recommends national requirements for periodic re-examination and recertification of all physicians and dentists by specialty boards and other appropriate bodies *(Higher Education and the Nation's Health)*.

INSTITUTIONAL ASSOCIATIONS

The American Council on Education may wish to consider establishing a Commission on Institutional Independence to be concerned with policies affecting independence and review of cases of alleged undue external influence. Such a commission should include members drawn from the public at large *(Governance of Higher Education)*.

Associations of professional schools, as well as individual professional schools in universities and comprehensive colleges, should undertake leadership and responsibility in more carefully planned integration of preprofessional and professional education *(Governance of Higher Education)*.

Associations of professional schools should collect annual data on enrollment of women and minority-group students and should stimulate programs designed to encourage and assist them. Within arts and science fields there should be similar efforts *(College Graduates and Jobs)*.

Associations of professional schools and professional societies should undertake the responsibility for careful studies of manpower supply and demand for graduates in their respective fields *(College Graduates and Jobs)*.

PRIVATE FOUNDATIONS

Private foundations that have traditionally provided support for health manpower education and research should continue to do so, and foundations that have not provided such support in the past should consider expanding their programs to include it. The Commission also recommends that foundations expand their support for research on the delivery of health care *(Higher Education and the Nation's Health)*.

More colleges founded for Negroes should provide education for adult members of the black community, and the federal government and foundations should give favorable consideration to requests for the support of such activities *(From Isolation to Mainstream)*.

Foundations, government agencies, and higher education associations should give special attention to funding studies and projects concerned with management problems of universities and colleges with effective utilization of available and potential resources *(The Capitol and the Campus)*.

An independent commission, supported either by an appropriate agency of the U.S. Department of Health, Education and Welfare or by one or more private foundations, should be created to make assessment of the instructional effectiveness and cost benefits of currently available instructional technology. Findings of the commission should be published and appropriately disseminated for the advice of institutions of higher education, such cooperative learning-technology centers as may be established, and governments and foundations supporting the advancement of instructional technology *(The Fourth Revolution)*.

EMPLOYERS

Employers, both private and public, should hire and promote on the basis of talent alone as well as on prior certification *(Less Time, More Options)*.

Employers should not raise educational requirements in response to changes in the job market for college graduates. We strongly recommend that educational requirements should not be imposed except where they are clearly indicated by job requirements *(College Graduates and Jobs)*.

We believe that the Urban Corps provides an excellent mechanism for giving opportunities to students to have experience in city government and recommend that cities that do not now have such programs seriously consider developing them *(The Campus and the City)*.

Business and industry, on a nationwide basis, should be fully informed about the rapid transitions occurring in colleges founded for Negroes. Representatives of business and industry should be invited to serve on advisory boards for the development programs of these colleges and should be asked to assist in planning effective communications between these institutions and the industrial community *(From Isolation to Mainstream)*.

SECONDARY SCHOOLS

The first priority in the nation's commitment to equal educational opportunity should be the increased effectiveness of our preelementary, elementary, and secondary school program *(A Chance to Learn)*.

High school students should be encouraged to study mathematics sequentially from grades 9 to 12 in order to keep options open to college programs, jobs, and careers requiring background in mathematics *(Continuity and Discontinuity)*.

Students in elementary and high school should be counseled through a variety of resources—counselors, written materials, community-based people, as well as college students (minority students and women, in particular) *(Continuity and Discontinuity)*.

Local school boards, with community and professional assistance, should identify the overall ends and objectives of the public schools, deliberately encourage experimentation with a diversity of means to those objectives, and insist upon accountability from teachers and administrators *(Continuity and Discontinuity)*.

Improvement of the nation's schools is the first educational priority in the nation; and within the schools, improvement in the basic skills, especially in large city schools, is the first priority. Colleges and universities should recognize this fact and help to provide the resources, incentives, and rewards for faculty members who commit themselves to this task *(Continuity and Discontinuity)*.

Schools and colleges should experiment with different structural models designed to provide a student with options that will enable him to find the right program at the right time. Such experimentation challenges the current structure and its traditional break between school and college at the end of grade 12. Liberal arts colleges should consider enrolling students at grade 11 and awarding the bachelor's degree after grade 14 or 15; there should be experimentation with public education at age 4; some school systems should eliminate a year from the K through 12 sequence; other school systems should stress general education equivalent to that found at good colleges; students should be able to "test out" of high school graduation requirements; there should be expanded programs of college credit for the senior year of high school, concurrent enrollment of students in school and college, and early admission to college; options other than college attendance should be made available for high school graduates *(Continuity and Discontinuity)*.

Greater emphasis should be placed on inservice education of a different kind from that traditionally available. Local teacher centers that focus on teachers' problems and that utilize the resources of the university should be encouraged and their effects carefully evaluated *(Continuity and Discontinuity)*.

Special efforts should be made to recruit able administrators from outside the field as well as members of minority groups and women into the profession of school administration *(Continuity and Discontinuity)*.

Given the diversity of school districts, there can be no single model of an administrator training program. Common elements in all programs should be the use of the resources of the whole university and experimentation with different ways of combining theory and practice in clinical settings *(Continuity and Discontinuity)*.

Greater emphasis should be placed on inservice training as a way of keeping administrators up-to-date and as a vehicle for school improvement *(Continuity and Discontinuity)*.

High schools that do not already do so should offer instruction in basic concepts and uses of computers and should encourage their students to obtain, as early as possible, other skills that will be helpful in the use of new media for learning *(The Fourth Revolution)*.

The first priority in the nation's commitment to equal educational opportunity for women should be placed on changing policies in preelementary, elementary, and secondary school programs that tend to deter women from aspiring to equality with men in their career goals. This will require vigorous pursuit of appropriate policies by state and local boards of education and implementation by school administrators, teachers, and counselors *(Opportunities for Women in Higher Education)*.

High school counseling programs should be strengthened and improved, not only for the purpose of guiding students to appropriate jobs or occupational programs, but also to dissuade poorly motivated students from entering college *(The More Effective Use of Resources)*.

OBJECTIVES FOR THE FUTURE

The current system of accreditation by institutional associations will be supplemented by a second system instituted by state and federal governments for the purpose of verifying fiscal stability, legitimacy of advertising claims, and general quality of instruction. Those responsible for administering such accreditation will be restrained, by all means feasible, from regulation of postsecondary education and will seek to establish minimum rather than optimum standards for the accreditation they are empowered to bestow *(Toward a Learning Society)*.

Elementary and secondary schools will continue to play a significant role in the provision of educational opportunities to persons of all ages in the communities where they are located *(Toward a Learning Society)*.

When they do not have skill-training expertise in their own companies, businesses will seek agreements with educational institutions to provide technical aid for the development of industry-based skill-training programs and for the evaluation of such programs *(Toward a Learning Society)*.

INDEX
TO
RECOMMENDATIONS

This index has been prepared to facilitate reference to recommendations of the Carnegie Commission on Higher Education. In the interests of brevity, entries in the index are abridgements and segments of the full recommendations. Although they express the "sense" of the full recommendations, they should not be substituted for the full recommendations found in the original reports when reference is made to Commission policy.

ACADEMIC FREEDOM   Academic policies set by state agencies should be of a broad nature and should not interfere with the more specific professional academic judgments about faculty appointments, courses of study, admission of individual students, specific research projects, appointment of academic and administrative staff and leadership, and protection of academic freedom *(Governance of Higher Education).*

The principles of academic freedom for faculty members should be preserved where they are now effective and extended into areas where they do not now prevail, and the essential institutional independence of the campus should be fully protected by society to assure the continuance of the possibilities of critical evaluation of society by individual faculty members and students *(The Purposes and the Performance of Higher Education in the United States).*

Each institution of higher education should establish a policy against selection and promotion of faculty members in accordance with their political beliefs *(The Purposes and the Performance of Higher Education in the United States).*

ACCESS   Each state should plan to provide universal access to its total system, but not necessarily to each of its institutions, since they vary greatly in their nature and purposes *(A Chance to Learn).*

Community colleges or equivalent facilities should be established within commuting range of potential students in all populous areas *(A Chance to Learn).*

All states should enact legislation providing admission to public community colleges of all applicants who are high school graduates or persons over 18 years of age who are capable of benefiting from continuing education *(The Open-Door Colleges).*

Through the coordinated efforts of federal, state, and local governments, the goal of providing a community college within commuting distance of every potential student should be attained by 1980 *(The Open-Door Colleges).*

Alternative avenues by which students can earn degrees or complete a major portion of their work for a degree should be expanded to increase accessibility of higher education for those to whom it is now unavailable because of work schedules, geographic location, or responsibilities in the home *(Less Time, More Options).*

States having a ratio of less than 30 places in both public and private higher education in the state for every 100 18-to 21-year-olds in the state should take emergency measures to increase the availability of higher education in the state *(The Capitol and the Campus).*

Appropriate state and local agencies should undertake an evaluation of the adequacy of the number of higher education student places in those areas with a ratio of between 2.5 and 3.5 student places per 100 population *(The Campus and the City).*

Appropriate state and local agencies should take steps to improve availability of student places in colleges and universities in those areas that now have less than 2.5 places available per 100 population *(The Campus and the City).*

ACCREDITATION   There should be a single program of institutional accreditation for two-year colleges, and the accreditation of specialties should be eliminated.

The contribution of professional associations in the evaluation of specialized programs should be made through cooperation with the regional accrediting bodies *(The Open-Door Colleges).*

The current system of accreditation by institutional associations will be supplemented by a second system instituted by state and federal governments for the purpose of validating fiscal stability, legitimacy of advertising claims, and general quality of instruction. Those responsible for administering such validation will be restrained, by all means feasible, from regulation of postsecondary education and will seek to establish minimum rather than optimum standards for the accreditation they are empowered to bestow *(Toward a Learning Society).*

ADMINISTRATION　University administrations should appoint appropriate officers to develop plans for the expansion of university health science centers and area health education centers. To accomplish this will often require administrative changes in the university and in the health science center *(Higher Education and the Nation's Health).*

Presidents should be given the authority to deal with emergency situations, and they should seek advice from preexisting consultative groups drawn from the campus community *(Dissent and Disruption).*

The administration should keep the campus and its trustees informed of the decisions it makes and the rationale behind them *(Dissent and Disruption).*

Institutions of higher education should contribute to the advancement of instructional technology by placing responsibility for its introduction and utilization at the highest possible level of academic administration *(The Fourth Revolution).*

All institutions of higher education, especially those with relatively high administrative costs, should conduct analyses of these costs with a view to identifying functions or parts of the institution in which these costs may be excessive or in which there is evidence of administrative inefficiency *(The More Effective Use of Resources).*

All universities with university health science centers should seek to ensure that management of these centers is effective by establishing separate, but coordinated, administration of health science centers and teaching hospitals, and by the development of an able core of middle managers to assume responsibility for the more routine administrative functions *(The More Effective Use of Resources).*

Boards should seek active presidents and give them the authority and the staff they need to provide leadership in a period of change and conflict *(Governance of Higher Education).*

Boards may wish to consider the establishment of stated review periods for presidents so that withdrawal by the president or reaffirmation of the president may be managed in a more effective manner than is often now the actual situation. Faculty members and students should be associated in an advisory capacity with the process of review as they are in the initial appointment *(Governance of Higher Education).*

Colleges and universities have a responsibility to develop policies specifically designed to bring about changes in the attitudes of administrators and faculty members, where these have been antagonistic to enrollment of women in traditionally male fields *(Opportunities for Women in Higher Education).*

Colleges and universities should take especially vigorous steps to overcome a pervasive problem of absence of women in top administrative positions. Women should be given opportunities by their departments to serve as department chairmen, because academic administrators are usually selected from among persons who have served ably as department chairmen. Most important is an administrative stance that is highly positive toward providing opportunities for women to rise in the administrative hierarchy. Also very important is the provision of management training opportunities for both men and women who have potential administrative ability but do not hold administrative positions *(Opportunities for Women in Higher Education)*.

ADMISSIONS POLICIES AND PROCEDURES
Whenever public four-year institutions are forced, because of inadequacies of budgets, to reject students who meet their admission requirements, top priority for admission should be given to qualified students transferring from community colleges within the states. Private colleges and universities should also develop policies encouraging admission of community college graduates *(The Open-Door Colleges)*.

Admissions policies should be examined to assure that they serve both the cause of diversity within higher education and also the possibilities for diversity at the high school level *(Reform on Campus)*.

Private colleges should reexamine their admissions policies to determine whether expansion of open-admission or flexible-admission student places in their institutions would be compatible with their particular educational missions *(The Campus and the City)*.

Admissions standards should be relaxed for members of disadvantaged groups, provided that the chances are good that such students can meet graduation requirements in full *(The Purposes and the Performance of Higher Education in the United States)*.

Both public and private institutions should give careful attention to admissions policies suitable to an era characterized by universal access to the total system of higher education and by a no-growth enrollment trend. Public agencies, including coordinating councils and state planning commissions, should determine general policies on student admissions within state systems, including policies with respect to number of places, equality of access by race, age, and sex, and the level of academic admissibility among types of institutions. Decisions on individual students should be left to each campus *(Continuity and Discontinuity)*.

Colleges should develop admissions programs to seek out new constituencies, including high school juniors as well as adults and transfers from two-year colleges *(Continuity and Discontinuity)*.

Colleges should review their admissions requirements and, except for competence in the basic skills of reading, writing, and arithmetic, should not require or suggest particular courses of study at the secondary level unless such requirements or suggestions are tied explicitly to the colleges' own degree requirements, or to those of the system of which they are a part *(Continuity and Discontinuity)*.

Colleges should closely examine their admissions policies with respect to sex, race, and age. They should then be certain that their admissions practices implement those policies that relate to social justice in higher education. Separate prediction equations for men and women, minority students, and adults should be developed and, where feasible, differential prediction by general field of study should be used *(Continuity and Discontinuity)*.

Testing agencies should initiate the development of a family of admissions and placement tests, with special versions prepared for individuals with particular educational and career aspirations *(Continuity and Discontinuity)*.

In those areas where multiple college applications are a problem, clearinghouse operations utilizing single application forms, transcripts, and school report forms should be developed *(Continuity and Discontinuity)*.

Experimentation with college admissions practices should be encouraged. In particular, more experimentation is needed to determine the quality of testing as a basis for admission and placement, the importance of student motivation and life experience as indicators of promise, and the feasibility of deferred admissions as a means of providing educational flexibility for students *(Continuity and Discontinuity)*.

There should be no discrimination on the basis of sex in the use of either high school grades or test scores as admissions criteria *(Opportunities for Women in Higher Education)*.

Departments and schools should be required to maintain complete records on all applicants for admission to graduate and professional education and to make these records available to administrative officers on request. They should also be required to maintain records indicating that, in any programs designed to recruit able graduate students, equal efforts have been made to recruit women as well as men *(Opportunities for Women in Higher Education)*.

Rules and policies that discriminate against the part-time graduate or professional student should allow for exceptions to accommodate men or women whose family circumstances require them to study on a part-time basis. Any limitation on the total number of graduate or professional students admitted by departments or schools and by the institution as a whole should be applied on a full-time-equivalent rather than on a head-count basis *(Opportunities for Women in Higher Education)*.

A woman desiring to enter graduate or professional school after some years away from higher education, and generally meeting departmental standards for admission, should be given an opportunity to make up for her inability to meet any special requirements, such as specific mathematical requirements. Under no circumstances should she be denied admission because her undergraduate education occurred some years earlier *(Opportunities for Women in Higher Education)*.

Policies that discriminate against admission of adults desirous of continuing their education should be liberalized to permit enrollment of qualified mature men and women whose education has been interrupted because of family responsibilities or for other reasons. High school or college records should not be ruled inapplicable as evidence of eligibility for admission simply because the records were acquired some years earlier *(Opportunities for Women in Higher Education)*.

ADULT EDUCATION *(See* Continuing education)

AFFIRMATIVE ACTION *(See also* Equal opportunity, Sexual discrimination)
All colleges and universities covered by federal affirmative action requirements relating to employment should proceed to develop adequate written statements of affirmative action policy and should take active steps to see that the goals of the affirmative action policy are achieved within a reasonable period of time. To expedite achieving such goals, every large college or university should appoint one or more affirmative action officers, whose policies should be guided by an appropriately constituted advisory committee or council. Small colleges may find it preferable to assign affirmative action responsibilities to an existing administrator or faculty member.

Every affirmative action policy, as it concerns the employment of faculty members, should include at least the following provisions relating to sex discrimination:

1 Departments and schools should actively recruit women and maintain rec-

ords that indicate the steps they have taken in this recruitment program. Serious consideration should be given to appointing qualified women lecturers to regular faculty positions.

2   Every department and school in an academic institution should establish, in consultation with the administration of the college or university, a goal relating to the relative representation of women on its regular faculty (assistant professor to full professor). In determining these goals, every appropriate source of information on the relative size of available pools of qualified women and men should be consulted—not just those indicated in the federal guidelines. A reasonable timetable for achieving the goals should be developed, but allowance should be made for special difficulties that may be encountered in adhering to the timetable, especially in fields in which there are currently relatively few women with doctor's degrees and in which competition among institutions for this limited pool of talent is likely to be intense. Special consideration should be given to women who meet the institution's standards of competence in terms of both realized and potential ability, even though they may have had a less substantial record of achievement in terms of research and publication than men who are being considered for the same positions. Standards of competence vary by type of institution. In practice, however, they are often only vaguely defined. Where this is a problem, they should be made more explicit.

3   Part-time appointments should not be discouraged for men and women whose family circumstances make such appointments desirable. Institutions may find it advantageous to distinguish, as some have done, between *(a)* such part-time appointments and *(b)* appointments to the faculty of persons whose principal employment is elsewhere and who come to the campus to give one or two specialized courses. For example, fringe benefits, pro-rated on the basis of the proportion of a full-time appointment, are more appropriate for the first type of part-time employee.

4   There should be no antinepotism rules applying to employment within the institution or campus as a whole, or within individual units, such as departments, schools, and institutes. However, a husband or wife should not be involved in a decision relating to his or her spouse.

5   Policies requiring decisions on the granting of tenure to be made within a given period of years should permit a limited extension of the time period for persons holding part-time appointments. Men and women holding part-time appointments for family reasons should be permitted to achieve tenure on a part-time basis. In such cases, tenure on a full-time basis at some future time would not be ensured, but the institution should attempt to shift the individual's status to a full-time tenured position when desired if budgetarily possible and academically appropriate.

6   Faculty members holding part-time appointments for family reasons should not be barred from service on departmental or campus committees and should, if holding an appropriate faculty rank, be eligible for membership in the academic senate.

7   There should be equal treatment of men and women in all matters relating to salary, fringe benefits, and terms and conditions of employment.

8   Women should be entitled to maternity leave for a reasonable length of time, and affirmative action plans should include specific provisions relating to the definition of a reasonable length of time, rights to accumulated leave, and other relevant considerations *(Opportunities for Women in Higher Education)*.

The affirmative action program should provide for an effective internal grievance procedure, if the institution does not already have one. An effective grievance procedure should result in minimizing litigation *(Opportunities for Women in Higher Education)*.

We support the objectives of federal policies aimed at ensuring that institutions of higher education having contracts with the federal government pursue effective affirmative action programs, but we believe that these federal policies should be carried out in relation to each institution with due regard for the sensitive characteristics of academic employment, and for the difficulties that may be encountered by individual departments and schools in meeting affirmative action goals and timetables.

We define a pattern of discrimination as involving one or more of the following situations: *(a)* failure to develop an adequate affirmative action plan within a reasonable period of time; *(b)* lack of evidence that the institution is making an effort to achieve its affirmative action goals; or evidence of widespread faculty or administrative attitudes that are antagonistic to the achievement of the affirmative action goals; or *(c)* lack of progress in achieving its affirmative action goals within a reasonable period of time *(Opportunities for Women in Higher Education)*.

ALLIED HEALTH PROFESSIONS *(See* Health care personnel)

APPRENTICESHIPS Apprenticeship, internship, and inservice training will be used more widely than they are today to prepare persons for their life work in many professions, paraprofessions, and occupations *(Toward a Learning Society)*.

AREA HEALTH EDUCATION CENTERS Area health education centers should be developed in areas at some distance from university health science centers that do not have sufficiently large populations to support university health science centers of their own and in a few metropolitian areas needing additional training facilities but not full health science centers. These area centers would be affiliated with the nearest appropriate university health science center and would perform somewhat the same functions recommended for university health science centers, except that the education of M.D. and D.D.S. candidates would be restricted to a limited amount of clinical education on a rotational basis, and research programs would be largely restricted to the evaluation of local experiments in health care delivery systems.

One hundred twenty-six new area health education centers should be developed and located on the basis of careful regional planning *(Higher Education and the Nation's Health)*.

Area health education centers should provide leadership in encouraging the development and expansion of continuing education programs for nurses and allied health workers in appropriate educational institutions *(College Graduates and Jobs)*.

AUTONOMY State legislation should provide for the formation of local community college districts and should prohibit inclusion of community colleges within K–12 local school districts *(The Open-Door Colleges)*.

Public and private institutions should seek to establish guidelines clearly defining the limitations on state concern and state regulation or control *(The Capitol and the Campus)*.

A special commission on institutional independence should be established within the American Council on Education; this commission would be assigned responsibility for reviewing external interference with institutional independence and issuing findings after such reviews *(The Capitol and the Campus* and *Governance of Higher Education).*

Coordinating agencies should serve as a buffer and communicator, protecting the institutions, when necessary, from legislative, executive, or public interference in carrying out their educational functions *(The Capitol and the Campus).*

Institutions should examine their own levels of cooperativeness to determine whether failures to respond to advisory agencies might lead more surely and quickly to establishment of regulatory agencies *(The Capitol and the Campus).*

Higher education should undertake internally the constructive actions necessary to get more effective use of resources and not wait for actions to be required because of external initiative *(The More Effective Use of Resources).*

Higher education should take responsibility and undertake needed reforms internally rather than wait for them to be imposed externally *(Reform on Campus).*

Academic policies set by state agencies should be of a broad nature and should not interfere with the more specific professional academic judgments about faculty appointments, courses of study, admission of individual students, grades and degrees for individual students, specific research projects, appointment of academic and administrative staff and leadership, and protection of academic freedom *(Governance of Higher Education).*

Innovations in programs and in policies should be encouraged by public authorities by influence and not by control *(Governance of Higher Education).*

Coordinating agencies at the state level should seek to establish, in cooperation with public and private institutions of higher education, guidelines defining areas of state concern and areas of institutional independence that avoid detailed control *(Governance of Higher Education).*

In those areas where multiple college applications are a problem, clearinghouse operations utilizing single application forms, transcripts, and school report forms should be developed. Concern for the small amount of college autonomy involved should be less important than better service to students *(Continuity and Discontinuity).*

AUXILIARY SERVICES All colleges and universities should seek maximum economies in the operation of auxiliary services. These may be achieved through (1) contracting out, especially in small colleges and universities, (2) the development of student cooperative housing, and (3) employing students in food and room service activities. Students should be charged for services on a full-cost basis *(The More Effective Use of Resources).*

BASIC OPPORTUNITY GRANTS The present program of educational opportunity grants based on need should be strengthened and expanded by providing (1) that the level of funding be increased so that all college students with demonstrated need will be assured of some financial aid to meet expenses at institutions that they select and (2) that grants based on need be available for a period not to exceed four years of undergraduate study and two years of study toward a graduate degree *(Quality and Equality).*

An undergraduate student holding an educational opportunity grant and receiving added grants from nonfederal sources should be given a supplementary federal grant in an amount matching the nonfederal grants but not exceeding one-quarter of the student's original educational opportunity grant *(Quality and Equality)*.

Each college and university should be given a scholarship fund for needy students equal to 10 percent of the total sum of educational opportunity grants (not including supplementary matching grants) held by students at that institution. Such funds are to be allocated by the institution to students as determined by the institution's own definition of student need *(Quality and Equality)*.

The Basic Opportunity Grants program should be fully funded. This legislation, already on the books, is a major step in providing critically needed assistance to both students and institutions of higher education *(Higher Education: Who Pays? Who Benefits? Who Should Pay?)*.

In the future the $1,400 ceiling on Basic Opportunity Grants should be raised gradually in line with increases in educational and subsistence costs *(Higher Education: Who Pays? Who Benefits? Who Should Pay?)*.

BILL OF RIGHTS AND RESPONSIBILITIES The time has come for campuses to develop bills of rights and responsibilities for *all* their members *(Dissent and Disruption)*.

Members of a campus should be tried or punished only for alleged violations of existing codes or regulations. Such regulations should be consistent with the bill of rights and responsibilities adopted by a campus *(Dissent and Disruption)*.

BLACK COLLEGES The governing boards, administrations, and faculties of most colleges founded for Negroes should plan to accommodate enrollments that may double on the average, certainly by the year 2000 and possibly by 1980. These colleges should utilize the present period of transition for curriculum innovation and enrichment. Most of them should concentrate on developing, in addition to general liberal arts courses, strong comprehensive undergraduate programs in preprofessional subjects and in subjects that prepare students for advance education and high-demand occupations *(From Isolation to Mainstream)*.

Colleges founded for Negroes should initiate proposals for the support and development of seminars, special training institutes, and classes to improve the skills of elementary and secondary schoolteachers *(From Isolation to Mainstream)*.

Those Negro colleges with strong resources and successful operating programs of Afro-American instruction and research should be encouraged to seek special financial support for the further development of such endeavors *(From Isolation to Mainstream)*.

More colleges founded for Negroes should provide education for adult members of the black community *(From Isolation to Mainstream)*.

By the year 2000, colleges founded for Negroes should have enrollments in keeping with the guidelines suggested for all institutions of higher education of comparable types. Comprehensive colleges should have 5,000 students. Liberal arts colleges should have at least 1,000 students. Public community colleges should have at least 2,000 students. Colleges with very low enrollments and with little prospect of meeting these goals should consider relocation or merging with other institutions that have complementing programs and facilities *(From Isolation to Mainstream)*.

The examples of special effort made by North Carolina and certain other states to overcome the historical disadvantages of their colleges founded for Negroes should be followed by other states in which such institutions are located *(From Isolation to Mainstream)*.

To meet many of the basic financial problems of black colleges, the federal government should adopt the full program of recommendations in *Quality and Equality* as revised June 1970 and in *Higher Education and the Nation's Health (From Isolation to Mainstream)*.

In recognition of the special urgency and problems involved in the planning and development tasks that face colleges founded for Negroes, we recommend a special subdivision for the development of black colleges and universities be created within the proposed National Foundation for the Development of Higher Education. The purpose of this division, in which Negroes should have a vital role in advisory and management capacities, would be to aid colleges and universities founded for Negroes to develop and implement new programs and activities that respond to the challenges that confront them as institutions in transition *(From Isolation to Mainstream)*.

Business and industry, on a nationwide basis, should be fully informed about the rapid transitions occurring in colleges founded for Negroes. Representatives of business and industry should be invited to serve on advisory boards for the development programs of these colleges and should be asked to assist in planning effective communications between these institutions and the industrial community *(From Isolation to Mainstream)*.

Colleges founded for Negroes should seek assistance from state governments and foundations for programs that will pay the salaries of their faculty members while they complete work for their doctorates at other institutions. Until qualified scholars and teachers become more plentiful, exchanges of visiting professors, joint appointments, and other arrangements that enable talented people to serve more than one institution should be attempted as a means of expanding the pool of teaching talent available to these colleges.

Organization of advanced management seminars and short courses for administrators at colleges founded for Negroes, supported at least in part by foundations and business firms, is also recommended *(From Isolation to Mainstream)*.

BROAD LEARNING EXPERIENCES *(See also* General education)

Consideration should be given to establishing campus by campus a series of coherent options for a broad learning experience among which students may choose *(Reform on Campus)*.

More broad learning experiences should be made available to students, and more opportunities for creative activity should be provided as through independent study and the creative arts *(The Purposes and the Performance of Higher Education in the United States)*.

BUDGETING States should strongly resist investing coordinating agencies with administrative authority, particularly over budget matters. If an existing state agency such as the budget office or finance office undertakes budget review for higher education, the coordinating agency should not be given the responsibility for an independent budget review, but should, instead, be involved in the budget review process of the other state agency. If there is no existing state agency which does or can undertake budget review for higher education, budget review, as opposed to budget control, could be assigned to the coordinating agency *(The Capitol and the Campus)*.

All appropriate agencies should give high priority to the development of more adequate data on the behavior of costs, income, and output in higher education *(The More Effective Use of Resources)*.

All institutions of higher education should place emphasis on policies that will ensure budgetary flexibility. Combinations of policies that will achieve this goal will vary from institution to institution but may well include elements of (1) selective cutbacks, (2) across-the-board budgetary cuts, (3) consolidation of existing programs, (4) readaptation of existing programs, (5) "every tub on its own bottom," and (6) central reassignment of positions vacated due to resignation, retirement, or death *(The More Effective Use of Resources)*.

Institutions of higher education should consider the establishment of committees including faculty, students, and administrators to serve in an advisory capacity in relation to the preparation of the budget when severe cuts must be made. Where it is not considered feasible or desirable to establish such committees, the more traditional practice of holding hearings on major budgetary decisions can provide faculty and students with opportunities to express their views *(The More Effective Use of Resources)*.

Institutions of higher education should seek to alter their budgetary procedures in such a way as to induce cost-saving change, giving special attention to the possibilities of permitting departments and schools to carry over from year to year significant proportions of unspent balances in their budgets and of permitting them to retain a portion of the budgetary savings resulting from innovation or investment in more efficient equipment *(The More Effective Use of Resources)*.

Long-range plans for capital expansion should be continually revised to meet changing circumstances. Adequate allowance should be made for meeting increased debt service and maintenance costs on the basis of several alternative and relatively conservative estimates of the behavior of future income. Capital and operating budgets should be consolidated (with the capital budget converted to a rental cost basis), so that shifts can be made from one allocation to the other *(The More Effective Use of Resources)*.

Institutions of higher education should develop plans for gradually shifting to a practice of requiring budgets of departments and other units to include a rental charge for the space they occupy and the equipment they use *(The More Effective Use of Resources)*.

All institutions of higher education should seek economies in computer expenditures by charging the full costs of computer services used in instruction and departmental research against departmental budgets and charging the full costs of computer services used in extramurally financed research against the relevant research budgets *(The More Effective Use of Resources)*.

One to three percent of all funds should be taken each year from existing programs, set aside as a self-renewal fund, and directed to new or expanded programs *(The More Effective Use of Resources and Reform on Campus)*.

Elected officials with the power of budgetary review should not serve as members of governing boards of public institutions over which they exercise such review *(Governance of Higher Education)*.

BUSINESS AND INDUSTRY Business and industry, on a nationwide basis, should be fully informed about the rapid transitions occurring in colleges and universities founded for Negroes. Representatives of business and industry should be invited to serve on advisory boards for the development programs of these colleges and should be asked to assist in planning effective communications between these institutions and the industrial community *(From Isolation to Mainstream)*.

Management seminars and short courses for administrators at black colleges, supported at least partially by business firms, are recommended *(From Isolation to Mainstream)*.

Industry will continue to accept responsibility for training persons to perform skills required by specific tasks on the job *(Toward a Learning Society)*.

When they do not have skill-training expertise in their own companies, businesses will seek agreements with educational institutions to provide technical aid for the development of industry-based skill-training programs and for the evaluation of such programs *(Toward a Learning Society)*.

Research and development funds will be made available by the Office of Education and the Department of Labor to facilitate the development of the theoretical knowledge and technical expertise needed to service agreements between postsecondary educational institutions and industry for the development of skill-training programs *(Toward a Learning Society)*.

Educational institutions that have well-developed instructional technology will avail businesses and industry of opportunities to tie plant-site classrooms to televised instruction originating on the campus, and will make available audio-video-tape instruction or computer-assisted instruction on subjects relevant to business and industry training programs *(Toward a Learning Society)*.

CAMPUS SIZE *(See* Enrollment)

CAPITAL INVESTMENT All capital investment plans should give full advance consideration to the possible impact of accelerated degree programs *(The More Effective Use of Resources)*.

CERTIFICATION There should be national requirements for periodic reexamination and recertification of all physicians and dentists by specialty boards and other appropriate bodies *(Higher Education and the Nation's Health)*.

A National Health Manpower Commission should be appointed to make a thorough study of the feasibility of national licensing requirements for all health manpower *(Higher Education and the Nation's Health)*.

Employers, both private and public, should hire and promote on the basis of talent alone as well as on prior certification *(Less Time, More Options)*.

Institutions of postsecondary education will grant degrees, certificates, and honors at more frequent intervals than they now do *(Toward a Learning Society)*.

Undergraduate and professional degrees will increasingly become only a part of the cumulative record of an individual's educational accomplishments. Ultimately, the degrees will become less important than the total record as evidence of such accomplishment *(Toward a Learning Society)*.

CHILD-CARE SERVICES Colleges and universities should be responsive to campus groups seeking to develop child-care services. An essential step is to appoint a carefully selected committee to study various possible types of child-care services, including those already available in the community, and to recommend a plan for making such services available to students and employees of the institution. The committee should include faculty members drawn from appropriate departments, parents, and persons knowledgeable about community resources.

We believe that in most situations, especially for smaller campuses, it will be preferable for the academic institution to cooperate with other community groups in ensuring the availability of adequate child-care services in the community. If campus facilities are desired on or near large campuses, we believe, consistent with our general view that an academic institution should not assume functions that are not central to its main purposes, that it will usually be preferable to seek an arrangement under which the child-care services will be provided under the auspices of a separate board of directors and not as a direct function of the academic institution. The board of directors would be expected to ensure adequate financing and adequate standards for the child-care services.

We believe that student-parents should be expected to pay for child-care services on the basis of sliding scale fees according to their incomes and that parents who are employees of the institution would normally be expected to pay for the full cost of services. Subsidies to meet the needs of low-income student-parents should be sought from extramural public and private sources and should not normally be sought from the academic institution's regular budget *(Opportunities for Women in Higher Education)*.

CLUSTER COLLEGES Universities, colleges, and state planning agencies should carefully study and adopt plans for the development of cluster colleges. The federal government, the states, and private foundations should make funds available for research evaluating the comparative experience of these colleges *(New Students and New Places)*.

Cluster colleges within large institutions should provide particularly good opportunities for diversity *(Reform on Campus)*.

COLLECTIVE BARGAINING Institutions of higher education engaged with faculty unionism should employ staff members or consultants who are experienced in collective bargaining negotiations and should consider the possibility of agreements that will induce increases in the productivity of faculty members and other academic employees without impairing educational effectiveness *(The More Effective Use of Resources)*.

State laws, where they do not now permit it, should provide faculty members in public institutions the opportunity of obtaining collective bargaining rights. One alternative under such laws should be choice of no bargaining unit *(Governance of Higher Education)*.

Faculties in each institution should undertake the most careful analysis of the implications of collective bargaining and, more broadly, of which of the alternative forms of governance they prefer *(Governance of Higher Education)*.

Representation and bargaining units should be composed of faculty members, including department chairmen *(Governance of Higher Education)*.

The approach to contract coverage should be one of restraint, with the contract covering economic benefits and with academic affairs left (or put) in the hands of the faculty senate or equivalent council *(Governance of Higher Education)*.

A separate federal law and separate state laws should be enacted governing collective bargaining by faculty members in both private and public institutions and should be responsive to the special circumstances that surround their employment. If this is not possible, then separate provisions should be made in more general laws, or leeway should be provided for special administrative interpretations *(Governance of Higher Education)*.

COMMUNITY COLLEGES *(See also* Postsecondary education)

To stimulate cooperative programs among community colleges and universities for the preparation and reeducation of community college teachers and counselors, $25 million is recommended in 1970–71 for an expanded special program of federal training grants *(Quality and Equality)*.

Community colleges or equivalent facilities should be established within commuting range of potential students in all populous areas *(A Chance to Learn)*.

All states should enact legislation providing admission to public community colleges of all applicants who are high school graduates or are persons over 18 years of age who are capable of benefiting from continuing education *(The Open-Door Colleges)*.

The comprehensive community college has a unique and important role to play in higher education, and two-year colleges should be actively discouraged by state planning and financing policies from converting to four-year institutions *(The Open-Door Colleges)*.

All state plans for the development of two-year institutions of higher education should provide for comprehensive community colleges that will offer meaningful options for college-age students and adults among a variety of educational programs, including transfer education, general education, remedial courses, occupational programs, continuing education for adults, and cultural programs designed to enrich the community environment. Within this general framework there should be opportunities for varying patterns of development and for the provision of particularly strong specialties in selected colleges *(The Open-Door Colleges)*.

All two-year colleges should award an associate in arts or associate in applied science degree to all students who satisfactorily complete a two-year prescribed curriculum, and students who enter with adequate advanced standing should have the option of earning the associate degree in less than two years. Non-degree-credit courses should be confined to short-term courses and to training of the skilled craftsman type, for which certificates should be provided, and to remedial work *(The Open-Door Colleges)*.

All community colleges should provide adequate resources for effective guidance, including not only provision for an adequate professional counseling staff, but also provision for involvement of the entire faculty in guidance of students enrolled in their courses. All community college districts should provide for effective coordination of their guidance services with those of local high schools and for coordination of both counseling and placement services with those of the public employment offices and other appropriate agencies *(The Open-Door Colleges)*.

The continuing existence of specialized two-year institutions should not stand in the way of the establishment of comprehensive community colleges in the same areas. State plans should place major emphasis on the allocation of vocational education funds to comprehensive community colleges rather than to post–high school area vocational schools or other noncollegiate institutions *(The Open-Door Colleges)*.

For the sake of quality of program, economy of operation, and easy availability, state plans should provide for community colleges generally ranging in size from about 2,000 to 5,000 daytime students, except in sparsely populated areas where institutions may have to be somewhat smaller, and in very large cities, where they may have to be somewhat larger *(The Open-Door Colleges)*.

Through the coordinated efforts of federal, state, and local governments, the goal of providing a community college within commuting distance of every potential student should be attained by 1980. In sparsely populated areas, where it is not feasible to provide institutions within commuting distance of every student, residential community colleges are needed. State plans should also designate selected urban community colleges to provide housing arrangements for students from smaller communities and rural areas, in order to encourage maximum access to specialized occupational programs. To achieve this goal, about 230 to 280 new, carefully planned community colleges will be needed by 1980 *(The Open-Door Colleges)*.[1]

The federal government should assist community colleges by providing (1) funds for state planning; (2) start-up grants for new campuses; (3) construction funds; (4) cost-of-education allowances for low-income students attending the colleges; (5) grants, work-study opportunities, and loans for students; and (6) an expanded program of federal training grants to stimulate expansion and improvement of graduate education programs for community college teachers, counselors, and administrators *(The Open-Door Colleges)*.

States should expand their contribution to the financing of community colleges so that the state's share amounts, in general, to one-half or two-thirds of the total state and local financial burden, including operational and capital outlay costs *(The Open-Door Colleges)*.

States should revise their legislation, wherever necessary, to provide for uniform low tuition or no tuition charges at public two-year colleges *(The Open-Door Colleges)*.

States with community college systems should undertake continuing evaluation studies of the experiences of these colleges, with particular reference to student achievement during the two-year educational period and their subsequent education and employment *(The Open-Door Colleges)*.

State legislation should provide for the formation of local community college districts and should prohibit inclusion of community colleges within K–12 local school districts. In every local community college district there should be an elected or appointed board of directors with substantial powers relating to the development and administration of community colleges within the district. These local boards should delegate substantial responsibility to the administration and faculty and provide for student participation in decisions relating to educational policy and student affairs. When community colleges are part of the state university system, there should be local advisory boards with substantial influence *(The Open-Door Colleges)*.

Community colleges should develop and expand their curricula in the allied health professions where this has not been done. They should also seek and accept guidance from university health science centers in the planning and evaluation of these educational programs *(Higher Education and the Nation's Health)*.

State and local planning bodies should develop plans for the establishment by 1980 of about 80 to 125 new community colleges in large metropolitan areas with populations of 500,000 or more. Including these new institutions, there should be about 175 to 235 new community colleges in all *(New Students and New Places)*.

---

[1] Because of the establishment of many new colleges and the availability of new information, the Commission revised its estimate of new community colleges needed by 1980. In *New Students and New Places* it estimates a need for 175 to 235 new community colleges.

State plans should, in general, incorporate a minimum FTE enrollment objective of 2,000 students and a maximum FTE enrollment objective of 5,000 students for community colleges *(New Students and New Places)*.

State financing authorities and local agencies should review their policies for funding community colleges to determine whether adequate funds are being made available for this segment of higher education *(The Campus and the City)*.

Urban community colleges, in order to serve more fully their urban clientele, should give careful consideration to the (1) establishment of multiple campuses in a metropolitan area rather than concentration of all students on one campus, and the development of some specialization of educational missions among the various campuses; (2) systematic experimentation and evaluation of remedial and developmental programs; (3) possible early admission of urban high school students requiring remedial work or seeking immediate entry into vocational training *(The Campus and the City)*.

Commuter institutions should make available lockers, study and lounge areas, and other physical facilities designed to meet the special needs of commuters, and the scheduling of educational programs and activities should be undertaken with the commuter in mind *(The Campus and the City)*.

Community college districts should conduct follow-up studies that would provide information on employment patterns of their former students by occupation and industry *(College Graduates and Jobs)*.

Professional schools in universities and colleges should undertake the responsibility for cooperating with and providing guidance for community colleges in the development of paraprofessional training programs *(College Graduates and Jobs)*.

Community colleges should maintain a relatively low-tuition policy for the first two years of higher education *(Higher Education: Who Pays? Who Benefits? Who Should Pay?)*.

COMMUNITY RELATIONS A substantial program of federal aid for medical education and health services should be established to increase the availability of health services in the community of the medical school and the quality of health care delivery *(Quality and Equality)*.

In communities where effective desegregation of local school systems has not been achieved, institutions of higher education should offer their resources of research and consultation to local school administrators and other community leaders *(A Chance to Learn)*.

Institutions of higher education, either alone or in conjunction with local school districts, should establish educational opportunity centers to serve areas with major concentrations of low-income populations *(A Chance to Learn)*.

Institutions of higher education should devote a portion of their summer schedule and facilities to camps for educationally disadvantaged children *(A Chance to Learn)*.

Experimental programs for the early development of verbal skills should be established, to be sponsored and administered by institutions of higher education with active participation from members of the community *(A Chance to Learn)*.

All state plans for the development of two-year institutions of higher education should provide for comprehensive community colleges that will offer cultural programs designed to enrich the community environment *(The Open-Door Colleges)*.

Dissatisfactions on campuses and their public expression should be viewed as the reflection of many problems and conditions both in society and on the campuses. Both campus and society share responsibility. Dissenters are also responsible for their choice of tactics in advancing their goals—for some of their tactics are the source of the dissatisfactions and negative reactions of the public at large.

Actions by society in response to coercion and violence, however, should be undertaken only with reference to those specific individuals and groups who engage in it. A campus as a whole, or a system as a whole, or higher education as a whole, should not be penalized *(Dissent and Disruption)*.

Representatives of the administration, the faculty, and the students should participate in establishing guidelines and procedures for relations between the campus and law enforcement authorities. These guidelines should be made public *(Dissent and Disruption)*.

Universities should develop long-range plans that give adequate attention to the interaction between the campus and the neighborhood in which it is located. Where appropriate, colleges and universities should participate actively in urban-renewal activities, but only in unusual circumstances should this participation extend to investment of scarce institutional resources in housing development for the general community. Institutions should limit their need for expansion into scarce urban space by better use of existing space *(The Campus and the City)*.

Colleges and universities should seek to assist the surrounding areas through the operation of their employment and purchasing policies. Regardless of rights given them by charter, colleges and universities should pay the usual taxes on any property held by them for noneducational purposes, and when expanding their campuses, should make every effort to develop the property in such a way as to permit its continuation on the tax rolls *(The Campus and the City)*.

The National Foundation on the Arts and Humanities should provide grants for university-based cultural activities available to both the campus and its neighbors and for cooperative endeavors involving higher education and city museums and performing arts centers *(The Campus and the City)*.

Large universities located in urban areas should appoint a vice-president or vice-chancellor for urban affairs who would be concerned with the university-urban interface in terms of the urban impact of the university's educational, service, research, and corporate functions *(The Campus and the City)*.

Mayors of major cities should assign someone on their staff primary responsibility for liaison with higher education in the city *(The Campus and the City)*.

Cultural and "lifelong learning" facilities and opportunities should be made available to the general public on an expanded basis *(The Purposes and the Performance of Higher Education in the United States)*.

COMPENSATORY EDUCATION   Experimental programs for the early development of verbal skills should be established, to be sponsored and administered by institutions of higher education with active participation from members of the community and of programs for remedying verbal skill deficiencies at the secondary and higher levels of education *(A Chance to Learn)*.

Programs should be initiated for an individualized "foundation year" to be available on an optional basis to all interested students *(A Chance to Learn* and *The Open-Door Colleges)*.

Every student accepted into a program requiring compensatory education should receive the necessary commitment of resources to allow his engagement in an appropriate level of course work by the end of no more than two years *(A Chance to Learn)*.

All state plans for the development of two-year institutions of higher education should provide for comprehensive community colleges that will offer remedial courses *(The Open-Door Colleges)*.

Community colleges should provide remedial education that is flexible and responsive to the individual student's needs; such programs should be subject to continual study and evaluation; and community colleges should seek the cooperation of other educational institutions in providing for remedial education *(The Open-Door Colleges)*.

Colleges enrolling large numbers of disadvantaged or minority students should review their institutional programs to determine if they are designed to meet the educational needs of the students involved *(The Campus and the City)*.

Urban community colleges should give careful consideration to systematic experimentation and evaluation of remedial and developmental programs and the possible early admission of urban high school students requiring remedial work *(The Campus and the City)*.

The new National Institute of Education should make grants available to those institutions that are conducting systematic experiments with remedial education *(The Campus and the City)*.

Because of the evidence that many women enter college with inadequate mathematical training, special provision should be made to ensure that women desiring to major in fields calling for extensive use of mathematics are encouraged to make up this deficiency *(Opportunities for Women in Higher Education)*.

COMPREHENSIVE COLLEGES   Comprehensive colleges should develop and expand their curricula in the allied health professions where this has not been done. They should also seek and accept guidance from university health science centers in the planning and evaluation of these educational programs *(Higher Education and the Nation's Health)*.

State and local planning bodies should develop plans for the establishment by 1980 of about 60 to 70 new comprehensive colleges in large metropolitan areas with populations of 500,000 or more *(New Students and New Places)*.

State plans should, in general, incorporate a minimum FTE enrollment objective of 5,000 students for comprehensive colleges and a maximum FTE enrollment objective of 10,000 for these colleges *(New Students and New Places)*.

Professional schools in universities and colleges should undertake the responsibility for cooperating with and providing guidance for comprehensive colleges in the development of paraprofessional training *(College Graduates and Jobs)*.

CONSOLIDATION   All new medical and dental schools should be parts of university health science centers and, wherever feasible, existing separate medical and dental schools should likewise become parts of university health science centers *(Higher Education and the Nation's Health)*.

Similarly, public health schools should be made parts of university health science centers *(Higher Education and the Nation's Health)*.

Black colleges with very low enrollments and with little prospect of meeting recommended enrollment goals should consider relocation or merging with other institutions that have complementing programs and facilities *(From Isolation to Mainstream).*

Consolidation of teacher education into a more limited number of institutions would be generally preferable to a cutting back of teacher education on an across-the-board basis. Many state colleges that have largely concentrated on teacher education will need to develop more comprehensive programs, and in sparsely populated states this will in some cases require a merger of two or more such state colleges into a single location *(College Graduates and Jobs).*

CONSORTIA Existing consortia should make continuous efforts toward increasing the effectiveness of the cooperative programs. Institutions—especially small colleges—that are not now members of consortia should carefully consider possibilities for forming consortia with neighboring institutions *(New Students and New Places).*

Consortia should be developed and strengthened in higher education *(The More Effective Use of Resources).*

Far more extensive use of consortium arrangements should be made that involve planning for concentration of development of Ph.D. programs in particular fields in individual members of the consortium as well as the rights of students to cross-register for individual courses or fields of concentration *(College Graduates and Jobs).*

Consortia should adopt policies of clear differentiation of functions among campuses and of assigned specialization among fields *(The Purposes and the Performance of Higher Education in the United States).*

CONSTRUCTION GRANTS AND LOANS (See also Cost-of-education supplements, Federal support, Institutional aid)

Construction grants should be made available to provide one-third of the total costs for construction and needed renovation of academic facilities. Funding levels for the academic facilities construction program should be increased to provide sufficient loan funds for an additional one-third of needed new construction costs *(Quality and Equality).*

The federal government should provide construction grants and loans for university health science centers and area health education centers and start-up grants for health science centers *(Higher Education and the Nation's Health).*

Those states that do not already have programs enabling private institutions to borrow construction funds through a state-created bond-issuing corporation should take steps to develop such agencies if the private institutions can demonstrate the need for them *(The Capitol and the Campus).*

CONTINUING EDUCATION (See also Further education, Postsecondary education)

All states should enact legislation providing admission to public community colleges of all applicants who are over 18 years of age and capable of benefiting from continuing education *(The Open-Door Colleges).*

Continuing education for adults should be provided in community colleges *(The Open-Door Colleges).*

Continuing education of health manpower should be a major concern of the university health science centers and area health education centers *(Higher Education and the Nation's Health).*

Opportunities should be created for persons to reenter higher education throughout their active careers in regular daytime classes, nighttime classes, summer courses, and special short-term programs *(Less Time, More Options).*

All persons, after high school graduation, should have two years of postsecondary education placed "in the bank" for them to be withdrawn at any time in their lives when it best suits them *(Less Time, More Options)*.

More colleges founded for Negroes should provide education for adult members of the black community. The federal government and foundations should give favorable consideration to requests for the support of such activities *(From Isolation to Mainstream)*.

University health science centers and area health education centers should provide leadership in encouraging the development and expansion of continuing education programs for nurses and allied health workers in appropriate educational institutions *(College Graduates and Jobs)*.

Professional schools in universities and colleges should also undertake the responsibility for providing guidance and advice in connection with programs of continuing education for members of their professions *(College Graduates and Jobs)*.

There should be a greater mixing of age groups on campus through providing more opportunities for older persons to take classes and to obtain needed financial support *(The Purposes and the Performance of Higher Education in the United States)*.

Cultural and "lifelong learning" facilities and opportunities should be made available to the general public on an expanded basis *(The Purposes and the Performance of Higher Education in the United States)*.

Colleges should develop admissions programs to seek out new constituencies, including adults *(Continuity and Discontinuity)*.

Policies that discriminate against admission of adults desirous of continuing their education should be liberalized to permit enrollment of qualified mature men and women whose education has been interrupted because of family responsibilities or for other reasons *(Opportunities for Women in Higher Education)*.

External degree and other nontraditional study programs of high quality are especially important in relation to the special needs of mature married women for continuing education *(Opportunities for Women in Higher Education)*.

Large campuses should have an administrative officer specifically concerned with ensuring that qualified adults are given opportunities to pursue undergraduate or graduate study. Whether there should be a separate center for continuing education of women should be decided in the light of the circumstances prevailing on any given campus *(Opportunities for Women in Higher Education)*.

Every person will have available to him, throughout his life, financial assistance for at least two years of postsecondary education *(Toward a Learning Society)*.

Wherever academic programs are offered for students who are adults of all ages, the rules for student conduct, campus traditions, and the learning environment will be hospitable to them, and will not discriminate against older students *(Toward a Learning Society)*.

Learning pavilions designed and operated to encourage and facilitate independent adult learning will be developed in urban centers and in areas that are remote from institutions of postsecondary education *(Toward a Learning Society)*.

CONVERSION OF INSTITUTIONS Public two-year colleges should be actively discouraged by state planning and financing policies from converting to four-year institutions *(The Open-Door Colleges)*.

Schools of osteopathy should be converted to schools of medicine, wherever feasible *(Higher Education and the Nation's Health)*.

Existing two-year medical schools that do not lead to M.D.-candidate education within the same university system should be converted to provide full M.D.-candidate education as soon as possible *(Higher Education and the Nation's Health)*.

COOPERATION Institutions should examine their own levels of cooperativeness to determine whether failures to respond to advisory agencies might lead more surely and quickly to establishment of regulatory agencies *(The Capitol and the Campus)*.

Colleges and universities should continue to seek ways of sharing facilities, courses, and specialized programs through cooperative arrangements *(New Students and New Places)*.

Developments that are occurring in several states in the direction of increased cooperation and sharing of facilities by public and private institutions of higher education are welcome. Such collaboration should be considered in all states *(The More Effective Use of Resources)*.

Relatively small institutions should seek to enter into arrangements with nearby similar institutions to conduct jointly sponsored programs of institutional research *(The More Effective Use of Resources)*.

All institutions of higher education should seek economies in computer expenditures by sharing computer facilities with nearby institutions of higher education where this appears to be a more advantageous solution than contracting out *(The More Effective Use of Resources)*.

Professional schools and academic departments should cooperate in the development of joint degree programs *(College Graduates and Jobs)*.

Before taking on a new educational function, institutions should determine the relationship of that function to their educational mission and should ascertain whether there are existing alternative educational resources to meet the particular educational need to be served. If such alternative resources exist, the possibility of contractual agreements with other institutions to secure the services, or the possibility of joint enrollment of the learner, should be explored before a new program is developed *(Toward a Learning Society)*.

COOPERATIVE LEARNING- (See also Instructional technology)
TECHNOLOGY CENTERS By 1992, at least seven cooperative learning-technology centers, voluntarily organized on a regional basis by participating higher education institutions and systems should be established for the purpose of sharing costs and facilities for the accelerated development and utilization of instructional technology in higher education.

The federal government should assume full financial responsibility for the capital expenditures required initially to establish one cooperative learning-technology center every three years between 1973 and 1992. The government should also provide at least one-third of the funds required for the operation of cooperative learning-technology centers for the first 10 years of their operation *(The Fourth Revolution)*.

COORDINATING The Commissioner of Education should designate a unit within the U.S. Office of
AGENCIES Education to develop standard definitions and methods of reporting to ensure the coordination, evaluation, and dissemination of available data on educational opportunity *(A Chance to Learn)*.

University health science centers should be responsible, in their respective geographic areas, for coordinating the education of health care personnel and for cooperation with other community agencies in improving the organization of health care delivery *(Higher Education and the Nation's Health)*.

Coordinating agencies in the several states where there are black colleges should make studies of compensation paid to faculty members in comparable ranks at all state-supported institutions and advise legislative bodies of inadequacies where they exist *(From Isolation to Mainstream)*.

Elected officials (unless elected for that specific purpose) should not serve as members of coordinating agencies. Governors should not serve as chairmen or voting members of state coordinating agencies *(The Capitol and the Campus)*.

Although there is a need for more effective coordination of post secondary education at the state level, states should strongly resist investing coordinating agencies with administrative authority, particularly over budget matters *(The Capitol and the Campus)*.

If an existing state agency such as the budget office or finance office undertakes budget review for higher education, the coordinating agency should not be given the responsibility for an independent budget review, but should instead be involved in the budget review process of the other state agency. If there is no existing state agency that does or can undertake budget review for higher education, budget review, as opposed to budget control, could be assigned to the coordinating agency *(The Capitol and the Campus)*.

Although coordinating agencies should not be invested with authority to control institutional budgets, states should grant to coordinating agencies some funds which the agency itself can grant to institutions to encourage quality improvement, and experimentation and innovation consistent with the state's long-range educational goals. Agencies allocating funds for these purposes should regularly evaluate the programs developed with such funds *(The Capitol and the Campus)*.

Coordinating agencies should be assigned certain program review responsibilities and authority consistent with their educational planning functions. These agencies should act in an advisory capacity on such matters as effective use of resources, educational quality, access to postsecondary education, appropriate functions for the various types of institutions, and articulation among the various elements within postsecondary education.

Coordinating agencies should serve as a buffer and communicator explaining the above matters to agencies of the state government and to the public; developing mutual understanding of common goals among the elements of postsecondary education; protecting the institutions, when necessary, from legislative, executive, or public interference in carrying out their educational functions *(The Capitol and the Campus)*.

States should review the funding levels of their coordinating agencies to determine if the levels permit attention to the broader functions of coordination or only to those minimal duties legally required of the agencies. States should take steps to attract staff members of the ability, stature, and sensitivity required to carry out the complex tasks of the agencies (e.g., salary level increases, opportunities for educational and research leaves, and adoption of certain other fringe benefits usually available to members of the academic community) *(The Capitol and the Campus)*.

Coordinating agencies should be granted the following authorities to be exercised within the context of the long-range plans or guidelines established for the state: To approve or disapprove new institutions, branches or centers, and where appropriate, to take active steps toward the establishment of new institutions; to approve all new degree programs at the doctoral level, and new master's and baccalaureate programs in general fields not previously offered, and in high-cost fields; and to allocate funds under state-administered federal programs *(The Capitol and the Campus)*.

Coordinating agencies should encourage pilot projects designed to demonstrate that changes in procedures will yield economies *(The More Effective Use of Resources)*.

State coordinating agencies should develop strong policies (where these do not now exist) for preventing the spread of Ph.D. programs to institutions that do not now have them *(College Graduates and Jobs)*.

Academic policies set by state agencies should be of a broad nature and should not interfere with the more specific professional academic judgments about faculty appointments, courses of study, admission of individual students, grades and degrees for individual students, specific research projects, appointment of academic and administrative staff and leadership, and protection of academic freedom *(Governance of Higher Education)*.

Coordinating agencies at the state level should seek to establish, in cooperation with public and private institutions of higher education, guidelines defining areas of state concern and areas of institutional independence that avoid detailed control *(Governance of Higher Education)*.

Coordinating councils should adopt policies of clear differentiation of functions among campuses and of assigned specializations among fields *(The Purposes and the Performance of Higher Education in the United States)*.

Public agencies, including coordinating councils, should determine general policies on student admissions within state systems. Decisions on individual students should be left to each campus *(Continuity and Discontinuity)*.

Each state through its coordinating mechanisms should study carefully and define the roles of public high schools, vocational schools, community colleges, and proprietary schools with respect to vocational and technical programs *(Continuity and Discontinuity)*.

State coordinating agencies will become increasingly aware of the resources of all postsecondary educational institutions in their states, and, in partnership with those affected, will utilize their influence to assure adequate financial support of their institutions and to minimize unnecessary duplication of specialized programs in colleges and universities and other institutions offering postsecondary education *(Toward a Learning Society)*.

COST-OF-EDUCATION SUPPLEMENTS (See also Federal support, Institutional aid, Student aid)

The federal government should grant cost-of-education supplements to colleges and universities based on the numbers and levels of students holding federal grants enrolled in the institution *(Quality and Equality)*.

Cost-of-instruction supplements should be granted to university health science centers for each medical and dental student enrolled and to these centers and their affiliated hospitals for each house officer *(Higher Education and the Nation's Health)*.

For those states in which our recommendations prove inadequate, each resident student should be given cost-of-education vouchers that would entitle any private institution selected by the student to receive a state payment increasing gradually each year up to an amount equal to one-third of the subsidy granted by the state for students at the same levels attending comparable public institutions *(The Capitol and the Campus).*

Cost-of-education supplements accompanying doctoral fellowships should be available only to those institutions that charge the doctoral recipient a fee that is not affected by his residency status *(The Capitol and the Campus).*

The federal government should establish a program of cost-of-education supplements to colleges and universities based on the numbers of students enrolled in the institutions who hold grants awarded on the basis of financial need. Under this program, it is recommended that any college or university officially recognized as being eligible for participation in this program by the U.S. Office of Education be paid $500 for each undergraduate student at the institution that is a recipient of a grant from the federal government which was made to the student because of this financial need. Proportionate cost-of-education supplements would be paid to institutions for any part-time students who are enrolled at that institution and who hold such grants.

Colleges and universities officially recognized as eligible for participation in this program by the U.S. Office of Education shall receive a grant of $200 for each student who receives a subsidized loan provided, however, that no such payment shall be made for students who hold federal grants or for students who borrow less than $200 during the fiscal year *(Institutional Aid).*

Institutions should be paid a cost-of-education supplement amounting to $5,000 for each federal doctoral fellow enrolled at that institution *(Institutional Aid).*

COUNSELING *(See* Guidance and counseling)

CURRICULUM A National Foundation for the Development of Higher Education should be established, whose functions would be to encourage, advise, review, and provide financial support for institutional programs designed to give new directions in curricula, to strengthen essential areas that have fallen behind or never been adequately developed because of inadequate funding, and to develop programs for improvement of educational processes and techniques *(Quality and Equality).*

Comprehensive colleges and community colleges should develop and expand their curricula in the allied health professions where this has not been done *(Higher Education and the Nation's Health).*

Colleges founded for Negroes should utilize the present period of transition for curriculum innovation and enrichment. Most of them should concentrate on developing, in addition to general liberal arts courses, strong comprehensive undergraduate programs in preprofessional subjects and in subjects that prepare students for advanced education and high-demand occupations *(From Isolation to Mainstream).*

Colleges and universities that are responsible for the training of prospective university, college, and high school teachers should begin now to incorporate in their curricula instruction on the development of teaching-learning segments that appropriately utilize the expanding technologies of instruction *(The Fourth Revolution).*

Prevention of undue proliferation of courses should be sought by periodic review of the totality of course offerings in a department *(The More Effective Use of Resources)*.

Greater attention in the curriculum should be given to (1) the creative arts and (2) world cultures *(Reforms on Campus)*.

The curriculum as a whole should be reviewed, campus by campus, in consultation with high school leaders, to assess its broad relevance not only to appropriate student interests but also to prior and subsequent learning experiences *(Reform on Campus)*.

Professional schools in universities and colleges should undertake the responsibility for cooperating with and providing guidance for comprehensive colleges and community colleges in the development of paraprofessional training programs *(College Graduates and Jobs)*.

Governance arrangements should provide adequate academic options from among which students may choose *(Governance of Higher Education)*.

Curricula should be examined to be certain they reflect the history, culture, and current roles of minority groups *(The Purposes and the Performance of Higher Education in the United States)*.

Because of the evidence that many women enter college with inadequate mathematical training, special provision should be made to ensure that women desiring to major in fields calling for extensive use of mathematics are encouraged to make up this deficiency *(Opportunities for Women in Higher Education)*.

DEGREE PROGRAMS, ACCELERATED   *(See also* Early admissions)

All universities with health science centers should develop plans for accelerating premedical and medical education and for predental and dental education. They should especially consider programs calling for three years (instead of four) after the B.A. to obtain the M.D. or D.D.S. and a three-year residency (instead of the typical four years of internship and residency) *(Higher Education and the Nation's Health)*.

Medical and dental schools with three-year programs should receive the same amount of institutional aid as they would if they were four-year schools *(Higher Education and the Nation's Health)*.

The time to get a degree should be shortened by one year to the B.A. and by one or two more years to the Ph.D. and to M.D. practice *(Less Time, More Options)*.

DEGREES   All two-year colleges should award an associate in arts or associate in applied science degree to all students who satisfactorily complete a two-year prescribed curriculum, and students who enter with adequate advanced standing should have the option of earning the associate degree in less than two years *(The Open-Door Colleges)*.

A master's degree should be awarded at the end of the basic training period in the health-related sciences *(Higher Education and the Nation's Health)*.

The master of philosophy and doctor of arts degrees should be widely accepted *(Less Time, More Options)*.

A degree (or other form of credit) should be made available to students at least every two years in their careers (and in some cases every year) *(Less Time, More Options)*.

Opportunities should be created for persons to reenter higher education through out their active careers in regular daytime classes, nighttime classes, summer courses, and special short-term programs, with degrees and certificates available as appropriate *(Less Time, More Options)*.

Coordinating agencies should be granted the authority to approve all new degree programs at the doctoral levels, and new master's and baccalaureate programs in general fields not previously offered, and in high-cost fields *(The Capitol and the Campus)*.

The number of different types of degrees awarded in higher education should be greatly reduced *(The More Effective Use of Resources)*.

Colleges and universities should use great caution in adopting new degree programs and conduct periodic reviews of existing degree programs, with a view to eliminating those in which very few degrees are awarded. In multicampus institutions, there is a strong case for confining highly specialized degree programs to only one or two campuses within the system *(The More Effective Use of Resources)*.

Professional schools and academic departments should cooperate in the development of joint degree programs in response to emerging societal problems and in response to the advancement of knowledge or technological change *(College Graduates and Jobs)*.

Liberal arts colleges should consider enrolling students as early as grade 11 and awarding the bachelor's degree after grade 14 or 15 *(Continuity and Discontinuity)*.

Colleges and universities will successfully resist pressures to grant degree credit for those activities and experiences that are not clearly planned as part of an academic learning program designed to meet the educational goals recognized by the degrees offered *(Toward a Learning Society)*.

Institutions of postsecondary education will grant degrees, certificates, and honors at more frequent intervals than they now do *(Toward a Learning Society)*.

Undergraduate and professional degrees will increasingly become only a part of the cumulative record of an individual's educational accomplishments. Ultimately, the degrees will become less important than the total record as evidence of such accomplishment *(Toward a Learning Society)*.

DISRUPTION Evaluation of and response to events on a campus should be based upon the distinction between dissent and disruption. Disruption should be met by the full efforts of the campus to end it and, where necessary, by the general law *(Dissent and Disruption)*.

Students and faculty members are divided, as is American society, about means and ends; but they stand predominantly, as does American society, against disruption and violence and for ordered change *(Dissent and Disruption)*.

Actions by society in response to coercion and violence should be undertaken only with reference to those specific individuals and groups who engage in it. A campus as a whole, or a system as a whole, or higher education as a whole, should not be penalized *(Dissent and Disruption)*.

Violent actions, involving injury to persons or more than incidental damage to property, should be met immediately by enforcement of the law. In cases of nonviolent disruption, to the extent possible, procedures internal to a campus should be used initially. Nonviolent actions should be met by responses that do not use force *(Dissent and Disruption).*

Each institution of higher education should establish a policy of self-restraint against disruptive activities *(The Purposes and the Performance of Higher Education in the United States).*

DISSENT Evaluation of and response to events on a campus should be based upon the distinction between dissent and disruption. Dissent should be protected as a democratic right and a major means of renewal for society; repression should be rejected.

Dissatisfactions on campuses and their public expression should be viewed as the reflections of many problems and conditions both in society and on the campuses. Both campus and society share responsibility. Dissenters are also responsible for their choice of tactics in advancing their goals—for some of their tactics are the source of the dissatisfactions and negative reactions of the public at large *(Dissent and Disruption).*

Campus rules should be formulated that regulate the time, place, and manner of peaceful assemblies. On campuses where organized protest does occur, faculty and student marshals might be available to monitor these events and to report on violations of campus rules and excessive actions by law enforcement officers *(Dissent and Disruption).*

DIVERSITY Diversity among institutions and within them should be a major goal of higher education, and one test of institutions and of their major segments should be how successful they have been in defining their special characters and how successful they are in achieving them *(Reform on Campus).*

Cluster and theme colleges within large institutions should provide particularly good opportunities for diversity *(Reform on Campus).*

State plans and multicampus-system plans should provide for specialization by field and for differentiation of general functions among campuses and groups of campuses *(Reform on Campus).*

Admissions policies should be examined to assure that they serve both the cause of diversity within higher education and also the possibilities for diversity at the high school level *(Reform on Campus).*

To help maintain differentiation of function and to reduce excessive tension within state systems, two steps should be taken: (1) There should be experimentation on a large scale with doctor of arts degrees as a teaching alternative to the research Ph.D.; and (2) There should be a redefinition of institutional quality to focus upon the value added by the college experience itself *(Continuity and Discontinuity).*

The National Council for the Accreditation of Teacher Education and state accrediting agencies should encourage diversity in teacher training programs *(Continuity and Discontinuity).*

DOCTOR OF ARTS The doctor of arts degree should be widely accepted *(Less Time, More Options).*

We do not believe that there is a need for any new Ph.D.-granting institutions, although some or even many institutions will be introducing the D.A. degree *(The More Effective Use of Resources).*

The continued development of doctor of arts programs should be encouraged.

We consider the doctor of arts a more suitable degree than the Ph.D. for many types of employment *(College Graduates and Jobs)*.

To help maintain differentiation of function and to reduce excessive tension within state systems, there should be experimentation on a large scale with doctors of arts degrees as a teaching alternative to the research Ph.D. *(Continuity and Discontinuity)*.

DOCTORAL-GRANTING INSTITUTIONS (See also Graduate and professional education)

State plans should, in general, incorporate a minimum FTE enrollment objective of 5,000 students and a maximum FTE enrollment objective of 20,000 students for doctoral-granting institutions *(New Students and New Places)*.

Institutions should be paid a cost-of-education supplement amounting to $5,000 for each federal doctoral fellow enrolled at that institution *(Institutional Aid)*.

Institutions with less emphasis on research than the leading research universities should consider curtailment or elimination, on a selective basis, of Ph.D. programs that are not of high quality or that are too small to be operated economically. We urge great caution in the development of new Ph.D. programs in particular fields at existing doctoral-granting institutions and do not believe there is a need for any new Ph.D.-granting institutions *(The More Effective Use of Resources)*.

State coordinating councils and similar agencies should develop strong policies for preventing the spread of Ph.D. programs to institutions that do not now have them. In addition, every effort should be made to prevent the establishment of new Ph.D. programs in particular fields of study in institutions that now have Ph.D. programs unless an exceptionally strong case can be made for them. There should also be a continuous review of existing degree programs with a view to eliminating those that are very costly or of low quality. Highly specialized degree programs should be concentrated on only one or two campuses of multicampus institutions *(College Graduates and Jobs)*.

Regional plans for the development of Ph.D. programs along the lines of those of the New England Board of Higher Education and the Southern Regional Education Board should be strengthened and extended to regions that do not now have them. Far more extensive use should be made of consortium arrangements that involve planning for concentration of development of Ph.D. programs in particular fields in individual members of the consortium as well as the right of students to cross-register for individual courses or fields of concentration *(College Graduates and Jobs)*.

EARLY ADMISSIONS (See also Degree programs, accelerated)

Urban community colleges should give careful consideration to the possible early admission of urban high school students requiring remedial work or seeking immediate entry into vocational training *(The Campus and the City)*.

Colleges should develop admissions programs to seek out new constituencies, including high school juniors *(Continuity and Discontinuity)*.

EDUCATION IN THE ARMED SERVICES The expansion of postsecondary educational opportunities should be encouraged outside the formal college in military programs. Appropriate educational credit should be given for the training received, and participants should be eligible, where appropriate, for federal and state assistance available to students in formal colleges *(Less Time, More Options)*.

Educational activity provided by the armed forces to officers and enlisted men at postsecondary levels will yield credit that is widely accepted as servicemen are transferred from military base to military base. Some of this instruction will be of a quality that is widely accepted for course-credit in civilian educational institutions after the serviceman student is discharged *(Toward a Learning Society)*.

The efforts of community colleges and four-year colleges to provide degree-credit instruction for military personnel and civilians living within commuting distance of such installations will be encouraged and increased *(Toward a Learning Society)*.

Enlisted men, as well as officers, will have increasing opportunities to participate in postsecondary education at civilian centers of postsecondary learning through educational leave programs subsidized by the armed forces *(Toward a Learning Society)*.

EDUCATIONAL OPPORTUNITY BANK An Educational Opportunity Bank should be established for medical and dental students, including house officers, with repayment excused during periods of house officer training and during two years of military service *(Higher Education and the Nation's Health)*.

EDUCATIONAL OPPORTUNITY CENTERS Institutions of higher education, either alone or in conjunction with local school districts, should establish educational opportunity centers to serve areas with major concentrations of low-income populations *(A Chance to Learn)*.

EDUCATIONAL OPPORTUNITY COUNSELING CENTERS In each metropolitan area with population in excess of 1 million, a metropolitan educational opportunity counseling center should be established. These centers should be funded one-half from local sources and one-half from state and federal sources *(The Campus and the City)*.

Educational opportunity counseling centers will have as one of their responsibilities the development and distribution of information about postsecondary educational resources including, but also in addition to, colleges and universities *(Toward a Learning Society)*.

EDUCATIONAL OPPORTUNITY GRANTS *(See* Basic opportunity grants, Student aid)

ELEMENTARY EDUCATION *(See* Precollege education)

EMERGENCY SITUATIONS Presidents should be given the authority to deal with emergency situations, and they should seek advice from preexisting consultative groups drawn from the campus community *(Dissent and Disruption)*.

ENROLLMENT *(See also* Expansion)

State plans should provide for community colleges generally ranging in size from about 2,000 to 5,000 daytime students, except in sparsely populated areas where institutions may have to be somewhat smaller, and in very large cities, where they may have to be somewhat larger *(The Open-Door Colleges)*.

The number of medical school entrants should be increased to 15,300 by 1976 and to 16,400 by 1978. The number of dental school entrants should be increased at least to 5,000 by 1976 and to 5,400 by 1980 *(Higher Education and the Nation's Health)*.

Governing boards, administrations, and faculties of most colleges founded for Negroes should plan to accommodate enrollments that may double on the average, certainly by the year 2000 and possibly by 1980.

By the year 2000, these colleges should have enrollments in keeping with the guidelines suggested for all institutions of higher education of comparable types. Comprehensive colleges should have 5,000 students. Liberal arts colleges should have at least 1,000 students. Public community colleges should have at least 2,000 students. Colleges with very low enrollments and with little prospect of meeting these goals should consider relocation or merging with other institutions that have complementing programs and facilities *(From Isolation to Mainstream).*

State plans for the growth and development of public institutions of higher education should, in general, incorporate minimum FTE enrollment objectives of (1) 5,000 students for doctoral-granting institutions, (2) 5,000 students for comprehensive colleges, (3) 1,000 students for liberal arts colleges, and (4) 2,000 students for two-year (community) colleges. Similarly, state plans should generally incorporate maximum FTE enrollment objectives of (1) about 20,000 students for doctoral-granting institutions, (2) about 10,000 students for comprehensive colleges, (3) about 2,500 students for liberal arts colleges, and (4) about 5,000 students for two-year (community) colleges *(New Students and New Places).*

Institutions of higher education and governments at all levels should not restrict undergraduate opportunities to enroll in college or to receive student aid because of less favorable trends in the job market for college graduates than have prevailed in the recent past *(College Graduates and Jobs).*

There is a need for revised estimates of supply that take account of the declining enrollment in undergraduate education programs and of a possible future decline in enrollment in master's-degree-in-education programs *(College Graduates and Jobs).*

EQUAL OPPORTUNITY The first priority in the nation's commitment to equal educational opportunity should be placed upon the increased effectiveness of our pre-elementary, elementary, and secondary school programs *(A Chance to Learn).*

Recruiting and counseling pools should be established among neighboring colleges and universities to coordinate resources and staff efforts for admitting educationally disadvantaged candidates *(A Chance to Learn).*

Institutions of higher education should devote a portion of their summer schedule and facilities to camps for educationally disadvantaged children *(A Chance to Learn).*

Each state should plan to provide universal access to its total system, but not necessarily to each of its institutions, since they vary greatly in their nature and purposes *(A Chance to Learn).*

All institutions should accept responsibility to serve the disadvantaged minorities at each of the levels at which they provide training *(A Chance to Learn).*

The Commissioner of Education should designate a unit within the U.S. Office of Education to develop standard definitions and methods of reporting to ensure the coordination, evaluation, and dissemination of available data on educational opportunity *(A Chance to Learn).*

Each institution should issue an annual report on its present and potential contributions to equality of opportunity *(A Chance to Learn).*

Open-access opportunities should be provided into most and perhaps all channels into adult life, and such access should be subject to public financial support where and as appropriate, and not restricted to college attendance alone *(The Purposes and the Performance of Higher Education in the United States).*

The first priority in the nation's commitment to equal educational opportunity for women should be placed on changing policies in preelementary, elementary, and secondary school programs that tend to deter women from aspiring to equality with men in their career goals *(Opportunities for Women in Higher Education).*

ETHNIC STUDIES Those Negro colleges with strong resources and successful operating programs of Afro-American instruction and research should be encouraged to seek special financial support for the further development of such endeavors. Foundations and governments should favorably consider requests for such support *(From Isolation to Mainstream).*

Curricula should be examined to be certain they reflect the history, culture, and current roles of minority groups *(The Purposes and the Performance of Higher Education in the United States).*

EXPANSION A substantial program of federal aid for medical education and health services should be established to stimulate the expansion of capacity at existing medical schools *(Quality and Equality).*

There should be increased federal funding for aid to developing institutions—$100 million in 1970–71 *(Quality and Equality).*

The federal government should award bonuses to university health science centers for expansion of enrollment *(Higher Education and the Nation's Health).*

Any further expansion of graduate education should proceed only after the most careful consideration *(Reform on Campus).*

Careful studies should be made in the areas noted to determine whether present patterns of nonresident enrollment correspond closely with those of 1968 and, if so, to take whatever steps are necessary to expand facilities for higher education *(The Campus and the City).*

Private colleges should reexamine their admission policies to determine whether expansion of open-admission or flexible-admission student places in their institutions would be compatible with their particular educational missions *(The Campus and the City).*

Institutions should limit their need for expansion into scarce urban space by better use of existing space *(The Campus and the City).*

EXTERNAL DEGREES *(See* Nontraditional study)

EVALUATION AND REVIEW *(See also* Planning, Reform)

Remedial education programs provided by community colleges should be subject to continual study and evaluation *(The Open-Door Colleges).*

All states with community college systems should undertake continuing evaluation studies of the experiences of these colleges, with particular reference to student achievement during the two-year educational period and their subsequent education and employment *(The Open-Door Colleges).*

States showing a low proportion of their students within commuting distance of free-access colleges should immediately undertake an evaluation of their higher education system to determine if, in fact, it lacks open access as a system and, if so, what steps need be taken to achieve reasonable open access *(The Capitol and the Campus).*

Each state should review the implementation of residence requirements of its institutions to ensure similar application of the criteria among public institutions *(The Capitol and the Campus).*

A basic reassessment of a state's postsecondary educational plan should be undertaken by the advisory coordinating board, if such exists, or by a commission appointed for that purpose, every five or ten years or whenever it becomes apparent that such a reassessment is essential to reflect adequately the totality and interaction of changing conditions and educational needs *(The Capitol and the Campus).*

Colleges and universities should examine their utilization of faculty time and in particular if their student-faculty ratios fall below the median levels for their categories *(The More Effective Use of Resources).*

Colleges and universities should conduct periodic reviews of existing degree programs with a view toward eliminating those in which very few degrees are awarded *(The More Effective Use of Resources).*

Institutions of higher education should carefully consider programs of year-round operation, but the conditions that determine whether net savings will be achieved through year-round operation are complex and require careful study and planning *(The More Effective Use of Resources).*

There should be careful study of space utilization standards and their reasonable application *(The More Effective Use of Resources).*

All institutions of higher education, especially those with relatively high administrative costs, should conduct analyses of these costs with a view to identifying functions or parts of the institution in which these costs may be excessive or in which there is evidence of administrative inefficiency *(The More Effective Use of Resources).*

Colleges and universities should review their student services, with particular reference to reducing the extent of subsidization of these services where it seems justified *(The More Effective Use Of Resources).*

Existing graduate education warrants a thorough review *(Reform on Campus).*

The process of change in each institution should be examined to assure that all innovations of significance are subject to subsequent evaluation and review *(Reform on Campus).*

Appropriate state and local agencies should undertake an evaluation of the adequacy of the number of higher education student places in those areas with a ratio of between 2.5 and 3.5 student places per 100 population *(The Campus and the City).*

Careful studies should be made in the areas noted to determine whether present patterns of nonresident enrollment correspond closely with those of 1968 *(The Campus and the City).*

Private colleges should reexamine their admission policies to determine whether expansion of open-admission or flexible-admission student places in their institutions would be compatible with their particular educational missions *(The Campus and the City).*

Colleges enrolling large numbers of disadvantaged or minority students should review their institutional programs to determine if they are designed to meet the educational needs of the students involved *(The Campus and the City).*

State financing authorities and local agencies should review their policies for funding community colleges to determine whether adequate funds are being made available for this segment of higher education with its difficult and important tasks *(The Campus and the City).*

Both planning agencies and urban-located institutions should review and analyze the educational resources in their areas and the educational needs of urban students to determine whether experimental approaches are desirable to expand effective options for postsecondary educational opportunities in the metropolitan areas *(The Campus and the City).*

A continuous review should be made of existing degree programs with a view to eliminating those that are very costly or of low quality and the concentration of highly specialized degree programs on only one or two campuses of multicampus institutions *(College Graduates and Jobs).*

Boards should periodically review the arrangements for governance—perhaps every four or five years—to be certain that they fit the current needs of the institution and are appropriate to the various functions being performed *(Governance of Higher Education).*

Each institution of higher education should survey periodically the totality of the functions it performs to be sure that none of them contradict the ethos of academic life, and that none of the nonacademic functions could be as well or better performed by some quasi-univeristy or external agency *(The Purposes and the Performance of Higher Education in the United States).*

Each state should undertake a review and analysis of the general education requirements for graduation from high school *(Continuity and Discontinuity).*

Schools and colleges alike should remember that experimentation carries with it the price of accountability. No new programs at either level should be initiated without clear criteria for evaluation *(Continuity and Discontinuity).*

States will periodically review their statutes to make certain that they adequately protect students against fraudulent claims and unfair business practices that may characterize operations of some private specialty schools *(Toward a Learning Society).*

EXTERNAL LAW ENFORCEMENT Disruption should be met by the full efforts of the campus to end it and, where necessary, by the general law, while guarding against excessive force by law enforcement personnel *(Dissent and Disruption).*

The view that a campus is a sanctuary from the processes of the law and law enforcement should be totally rejected *(Dissent and Disruption).*

We generally endorse the recommendation of the Scranton Commission in their chapter on "The Law Enforcement Response," while noting the variety of situations on different campuses and on the same campus at different moments of time *(Dissent and Disruption).*

Campus personnel chosen to communicate with law enforcement agencies should consist of persons who not only can achieve rapport, but also can effectively present the views of the campus community *(Dissent and Disruption)*.

Significant actions that could be construed as violations of the general law should be handled by the outside courts. A corollary to this is that campus authorities have an obligation to report significant violations of the general law that come to their attention *(Dissent and Disruption)*.

FACULTY Until qualified scholars and teachers become more plentiful, exchanges of visiting professors, joint appointments, and other arrangements that enable talented people to serve more than one institution should be attempted as a means of expanding the pool of teaching talent available to colleges founded for Negroes *(From Isolation to Mainstream)*.

Colleges and universities should provide incentives to faculty members who contribute to the advancement of instructional technology *(The Fourth Revolution)*.

Standards should be established relating to a reasonable maximum amount of time to be spent in consulting activities *(The More Effective Use of Resources)*.

Reasonable and equitable policies should be maintained relating to sabbatical leaves for all career members of the faculty, including assistant professors *(The More Effective Use of Resources)*.

Institutions of higher education should consider the establishment of committees including faculty to serve in an advisory capacity in relation to the preparation of the budget when severe cuts must be made. The more traditional practice of holding hearings on major budgetary decisions can also provide faculty with opportunities to express their views *(The More Effective Use of Resources)*.

Campuses should consider the following special policies for increasing their flexibility to adjust to a period of a declining rate of growth: (1) recapturing certain vacated positions for central reassignment; (2) hiring temporary and part-time faculty members; (3) requiring that tenure does not necessarily apply only to the specific original assignment of specialized field and location; (4) employing persons with subject-matter flexibility, as made easier in the training for the doctor of arts degree, and by encouraging persons to shift fields where this is desirable and possible; (5) providing opportunities for early retirements on a full-time or part-time basis *(The More Effective Use of Resources)*.

All colleges and universities should examine their utilization of faculty time and in particular if their student-faculty ratios fall below the median levels for their categories *(The More Effective Use of Resources)*.

The mixture of class sizes at the different levels of instruction should be varied. Appropriate average class sizes that different departments may be expected to meet should be established *(The More Effective Use of Resources)*.

Faculty should be involved in developing policies directed toward achieving appropriate and equitable teaching loads *(The More Effective Use of Resources)*.

Institutions of higher education should consider the possibility of agreements that will induce increases in the productivity of faculty members and other academic employees without impairing educational effectiveness *(The More Effective Use of Resources)*.

More faculty attention should be devoted to lower-division students *(Reform on Campus)*.

Teaching performance should be the basic criterion for rewards to faculty members, except in research universities where research, of necessity, is of equal or greater importance *(Reform on Campus)*.

Students should be given the opportunity to evaluate the teaching performance of faculty members, and students should be involved in periodic reviews of the performance of departments *(Governance of Higher Education)*.

Boards should consider faculty membership on appropriate board committees, or the establishment of parallel committees with arrangements for joint consultation *(Governance of Higher Education)*.

Faculties should be granted, where they do not already have it, the general level of authority as recommended by the American Association of University Professors *(Governance of Higher Education)*.

Faculty members should be associated in an advisory capacity with the process of review as they are in the initial appointment of presidents *(Governance of Higher Education)*.

Special efforts should be made to find qualified members of minority groups and women for inclusion in the "pool" of candidates for consideration when faculty appointments are being made, and such persons should be given special consideration in employment for faculty positions where their employment will lead to the creation of a more effective total academic environment for the entire student group that will be affected *(The Purposes and the Performance of Higher Education in the United States)*.

The principles of academic freedom for faculty members should be preserved where they are now effective and extended into areas where they do not now prevail *(The Purposes and the Performance of Higher Education in the United States)*.

Each institution of higher education should establish a policy against selection and promotion of faculty members in accordance with their political beliefs *(The Purposes and the Performance of Higher Education in the United States)*.

There should be equal treatment of men and women in all matters relating to salary, fringe benefits, and terms and conditions of employment.

Women should be entitled to maternity leave for a reasonable length of time, and affirmative action plans should include specific provisions relating to the definition of a reasonable length of time, rights to accumulated leave, and other relevant considerations.

There should be no antinepotism rules applying to employment within the institution or campus as a whole, or within individual units, such as departments, schools, and institutes. However, a husband or wife should not be involved in a decision relating to his or her spouse *(Opportunities for Women in Higher Education)*.

Every department and school in an academic institution should establish, in consultation with the administration of the college or university, a goal relating to the relative representation of women on its regular faculty.

Serious consideration should be given to appointing qualified women lecturers to regular faculty positions *(Opportunities for Women in Higher Education)*.

Faculty members holding part-time appointments for family reasons should not be barred from service on departmental or campus committees and should, if holding an appropriate faculty rank, be eligible for membership in the academic senate *(Opportunities for Women in Higher Education).*

Policies requiring decisions on the granting of tenure to be made within a given period of years should permit a limited extension of the time period for persons holding part-time appointments. Men and women holding part-time appointments for family reasons should be permitted to achieve tenure on a part-time basis. In such cases, tenure on a full-time basis at some future time would not be ensured, but the institutions should attempt to shift the individual's status to a full-time tenured position when desired if budgetarily possible and academically appropriate *(Opportunities for Women in Higher Education).*

Part-time appointments should not be discouraged for men and women whose family circumstances make such appointments desirable. Institutions may find it advantageous to distinguish, as some have done, between (1) such part-time appointments and (2) appointments to the faculty of persons whose principal employment is elsewhere and who come to the campus to give one or two specialized courses. For example, fringe benefits, prorated on the basis of the proportion of a full-time appointment involved, are more appropriate for the first type of part-time employee *(Opportunities for Women in Higher Education).*

FACULTY PRODUCTIVITY   All colleges and universities should examine their utilization of faculty time—in particular if their student-faculty ratios fall below the median levels for their categories *(The More Effective Use of Resources).*

The mixture of class sizes at the different levels of instruction should be varied. Appropriate average class sizes that different departments may be expected to meet should be established *(The More Effective Use of Resources).*

Faculty should be involved in developing policies directed toward achieving appropriate and equitable teaching loads *(The More Effective Use of Resources).*

Institutions of higher education should consider the possibility of agreements that will induce increases in the productivity of faculty members and other academic employees without impairing educational effectiveness *(The More Effective Use of Resources).*

Teaching performance should be the basic criterion for rewards to faculty members, except in research universities where research, of necessity, is of equal or greater importance *(Reform on Campus).*

Students should be given the opportunity to evaluate the teaching performance of faculty members, and students should be involved in periodic reviews of the performance of departments *(Governance of Higher Education).*

FACULTY SALARIES   Coordinating agencies and boards of higher education in the several states where there are black colleges should make studies of compensation paid to faculty members in comparable ranks at all state-supported institutions and advise legislative bodies of inadequacies where they exist *(From Isolation to Mainstream).*

Colleges founded for Negroes should seek assistance from state governments and foundations for programs that will pay the salaries of their faculty members while they complete work for their doctorates at other institutions *(From Isolation to Mainstream).*

Colleges and universities should provide incentives to faculty members who contribute to the advancement of instructional technology. Released time for the development of instructional materials and promotions and salary improvement for successful achievement in such endeavors should be part of that encouragement *(The Fourth Revolution)*.

Teaching performance should be the basic criterion for rewards to faculty members, except in research universities, where research, of necessity, is of equal or greater importance *(Reform on Campus)*.

FEDERAL AGENCIES AND PROGRAMS, PROPOSED

A National Foundation for the Development of Higher Education should be established whose functions would be to encourage, advise, review, and provide financial support for institutional programs designed to give new directions in curricula, to strengthen essential areas that have fallen behind or never been adequately developed because of inadequate funding, and to develop programs for improvement of educational processes and techniques.

The Foundation should be granted $50 million, to be allocated to states and regions which would, working with the advice and assistance of the Foundation, make further plans for the effective growth of the states' postsecondary educational system. In the development of these plans, the Foundation and the states should give particular attention to the creation of an adequate system of community colleges and to the stimulation and coordination of the states' occupational and technical educational resources *(Quality and Equality)*.

An Educational Opportunity Bank should be established for medical and dental students, including house officers, with repayment excused during periods of house officer training and during two years of military service *(Higher Education and the Nation's Health)*.

A National Health Manpower Commission should be appointed to make a thorough study of changing patterns of education and utilization of health manpower, with particular reference to new types of allied health workers, of changing patterns of health care delivery, and of the feasibility of national licensing requirements for all health manpower *(Higher Education and the Nation's Health)*.

Because of the special urgency and problems involved in the planning and development tasks that face colleges founded for Negroes, a special subdivision for the development of black colleges and universities should be created within the National Foundation for the Development of Higher Education. The purpose of this division, in which Negroes should have a vital role in advisory and management capacities, would be to aid colleges and universities founded for Negroes to develop and implement new programs and activities that respond to the challenges that confront them as institutions in transition. To fund this division, an average of $40 million annually in the 1970s from the proposed funding to the Developing Institutions Program should be channeled through the division for allocation to those black colleges working with the division toward the development and implementation of specific proposals for modification and expansion of the range of curricular offerings at the institution, or for the development of consortia to facilitate such changes, or to effect mergers among institutions to enable the desirable transition. Further, $1 million annually should be earmarked from planning funds assigned to the National Foundation for the Development of Higher Education to aid states and black colleges to plan for their growth and transition.

If the Foundation is not established at an early date, thus delaying the creation of the subdivision with the Foundation, the above-described responsibilities should be assigned to a special commission appointed by the President of the United States in consultation with representatives of institutions founded for Negroes.

The funds that would have been channeled through the subdivision should be assigned to this special commission *(From Isolation to Mainstream)*.

The proposed National Foundation for the Development of Higher Education should aid in planning liberal arts centers to be established by groups of colleges for the purpose of increasing quality, scope, and diversity of undergraduate education; of stimulating more economical and effective use of administrative and teaching personnel; and of sharing library and computer facilities *(New Students and New Places)*.

The proposed National Foundation for Postsecondary Education and the proposed National Institute of Education should be established. The National Foundation for Postsecondary Education should be assigned responsibility for administering loans and the provision of capital investment funds and grants for the utilization of instructional technology. Grants to support research and development activities in the field of instructional technology for higher education should be made by the proposed National Institute of Education *(The Fourth Revolution)*.

An independent commission, supported either by an appropriate agency of the U.S. Department of Health, Education and Welfare or by one or more private foundations should be created to make assessments of the instructional effectiveness and cost benefits of currently available instructional technology. Findings of the commission should be published and appropriately disseminated for the advice of institutions of higher education, such cooperative learning-technology centers as may be established, and governments and foundations supporting the advancement of instructional technology *(The Fourth Revolution)*.

An Urban-Grant program should be established to provide 10 grants to carefully selected institutions for the purpose of undertaking a comprehensive urban commitment for their institutions. These grants should not exceed $10 million each for a 10-year period with reviews every two years *(The Campus and the City)*.

The federal government should charter a National Student Loan Bank as a nonprofit corporation financed by the sale of governmentally guaranteed securities, which would serve all eligible students regardless of need. The fund should be self-sustaining, except for catastrophic risks, and should permit borrowing up to a reasonable limit that would reflect both tuition charges and subsistence costs. Loan repayments should be based upon income currently earned, and up to 40 years should be permitted for repayment. Provision should be made for public subsidy of catastrophic risks *(Higher Education: Who Pays? Who Benefits? Who Should Pay?)*.

FEDERAL SUPPORT *(See also* Construction grants and loans, Cost-of-education supplements, Institutional aid, Student aid, and others)

The work-study program should be continued and expanded with federal funding sufficient to enable those undergraduate students who meet, in general terms, the federal need criteria to earn up to $1,000 during the academic year, working not more than the equivalent of two days per week *(Quality and Equality)*.

The present federal aid program of guidance, counseling, and testing for identification and encouragement of able students should be expanded, and funding for the program should be increased to $30 million in 1970–71, rising to $40 million in 1976–77 *(Quality and Equality)*.

Certain universities should be selected on the basis of program proposals submitted to national panels to undertake specific graduate talent search and development programs, and federal funding should be made available for such programs in the amount of $25 million in 1970–71, rising to $100 million in 1976–77 *(Quality and Equality)*.

A substantial program of federal aid for medical education and health services should be established *(Quality and Equality)*.

Federal grants for university-based research (not including federal contract research centers), regardless of changing priorities for defense and space research, should be increased annually (using grants in 1967–68 as a base) at a rate equal to the five-year moving average annual rate of growth in the gross national product *(Quality and Equality)*.

There should be increased funding for the following three programs: aid to developing institutions ($100 million in 1970–71), library support ($100 million in 1970–71), and international studies ($25 million in 1970–71). To stimulate cooperative programs among community colleges and universities for the preparation and re-education of community college teachers and counselors, $25 million is recommended in 1970–71 for an expanded special program of federal training grants *(Quality and Equality)*.

Federal funds should be allocated to colleges and universities for specific programs to meet the present needs of inner-city schools, and of desegregated schools with heterogeneous classroom enrollments *(A Chance to Learn)*.

Federal funds should be allocated to meet the present needs of rural schools in disadvantaged areas *(A Chance to Learn)*.

The federal government should assist community colleges by providing (1) funds for state planning; (2) start-up grants for new campuses; (3) construction funds; (4) cost-of-education allowances for low-income students attending the colleges; (5) grants, work-study opportunities, and loans for students; and (6) an expanded program of federal training grants to stimulate expansion and improvement of graduate education programs for community college teachers, counselors, and administrators *(The Open-Door Colleges)*.

Federal support for university health science centers and area health education centers is recommended in the form of (1) construction grants in amounts up to 75 percent of total construction costs, with the remaining 25 percent available in the form of loans and (2) start-up grants for new university health science centers in amounts not exceeding $10 million per center *(Higher Education and the Nation's Health)*.

Federal financial support of research in university health science centers should be maintained at its present percentage of the GNP; federal allocations should cover the total cost of research projects *(Higher Education and the Nation's Health)*.

Continuing education of health manpower should be a major concern of the university health science centers and area health education centers with federal funds providing 50 percent of the financial support for such programs *(Higher Education and the Nation's Health)*.

To meet many of the basic financial problems of black colleges, the federal government should adopt the full program of recommendations in *Quality and Equality* as revised in June 1970 and the funding proposals in *Higher Education and the Nation's Health (From Isolation to Mainstream)*.

The federal and state governments should develop and implement policies to preserve and strengthen private institutions of higher education. The federal aid recommended in *Quality and Equality* would be available to public and private institutions alike *(New Students and New Places)*.

The federal government should make funds available for research evaluating the comparative experience of cluster colleges *(New Students and New Places)*.

The federal government should establish a program of cost-of-education supplements to colleges and universities based on the numbers of students enrolled in the institutions who hold grants awarded on the basis of financial need *(Institutional Aid)*.

The federal government should reverse its recent trend away from institutional support, increasing its assistance from $850 million in 1971 to about $1,100 million in 1976—excluding aid to medical schools *(Institutional Aid)*.

The federal government should assume full financial responsibility for the capital expenditures required initially to establish one cooperative learning-technology center every three years between 1973 and 1992. It should also provide at least one-third of the funds required for the operation of cooperative learning-technology centers for the first 10 years of their operation *(The Fourth Revolution)*.

The federal government should continue to provide a major share of expenditures required for research and development in instructional technology and for introduction of new technologies more extensively into higher education at least until the end of the century. The total level of federal government support for these purposes should be at least $100 million in 1973 and should rise to 1 percent of the total expenditures of the nation on higher education by 1980 *(The Fourth Revolution)*.

Within the level of research funding previously recommended in *Quality and Equality,* high priority should be given to both basic and applied social science research.

The network of urban observatories should be continued. Each observatory should be funded at approximately $100,000 per year *(The Campus and the City)*.

The new National Institute of Education should make grants available to those institutions that are conducting systematic experiments with remedial education *(The Campus and the City)*.

The Educational Opportunity Counseling Centers should be funded one-half from state and federal sources. Funding for administrative expenses of the metropolitan higher education councils should be similarly shared, with one-half from state and federal sources *(The Campus and the City)*.

The Urban Grants program should have a funding of $10 million annually for 10 years *(The Campus and the City)*.

As long as shortages continue in health manpower, federal funds to support the training of health personnel should not be cut back, as under the proposed federal budget for 1973–74 *(College Graduates and Jobs)*.

The federal government should not only stabilize its support of graduate training and research, but should attempt to stabilize the scope of activities, like the space program, that have in the past involved sudden and sharp shifts in the demand for scientists and engineers *(College Graduates and Jobs)*.

Federal research funds expended within higher education should be maintained steadily at a level of about 0.3 percent of the gross national product *(The Purposes and the Performance of Higher Education in the United States)*.

Federal research funds should be substantially increased for the social sciences, humanities, and creative arts from their current level of about 7 percent of the amount for science *(The Purposes and the Performance of Higher Education in the United States)*.

Over the next few years, the taxpayer share of monetary outlays in higher education should be increased modestly, as student-aid funds expand to assist students from low-income families *(Higher Education: Who Pays? Who Benefits? Who Should Pay?)*.

Federal funds should partially relieve the states of added financial burdens resulting from the expected expansion in higher education. Federal support of higher education should gradually expand to about one-half of the total governmental contributions by the early 1980s *(Higher Education: Who Pays? Who Benefits? Who Should Pay?)*.

The Basic Opportunity Grants program should be fully funded. This legislation, already on the books, is a major step in providing critically needed assistance to both students and institutions of higher education *(Higher Education: Who Pays? Who Benefits? Who Should Pay?)*.

The federal government should appropriate full funding for state student incentive matching grants. The federal program should be modified in the next several years to provide one-fourth of all state awards that meet the criterion of making up, for students with full need, the difference between federal Basic Opportunity Grants and the full cost of attending college in the first two years at public institutions, and a significant fraction of the difference in upper-division years. The awards would be reduced by appropriate amounts for students with less than full need *(Higher Education: Who Pays? Who Benefits? Who Should Pay?)*.

FOREIGN STUDENTS The international migration of students and professional personnel should be explicitly incorporated into analyses of changes in demand and supply, and opportunities for student places and student aid for foreign students in the United States should not be curtailed *(College Graduates and Jobs)*.

FOUNDATIONS Private foundations that have traditionally provided support for health manpower education and research should continue to do so, and foundations that have not provided such support in the past should consider expanding their programs to include it. Foundations should also expand their support for research on the delivery of health care *(Higher Education and the Nation's Health)*.

Foundations should favorably consider requests for support of Afro-American instruction and research *(From Isolation to Mainstream)*.

Foundations should give favorable consideration to requests for the support of black colleges to provide education for adult members of the black community *(From Isolation to Mainstream)*.

Colleges and universities should develop programs and prepare proposals to foundations for support of administrative intern programs for black students. Organization of advanced management seminars and short courses for administrators at colleges founded for Negroes, supported at least partially by foundations, is also recommended *(From Isolation to Mainstream)*.

Foundations should give special attention to funding studies and projects concerned with management problems of universities and colleges with effective utilization of available and potential resources *(The Capitol and the Campus)*.

seminars or workshops focused on state educational concerns *(The Capitol and the Campus).*

States with heavy institutional representation in the composition of their boards should take steps to increase the proportion of lay members *(The Capitol and the Campus).*

Elected officials with the power of budgetary review should not serve as members of governing boards of public institutions over which they exercise such review *(Governance of Higher Education).*

Members of governing boards of public institutions (where the governor makes the appointments) should be subject to appropriate mechanisms for nominating and screening individuals before appointment by the governor to assure consideration of properly qualified individuals, or to subsequent legislative confirmation to reduce the likelihood of purely politically partisan appointments, or both *(Governance of Higher Education).*

Faculty members, students, and alumni should be associated with the process of nominating at least some board members in private and public institutions, but faculty members and students should not serve on the boards of institutions where they are enrolled or employed *(Governance of Higher Education).*

Board membership should reflect the different age, sex, and racial groups that are involved in the concerns of the institution. Faculty members from other institutions and young alumni should be considered for board memberships *(Governance of Higher Education).*

Boards should consider faculty and student membership on appropriate board committees, or the establishment of parallel committees with arrangements for joint consultation *(Governance of Higher Education).*

Boards should periodically review the arrangements for governance—perhaps every four or five years—to be certain that they fit the current needs of the institution and are appropriate to the various functions being performed *(Governance of Higher Education).*

Boards should seek active presidents and give them the authority and the staff they need to provide leadership in a period of change and conflict *(Governance of Higher Education).*

Boards may wish to consider the establishment of stated review periods for presidents so that withdrawal by the president or reaffirmation of the president may be managed in a more effective manner than is often now the actual situation *(Governance of Higher Education).*

Universities, in conjunction with state school boards associations, should experiment with various means of providing school board members with information on crucial issues *(Continuity and Discontinuity).*

GRADUATE AND PROFESSIONAL EDUCATION *(See also* Doctoral-granting institutions)

Universities should accept a special responsibility to serve a substantially greater representation of currently disadvantaged minorities in their graduate programs. Graduate and professional departments should coordinate recruiting of disadvantaged students *(A Chance to Learn).*

Professions, wherever possible, should create alternate routes of entry other than full-time college attendance *(Less Time, More Options).*

To encourage the continued development of quality in graduate education at public institutions, students of high ability should be permitted to attend public institutions without reference to their residency *(The Capitol and the Campus).*

Leading research universities should refrain from cutbacks in graduate programs except on a carefully considered, selective basis *(The More Effective Use of Resources).*

Existing graduate education warrants a thorough review *(Reform on Campus).*

Any further general expansion of graduate education should proceed only after the most careful consideration *(Reform on Campus).*

Professional schools in universities and colleges should undertake the responsibility for cooperating with and providing guidance for community colleges and comprehensive colleges in the development of paraprofessional training programs *(College Graduates and Jobs).*

Associations of professional schools should undertake the responsibility for careful studies of manpower supply and demand for graduates in their respective fields *(College Graduates and Jobs).*

Associations of professional schools should collect annual data on enrollment of women and minority-group students and should stimulate programs designed to encourage and assist them. Within arts and science fields there should be similar efforts *(College Graduates and Jobs).*

Professional schools in universities and colleges should undertake the responsibility for providing guidance and advice in connection with programs of continuing education for members of their professions, whether these are provided under the auspices of extension divisions, evening school programs of the professional schools, or in other ways *(College Graduates and Jobs).*

Associations of professional schools, as well as individual professional schools in universities and comprehensive colleges, should undertake leadership and responsibility in more carefully planned integration of preprofessional and professional education *(College Graduates and Jobs).*

In virtually all professional fields, increased attention should be devoted to providing students with opportunities to proceed along carefully planned and at the same time flexible career training ladders *(College Graduates and Jobs).*

In all professional fields, careful and sustained attention needs to be given to adaptation of educational programs to the advancement of knowledge and technological change, and to society's changing problems and needs *(College Graduates and Jobs).*

All programs of professional education involving human services should seek to incorporate clinical or operational experience in the student's training. Successful clinical training requires careful planning, evaluation, and adaptation to changing needs *(College Graduates and Jobs).*

Professional schools and academic departments should cooperate in the development of joint degree programs in response to emerging societal problems and in response to the advancement of knowledge or technological change *(College Graduates and Jobs).*

The federal government should stabilize its support of graduate training and research *(College Graduates and Jobs).*

Federal and state government agencies and other appropriate bodies should undertake studies of the implications of the changing job market for enrollment in master's programs *(College Graduates and Jobs)*.

Professional schools should maintain their own placement programs for those receiving master's, first-professional, and doctor's degrees, while arts and science departments should have their own placement programs for students at the doctoral level *(College Graduates and Jobs)*.

There should be no discrimination on the basis of sex or marital status in admitting students to graduate and professional schools *(Opportunities for Women in Higher Education)*.

Departments and schools should be required to maintain complete records on all applicants for admission to graduate and professional education and to make these records available to administrative officers on request. They should also be required to maintain records indicating that, in any programs designed to recruit able graduate students, equal efforts have been made to recruit women as well as men *(Opportunities for Women in Higher Education)*.

Rules and policies that discriminate against the part-time graduate or professional student should allow for exceptions to accommodate men or women whose family circumstances require them to study on a part-time basis. Any limitation on the total number of graduate or professional students admitted by departments or schools and by the institution as a whole should be applied on a full-time-equivalent rather than on a head-count basis *(Opportunities for Women in Higher Education)*.

Policies requiring students to obtain advanced degrees within a certain number of years should allow for a limited extension of the period for those graduate students whose family circumstances require them to study on a part-time basis *(Opportunities for Women in Higher Education)*.

A woman desiring to enter graduate or professional school after some years away from higher education should be given an opportunity to make up for her inability to meet any special requirements, such as specific mathematical requirements *(Opportunities for Women in Higher Education)*.

Apprenticeship, internship, and inservice training will be used more widely than they are today to prepare persons for their life work in many professions, paraprofessions, and occupations *(Toward a Learning Society)*.

GRADUATE AND PROFESSIONAL STUDENT AID Grants based on need should be available for a period not to exceed two years of study toward a graduate degree *(Quality and Equality)*.

$2,000 per year is the maximum grant recommended for students working toward a graduate degree or postgraduate certificate or credential, generally for no more than two years, but for a longer period up to a maximum of three years for students in professional programs requiring three years beyond the bachelor's degree *(Quality and Equality)*.

A doctoral fellowship program should be established with selection based upon demonstrated academic ability without reference to need, with fellowships in the amount of $3,000 annually for a maximum of two years to graduate students advanced to candidacy for a Ph.D. or equivalent research doctorate.

The total number of such first-year fellowships awarded should equal one-half of the average of the national total of doctorates earned in the fourth, third, and second year preceding the year in which the fellowships are awarded. In each year an additional number of fellowships equal to 10 percent of the total just described would be allocated for expansion into neglected or developing fields *(Quality and Equality)*.

A federal program of grants should be established for amounts up to $4,000 a year for medical and dental students from low-income families and for students from low-income families enrolled in associate and assistant programs in medical and dental schools *(Higher Education and the Nation's Health)*.

An Educational Opportunity Bank should be established for medical and dental students, including house officers, with repayment excused during periods of house officer training *(Higher Education and the Nation's Health)*.

We reaffirm our recommendations that federal grants and loans be provided to assist students from low-income families who enroll in graduate and professional schools *(From Isolation to Mainstream)*.

Colleges founded for Negroes should seek assistance from state governments and foundations for programs that will pay the salaries of their faculty members while they complete work for their doctorates at other institutions *(From Isolation to Mainstream)*.

GRIEVANCE PROCEDURES Regular procedures and channels for hearing grievances and suggestions directed to a campus should be established and be well publicized. Decisions should be based on wide consultation with those segments of the campus affected by them, and decisions and the rationale behind them should be made widely known *(Dissent and Disruption)*.

It should be unlawful to interfere in any way with any person's exercise of his constitutional rights. Aggrieved persons should be able to bring civil action for appropriate relief, and United States district courts should be given original jurisdiction to grant permanent or temporary injunctions, temporary restraining orders, or any other orders, and to award damages *(Dissent and Disruption)*.

In serious cases involving "rights and responsibilities" of members of the campus community and possible campus penalties beyond those for violation of the external law, campus judicial tribunals should be composed partially or wholly of external persons, defined as persons drawn from outside the particular school or college or campus whose members are involved in the dispute *(Dissent and Disruption)*.

Careful consideration should be given to use of (1) ombudsmen, (2) hearing officers, and (3) campus attorneys *(Dissent and Disruption)*.

Conduct codes should be prepared with student involvement in the process of their preparation, ombudsmen or the equivalent should be appointed, and formal grievance machinery should be available and should end in impartial judicial tribunals *(Governance of Higher Education)*.

The affirmative action program for women should provide for an effective internal grievance procedure, if the institution does not already have one *(Opportunities for Women in Higher Education)*.

GUIDANCE AND COUNSELING The present federal aid program of guidance, counseling, and testing for identification and encouragement of able students should be expanded, and funding for the program should be increased to $30 million in 1970–71, rising to $40 million in 1976–77 *(Quality and Equality)*.

All community colleges should provide adequate resources for effective guidance, including not only provision for an adequate professional counseling staff but also provision for involvement of the entire faculty in guidance of students enrolled in their courses.

All community college districts should provide for effective coordination of their guidance services with those of local high schools and for coordination of both counseling and placement services with those of the public employment offices and other appropriate agencies *(The Open-Door Colleges)*.

Institutions of higher education should seek to increase their retention rates through improved counseling programs, where these are deficient, and through establishing the practice of conducting an "exit interview" with every student who plans to withdraw *(The More Effective Use of Resources)*.

Colleges and universities should inaugurate programs designed to discourage poorly motivated students from entering and from continuing once they have entered. These programs should be designed to include appropriate counseling of applicants, generally through the admissions office, as well as counseling of all undergraduate students, perhaps through the medium of a regular annual interview *(The More Effective Use of Resources)*.

In view of the critical need for counseling services for disadvantaged students, the changes that are occurring in patterns of participation in higher education, and the complex shifts that are taking place in the labor market for college graduates, counseling services will need to be expanded rather than contracted in many colleges and universities *(The More Effective Use of Resources)*.

Reasonable efforts should be made to reduce the ranks of the reluctant attenders *(Reform on Campus)*.

Enhanced emphasis should be placed on advising as an increasingly important aspect of higher education *(Reform on Campus)*.

Professional schools in universities and colleges should undertake the responsibility for providing guidance and advice in connection with programs of continuing education for members of their professions *(College Graduates and Jobs)*.

Federal government agencies should take steps to improve the flow of current occupational information and to make it available more promptly *(College Graduates and Jobs)*.

Colleges and universities should take immediate steps to strengthen occupational counseling programs available to their students *(College Graduates and Jobs)*.

More attention should be paid to the occupational training interests of students and to occupational counseling and guidance as students and adults seek to adjust to changing labor market conditions *(The Purposes and the Performance of Higher Education in the United States)*.

Students in elementary and high school should be counseled through a variety of resources—counselors, written materials, community-based people, as well as college students—minority students and women, in particular *(Continuity and Discontinuity)*.

Not only should colleges and universities take immediate steps to strengthen occupational counseling programs generally in this era of a changing job market for college graduates, but they should also take special steps to strengthen career counseling programs for women. Counselors should be trained to discard outmoded concepts of male and female careers and to encourage women in their abilities and aspirations *(Opportunities for Women in Higher Education).*

HEALTH CARE PERSONNEL
University health science centers should consider the development of programs for the training of physician's and dentist's associates and assistants *(Higher Education and the Nation's Health).*

A voluntary national health service corps should be developed *(Higher Education and the Nation's Health).*

States should provide major financial support for house officer training and for the education of allied health personnel *(Higher Education and the Nation's Health).*

The health manpower research programs in the Department of Health, Education and Welfare, in cooperation with the Department of Labor, should be expanded to encompass broad continuous studies of health manpower supply and demand *(Higher Education and the Nation's Health).*

A National Health Manpower Commission should be appointed to make a thorough study of changing patterns of education and utilization of health manpower, with particular reference to new types of allied health workers, and of the feasibility of national licensing requirements for all health manpower *(Higher Education and the Nation's Health).*

Vigorous efforts should be made at the state level to develop training programs in nursing and allied health professions in state colleges and community colleges *(College Graduates and Jobs).*

Federal government agencies involved in studies of health manpower should continuously review projections of supply and demand during the 1970s. As long as shortages continue, federal funds to support the training of health personnel should not be cut back *(College Graduates and Jobs).*

There should be increased emphasis on encouraging research on alternative ways of utilizing health manpower. There is a need for studies evaluating innovations in health care delivery and for comparative studies on differing patterns of utilization of health manpower in selected countries *(College Graduates and Jobs).*

The training of health care personnel should be substantially expanded for the immediate future to eliminate the one remaining major deficit in highly trained manpower *(The Purposes and the Performance of Higher Education in the United States).*

HEALTH SCIENCE CENTERS
University health science centers should be responsible, in their respective geographic areas, for coordinating the education of health care personnel and for cooperation with other community agencies in improving the organization of health care delivery. Their educational and research programs should become more concerned with problems of health care delivery and the social and economic environment of health care. All new medical and dental schools should be parts of university health science centers, and, wherever feasible, existing separate medical and dental schools should likewise become parts of these centers.

All university health science centers should consider the development of programs for the training of physician's and dentist's associates and assistants, where they do not exist, and wherever feasible, such programs should be initiated forthwith.

In developing their plans for expansion, university health science centers should adopt programs designed to recruit more women and members of minority groups as medical and dental students.

All universities with health science centers should develop plans for accelerating premedical and medical education. In addition, all universities with health science centers, and especially those developing new centers, should consider plans for (1) greater integration of preprofessional and professional curricula, (2) increasing the students' options, (3) awarding a master's degree at the end of the basic training period, and (4) integrating instruction in the basic sciences on main university campuses.

New public health schools should be made parts of university health science centers, and existing public health schools should become parts of such centers as soon as possible.

New university health science centers should consider providing clinical instruction in selected hospitals on the British model. All such centers should give serious consideration to curriculum reforms. Their admission policies should be made more flexible and their programs more responsive to the expressed needs of students.

The following grants are recommended: (1) cost-of-instruction supplements for each medical and dental student enrolled; (2) bonuses for expansion of enrollment; (3) cost-of-instruction supplements to the university health science centers and their affiliated hospitals for each house officer; and (4) bonuses for curriculum reform. Construction grants are recommended in amounts up to 75 percent of total construction costs, with the remaining 25 percent available in the form of loans. Start-up grants are recommended for new university health science centers in amounts not exceeding $10 million per center.

Federal support of research in university health science centers should be maintained at its present percentage of the GNP. Research funds should be made available for specialized studies of health manpower supply and demand in university health science centers.

Nine new health science centers should be developed. The states, in cooperation with universities and with regional and local planning bodies, should play a major role in the development of plans for the location of these centers.

University administrations should appoint appropriate officers to develop plans for the expansion of university health science centers and for their transformation to perform broad educational, research, and community service functions.

University health science centers should have central responsibility for the planning of health manpower education (Higher Education and the Nation's Health).

All universities with university health science centers should seek to ensure that management of these centers is organized in such a way as to enable the centers to meet the greatly increased responsibilities they are asked to fulfill (The More Effective Use of Resources).

University health science centers and area health education centers should provide leadership in encouraging the development and expansion of continuing education programs for nurses and allied health workers in appropriate educational institutions (College Graduates and Jobs).

HEALTH SCIENCE EDUCATION A substantial program of federal aid for medical education and health services should be established for the purposes of stimulating expansion of capacity at existing medical schools, planning additional medical schools distributed on a geographical basis to provide needed service to areas not now served, expanding educational facilities and developing new programs for the training of medical care support personnel, and increasing availability of health services in the community of the medical school and the quality of health care delivery *(Quality and Equality)*.

The number of medical school entrants should be increased to 15,300 by 1976 and to 16,400 by 1978. The number of dental school entrants should be increased at least to 5,000 by 1976 and to 5,400 by 1980 *(Higher Education and the Nation's Health)*.

All universities with health science centers should develop plans for accelerating premedical and medical education. Plans should also be developed for shortening the total duration of predental and dental education where it is unnecessarily prolonged *(Higher Education and the Nation's Health)*.

All universities with health science centers, and especially those developing new centers, should consider plans for (1) greater integration of preprofessional and professional curricula, (2) increasing the students' options so that basic training in health-related sciences can lead on to training for a variety of health-related professions as well as medicine and dentistry, (3) awarding a master's degree at the end of this basic training period, and (4) integrating instruction in the basic sciences on main university campuses if this can be accomplished without major costs associated with the shift, without interfering with integration of basic science and clinical science instruction, and without delaying the opportunities for students to have early contact with patients *(Higher Education and the Nation's Health)*.

New university health science centers should consider providing clinical instruction in selected hospitals on the British model *(Higher Education and the Nation's Health)*.

All university health science centers should give serious consideration to curriculum reforms. Their admissions policies should be made more flexible and their programs more responsive to the expressed needs of students. Greater emphasis should be placed on comprehensive medicine in both the M.D.-candidate programs and in graduate medical education. In all phases of medical and dental education, including residency programs, there should be more careful integration of abstract theory and clinical experience. Residency programs should be planned and reviewed by the entire faculty, and residency training should include experience in community hospitals, neighborhood clinics, and other facilities, as well as in teaching hospitals *(Higher Education and the Nation's Health)*.

A relatively low uniform national tuition policy is recommended for institutions providing medical and dental education *(Higher Education and the Nation's Health)*.

Existing federal legislation for regional, state, and local health planning should be strengthened to encompass regional planning of all health manpower education and health care facilities. Continuing education of health manpower should be a major concern of the university health science centers and area health education centers *(Higher Education and the Nation's Health)*.

A National Health Manpower Commission should be appointed to make a thorough study of changing patterns of education and utilization of health manpower *(Higher Education and the Nation's Health)*.

Careful integration of instruction in the biomedical sciences and social sciences between university health science centers and departments on major university campuses should be achieved *(Higher Education and the Nation's Health)*.

Comprehensive colleges and community colleges should develop and expand their curricula in the allied health professions where this has not been done *(Higher Education and the Nation's Health)*.

Medical and dental schools with three-year programs should receive the same amount of institutional aid as they would if they were four-year schools *(Higher Education and the Nation's Health)*.

There should be increased emphasis on basic programs of education in the health sciences to provide a uniform core of training for nurses, allied health workers, physicians, dentists, and persons preparing themselves for administrative, educational, and research careers in the health field *(College Graduates and Jobs)*.

There should be increased emphasis in educational programs on providing experience in working with other health care personnel as a team *(College Graduates and Jobs)*.

Federal funds to support the training of health personnel should not be cut back as long as shortages continue *(College Graduates and Jobs)*.

University health science centers and area health education centers should provide leadership in encouraging the development and expansion of continuing education programs for nurses and allied health workers in appropriate educational institutions *(College Graduates and Jobs)*.

HIGH SCHOOL ADMINISTRATION Special efforts should be made to recruit able administrators from outside the field as well as members of minority groups and women into the profession of school administration *(Continuity and Discontinuity)*.

Given the diversity of school districts, there can be no single model of an administrator training program. Common elements in all programs should be the use of the resources of the whole university and experimentation with different ways of combining theory and practice in clinical settings *(Continuity and Discontinuity)*.

Greater emphasis should be placed on inservice training as a way of keeping administrators up-to-date and as a vehicle for school improvement *(Continuity and Discontinuity)*.

HIGH SCHOOL CURRICULUM High schools that do not already do so should offer instruction in basic concepts and uses of computers and should encourage their students to obtain, as early as possible, other skills that will be helpful in the use of new media for learning *(The Fourth Revolution)*.

High school students should be encouraged to study mathematics sequentially throughout secondary school in order to keep options open to college programs, jobs, and careers requiring background in mathematics *(Continuity and Discontinuity)*.

Improvement of the nation's schools is the first educational priority in the nation; and within the schools improvement in the basic skills, especially in large city schools, is the first priority *(Continuity and Discontinuity)*.

Each state should undertake a review and analysis of the general education requirements for graduation from high school.

More of the responsibility for general education should be assumed by the high schools *(Continuity and Discontinuity)*.

Curriculum development in the humanities and social studies has lagged behind mathematics and science. Schools and colleges, together with funding agencies, should foster new programs and approaches *(Continuity and Discontinuity)*.

HIGH SCHOOLS *(See also* Precollege education, School-college relations)
All states, but particularly those with ratios below 70 percent, should take steps to increase the percentage of high school students who remain in high school and successfully complete the high school program *(The Capitol and the Campus)*.

High school counseling programs should be strengthened and improved, not only for the purpose of guiding students to appropriate colleges or jobs or occupational programs, but also to dissuade poorly motivated students from entering college *(The More Effective Use of Resources)*.

Admissions policies should be examined to assure that they serve both the cause of diversity within higher education and also the possibilities for diversity in the high school *(Reform on Campus)*.

The curriculum as a whole should be reviewed, campus by campus, in consultation with high school leaders, to assess its broad relevance not only to appropriate student interests but also to prior and subsequent learning experiences *(Reform on Campus)*.

Local school boards, with community and professional assistance, should identify the overall ends and objectives of the public schools, deliberately encourage experimentation with a diversity of means to those objectives, and insist upon accountability from teachers and administrators *(Continuity and Discontinuity)*.

Schools and colleges should experiment with different structural models designed to provide a student with options that will enable him to find the right program at the right time. Such experimentation challenges the current structure and its traditional break between school and college at the end of grade 12. Some school systems should eliminate a year from the K through 12 sequence; other school systems should stress general education equivalent to that found at good colleges; students should be able to "test out" of high school graduation requirements; there should be expanded programs of college credit for the senior year of high school, and concurrent enrollment of students in school and college. Options other than college attendance should be made available for high school graduates *(Continuity and Discontinuity)*.

INFORMATION SYSTEMS Schools, colleges, and testing agencies should work together in developing a complete and coherent information system that enables sound decision making by both students and colleges. Colleges should prepare frank, accurate, and complete descriptive materials, so that students will know as much about colleges as the colleges know about students *(Continuity and Discontinuity)*.

Educational Opportunity Counseling Centers and other appropriate local agencies will have as one of their responsibilities the development and distribution of information about postsecondary educational resources including, but also in addition to, colleges and universities *(Toward a Learning Society)*.

INSTITUTIONAL AID *(See also* Construction grants and loans, Cost-of-education supplements, Federal support, Student aid)
Each college and university should be given a scholarship fund for needy students equal to 10 percent of the total sum of educational opportunity grants (not includ-

ing supplementary matching grants) held by students at that institution *(Quality and Equality).*

A grant amounting to 10 percent of the total research grants received annually by an institution should be made to that institution to be used at its discretion *(Quality and Equality).*

There should be increased funding for developing institutions—$100 million in 1970–71 *(Quality and Equality).*

Medical and dental schools and three-year programs should receive the same amount of institutional aid as they would if they were four-year schools *(Higher Education and the Nation's Health).*

The federal government should reverse its recent trend away from institutional support, increasing its assistance from $850 million in 1971 to about $1,100 million in 1976—excluding aid to medical schools *(Institutional Aid).*

State grants to institutions for general support should be based on broad formulas and not line-item control *(Governance of Higher Education).*

The Basic Opportunity Grants program should be fully funded. This legislation is a major step in providing critically needed assistance to institutions of higher education *(Higher Education: Who Pays? Who Benefits? Who Should Pay?).*

INSTITUTIONAL FUNCTIONS

State plans and multicampus system plans should provide for specialization by field and for differentiation of general functions among campuses and groups of campuses *(Reform on Campus).*

Institutional service should be extended on a more even-handed basis to groups and persons in connection with problems where it may be helpful, subject to the major limitation that any service should be appropriate to the educational functions of higher education *(The Purposes and the Performance of Higher Education in the United States).*

Each institution of higher education should establish a policy of self-restraint against disruptive activities, against improper use of campus facilities, against improper political indoctrination of students, against selection and promotion of faculty members in accordance with their political beliefs, and against commitment of the institution as such to the pursuit of specific external political and social changes; each institution should be prepared to defend its own integrity *(The Purposes and the Performance of Higher Education in the United States).*

Each institution of higher education should survey periodically the totality of the functions it performs to be sure that none of them contradict the ethos of academic life and that none of the nonacademic functions could be as well or better performed by some quasi-university or external agency *(The Purposes and the Performance of Higher Education in the United States).*

Campuses should not add and, where feasible, should eliminate, operational, custodial, and service functions which are not directly tied to academic and educational activities and which can be performed as well or better by other agencies *(The Purposes and the Performance of Higher Education in the United States).*

Institutions of higher education should seek to avoid and to eliminate noncomplementary functions *(The Purposes and the Performance of Higher Education in the United States).*

Coordinating councils, consortia, and multicampus systems should adopt policies of clear differentiation of functions among campuses and of assigned specializations among fields. Such differentiation of functions should follow the logic of complementarity of interests *(The Purposes and the Performance of Higher Education in the United States).*

Before taking on a new educational function, institutions should determine the relationship of that function to their educational mission and should ascertain whether there are existing alternative educational resources to meet the particular educational need to be served. If such alternative resources exist, the possibility of contractual agreements with other institutions to secure the services, or the possibility of joint enrollment of the learner, should be explored before a new program is developed *(Toward a Learning Society).*

INSTITUTIONAL QUALITY To encourage the continued development of quality in graduate education at public institutions, students of high ability should be permitted to attend public institutions without reference to their residency *(The Capitol and the Campus).*

More faculty attention and more funds, on a comparative basis, should be devoted to lower-division students *(Reform on Campus).*

There should be a redefinition of institutional quality to focus upon the value added by the college experience itself.

Colleges and testing agencies should work together in developing appropriate criteria and measures of value added to reflect a diversity of institutional objectives and outcomes *(Continuity and Discontinuity).*

INSTITUTIONAL RESEARCH All relatively large institutions should maintain an office of institutional research or its equivalent and relatively small institutions should seek to enter into arrangements with nearby similar institutions to conduct jointly sponsored programs of institutional research *(The More Effective Use of Resources).*

INSTRUCTIONAL MATERIALS Since a grossly inadequate supply of good quality instructional materials now exists, a major thrust of financial support and effort on behalf of instructional technology for the next decade should be toward the development and utilization of outstanding instructional programs and materials. Academic disciplines should follow the examples of physics and mathematics in playing a significant role in such efforts *(The Fourth Revolution).*

A major national study should be conducted of the entire set of relationships that exists among school systems, state bureaucracies, school and college teachers, and the educational materials industry in the production and selection of materials. The purpose of the study would be to seek ways to improve the system by which curricular materials are chosen, created, and marketed *(Continuity and Discontinuity).*

INSTRUCTIONAL TECHNOLOGY *(See also* Cooperative learning-technology centers)
Because expanding technology will extend higher learning to large numbers of people who have been unable to take advantage of it in the past, because it will provide instruction in forms that will be more effective than conventional instruction for some learners in some subjects, because it will be more effective for all learners and many teachers under many circumstances, and because it will significantly reduce costs of higher education in the long run, its early advancement should be encouraged by the adequate commitment of colleges and universities to its utilization and development and by adequate support from governmental and other agencies concerned with the advancement of higher learning *(The Fourth Revolution).*

Since a grossly inadequate supply of good quality instructional materials now exists, a major thrust of financial support and effort on behalf of instructional technology for the next decade should be toward the development and utilization of outstanding instructional programs and materials. The academic disciplines should follow the examples of physics and mathematics in playing a significant role in such efforts *(The Fourth Revolution)*.

Institutions of higher education should contribute to the advancement of instructional technology not only by giving favorable consideration to expanding its use, whenever such use is appropriate, but also by placing responsibility for its introduction and utilization at the highest possible level of academic administration *(The Fourth Revolution)*.

The introduction of new technologies to help libraries continue to improve their services to increasing numbers of users should be given first priority in the efforts of colleges and universities, government agencies and other agencies seeking to achieve more rapid progress in the development of instructional technology *(The Fourth Revolution)*.

Major funding sources, including states, the federal government, and foundations, should recognize not only the potential of new and developing extramural education systems for expanding learning opportunities, but also the crucial role such systems should play in the ultimate development of instructional technologies. Requests of these systems for funds with which to introduce and use new instructional programs, materials, and media should be given favorable consideration *(The Fourth Revolution)*.

By 1992, at least seven cooperative learning-technology centers, voluntarily organized on a regional basis by participating higher educational institutions and systems, should be established for the purpose of sharing costs and facilities for the accelerated development and utilization of instructional technology in higher education *(The Fourth Revolution)*.

The federal government should continue to provide a major share of expenditures for research and development in instructional technology and for introduction of new technologies more extensively into higher education at least until the end of the century. The total level of federal government support for these purposes should be at least $100 million in 1973 and should rise to 1 percent of the total expenditures of the nation on higher education by 1980 *(The Fourth Revolution)*.

The proposed National Foundation for Postsecondary Education and the proposed National Institute of Education should be established, and the proposed National Foundation for Postsecondary Education should be assigned responsibility for administering loans and the provision of capital investment funds and grants for the utilization of instructional technology. Grants to support research and development activities in the field of instructional technology for higher education should be made by the proposed National Institute of Education *(The Fourth Revolution)*.

Colleges and universities should provide incentives to faculty members who contribute to the advancement of instructional technology. Released time for the development of instructional materials and promotions and salary improvement for successful achievement in such endeavors should be part of that encouragement *(The Fourth Revolution)*.

Colleges and universities that are responsible for the training of prospective university, college, and high school teachers should begin now to incorporate in their curriculum instruction on the development of teaching-learning segments that appropriately utilize the expanding technologies of instruction *(The Fourth Revolution)*.

Colleges and universities should supplement their instructional staffs with qualified technologists and specialists to assist instructors in the design, planning, and evaluation of teaching-learning units that can be used with the expanding instructional technologies. Institutions of higher education at all levels should develop their potentials for training specialists and professionals needed to perform the new functions that are associated with the increasing utilization of instructional technology on the nation's college and university campuses *(The Fourth Revolution)*.

An Independent commission, supported either by an appropriate agency of the U.S. Department of Health, Education and Welfare or by one or more private foundations, should be created to make assessments of the instructional effectiveness and cost benefits of currently available instructional technology. Findings of the commission should be published and appropriately disseminated for the advice of institutions of higher education, such cooperative learning-technology centers as may be established, and governments and foundations supporting the advancement of instructional technology *(The Fourth Revolution)*.

All institutions of higher education should seek economies in computer expenditures by (1) contracting for computer services where this is found to be advantageous, (2) charging the full costs of computer services used in instruction and departmental research against departmental budgets, (3) charging the full costs of computer services used in extramurally financed research against the relevant research budgets, and (4) sharing computer facilities with nearby institutions of higher education where this appears to be a more advantageous solution than contracting out *(The More Effective Use of Resources)*.

A major national study should be conducted on the entire set of relationships that exist among school systems, state bureaucracies, school and college teachers, and the educational materials industry in the production and selection of materials. Such a study would shed light upon the difficulties and problems associated with the widespread adoption of educational technology *(Continuity and Discontinuity)*.

Educational institutions that have well-developed instructional technology will avail businesses and industry of opportunities to tie plant-site classrooms to televised instruction originating on the campus, and will make available audio-video-tape instruction or computer-assisted instruction on subjects relevant to business and industry training programs *(Toward a Learning Society)*.

Educational institutions located within accessible range of prisons and having at their disposal well-developed instructional technology will make remote-access instruction and independent learning materials available to prison education programs at minimum costs *(Toward a Learning Society)*.

THE LABOR MARKET Efforts should be coordinated at the federal, state, and local levels to stimulate the expansion of occupational education in community colleges and to make it responsive to changing manpower requirements *(The Open-Door Colleges)*.

The health manpower research programs in the Department of Health, Education and Welfare should be expanded to encompass broad continuous studies of health manpower supply and demand *(Higher Education and the Nation's Health)*.

In view of the complex shifts that are taking place in the labor market for college graduates, we believe that counseling services will need to be expanded in many colleges and universities *(The More Effective Use of Resources)*.

Institutions of higher education and governments at all levels should not restrict undergraduate opportunities to enroll in college or to receive student aid because of less favorable trends in the job market for college graduates than have prevailed in the recent past *(College Graduates and Jobs)*.

Individual institutions of higher education and state planning agencies should place high priority in the 1970s and 1980s on adjusting their programs to changing student choices of fields that will occur in response both to pronounced occupational shifts in the labor market and to changing student interests and concerns. High priority should also be placed on continued flexibility in the use of resources in order to facilitate such adjustments *(College Graduates and Jobs)*.

Federal government agencies should develop more adequate data on occupational and industrial employment patterns of graduates of two-year colleges and of dropouts from institutions of higher education. Community college districts should conduct follow-up studies that would provide information on employment patterns of their former students by occupation and industry *(College Graduates and Jobs)*.

State planning agencies should give very high priority in the next few years to careful adaptation of teacher education to the changing needs of a period of shrinking job opportunities for elementary and secondary school teachers *(College Graduates and Jobs)*.

Associations of professional schools and professional societies should undertake the responsibility for careful studies of manpower supply and demand for graduates in their respective fields *(College Graduates and Jobs)*.

Agencies and individuals that have been conducting studies of future supply and demand for Ph.D.'s should continue to review and update their work. We are impressed by the differences in outlook among fields and believe that the time has come for increased emphasis on projections relating to individual fields or groups of fields and less reliance on broad aggregative studies *(College Graduates and Jobs)*.

Federal and state government agencies and other appropriate bodies should undertake studies of the implications of the changing job market for holders of master's degrees and for enrollment in master's program *(College Graduates and Jobs)*.

Employers should not raise educational requirements in response to changes in the job market for college graduates. We strongly recommend that educational requirements should not be imposed except where they are clearly indicated by job requirements *(College Graduates and Jobs)*.

More attention should be paid to the occupational training interests of students, and to occupational counseling and guidance as students and adults seek to adjust to changing labor market conditions *(The Purposes and the Performance of Higher Education in the United States)*.

LEARNING PAVILIONS   We recommend consideration of the establishment of *learning pavilions* at community colleges and comprehensive colleges located in central cities *(The Campus and the City)*.

Learning pavilions designed and operated to encourage and facilitate independent adult learning will be developed in urban centers and in areas that are remote from institutions of postsecondary education. Funding responsibility for construction and operation of such facilities will reside with metropolitan or county governments *(Toward a Learning Society)*.

LIBERAL ARTS CENTERS The proposed National Foundation for the Development of Higher Education should aid in planning liberal arts centers to be established by groups of colleges for the purpose of increasing quality, scope, and diversity of undergraduate education; of stimulating more economical and effective use of administrative and teaching personnel; and of sharing library and computer facilities *(New Students and New Places)*.

LIBERAL ARTS COLLEGES State plans, in general, should incorporate a minimum FTE enrollment objective of 1,000 students and a maximum FTE enrollment objective of 2,500 students for liberal arts colleges *(New Students and New Places)*.

Liberal arts colleges should consider enrolling students as early as grade 11 and awarding the bachelor's degree after grade 14 or 15 *(Continuity and Discontinuity)*.

LIBERAL EDUCATION *(See* General education)

LIBRARIES There should be increased funding for library support—$100 million in 1970–71 *(Quality and Equality)*.

The introduction of new technologies to help libraries continue to improve their services to increasing numbers of users should be given first priority in the efforts of colleges and universities, government agencies, and other agencies seeking to achieve more rapid progress in the development of instructional technology *(The Fourth Revolution)*.

The library should become a more active participant in the instructional process with an added proportion of funds, perhaps as much as a doubling *(Reform on Campus)*.

Public libraries and museums will increasingly recognize their potentials as sources for guidance and independent study that can be utilized to meet the standards and objectives of postsecondary-level instruction *(Toward a Learning Society)*.

LOCAL AGENCIES AND PROGRAMS, PROPOSED In each metropolitan area with population in excess of 1 million, we recommend establishment of a metropolitan higher education council and a metropolitan educational opportunity counseling center *(The Campus and the City)*.

Educational opportunity counseling centers should be funded one-half from local sources and one-half from state and federal sources.
Funding for administrative expenses of the metropolitan higher education councils should be similarly shared, with one-half from local sources and one-half from state and federal sources *(The Campus and the City)*.

Educational opportunity counseling centers and other appropriate local agencies will have as one of their responsibilities the development and distribution of information about postsecondary educational resources including, but also in addition to, colleges and universities *(Toward a Learning Society)*.

Learning pavilions designed and operated to encourage and facilitate independent adult learning will be developed in urban centers and in areas that are remote from institutions of postsecondary education. Funding responsibility for construction and operation of such facilities will reside with metropolitan or county governments *(Toward a Learning Society)*.

LOCAL RESPONSIBILITY The elimination of any local share of the financing of community colleges is opposed on the grounds that, if local policy-making responsibility is to be meaningful, it should be accompanied by some substantial degree of financial responsibility *(The Open-Door Colleges)*.

Appropriate state and local agencies should undertake an evaluation of the adequacy of the number of higher education student places in those areas with a ratio of between 2.5 and 3.5 student places per 100 population *(The Campus and the City)*.

Appropriate state and local agencies should take steps to improve availability of student places in colleges and universities in those areas which now have less than 2.5 places available per 100 population *(The Campus and the City)*.

Local agencies should review their policies for funding community colleges to determine whether adequate funds are being made available for this segment of higher education with its difficult and important tasks *(The Campus and the City)*.

Educational opportunity community centers should be funded one-half from local sources. Funding for administrative expenses of the metropolitan higher education councils should be similarly shared, with one-half from local sources *(The Campus and the City)*.

Local school boards, with community and professional assistance, should identify the overall ends and objectives of the public schools, deliberately encourage experimentation with a diversity of means to those objectives, and insist upon accountability from teachers and administrators *(Continuity and Discontinuity)*.

Learning pavilions designed and operated to encourage and facilitate independent adult learning will be developed in urban centers and in areas that are remote from institutions of postsecondary education. Funding responsibility for construction and operation of such facilities will reside with metropolitan or county governments *(Toward a Learning Society)*.

MEDICAL EDUCATION *(See Health science education)*

NATIONAL AND COMMUNITY SERVICE A national service educational benefit program should be established making educational grants available for service in various programs such as the Peace Corps or Vista, with the amount of the benefits set at some percentage of veterans' educational benefits *(Quality and Equality)*.

A voluntary national health service corps should be developed *(Higher Education and the Nation's Health)*.

Service opportunities should be created for students between high school and college and at stop-out points in college through national, state, and municipal youth programs *(Less Time, More Options)*.

More opportunities should be created for students to gain community service and work experience *(Reform on Campus)*.

The Urban Corps provides an excellent mechanism for giving opportunities to students to have experience in city government, and cities that do not now have such programs should seriously consider developing them *(The Campus and the City)*.

Institutions of higher education should undertake those community service activities that revitalize its educational functions and constitute an integral part of its educational program, are within the institutional capacity both in terms of personnel and resources, and are not duplicative of the services of other urban institutions *(The Campus and the City)*.

Quasi-university agencies should be established through which faculty members and/or students could provide services, even on controversial matters, without directly involving the university or college in its corporate capacity *(The Campus and the City)*.

States should recognize the public-service demands made on public institutions and provide funds for such services *(The Campus and the City)*.

As debates inevitably proceed in the coming years over the reordering of national goals, the goal of fulfilling the aspirations of many young people for more useful roles in our society should be given high priority, along with the more widely recognized goals of overcoming human, urban, and environmental problems *(College Graduates and Jobs)*.

More work and service opportunities should be created for students by government and industry and nonprofit agencies, and students should be encouraged to pursue these opportunities, including, occasionally, through "stop-outs" *(The Purposes and the Performance of Higher Education in the United States)*.

Institutional service should be extended on a more even-handed basis to groups and persons in connection with problems where it may be helpful, subject to the major limitation that any service should be appropriate to the educational functions of higher education *(Institutional Aid)*.

Local, state, and national governments will provide opportunities for persons to render public service through well-organized programs, and those who engage in national service will be able to earn financial benefits toward education in addition to their regular inservice compensation *(Toward a Learning Society)*.

NATIONAL FOUNDATION FOR THE DEVELOPMENT OF HIGHER EDUCATION A National Foundation for the Development of Higher Education should be established, whose functions would be to encourage, advise, review, and provide financial support for institutional programs designed to give new directions in curricula, to strengthen essential areas that have fallen behind or never been adequately developed because of inadequate funding, and to develop programs for improvement of educational processes and techniques.

$50 million should be granted to the Foundation to be allocated to states and regions which would, working with the advice and assistance of the Foundation, make further plans for the effective growth of the states' postsecondary educational system. In the development of these plans, the Foundation and the states should give particular attention to creation of an adequate system of community colleges and to stimulation and coordination of the states' occupational and technical educational resources *(Quality and Equality)*.

A special subdivision for the development of black colleges and universities should be created within the National Foundation for the Development of Higher Education. The purpose of this division would be to aid colleges and universities founded for Negroes to develop and implement new programs and activities that respond to the challenges that confront them as institutions in transition *(From Isolation to Mainstream)*.

The proposed National Foundation for the Development of Higher Education should aid in planning liberal arts centers to be established by groups of colleges for the purpose of increasing quality, scope, and diversity of undergraduate education; of stimulating more economical and effective use of administrative and teaching personnel; and of sharing library and computer facilities *(New Students and New Places)*.

NATIONAL FOUNDATION FOR POSTSECONDARY EDUCATION The proposed National Foundation for Postsecondary Education[2] should be established, and assigned responsibility for administering loans and the provision of capital investment funds and grants for the utilization of instructional technology *(The Fourth Revolution)*.

NATIONAL INSTITUTE OF EDUCATION The proposed National Institute of Education should be established, and should make grants to support research and development activities in the field of instructional technology for higher education *(The Fourth Revolution)*.

The new National Institute of Education should make grants available to those institutions that are conducting systematic experiments with remedial education *(The Campus and the City)*.

NATIONAL STUDENT LOAN BANK The federal government should charter a National Student Loan Bank as a non-profit corporation financed by the sale of governmentally guaranteed securities, which would serve all eligible students regardless of need. The fund should be self-sustaining, except for catastrophic risks, and should permit borrowing up to a reasonable limit that would reflect both tuition charges and subsistence costs. Loan repayments should be based upon income currently earned, and up to 40 years should be permitted for repayment. Provision should be made for public subsidy of catastrophic risks *(Higher Education: Who Pays? Who Benefits? Who Should Pay?)*.

NEW INSTITUTIONS Additional medical schools should be distributed on a geographical basis to provide needed service to areas not now served *(Quality and Equality)*.

State plans for two-year institutions should not provide for new two-year strictly academic branches of universities or new specialized two-year technical institutes, although there may be a case for exceptions under special circumstances prevailing in some of the states *(The Open-Door Colleges)*.

To achieve the goal of a community college within commuting distance of every potential student, about 230 to 280 new, carefully planned, community colleges will be needed by 1980 *(The Open-Door Colleges* and *The Capitol and the Campus)*.[3]

No new two-year medical schools should be established that do not lead on to M.D.-candidate education *(Higher Education and the Nation's Health)*.

[2] This is the same agency referred to in earlier reports as National Foundation for the Development of Higher Education.

[3] Because of the establishment of many new colleges and the availability of new information, the Commission revised its estimate of new community colleges needed by 1980. In *New Students and New Places* it estimates a need for 175 to 235 new community colleges.

Nine new university health science centers should be developed *(Higher Education and the Nation's Health)*.

Coordinating agencies should be granted the authority to approve new institutions, branches, or centers, and where appropriate, to take active steps toward the establishment of new institutions *(The Capitol and the Campus)*.

States that do not presently have a strong private sector should consider the desirability of making the equivalent of land grants to responsible groups who can demonstrate financial ability to operate new private institutions. Such grants should encourage groups to start new institutions or to open branches of existing well-established private institutions in the granting state *(The Capitol and the Campus)*.

State and local planning bodies should develop plans for the establishment by 1980 of about 80 to 125 new community colleges in large metropolitan areas with populations of 500,000 or more. Including these institutions, there should be about 175 to 235 new community colleges in all *(New Students and New Places)*.

State and local planning bodies should also develop plans for the establishment by 1980 of about 60 to 70 new comprehensive colleges in large metropolitan areas with populations of 500,000 or more. Including these institutions, there should be about 80 to 105 new comprehensive colleges in all *(New Students and New Places)*.

In view of the very recent movement to establish external degree programs and open universities, state and local planning bodies should continuously study the impact of these innovations on patterns of enrollment and modify estimates of needs for new institutions accordingly *(New Students and New Places)*.

We do not believe that there is a need for any new Ph.D.-granting institutions, although some or even many institutions will be introducing the D.A. degree *(The More Effective Use of Resources)*.

NONTRADITIONAL EDUCATION   Alternative avenues by which students can earn degrees or complete a major portion of their work for a degree should be expanded to increase accessibility of higher education for those to whom it is now unavailable because of work schedules, geographic location, or responsibilities in the home *(Less Time, More Options)*.

State and federal government agencies, as well as private foundations, should expand programs of support for the development of external degree systems and open universities along the lines of programs initiated within the last year or so. It will also be important for governmental bodies and foundations to provide funds for evaluation of these innovative programs as they develop *(New Students and New Places)*.

Because expanding technology will extend higher learning to large numbers of people who have been unable to take advantage of it in the past, because it will provide instruction in forms that will be more effective than conventional instruction for some learners in some subjects, because it will be more effective for all learners and many teachers under many circumstances, and because it will significantly reduce costs of higher education in the long run, its early advancement should be encouraged by the adequate commitment of colleges and universities to its utilization and development and by adequate support from governmental and other agencies concerned with the advancement of higher learning *(The Fourth Revolution)*.

Major funding sources should recognize not only the potential of new and developing extramural education systems for expanding learning opportunities, but also the crucial role such systems should play in the ultimate development of instructional technologies. Requests of these systems for funds with which to introduce and use new instructional programs, materials, and media should be given favorable consideration *(The Fourth Revolution)*.

In view of the changes that are occurring in patterns of participation in higher education, counseling services will need to be expanded in many colleges and universities *(The More Effective Use of Resources)*.

Urban campuses, in appropriate instances, should offer certain portions of their programs in off-campus facilities—at industrial plants, in business and governmental offices, and at public libraries and schoolrooms in residential areas *(The Campus and the City)*.

Schools and colleges should experiment with different structural models designed to provide a student with options that will enable him to find the right program at the right time. Such experimentation challenges the current structure and its traditional break between school and college at the end of grade 12. Liberal arts colleges should consider enrolling students as early as grade 11 and awarding the bachelor's degree after grade 14 or 15; there should be experimentation with public education at age 4; some school systems should eliminate a year from the K through 12 sequence; other school systems should stress general education equivalent to that found at good colleges; students should be able to "test out" of high school graduation requirements; there should be expanded programs of college credit for the senior year of high school, concurrent enrollment of students in school and college, and early admission to college; options other than college attendance should be made available for high school graduates *(Continuity and Discontinuity)*.

The Commission reiterates its support of the development of external degree and other nontraditional study programs, emphasizing the need for high quality in such programs. They are especially important in relation to the special needs of mature married women for continuing education *(Opportunities for Women in Higher Education)*.

The existence of separate institutions for nontraditional study should not be used as an excuse for denying qualified adults of either sex the opportunity to study on traditional campuses on a full-time or part-time basis *(Opportunities for Women in Higher Education)*.

Educational institutions that have well-developed instructional technology will avail businesses and industry of opportunities to tie plant-site classrooms to televised instruction originating on the campus, and will make available audio-video-tape instruction or computer-assisted instruction on subjects relevant to business and industry training programs *(Toward a Learning Society)*.

OCCUPATIONAL EDUCATION *(See* Vocational and technical training)

OPEN UNIVERSITIES *(See* Nontraditional study)

appointments and (2) appointments to the faculty of persons whose principal employment is elsewhere and who come to the campus to give one or two specialized courses. For example, fringe benefits, prorated on the basis of the proportion of a full-time appointment involved, are more appropriate for the first type of part-time employee *(Opportunities for Women in Higher Education)*.

The provision of part-time learning opportunities will be considered a legitimate function of all colleges and universities, regardless of their level of instruction or type of control. After deliberation, some institutions will elect not to perform this function, but their decisions will be based on particular objectives they have set for themselves because of educational policy options, limitations of space, finances, or facilities, and not on a belief that such instruction is inherently inappropriate to colleges and universities *(Toward a Learning Society)*.

Once admitted to a college or university for academic studies, qualified part-time students will be eligible to take courses in the regular departments of the institution and will be accorded the same campus privileges that are accorded to full-time students *(Toward a Learning Society)*.

Institutions of higher education will not offer part-time students courses that exceed levels of instruction maintained in courses offered to full-time students. Two-year institutions will not offer upper-division or professional instruction to part-time students. Vocational schools that do not offer general education to full-time students will not offer it to part-time students *(Toward a Learning Society)*.

PERSONNEL On campuses where organized protest occurs, faculty and student marshals might be available to monitor these events and to report on violations of campus rules and excessive actions by law enforcement officers. The marshals should be organized so that they are available on a regular, ongoing basis *(Dissent and Disruption)*.

Campus personnel chosen to communicate with law enforcement agencies should consist of persons who not only can achieve rapport, but also can effectively present the views of the campus community *(Dissent and Disruption)*.

Careful consideration should be given to use of (1) ombudsmen, (2) hearing officers, and (3) campus attorneys *(Dissent and Disruption)*.

Colleges and universities should supplement their instructional staffs with qualified technologists and specialists to assist instructors in the design, planning, and evaluation of teaching-learning units that can be used with the expanding instructional technologies. Institutions of higher education at all levels should develop their potentials for training specialists and professionals needed to perform the new functions that are associated with the increasing utilization of instructional technology on the nation's college and university campuses *(The Fourth Revolution)*.

Costs of support personnel, in comparison with those of other similar institutions, should be analyzed with a view to identifying possible excessive costs in some aspects of support functions, but also of making certain that these functions are being conducted efficiently and that high-paid faculty members are not performing functions that could be delegated to lower-paid support personnel *(The More Effective Use of Resources)*.

Institutions of higher education engaged with faculty unionism should employ staff members or consultants who are experienced in collective bargaining negotiations *(The More Effective Use of Resources)*.

All universities with health science centers should consider the development of an able core of middle managers to assume responsibility for the more routine administrative functions of the management of these centers *(The More Effective Use of Resources)*.

Colleges and universities should delegate responsibility for portfolio management to an able professional *(The More Effective Use of Resources)*.

Large universities located in urban areas should appoint a vice-president or vice-chancellor for urban affairs who would be concerned with the university-urban interface in terms of the urban impact of the university's educational, service, research, and corporate functions *(The Campus and the City)*.

Ombudsmen or their equivalent should be appointed *(Governance of Higher Education)*.

College admissions officers should be appointed with great care because their work is intimately tied to the primary mission of the institution. If possible, they should have both faculty status and a prominent place in the administrative hierarchy *(Continuity and Discontinuity)*.

Every large college or university should appoint one or more affirmative action officers, whose policies should be guided by an appropriately constituted advisory committee or council. Small colleges may find it preferable to assign affirmative action responsibilities to an existing administrator or faculty member *(Opportunities for Women in Higher Education)*.

Large campuses should have an administrative officer specifically concerned with ensuring that qualified adults are given opportunities to pursue undergraduate or graduate study on a full-time or part-time basis *(Opportunities for Women in Higher Education)*.

PLANNING *(See also* Evaluation and review)

State plans for two-year institutions should not provide for new two-year strictly academic branches of universities or new specialized two-year technical institutes. State plans should also place major emphasis on the allocation of vocational education funds to comprehensive community colleges rather than to post-high school area vocational schools or other noncollegiate institutions *(The Open-Door Colleges)*.

All state plans for the development of two-year institutions of higher education should provide for comprehensive community colleges that will offer transfer education, general education, remedial courses, occupational programs, continuing education for adults, and cultural programs designed to enrich the community environment. Within this general framework there should be opportunities for varying patterns of development and for the provision of particularly strong specialties in selected colleges *(The Open-Door Colleges)*.

The states, in cooperation with universities and with regional and local planning bodies, should play a major role in the development of plans for the location of university health science centers, area health education centers, and comprehensive colleges and community colleges providing training for allied health personnel *(Higher Education and the Nation's Health)*.

Existing federal legislation for regional, state, and local health planning should be strengthened to encompass regional planning of all health manpower education and health care facilities. The university health science centers, along with their affiliated area health education centers, should have central responsibility for the planning of health manpower education, while the central responsibility for planning changes in the delivery of health care should be in the hands of regional agencies, in cooperation with state and local agencies, as well as appropriate private institutions *(Higher Education and the Nation's Health)*.

University administrations should appoint appropriate officers to develop plans for the expansion of university health science centers and for their transformation to perform broad educational, research, and community service functions *(Higher Education and the Nation's Health)*.

Governing boards, administrations, and faculties of most colleges founded for Negroes should plan to accommodate enrollments that may double on the average, certainly by the year 2000 and possibly by 1980 *(From Isolation to Mainstream)*.

A state's initial development of a broad postsecondary educational plan should be undertaken by a commission appointed for that purpose with a small staff augmented by special task forces as needed *(The Capitol and the Campus)*.

As minimum elements in any state planning effort, attention should be given to: (1) present and future access to postsecondary education, including need for student spaces, student financial aid programs, geographic availability of institutions, and admissions standards for types of institutions; (2) appropriate functions for the various types of institutions within postsecondary education, including degrees to be granted, research activities, and public service functions; (3) orderly growth of postsecondary education, including location of new campuses, development of new schools, and optimum size of institutions; and (4) articulation among the various elements of postsecondary education and within secondary education.

In setting the parameters for these planning functions, state agencies should take into account the present and potential contributions to state needs of all types of postsecondary institutions including universities, colleges, private trade and technical schools, area vocational schools, industry, and unions and other agencies providing various forms of postsecondary education. They should also take into account the entire timespan of a person's postsecondary education needs from immediately after high school throughout life.

In developing both their short- and longer-range plans, states should give greater attention to institutional diversity, and to building sufficient flexibility into both institutional and systemwide plans to permit adaptation as educational processes and needs change *(The Capitol and the Campus)*.

Universities, colleges, and state planning agencies should carefully study and adopt plans for the development of cluster colleges *(New Students and New Places)*.

In view of the very recent movement to establish external degree programs and open universities, state and local planning bodies should continuously study the impact of these innovations on patterns of enrollment and modify estimates of needs for new institutions accordingly *(New Students and New Places)*.

Both planning agencies and urban-located institutions should review and analyze the educational resources in their areas and the educational needs of urban students to determine whether experimental approaches are desirable to expand effective options for postsecondary educational opportunities in the metropolitan areas *(The Campus and the City)*.

Colleges and universities should develop overall policies concerning appropriate urban activities for their institutions to avoid response to new proposals on an ad hoc basis without reference to consistency with the educational mission of the institution *(The Campus and the City)*.

Individual institutions of higher education and state planning agencies should place high priority in the 1970s and 1980s on adjusting their programs to changing student choices of fields that will occur in response both to pronounced occupational shifts in the labor market and to changing student interests and concerns. High priority should also be placed on continued flexibility in the use of resources in order to facilitate such adjustments *(College Graduates and Jobs)*.

POSTSECONDARY EDUCATION

(See also Community colleges, Continuing education, Further education, Proprietary schools, Vocational and technical training)

Existing legislation should be revised to enable all postsecondary vocational and technical students to apply for grants on the basis of need regardless of whether such students are enrolled in community colleges, area vocational schools, or public adult schools. Work-study programs should also be available to vocational and technical students in all these institutions, and, in addition, to students in proprietary schools. To participate in either of these programs each institution should be officially recognized as providing a particular program in which the student is enrolled at an acceptable standard of instruction *(Quality and Equality)*.

The proposed National Foundation for the Development of Higher Education should be granted $50 million, to be allocated to states and regions that would, working with the advice and assistance of the Foundation, make further plans for the effective growth of the states' postsecondary educational systems. In the development of their plans, the Foundation and the states should give particular attention to the creation of an adequate system of community colleges and to the stimulation and coordination of the states' occupational and technical educational resources *(Quality and Equality)*.

State plans should place major emphasis on the allocation of vocational education funds to comprehensive community colleges rather than to post-high school area vocational schools or other noncollegiate institutions *(The Open-Door Colleges)*.

The expansion of postsecondary educational opportunities should be encouraged outside the formal college in apprenticeship programs, proprietary schools, in-service training in industry, and in military programs. Appropriate educational credit should be given for the training received, and participants should be eligible, where appropriate, for federal and state assistance available to students in formal colleges *(Less Time, More Options)*.

State governments should continue to exercise major responsibility, in cooperation with local governments and private institutions, for maintaining, improving, and expanding systems of postsecondary education adequate to meet the needs of the American people *(The Capitol and the Campus)*.

In setting the parameters for their planning functions, state agencies should take into account the present and potential contributions to state needs of all types of postsecondary institutions including universities, colleges, private trade and technical schools, area vocational schools, industry, and unions and other agencies providing various forms of postsecondary education. State plans should also encompass the entire timespan of a person's postsecondary education needs from immediately after high school throughout life *(The Capitol and the Campus)*.

Both planning agencies and urban-located institutions should review and analyze the educational resources in their areas and the educational needs of urban students to determine whether experimental approaches are desirable to expand effective options for postsecondary educational opportunities in the metropolitan areas *(The Campus and the City)*.

The total postsecondary age group should become more the subject of concern, and attention should be comparatively less concentrated on those who attend college *(The Purposes and the Performance of Higher Education in the United States)*.

Public policy should be directed to improvement of existing channels into adult life and to the creation of new channels—college being only one of several preferred channels *(The Purposes and the Performances of Higher Education in the United States)*.

Schools and colleges should experiment with different structural models designed to provide a student with options that will enable him to find the right program at the right time. Such experimentation challenges the current structure and its traditional break between school and college at the end of grade 12. Liberal arts colleges should consider enrolling students as early as grade 11 and awarding the bachelor's degree after grade 14 or 15. Options other than college attendance should be made available for high school graduates *(Continuity and Discontinuity)*.

Every person will have available to him, throughout his life, financial assistance for at least two years of postsecondary education. For at least part of the entitlement, there will be no restriction as to the type of educational institution the recipient might elect to attend *(Toward a Learning Society)*.

The states will make adequate provision, with the full spectrum of their postsecondary education resources, for educational opportunities adequate to the divergent needs of all of their citizens *(Toward a Learning Society)*.

State coordinating agencies will become increasingly aware of the resources of all postsecondary educational institutions in their states, and, in partnership with those affected, will utilize their influence to assure adequate financial support for their institution and to minimize unnecessary duplication of specialized programs in colleges and universities and other institutions offering postsecondary education *(Toward a Learning Society)*.

Collection and dissemination of information on all forms of postsecondary education will be given high priority by federal and state educational statistical agencies *(Toward a Learning Society)*.

Educational Opportunity Counseling Centers and other appropriate local agencies will have as one of their responsibilities the development and distribution of information about postsecondary educational resources including, but also in addition to, colleges and universities *(Toward a Learning Society)*.

The current system of accreditation by institutional associations will be supplemented by a second system instituted by state and federal governments for the purpose of validating fiscal stability, legitimacy of advertising claims, and general quality of instruction. Those responsible for administering such validation will be restrained, by all means feasible, from regulation of postsecondary education, and will seek to establish minimum rather than optimum standards for the accreditation they are empowered to bestow *(Toward a Learning Society)*.

Institutions of postsecondary education will grant degrees, certificates, and honors at more frequent intervals than they now do *(Toward a Learning Society)*.

PRECOLLEGE EDUCATION   *(See also* High schools, School-college relations)

The first priority in the nation's commitment to equal educational opportunity should be placed upon the increased effectiveness of our preelementary, elementary, and secondary school programs *(A Chance to Learn)*.

Experimental programs for the early development of verbal skills should be established, to be sponsored and administered by institutions of higher education with active participation from members of the community; and of programs for remedying verbal skill deficiencies at the secondary and higher levels of education *(A Chance to Learn)*.

States should give careful consideration to the adoption of policies encouraging a lower age of entrance into the public schools, specifically at the age of four *(College Graduates and Jobs)*.

Students in elementary and high school should be counseled through a variety of resources—counselors, written materials, community-based people, as well as college students—minority students and women, in particular *(Continuity and Discontinuity)*.

Improvement of the nation's schools is the first educational priority in the nation; and within the schools improvement in the basic skills, especially in large city schools, is the first priority. Colleges and universities should recognize this fact and help to provide the resources, incentives, and rewards for faculty members who commit themselves to this task *(Continuity and Discontinuity)*.

The first priority in the nation's commitment to equal educational opportunity for women should be placed on changing policies in preelementary, elementary, and secondary school programs that tend to deter women from aspiring to equality with men in their career goals *(Opportunities for Women in Higher Education)*.

Elementary and secondary schools will continue to play a significant role in the provision of educational opportunities appropriate to their resources to persons of all ages in the communities where they are located *(Toward a Learning Society)*.

PRESIDENCY Presidents should have authority to deal with emergency situations and should seek advice from preexisting consultative groups drawn from the campus community *(Dissent and Disruption)*.

Presidents should be given adequate assistance from a highly capable staff *(The More Effective Use of Resources)*.

Boards should seek active presidents and give them the authority and the staff they need to provide leadership in a period of change and conflict *(Governance of Higher Education)*.

Boards may wish to consider the establishment of stated review periods for presidents so that withdrawal by the president or reaffirmation of the president may be managed in a more effective manner than is often now the actual situation. Faculty members and students should be associated in an advisory capacity with the process of review as they are in the initial appointment *(Governance of Higher Education)*.

PRISON EDUCATION PROGRAMS Educational institutions located within accessible range of prisons and having at their disposal well-developed instructional technology will make remote-access instruction and independent learning materials available to prison education programs at minimum costs *(Toward a Learning Society)*.

PRIVATE INSTITUTIONS Private colleges and universities should develop policies encouraging admission of community college graduates *(The Open-Door Colleges)*.

States should provide financial support for medical and dental education in private institutions *(Higher Education and the Nation's Health)*.

States that do not presently have a strong private sector should consider the desirability of making the equivalent of land grants to responsible groups who can demonstrate financial ability to operate new private institutions. Such grants should encourage groups to start new institutions or to open branches of existing well-established private institutions in the granting state *(The Capitol and the Campus)*.

States should enter into agreements, or make grants, for the purpose of continuing certain educational programs at private institutions. These should be selected after consideration of special manpower needs, evaluation of existing student places for these programs in public institutions, and the relative costs of expanding public capacity or supporting and expanding private programs *(The Capitol and the Campus)*.

Those states that do not already have programs enabling private institutions to borrow construction funds through a state-created bond-issuing corporation should take steps to develop such agencies if the private institutions can demonstrate the need for them *(The Capitol and the Campus)*.

For those few states which rely heavily on private universities and colleges, and for which our recommendations prove inadequate, each resident student should be given cost-of-education vouchers that would entitle any private institution selected by the student to receive a state payment increasing gradually each year up to an amount equal to one-third of the subsidy granted by the state for students at the same levels attending comparable public institutions *(The Capitol and the Campus)*.

The federal and state governments should develop and implement policies to preserve and strengthen private institutions of higher education. The federal aid recommended in *Quality and Equality* would be available for public and private institutions alike. We also reiterate those recommendations for state aid to private higher education, with emphasis on student aid the major approach, that were set forth in *The Capitol and the Campus (New Students and New Places)*.

Private colleges should reexamine their admissions policies to determine whether expansion of open-admission or flexible-admission student places in their institutions would be compatible with their particular educational missions *(The Campus and the City)*.

Private colleges and universities should increase their tuition charges at a rate that is no more rapid than the increase in per capita disposable income. The rate of increase in tuition should be less pronounced than this, if at all possible *(Higher Education: Who Pays? Who Benefits? Who Should Pay?)*.

Private colleges and universities should carefully study their educational costs per student and consider restructuring their tuition charges, so that tuition is relatively low for lower-division students, somewhat higher for upper-division students, and considerably higher for graduate and professional students *(Higher Education: Who Pays? Who Benefits? Who Should Pay?)*.

PRIVATE SPECIALTY SCHOOLS States will periodically review their statutes to make certain that they adequately protect students against fraudulent claims and unfair business practices that may characterize operations of some private specialty schools *(Toward a Learning Society)*.

PROFESSIONAL SCHOOLS *(See* Graduate and professional education)

grams, set aside as a self-renewal fund, and directed to new or expanded programs *(The More Effective Use of Resources* and *Reform on Campus).*

From funds allocated to the Secretary of Health, Education and Welfare for innovation and reform in higher education, grants should be made available for development and testing of new techniques for assessing individual competencies *(Reform on Campus).*

In all professional fields, careful and sustained attention needs to be given to adaptation of educational programs to the advancement of knowledge and technological change, and to society's changing problems and needs *(College Graduates and Jobs).*

Innovations in programs and in policies should be encouraged by public authorities by influence and not by control *(Governance of Higher Education).*

Schools and colleges alike should remember that experimentation carries with it the price of accountability. No new programs at either level should be initiated without clear criteria for evaluation *(Continuity and Discontinuity).*

REMEDIAL EDUCATION *(See* Compensatory education)

RESEARCH Federal grants for university-based research (not including federal contract research centers), regardless of changing priorities for defense and space research, should be increased annually (using grants in 1967–68 as a base) at a rate equal to the five-year moving average annual rate of growth in the gross national product *(Quality and Equality).*

Federal financial support of research in university health science centers should be maintained at its present percentage of the GNP; funds should be made available to support research on methods of achieving greater efficiency in health manpower education and in the delivery of health care as well as for biomedical research. Federal allocations should cover the total cost of research projects, and not less than 10 percent and not more than 25 percent of the research grants to any university health science center should take the form of institutional grants rather than grants for specific research projects *(Higher Education and the Nation's Health).*

The health manpower research programs in the Department of Health, Education and Welfare, in cooperation with the Department of Labor, should be expanded to encompass broad continuous studies of health manpower supply and demand. Research funds should be made available for specialized studies of these problems in university health science centers and appropriate university research institutes *(Higher Education and the Nation's Health).*

Two or more regional centers should be established for research on the academically disadvantaged *(From Isolation to Mainstream).*

The federal government should continue to provide a major share of expenditures required for research and development in instructional technology and for introduction of new technologies more extensively into higher education at least until the end of the century. The total level of federal government support for these purposes should be at least $100 million in 1973 and should rise to 1 percent of the total expenditures of the nation on higher education by 1980 *(The Fourth Revolution).*

Within the level of research funding that was recommended in *Quality and Equal-*

ity, high priority should be given to both basic and applied social science research *(Campus and the City).*

Funds for basic research should be concentrated on highly productive centers and individuals, and money for applied research should be subject to periodic reassignment to reflect the decline of old and the rise of new potentialities *(The Purposes and the Performance of Higher Education in the United States).*

Federal research funds should be substantially increased for the social sciences, humanities, and creative arts from their current level of about 7 percent of the amount for science *(The Purposes and the Performance of Higher Education in the United States).*

All secret research should be eliminated from all campuses as a matter of national policy, except under quite unusual circumstances *(The Purposes and the Performance of Higher Education in the United States).*

Research and development funds will be made available by the U.S. Office of Education and the Department of Labor to facilitate the development of the theoretical knowledge and technical expertise needed to service agreements between postsecondary educational institutions and industry for the development of skill-training programs *(Toward a Learning Society).*

RESEARCH IN EDUCATION Two or more regional centers should be established for research on the academically disadvantaged *(From Isolation to Mainstream).*

The federal government should continue to provide a major share of expenditures required for research and development in instructional technology and for introduction of new technologies more extensively into higher education at least until the end of the century. The total level of federal government support for these purposes should be at least $100 million in 1973 and should rise to 1 percent of the total expenditures of the nation on higher education *(The Fourth Revolution).*

Research and development funds will be made available by the Office of Education and the Department of Labor to facilitate the development of the theoretical knowledge and technical expertise needed to service agreements between postsecondary educational institutions and industry for the development of skill-training programs *(Toward a Learning Society).*

RESIDENCY *(See also* Tuition)

States should carefully review their residence requirements and modify them if necessary for the purpose of granting immediate residence status to students whose families came to the state for other than educational reasons. States should cooperate for the purpose of developing relatively standard residence criteria, and each state should review the implementation of requirements of its own institutions to ensure similar application of the criteria among public institutions *(The Capitol and the Campus).*

To encourage the continued development of quality in graduate education at public institutions by permitting students of high ability to attend public institutions without reference to their residency, the cost-of-education supplements accompanying doctoral fellowships should be available only to those institutions that charge the doctoral recipent a fee that is not affected by his residency status. States should consider carefully the adverse effects of enrollment limits at the graduate level for out-of-state students *(The Capitol and the Campus).*

States should enter into reciprocity agreements for the exchange of both undergraduates and graduate students in those situations where the educational systems of each of the states will be enhanced by such an exchange agreement *(The Capitol and the Campus)*.

RESOURCE USE *(See also* Budgeting)

Foundations, government agencies, and higher education associations should give special attention to funding studies and projects concerned with management problems of universities and colleges with effective utilization of available and potential resources *(The Capitol and the Campus)*.

There should be careful study of space utilization standards and their reasonable application *(The More Effective Use of Resources)*.

Colleges and universities should (1) aim to maximize long-term return in the investment of endowment funds, (2) delegate responsibility for portfolio management to an able professional, and (3) generally follow modern principles of endowment management *(The More Effective Use of Resources)*.

Public institutions of higher education, as well as private institutions, should pursue systematic and vigorous policies aimed at attracting additions to their endowment funds *(The More Effective Use of Resources)*.

Higher education should undertake internally the constructive actions necessary to get more effective use of resources and not wait for actions to be required because of external initiative *(The More Effective Use of Resources)*.

Where appropriate, colleges and universities should participate actively in urban renewal activities, but only in unusual circumstances should this participation extend to investment of scarce institutional resources in housing development for the general community. Institutions should limit their need for expansion into scarce urban space by better use of existing space *(The Campus and the City)*.

Individual institutions of higher education and state planning agencies should place high priority in the 1970s and 1980s on adjusting their programs to changing student choices of fields that will occur in response both to pronounced occupational shifts in the labor market and to changing student interests and concerns. High priority should also be placed on continued flexibility in the use of resources in order to facilitate such adjustments *(College Graduates and Jobs)*.

RURAL SCHOOLS State and federal funds should be allocated to meet the present needs of rural schools in disadvantaged areas *(A Chance to Learn)*.

In sparsely populated areas, where it is not feasible to provide institutions within commuting distance of every student, residential community colleges are needed *(The Open-Door Colleges)*.

SCHOOL-COLLEGE RELATIONS *(See also* High schools, Precollege education)

In communities where effective desegregation of local school systems has not been achieved, institutions of higher education should offer their resources of research and consultation to local school administrators and other community leaders *(A Chance to Learn)*.

State and federal funds should be allocated to colleges and universities for specific programs to meet the present needs of inner-city schools and of desegregated schools with heterogeneous classroom enrollments *(A Chance to Learn)*.

All community college districts should provide for effective coordination of their guidance services with those of local high schools *(The Open-Door Colleges)*.

Admissions policies should be examined to assure that they serve both the diversity within higher education and also the possibilities for diversity at the high school level *(Reform on Campus)*.

The curriculum as a whole should be reviewed, campus by campus, in consultation with high school leaders, to assess its broad relevance not only to appropriate student interests but also to prior and subsequent learning experiences *(Reform on Campus)*.

Improvement of the nation's schools is the first educational priority in the nation; and within the schools improvement in the basic skills, especially in large city schools, is the first priority. Colleges and universities should recognize this fact and help to provide the resources, incentives, and rewards for faculty members who commit themselves to this task *(Continuity and Discontinuity)*.

The relationship of general education at the high school to that at the college level, especially in grades 13 and 14, should be explored with a view toward ways that the general education requirements at both levels might be linked together to provide continuity and to prevent wasteful overlap and duplication. School and college faculty members should work together on this set of problems under the sponsorship of local, state, and national organizations such as the College Board and professional associations. More of the responsibility for general education should be assumed by the high schools *(Continuity and Discontinuity)*.

Curriculum development in the humanities and social studies has lagged behind mathematics and science. Schools and colleges, together with funding agencies, should foster new programs and approaches *(Continuity and Discontinuity)*.

Universities, in conjunction with state school boards associations, should experiment with various means of providing school board members with information on crucial issues *(Continuity and Discontinuity)*.

Colleges and universities should encourage school-college collaboration on substantive matters through promotion and reward policies that recognize the importance of such activities *(Continuity and Discontinuity)*.

Though often different in temperament, training, and style, school and college teachers and administrators must work together to reduce many of the present undesirable discontinuities in the relationships between school and college *(Continuity and Discontinuity)*.

SECONDARY EDUCATION *(See* High schools, Precollege education)

SEXUAL DISCRIMINATION There should be no discrimination on the basis of sex in the use of either high school grades or test scores as admissions criteria *(Opportunities for Women in Higher Education)*.

Efforts to eliminate sex bias from vocational interest questionnaires should be encouraged, as should research designed to achieve a more adequate understanding of similarities and differences in patterns of vocational choices among men and women *(Opportunities for Women in Higher Education)*.

Colleges and universities have a responsibility to develop policies specifically designed to bring about changes in the attitudes of administrators and faculty members, where these have been antagonistic to enrollment of women in traditionally male fields *(Opportunities for Women in Higher Education)*.

There should be no discrimination on the basis of sex or marital status in admitting students to graduate and professional schools *(Opportunities for Women in Higher Education)*.

There should be no discrimination on the basis of sex or marital status in appointing teaching or research assistants or in awarding fellowships. In addition, there should be no antinepotism rules in connection with these appointments or awards *(Opportunities for Women in Higher Education)*.

Positive attitudes on the part of faculty members toward the serious pursuit of graduate study and research by women are greatly needed. College and university administrations should assume responsibility for adoption of policies that will encourage positive, rather than negative, attitudes of faculty members in all fields *(Opportunities for Women in Higher Education)*.

Colleges and universities should take especially vigorous steps to overcome a pervasive problem of absence of women in top administrative positions. Women should be given opportunities by their departments to serve as department chairmen, because academic administrators are usually selected from among persons who have served ably as department chairmen. Most important is an administrative stance that is highly positive toward providing opportunities for women to rise in the administrative hierarchy. Also very important is the provision of management training opportunities for both men and women who have potential administrative ability but do not hold administrative positions *(Opportunities for Women in Higher Education)*.

STATE AGENCIES AND PROGRAMS, PROPOSED States should establish a program of tuition grants for both public and private institutions to be awarded to students on the basis of financial need *(The Capitol and the Campus)*.

Those states that do not already have programs enabling private institutions to borrow construction funds through a state-created bond-issuing corporation should take steps to develop such agencies if the private institutions can demon-. strate the need for them *(The Capitol and the Campus)*.

A state's initial development of a broad postsecondary educational plan should be undertaken by a commission appointed for that purpose with a small staff augmented by special task forces as needed, selected so as to assure participation by both public representatives and leaders of educational constituencies *(The Capitol and the Campus)*.

STATE SUPPORT State funds should be allocated to colleges and universities for specific programs to meet the present needs of inner-city schools, and of desegregated schools with heterogeneous classroom enrollments *(A Chance to Learn)*.

State funds should also be allocated to meet the present needs of rural schools in disadvantaged areas *(A Chance to Learn)*.

States should expand their contributions to the financing of community colleges so that the state's share amounts, in general, to one-half or two-thirds of the total state and local financial burden, including operational and capital outlay costs. In providing its share, states should ensure that total appropriations for operating expenses are large enough to permit the institution to follow a policy of either no tuition or very low tuition *(The Open-Door Colleges)*.

States should continue to provide substantial financial support for medical and dental education. In addition, the states should provide major financial support for house officer training and for the education of allied health personnel *(Higher Education and the Nation's Health)*.

States that rank low in terms of the proportion of students going on to higher education should substantially increase their financial commitment to higher education *(The Capitol and the Campus)*.

States should establish a program of tuition grants for both public and private institutions to be awarded to students on the basis of financial need. Only after establishment of a tuition grants program should states consider raising tuition levels at public institutions *(The Capitol and the Campus)*.

States should enter into agreements, or make grants, for the purpose of continuing certain educational programs at private institutions *(The Capitol and the Campus)*.

States with a present expenditure of less than 0.6 percent of per capita personal income spent through state and local taxes for higher education should take immediate steps to increase their financial support of higher education *(The Capitol and the Campus, Institutional Aid)*.

For those states in which our recommendations prove inadequate, each resident student should be given cost-of-education vouchers that would entitle any private institution selected by the student to receive a state payment increasing gradually each year up to an amount equal to one-third of the subsidy granted by the state for students at the same levels attending comparable public institutions *(The Capitol and the Campus)*.

State governments should develop and implement policies to preserve and strengthen private institutions of higher education. The recommendations of *The Capitol and the Campus* are reiterated *(New Students and New Places)*.

States should make funds available for research evaluating the comparative experience of cluster colleges *(New Students and New Places)*.

State financing authorities and local agencies should review their policies for funding community colleges to determine whether adequate funds are being made available for this segment of higher education with its difficult and important tasks *(Campus and The City)*.

States should recognize the public-service demands made on public institutions and provide funds for such services *(The Campus and the City)*.

Educational opportunity counseling centers should be funded one-half from state and federal sources.

Funding for administrative expenses of the metropolitan higher education councils should be similarly shared, with one-half from state and federal sources *(The Campus and the City)*.

State grants to institutions for general support should be based on broad formulas and not line-item control *(Governance of Higher Education)*.

Over the next few years, the taxpayer share of monetary outlays in higher education should be increased modestly, as student-aid funds expand to assist students from low-income families *(Higher Education: Who Pays? Who Benefits? Who Should Pay?)*.

States with regressive tax structures should develop more progressive tax systems in the interest of greater equity and adequacy in the financing of education and other public services *(Higher Education: Who Pays? Who Benefits? Who Should Pay?)*.

State governments should take positive steps toward a gradual narrowing of the tuition differential between public and private institutions in their jurisdictions. This can be accomplished through adjustments in tuition levels at public institutions with an accompanying statewide program of student aid that will minimize the cost to the low-income student, by a program of direct or indirect support to private institutions to enable them to keep tuition charges from rising unduly rapidly, or by a combination of both *(Higher Education: Who Pays? Who Benefits? Who Should Pay?)*.

STATISTICS The Commissioner of Education should designate a unit within the U.S. Office of Education to develop standard definitions and methods of reporting to ensure the coordination, evaluation, and dissemination of available data on educational opportunity *(A Chance to Learn)*.

The U.S. Office of Education should develop a more accurate definition of enrollment in occupational programs and expand its statistics to include changes in enrollment by field of study *(The Open-Door Colleges)*.

All appropriate agencies—the U.S. Office of Education, the Southern Regional Education Board, the Western Interstate Commission on Higher Education, and similar bodies—should give high priority to the development of more adequate data on the behavior of costs, income, and output in higher education *(The More Effective Use of Resources)*.

Federal government agencies should develop more adequate data on occupational and industrial employment patterns of graduates of two-year colleges and of dropouts from institutions of higher education. Community college districts should conduct follow-up studies that would provide information on employment patterns of their former students by occupation and industry *(College Graduates and Jobs)*.

The U.S. Bureau of Labor Statistics and the U.S. Office of Education should develop revised estimates of the future demand for teachers that take account, as existing projections do not, of the growing demand for teachers in preelementary education and in such other settings as adult education programs. There is a need for revised estimates of supply that take account of the declining enrollment in undergraduate education programs and of a possible future decline in enrollment in master's-degree-in-education programs *(College Graduates and Jobs)*.

Federal government agencies involved in studies of health manpower should continuously review projections of supply and demand during the 1970s *(College Graduates and Jobs)*.

The federal government should give high priority to the development of more adequate, sophisticated, and coordinated programs of data gathering and analysis relating to highly educated manpower. Because professional associations can be particularly helpful in these efforts, we also believe that federal government agencies should develop programs designed to elicit and support the efforts of these associations *(College Graduates and Jobs)*.

Associations of professional schools should collect annual data on enrollment of women and minority-group students and should stimulate programs designed to encourage and assist them. Within arts and science fields there should be similar efforts *(College Graduates and Jobs)*.

Agencies and individuals that have been conducting studies of future supply and demand for Ph.D.'s should continue to review and update their work. We are impressed by the differences in outlook among fields and believe that the time has come for increased emphasis on projections relating to individual fields or groups of fields and less reliance on broad aggregative studies *(College Graduates and Jobs)*.

The international migration of students and professional personnel should be explicitly incorporated into analyses of changes in demand and supply *(College Graduates and Jobs)*.

Federal government agencies should take steps to improve the flow of current occupational information and to make it available more promptly *(College Graduates and Jobs)*.

Collection and dissemination of information on all forms of postsecondary education will be given high priority by federal and state educational statistical agencies *(Toward a Learning Society)*.

STOPPING OUT Service and other employment opportunities should be created for students between high school and college and at stop-out points in college, and students should be actively encouraged to participate *(Less Time, More Options)*.

Opportunities should be expanded for students to alternate employment and study, such as the "sandwich" programs in Great Britain and the programs at some American colleges *(Less Time, More Options)*.

Most professional schools and academic departments should be actively involved, along with their institutions, in developing policies that encourage students to stop out between high school and college, or after several years of undergraduate education, or between undergraduate and graduate work, and that assist those students to gain relevant work experience during periods away from school. Of equal importance are policies that facilitate part-time study for the working student *(College Graduates and Jobs)*.

More work and service opportunities should be created for students by government and industry and nonprofit agencies, and students should be encouraged to pursue these opportunities, including, occasionally, through "stop-outs" *(The Purposes and the Performance of Higher Education in the United States)*.

STUDENT AID *(See also* Cost of education supplements, Federal support, Institutional aid)
The present program of educational opportunity grants based on need should be strengthened and expanded by providing (1) that the level of funding be increased so that all college students with demonstrated need will be assured of some financial aid to meet expenses at institutions that they select and (2) that grants based on need be available for a period not to exceed four years of undergraduate study and two years of study toward a graduate degree *(Quality and Equality)*.

The maximum grant recommended is $1,000 per year for students working for a recognized undergraduate degree or certificate, generally for not more than four years, but for a longer period up to a maximum of six years *(Quality and Equality)*.

An undergraduate student holding an educational opportunity grant and receiving added grants from nonfederal sources should be given a supplementary federal grant in an amount matching the nonfederal grants but not exceeding one-quarter of the student's original educational opportunity grant *(Quality and Equality)*.

Existing legislation should be revised to enable all postsecondary vocational and technical students to apply for grants on the basis of need regardless of whether such students are enrolled in community colleges, area vocational schools, or public adult schools *(Quality and Equality)*.

A national service educational benefits program should be established making educational grants available for service in various programs such as the Peace Corps or Vista, with the amount of the benefits set at some percentage of veterans' educational benefits *(Quality and Equality)*.

There should be no discrimination against students transferring from community colleges in the allocation of student aid *(The Open-Door Colleges)*.

The federal government should assist community colleges by providing grants, work-study opportunities, and loans for students *(The Open-Door Colleges)*.

The expansion of postsecondary educational opportunities should be encouraged outside the formal college in apprenticeship programs, proprietary schools, in-service training in industry, and in military programs. Participants should be eligible, where appropriate, for federal and state assistance available to students in formal colleges *(Less Time, More Options)*.

Colleges and universities should seek maximum effectiveness in the allocation of student-aid funds through limiting aid given exclusively in the form of grants to the neediest and most disadvantaged students, while providing combinations of grants, loans, and work opportunities to less needy students *(The More Effective Use of Resources)*.

Institutions of higher education and governments at all levels should not restrict undergraduate opportunities to enroll in college or to receive student aid because of less favorable trends in the job market for college graduates than have prevailed in the recent past *(College Graduates and Jobs)*.

There should be a greater mixing of age groups on campus through providing more opportunities for older persons to take classes and to obtain needed financial support *(The Purposes and the Performance of Higher Education in the United States)*.

Over the next few years, the taxpayer share of monetary outlays in higher education should be increased modestly, as student-aid funds expand to assist students from low-income families *(Higher Education: Who Pays? Who Benefits? Who Should Pay?)*.

The Basic Opportunity Grants program should be fully funded. This legislation, already on the books, is a major step in providing critically needed assistance to both students and institutions of higher education *(Higher Education: Who Pays? Who Benefits? Who Should Pay?)*.

In keeping with the principles previously elaborated, the 50 percent of cost limitation for Basic Opportunity Grants for lower-division students should be raised, perhaps in steps, to 75 percent over the next few years *(Higher Education: Who Pays? Who Benefits? Who Should Pay?)*.

The $1,400 ceiling on Basic Opportunity Grants should be raised gradually in line with increases in educational and subsistence costs *(Higher Education: Who Pays? Who Benefits? Who Should Pay?).*

The federal government should appropriate full funding for state student incentive matching grants. We also recommend that the federal program be modified in the next several years to provide one-fourth of all state awards that meet the criterion of making up, for students with full need, the difference between federal Basic Opportunity Grants and the full cost of attending college in the first two years at public institutions, and a significant fraction of the difference in upper-division years. The awards would be reduced by appropriate amounts for students with less than full need *(Higher Education: Who Pays? Who Benefits? Who Should Pay?).*

State governments should take positive steps toward a gradual narrowing of the tuition differential between public and private institutions in their jurisdictions. This can be accomplished through adjustments in tuition levels at public institutions with an accompanying statewide program of student aid that will minimize the cost to the low-income student *(Higher Education: Who Pays? Who Benefits? Who Should Pay?).*

Every person will have available to him, throughout his life, financial assistance for at least two years of postsecondary education. For at least part of the entitlement, there will be no restrictions as to the type of educational institution the recipient might elect to attend *(Toward a Learning Society).*

STUDENT-FACULTY RATIOS All colleges and universities should examine their utilization of faculty time and in particular they should do so if their student-faculty ratios fall below the median levels for their categories *(The More Effective Use of Resources).*

Varying the mixture of class sizes at the different levels of instruction and establishing appropriate average class sizes that different departments may be expected to meet should be considered. The faculty should be involved in developing policies directed toward achieving appropriate and equitable teaching loads *(The More Effective Use of Resources).*

STUDENT LOAN BANK *(See* National Student Loan Bank)

STUDENT PARTICIPATION Local boards in community college districts should provide for student participation in decisions relating to educational policy and student affairs *(The Open-Door Colleges).*

Representatives of the students should participate in establishing guidelines and procedures for relations between a campus and law enforcement authorities *(Dissent and Disruption).*

Institutions of higher education should consider the establishment of committees, including students, to serve in an advisory capacity in relation to the preparation of the budget when severe cuts must be made. Where it is not considered feasible or desirable to establish such committees, the more traditional practice of holding hearings on major budgetary decisions can provide students with opportunities to express their views *(The More Effective Use of Resources).*

Students should be added more generally as voting members to curriculum committees in departments, group majors, and professional schools where they are majors, and on committees concerned with broad learning experiences. If they are not added as members they should be given some other forum for the expression of their opinions *(Reform on Campus)*.

Students should be associated with the evaluation of teaching performance *(Reform on Campus)*.

An *urban affairs advisory council,* including student representatives, should be appointed to consult with the vice-president or vice-chancellor of urban affairs *(The Campus and The City)*.

Students and alumni should be associated with the process of nominating at least some board members in private and public institutions, but they should not serve on the boards of institutions where they are enrolled or employed *(Governance of Higher Education)*.

Boards should consider faculty and student membership on appropriate board committees, or the establishment of parallel committees with arrangements for joint consultation *(Governance of Higher Education)*.

Boards may wish to consider the establishment of stated review periods for presidents so that withdrawal by the president or reaffirmation of the president may be managed in a more effective manner than is often now the actual situation. Students should be associated in an advisory capacity with the process of review as they are in the initial appointment *(Governance of Higher Education)*.

Governance arrangements should provide (1) adequate academic options from among which students may choose and (2) the right to be heard on important campus issues *(Governance of Higher Education)*.

Students should serve on joint faculty-student (or trustee-student or administrative-student) committees with the right to vote or should have their own parallel student committees with the right to meet with faculty, trustee, and administrative committees in areas of special interest and competence such as educational policy and student affairs. Students serving on such committees should be given staff assistance *(Governance of Higher Education)*.

Students should be given the opportunity to evaluate the teaching performance of faculty members, and students should be involved in periodic reviews of the performance of departments *(Governance of Higher Education)*.

Conduct codes should be prepared with student involvement in the process of their preparation *(Governance of Higher Education)*.

TEACHER TRAINING To stimulate cooperative programs among community colleges and universities for the preparation and reeducation of community college teachers and counselors, $25 million is recommended in 1970–71 for an expanded special program of federal training grants *(Quality and Equality)*.

An intensive research and experimental undertaking should be made in the area of education similar to that made possible in medical practice through the National Institutes of Health *(A Chance to Learn)*.

Two or more regional centers should be established for research on the academically disadvantaged and for training teachers for work with students thus defined. Such centers should be developed, wherever possible, with the cooperation of both predominantly black and predominantly white schools of education *(From Isolation to Mainstream)*.

Colleges founded for Negroes should initiate proposals to state coordinating councils, boards of education, and other education agencies for the support and development of seminars, special training institutes, and classes to improve the skills of elementary and secondary school teachers *(From Isolation to Mainstream)*.

All colleges and universities should make a special effort to identify and support, at all levels of their college and graduate preparation, young Negro men and women who show promise of becoming college teachers *(From Isolation to Mainstream)*.

Colleges and universities that are responsible for the training of prospective university, college, and high school teachers should begin now to incorporate in their curricula instruction on the development of teaching-learning segments that appropriately utilize the expanding technologies of instruction *(The Fourth Revolution)*.

State planning agencies should give very high priority in the next few years to careful adaptation of teacher education to the changing needs of a period of shrinking job opportunities for elementary and secondary school teachers. We believe that consolidation of teacher education into a more limited number of institutions that can offer high-quality training would be generally preferable to a cutting back of teacher education on an across-the-board basis. States should encourage the participation of private as well as public colleges and universities in such planning. Many state colleges that have largely concentrated on teacher education will need to develop more comprehensive programs if they are to serve students effectively, and in sparsely populated states this will require division of labor among such state colleges in adding new fields or in some cases a merger of two or more such state colleges into a single location *(College Graduates and Jobs)*.

High priority should be given to adaptation of teacher-training programs to changing needs. There should be increased emphasis on specialized training to prepare teachers for service in ghetto schools, in programs for mentally retarded or physically handicapped children, in early child development programs and day-care centers, and in vocational education programs *(College Graduates and Jobs)*.

The U.S. Bureau of Labor Statistics and the U.S. Office of Education should develop revised estimates of the future demand for teachers that take account, as existing projections do not, of the growing demand for teachers in preelementary education and in such other settings as adult education programs *(College Graduates and Jobs)*.

At present too many white, middle-class teachers are prepared in essentially nonspecific ways for general purpose assignments. The problems of the large urban schools, small rural schools, bilingual-bicultural schools, and wealthy suburban school districts require teachers trained for these separate constituencies. University faculties of arts and sciences and education should concentrate more upon training teachers for different kinds of schools. Because of the variety of tasks there can be no single model of a teacher training program, and the National Council for the Accreditation of Teacher Education and state accrediting associations should encourage diversity. A common element in all preservice programs should be an emphasis upon bringing theory and practice together in clinical settings *(Continuity and Discontinuity)*.

Greater emphasis should be placed on inservice education of a different kind from that traditionally available. Local teacher centers that focus on teachers'

TRANSFER Four-year colleges should generally be prepared to accept qualified transfer students and to give them appropriate credit for the work they have already completed *(A Chance to Learn)*.

All state plans for the development of two-year institutions of higher education should provide for comprehensive community colleges that will offer transfer education *(The Open-Door Colleges)*.

Policies should be developed in all states to facilitate the transfer of students from community colleges to public four-year institutions. Whenever public four-year institutions are forced, because of inadequacies of budgets, to reject students who meet their admission requirements, top priority should be given to qualified students transferring from community colleges within the state. Private colleges and universities should also develop policies encouraging admission of community college graduates. In addition, there should be no discrimination against students transferring from community colleges in the allocation of student aid *(The Open-Door Colleges)*.

Colleges should develop admissions programs to seek out new constituencies, including transfers from two-year colleges *(Continuity and Discontinuity)*.

TUITION *(See also* Residency)
In providing their share of the financing of community colleges, states should ensure that total appropriations for operating expenses are large enough to permit the institution to follow a policy of either no tuition or very low tuition. States should revise their legislation, wherever necessary, to provide for uniform low tuition or no tuition charges at public two-year colleges *(The Open-Door Colleges)*.

A relatively low uniform national tuition policy is recommended for institutions providing medical and dental education *(Higher Education and the Nation's Health)*.

Only after establishing a tuition grants program should states consider raising tuition levels at public institutions. To avoid upward pressures on private tuition from such grants, states would need to set a maximum tuition grant *(The Capitol and the Campus)*.

No tuition or very low tuition should be charged for the first two years in public institutions including community colleges, state colleges, and universities *(The Capitol and the Campus)*.

Public institutions—and especially the community colleges—should maintain a relatively low tuition policy for the first two years of higher education. Such tuition should be sufficiently low that no student, after receipt of whatever federal and state support he or she may be eligible for, is barred from access to some public institution by virtue of inadequate finances *(Higher Education)*.

Public colleges and universities should carefully study their educational costs per student and consider restructuring their tuition charges at upper-division and graduate levels to more nearly reflect the real differences in the cost of education per student, eventually reaching a general level equal to about one-third of educational costs *(Higher Education: Who Pays? Who Benefits? Who Should Pay?)*.

Private colleges and universities should increase their tuition charges at a rate that is no more rapid than the increase in per capita disposable income. The rate of increase in tuition should be less pronounced than this, if at all possible.

Private colleges and universities also should carefully study their educational costs per student and consider restructuring their tuition charges, so that tuition is relatively low for lower-division students, somewhat higher for upper-division students, and considerably higher for graduate and professional students *(Higher Education: Who Pays? Who Benefits? Who Should Pay?).*

URBAN INSTITUTIONS State and federal funds should be allocated to colleges and universities for specific programs to meet the present needs of inner-city schools and of desegregated schools with heterogeneous classroom enrollments *(A Chance to Learn).*

State plans should designate selected urban community colleges to provide housing arrangements for students from smaller communities and rural areas, in order to encourage maximum access to specialized occupational programs *(The Open-Door Colleges).*

State and local planning bodies should develop plans for the establishment by 1980 of about 60 to 70 new comprehensive colleges and 80 to 125 new community colleges in large metropolitan areas with populations of 500,000 or more *(New Students and New Places).*

A special effort should be made to develop new institutions in those metropolitan areas that have comparatively low ratios of enrollment to population *(New Students and New Places).*

Urban campuses, in appropriate instances, should offer certain portions of their programs in off-campus facilities—at industrial plants, in business and government offices, and at public libraries and schoolrooms in residential areas *(The Campus and the City).*

We recommend consideration of the establishment of *learning pavilions* at community colleges and comprehensive colleges located in central cities *(The Campus and the City).*

Urban community colleges, in order to serve more fully their urban clientele, should give careful consideration to the establishment of multiple campuses in a metropolitan area rather than concentration of all students on one campus, and the development of some specialization of educational missions among the various campuses; systematic experimentation and evaluation of remedial and developmental programs; and possible early admission of urban high school students requiring remedial work or seeking immediate entry into vocational training programs *(The Campus and the City).*

Commuter institutions should make available lockers, study and lounge areas, and other physical facilties designed to meet the special needs of commuters, and scheduling of educational programs and activities should be undertaken with the commuter in mind *(The Campus and the City).*

Institutions of higher education should undertake those community service activities that revitalize its educational functions and constitute an integral part of its educational program, are within the institutional capacity both in terms of personnel and resources, and are not duplicative of the services of other urban institutions *(The Campus and the City).*

Both planning agencies and urban-located institutions should review and analyze the educational resources in their areas and the educational needs of urban students to determine whether experimental approaches are desirable to expand effective options for postsecondary educational opportunities in the metropolitan areas *(The Campus and the City).*

Universities and colleges should develop long-range plans that give adequate attention to the interaction between the campus and the neighborhood in which it is located.

Where appropriate, colleges and universities should participate actively in urban-renewal activities, but only in unusual circumstances should this participation extend to investment of scarce institutional resources in housing development for the general community.

Institutions should limit their need for expansion into scarce urban space by better use of existing space *(The Campus and the City)*.

Large universities located in urban areas should appoint a vice-president or vice-chancellor for urban affairs who would be concerned with the university-urban interface in terms of the urban impact of the university's educational, service, research, and corporate functions *(The Campus and the City)*.

Colleges and universities should develop overall policies concerning appropriate urban activities for their institutions to avoid response to new proposals on an ad hoc basis without reference to consistency with the educational mission of the institution *(The Campus and the City)*.

An Urban Grant program should be established to provide 10 grants to carefully selected institutions for the purpose of undertaking a comprehensive urban commitment for their institution. These grants should not exceed $10 million each for a 10-year period with reviews every two years *(The Campus and the City)*.

The network of urban observatories should be continued and each observatory should be funded at approximately $100,000 per year *(The Campus and the City)*.

VETERANS' EDUCATIONAL BENEFITS The Veterans' Educational Benefits Programs should be continued, and benefits under such programs should be revised automatically to keep pace with rising living and educational costs *(Quality and Equality)*.

VOCATIONAL AND TECHNICAL EDUCATION *(See also* Community colleges, Continuing education, Further education, Postsecondary education, Proprietary schools)

All state plans for the development of two-year institutions of higher education should provide for comprehensive community colleges that will offer occupational programs *(The Open-Door Colleges)*.

Efforts should be coordinated at the federal, state, and local levels to stimulate the expansion of occupational education in community colleges and to make it responsive to changing manpower requirements *(The Open-Door Colleges)*.

The U.S. Office of Education should develop a more accurate definition of enrollment in occupational programs and expand its statistics to include changes in enrollment by field of study *(The Open-Door Colleges)*.

Urban community colleges should give careful consideration to the possible early admission of urban high school students seeking immediate entry into vocational training programs *(The Campus and the City)*.

More attention should be paid to the occupational training interests of students, and to occupational counseling and guidance as students and adults seek to adjust to changing labor market conditions *(The Purposes and the Performance of Higher Education in the United States)*.

Each state through its coordinating mechanisms should study carefully and define the roles of public high schools, area vocational schools, community colleges, and proprietary schools with respect to vocational and technical programs *(Continuity and Discontinuity).*

College- and school-based vocational education will emphasize general knowledge common to broad groups of occupations in addition to providing training for specific skills. Industry will continue to accept responsibility for training persons to perform skills required by specific tasks on the job *(Toward a Learning Society).*

When they do not have skill-training expertise in their own companies, businesses will seek agreements with educational institutions to provide technical aid for the development of industry-based skill-training programs and for the evaluation of such programs *(Toward a Learning Society).*

Research and development funds will be made available by the U.S. Office of Education and the Department of Labor to facilitate the development of the theoretical knowledge and technical expertise needed to service agreements between postsecondary educational institutions and industry for the development of skill-training programs *(Toward a Learning Society).*

Educational institutions that have well-developed instructional technology will avail businesses and industry of opportunities to tie plant-site classrooms to televised instruction originating on the campus, and will make available audio-videotape instruction or computer-assisted instruction on subjects relevant to business and industry training programs *(Toward a Learning Society).*

Apprenticeship, internship, and inservice training will be used more widely than they are today to prepare persons for their life work in many professions, paraprofessions, and occupations *(Toward a Learning Society).*

WORK-STUDY PROGRAMS The work-study program should be continued and expanded with federal funding sufficient to enable those undergraduate students who meet, in general terms, the federal need criteria to earn up to $1,000 during the academic year, working not more than the equivalent of two days per week. Off-campus assignments of educational importance, such as tutorial work, should be encouraged *(Quality and Equality).*

Work-study programs should be available to vocational and technical students in all postsecondary institutions *(Quality and Equality).*

WOMEN'S STUDIES The movement to introduce courses on women and interdisciplinary women's study programs should be encouraged by institutions of higher education, at least on a transitional basis, but these courses and programs should be organized within existing disciplines and not under separate departments of women's studies *(Opportunities for Women in Higher Education).*